Religious Freedom

Religious Freedom

The Contested History

of an American Ideal

TISA WENGER

THE UNIVERSITY OF NORTH CAROLINA PRESS
CHAPEL HILL

This book was published with the assistance of the
Thornton H. Brooks Fund of the University of North Carolina Press.

Library of Congress Cataloging-in-Publication Data
Names: Wenger, Tisa Joy, 1969- author.
Title: Religious freedom : the contested history of an American ideal / Tisa Wenger.
Description: Chapel Hill : University of North Carolina Press,
[2017] | Includes bibliographical references and index.
Identifiers: LCCN 2016059293 | ISBN 9781469634623 (cloth : alk. paper) |
ISBN 9781469634630 (ebook)
Subjects: LCSH: Freedom of religion—United States—History—20th century. |
United States—Race relations—History—20th century. | United States—
Race relations—Religious aspects. | United States—Foreign
relations—History—20th century. | United States—Foreign relations—
Philippines. | Philippines—Foreign relations—United States.
Classification: LCC BL2525 .W4145 2017 | DDC 323.44/20973—dc23
LC record available at https://lccn.loc.gov/2016059293

Portions of chapter 1 were previously published as "Indian Dances
and the Politics of Religious Freedom, 1870-1930," *Journal of the
American Academy of Religion* 79, no. 4 (2011): 850-78.

In memory of Christine Headings Wenger, 1944–2014

Contents

Acknowledgments

Writing a book is not really a solitary endeavor, no matter how much time I have spent alone at my computer. This is certainly the case for a book as troublesome and unruly as this one. There is no way I could have finished this project without the lifeline of family, friends, colleagues, and students who pointed me in the right direction and lifted my spirits when the going got tough.

The seeds of this project were sown at Arizona State University, where an interdisciplinary group of students, colleagues, and friends encouraged me to think expansively. In ways they may not even recognize, this book owes a great deal to Linell Cady, John Carlson, Myla Vicente Carpio, Doe Daughtrey, Anne Feldhaus, Joel Gereboff, Brett Hendrickson, Karen Leong, Moses Moore, Shahla Talebi, and especially Tracy Fessenden.

As a historian of religion in America, I have the good fortune to be part of what I am convinced must be the friendliest guild in the academy. This book is possible because of the brilliance and generosity, in big and little ways, of a long list of friends. They include James Bennett, Wallace Best, Edward J. Blum, Anthea Butler, Wendy Cadge, Leslie Callahan, Christopher Cantwell, Finbarr Curtis, Brandi Denison, Kate Carté Engel, Martha Finch, Linford Fisher, Timothy Fitzgerald, Spencer Fluhman, Eugene Gallagher, Shreena Gandhi, Rebecca Goetz, Naomi Goldenberg, Sarah Barringer Gordon, Daniel Greene, Jenna Gray-Hildenbrand, Paul Harvey, Matthew Hedstrom, Kathleen Holscher, Nicole Kirk, Kip Kosek, Jenny Wiley Legath, Laura Levitt, Laurie Maffly-Kipp, Michael McNally, Laura McTighe, Lori Meeks, Samira Mehta, Quincy Newell, Colleen O'Neill, Anthony Petro, Benji Rolsky, Kathleen Sands, Connie Shemo, Ronit Stahl, Winnifred Fallers Sullivan, Angela Tarango, Jonathan Walton, David Harrington Watt, Heather White, Melissa Wilcox, and many more. For their gracious hospitality on my research trips, and for stimulating conversation along the way, I am especially grateful to Susan Ridgely Bales, K. Healan Gaston, and Jana Riess.

I have had the privilege of presenting bits and pieces of this project in a variety of venues. Thanks go especially to Kathryn Gin Lum and the

Department of Religion at Princeton University; Pamela Moro, Charles Wallace, and Steven Green at Willamette University; Kevin Wanner and Stephen Covell at Western Michigan University; R. Marie Griffith and Leigh Schmidt at the Danforth Center on Religion and Politics, Washington University in St. Louis; Jeffrey Engel and the Center for Presidential History at Southern Methodist University; Jenna Reinbold and Christopher Vecsey at Colgate University; Justin Stein and Pamela Klassen at the University of Toronto; Kathleen Foody, M. Gail Hamner, Elizabeth Shakman Hurd, and Isaac Weiner at the American Academy of Religion, Religion and Media Pre-Conference Workshop; Patrick Mason at Claremont Graduate University; and Gale Kenny and Courtney Bender at Columbia University.

The Religion and U.S. Empire group, convened by Sylvester Johnson and Tracy Leavelle, came along at just the right time to help me shape many of the ideas in this book, especially on the Philippines. Along with Sylvester and Tracy, I am grateful to Julius Bailey, Ed Blum, Cara Burnidge, Emily Conroy-Krutz, Heather Curtis, Sarah Dees, Jonathan Ebel, Keith Feldman, Jennifer Graber, Michael Hawkins, Charles Strauss, and Karine Walther.

Friends, students, and colleagues at Yale have made this journey not just possible but enjoyable as well. Yale Divinity School students Heather Vermeulen and Kimberly Pendleton helped with the early stages of research; Kimberly George, Jason Craige Harris, and N'Kosi Oates all provided helpful comments. Current and former doctoral students Kati Curts, Tiffany Hale, Sarah Koenig, Cody Musselman, Shari Rabin, David Walker, and especially Lucia Hulsether (who did a big chunk of research and read several chapter drafts) have been among my most important interlocutors.

Thanks to YDS colleagues Joel Baden, Bruce Gordon, Rona Johnston Gordon, Jennifer Herdt, Mary Moschella, Carolyn Sharp, and Chloë Starr and my writing buddies Melanie Ross, Linn Tonstad, and Almeda Wright for keeping my spirits lifted and helping me stay on task. Across Yale, Ned Blackhawk, John Mack Faragher, Zareena Grewal, Briallen Hopper, Matthew Frye Jacobson, Birgit Brander Rasmussen, and Laura Wexler gave support and encouragement along the way. Clarence Hardy, Kathryn Lofton, Sally Promey, and Harry Stout are an American religious historian's dream team, brilliant colleagues who kept faith in me even when I lost it myself. Skip and Katie especially: I could not have made it this far without you.

These friends and colleagues deserve special gratitude for their comments on chapter drafts: Steven Green, K. Healan Gaston, Lucia Hulsether, Sylvester Johnson, Karen Leong, Kathryn Lofton, Samira Mehta, Leigh Schmidt, Harry Stout, Thomas Tweed, and Judith Weisenfeld. Linda Mehta provided excellent editorial assistance on the first full version of the manuscript. I do not think I could have written this book at all without Rona Johnston Gordon, who served as my writing consultant, a helpful guide and cheering presence over the last two and a half years. Finally, I am truly privileged to have as my editor Elaine Maisner at the University of North Carolina Press, whose judgment is always impeccable.

The research for this book took a number of unexpected turns. I owe an immense debt to the librarians and archivists who have helped me find resources at the Yale Divinity Library, the Beinecke and the Sterling Memorial Library at Yale, the Newberry Library in Chicago, the Southern Baptist Historical Library and Archives in Nashville, the American Jewish Archives in Cincinnati, the American Jewish Historical Society and the Schomburg Center for Research in Black Culture in New York, and the Catholic University of America in Washington, D.C. For supporting portions of my research I want to thank the Newberry Library, the Southern Baptist Historical Center and Archives, the Whitney Humanities Center at Yale University, the Association of Theological Schools, and above all Dean Gregory Sterling at Yale Divinity School.

Last and closest to my heart is my family. I am grateful to Aaron Wenger and Megan Maddox-Wenger for the laughter and good cheer. Thanks go to my dad, Harold Wenger, for having so much faith in me, and to my new stepmother, Elba Cardona Wenger, for her kindness. Thanks are due to Harold and Mary Ellen Groff for their support over the years. Jordan, Sophia, and Dylan have grown up with this book and lived with its stresses. I thank them for reminding me that there are more important things than work—but also for understanding when I needed to work. Rod Groff has made it all possible, in so many ways, and I don't think I'll ever be able to thank him enough.

This book is dedicated to my mother, Christine Headings Wenger, who always listened and always loved and left us much too soon. We miss you, Mom.

Religious Freedom

Introduction

Americans have long championed the freedom of religion as a defining national ideal. Since the time of the Revolution, pundits and politicians have celebrated this freedom as a pioneering achievement, a signal contribution to the larger causes of liberty and democracy around the world. Because they granted so much importance to religious freedom, Americans invoked it to defend a wide variety of practices, interests, and traditions. I began this book with questions about the kinds of cultural work that these diverse articulations performed. Rather than asking how adequately Americans had achieved this freedom or how rapidly it advanced—queries that assume we already know what it is and how to measure it—I wanted to know who appealed to religious freedom, for what purposes, and what it meant to them. Somewhat unexpectedly, race and empire quickly emerged as key themes in my analysis. I found that some of the most frequent and visible articulations of American religious freedom were exclusive, even coercive. The dominant voices in the culture linked racial whiteness, Protestant Christianity, and American national identity not only to freedom in general but often to this freedom in particular. The most audible varieties of religious freedom talk—the many ways in which people invoke this ideal— helped define American whiteness and make the case for U.S. imperial rule. But in response, the racialized and colonized subjects of U.S. empire also rearticulated this freedom to defend themselves and their traditions. For them, religious freedom became a way to redefine communal identities, to carve out space for themselves and their traditions within the confines of a racialized empire, and even at times to resist its mandates.

This book retells the story of American religious freedom as an illuminating lens into the intersections of race, religion, and empire in U.S. history. It focuses on the decades between the Spanish-American War of 1898 (or, more accurately, the Spanish-Cuban-Filipino-American War) and the Second World War, a pivotal period in our histories of race and empire but one that most scholarship on religious freedom has neglected. It asks how diverse groups of Americans and some of those who became the subjects of U.S.

imperial rule in this period—Protestants, Catholics, Jews, Filipinos, Native Americans, and African Americans of varied religious commitments—deployed the ideal of religious freedom. They did so variously, I argue, to assert racial and imperial prerogatives, to defend subaltern traditions and identities against the power of the majority, and to (re)categorize the terms of their peoplehood as they navigated the stormy civilizational waters of an imperial world.

Pundits, politicians, and some scholars have regularly denied that the United States, past or present, should be called an empire. But these denials, and the assurances of American benevolence that so often accompany them, are in no way distinctive to the United States. Rather, they have been part of the discursive mechanics of many empires around the world and help to sustain an exceptionalism that rationalizes the global exercise of U.S. military and economic power. In fact, the colonies that declared their independence from British rule in 1776 were founded in the crucible of empire, out of the mix of Europe's competitions for empire in the Atlantic world. Thomas Jefferson famously described the new republic as a distinctive "Empire of Liberty," and by the late nineteenth century it had joined in the European contest for imperial possessions around the globe. Through the early twentieth century—the period highlighted in this book—the United States expanded and consolidated its status as an imperial power. It would take an even more prominent role in the global reconfigurations of empire that followed the Second World War, when most of the nations of Asia and Africa formally won their independence.[1]

In the early twentieth century, American religious freedom talk functioned in various ways to shape and to navigate the imperial hierarchies of race, nation, and religion. Americans who could assert the racial status of whiteness claimed this freedom as a racial possession and used it to define a superiority that they tied both to their religion (Protestant) and to the secular modernity that it grounded. For others, especially Catholic and Jewish immigrants whose claims to American whiteness were not yet established, religious freedom talk could help secure a new racial status. By reclassifying their difference in the language of *religion*, some minorities could claim the protections of the First Amendment and escape the stigma of racial minority status in the United States. As racialized minorities and colonized peoples struggled to (re)define the terms of their peoplehood within the strictures of U.S. empire, this book argues, religious freedom talk worked to delineate what counted as religion and so helped map the distinctions of race, nation, and religion across the cultural landscapes of an imperial world.

Without attending to the civilizational assemblages of race and empire, we cannot fully understand the cultural meanings of religious freedom, its practical and theoretical limits, or the discursive terrains in which it has operated. The reverse is also true: the rhetorics of religious freedom have played largely unrecognized roles in the histories of race and empire. The principle of religious freedom—often coded as white and Protestant and set against the supposed bondage of the pagan and the Catholic—served as an imperial mechanism of classification and control, helping to define not only what counted as religion (or to delineate the good religion versus the bad religion) but also the contours of the racial. At the same time, it served as an ambivalent means of resistance, a tool for colonized and subordinated peoples to claim the status of religion and, however imperfectly, to define and defend their own traditions and identities in the face of empire.

KEYWORDS AND TRAJECTORIES: RACE, EMPIRE, RELIGION, FREEDOM

This book uses the Deleuzian concept of assemblage to highlight the heterogeneous, contingent, and contested conditions in which diverse groups of people shape their own identities and distinguish themselves from others as they navigate imperial relations of power in the modern world. Race, gender, sexuality, class, and religion are interlocking assemblages, forged and sustained through the discourses, institutions, and material relations of daily life as intersecting models of classification and control. Neither individually constructed nor simply ideological, assemblages involve the interplay of ideological, material, and institutional factors. "The idea of racializing assemblages," writes Alexander Weheliye, "construes race not as biological or cultural classification but as a set of sociopolitical processes that discipline humanity into full humans, not-quite-humans, and nonhumans."[2] Assemblage is a multilayered concept, so that we can speak of race, religion, and so forth as assemblages in their own right but also as dimensions of a broader assemblage of civilization. When I refer to civilizational assemblages, I mean the complex interplay of ideological and institutional processes that work together to define who and what counts as civilized and thus as fully human—and by contrast, who and what does not.

Assemblages shape the life prospects, perspectives, and experiences of everyone they touch. At the same time, their contingent and multifaceted qualities leave them open to constant challenge and subtle (or not-so-subtle) reconfigurations. I find the concept of assemblage useful because it brings together the processes of social classification, identity formation, and material relations of power. In so doing it provides a nuanced way to theorize the relations of power, highlighting the constrained conditions in which agency and resistance must emerge and the unpredictable (but also historically grounded) qualities of cultural change. Sometimes intentionally and sometimes not, minority and subaltern communities can push against and even reconfigure the elements of the civilizational assemblages that demean them. This process of reconfiguration or reassemblage is always constrained by the elements at hand and by the relations of power that are the warp and weft of any assemblage. Nevertheless, such reassemblages are the necessary foundation for cultural and political change.

Race is a powerful assemblage, a product of history rather than an unchanging essence or a biological given. Historians do not agree on the question of precisely when modern concepts of race emerged or when earlier forms of classification transitioned into something that should be called racial. But it is clear that race as we know it, which locates human difference primarily in the body, developed from the seventeenth century onward as a primary way to classify and control diverse human populations. Race in its modern sense provided a way to manage the disciplinary conundrums of slavery and colonialism. It has been one of the most important ways to organize relations of power in the modern world, indelibly shaping every dimension of American cultural, social, economic, and political life. This book contends that the cultural work of American religious freedom cannot adequately be understood without attending to its shifting formations.[3]

Race and other civilizational assemblages of modernity have inevitably taken shape in the context of empire. Empire can be defined as an expansionist political entity that effectively dominates other societies through mechanisms that may be either formal or informal, and that maintains hierarchical distinctions—often unacknowledged and made to appear natural—between its own people and those it controls. Edward Said describes imperialism as "the practice, the theory, and the attitudes" of the "dominating imperial center" and colonialism as "almost always a consequence of imperialism . . . the implanting of settlements on distant territory." Colonialism is thus one model of imperialism, and settler colonialism—in which the primary modes of imperial expansion are settlement and the displacement of indigenous peoples, rather than resource extraction and governance by a small cadre of colonial officials or local elites loyal to the empire—is one kind of colonialism. Against Said's definition, then, colonized territories and peoples need not be distant from an imperial metropole. The United

States began as a settler-colonial venture, but by the end of the nineteenth century its imperial expansions had incorporated a vast range of territories and peoples across the Atlantic and Pacific worlds.[4]

The civilizational assemblages of empire have been supported but also resisted by the quintessential modern ideology of freedom. Freedom as an elaborated ideal, defined as a basic individual right, developed during the Age of Enlightenment alongside modern notions of race and against the backdrop of Europe's expanding colonial endeavors. Ancient and medieval concepts of freedom had already been constructed against the condition of slavery. The status and the privileges of freedom had little meaning without the figure of the slave, whose subordination was the negative definition of freedom and whose service (along with the gendered role of the woman) enabled elite male conceits of individual autonomy.[5] During the centuries of imperial expansion, as race became the key rationale for colonial subjugation, these ideologies of freedom grew more and more elaborate. Those who articulated the Enlightenment's most stirring appeals for human liberty were often also the theorists and administrators of empire. This was no accident, since they constructed such liberal ideals as a story of humanity's progress from its allegedly primitive past. They construed the peoples who were the targets of empire as lagging behind in a racial march of progress, not yet having developed the civilizational capacities for reason, individuality, and freedom. The ideal of freedom could also be turned against empire, as colonized and subaltern peoples around the world have amply demonstrated. Yet ideologies of freedom continued to work powerfully as a rationale for imperial conquest, grounding assertions for *this* empire as a benevolent one, uniquely designed to bestow the blessings of freedom, democracy, and civilization.[6]

Religious freedom as an explicitly articulated principle rested both on these liberal ideologies of freedom and on the emergent modern category of religion, which also came into being through the violent upheavals and intellectual ferment of early modern Europe. The wars that raged across that continent in the sixteenth and seventeenth centuries were the birth pangs of distinct nations in the wake of the Holy Roman Empire as much as they were conflicts between Protestants and Catholics. As monarchs increasingly claimed total sovereignty over the lands they governed, Catholic as well as Protestant rulers denied the right of the pope to intervene in their domains. Naming these conflicts the "Wars of Religion" provided the foundation for early Enlightenment suspicions of religion—or rather out-of-bounds religion, the religion that transgressed its newly assigned sphere of the interior, the soul or the conscience—as a primary source of conflict and violence. In other words, this act of naming sought to limit the sphere of the religious to the spiritual and the otherworldly, as opposed to the political and material domain of the state.[7]

The modern category of religion along with the ideal of religious freedom developed further through European attempts to understand and then to subjugate newly encountered peoples around the world. Anglo-American imperial theorists and administrators employed evaluative criteria that privileged Protestant Christianity as rational, ethical, and free: the optimal religion for modernity. In contrast the targets of colonial conquest were often said to have no religion or were denigrated for what colonial theorists of religion considered a blindingly superstitious "paganism," opposed by definition to the modern virtues of freedom and progress. English Protestants developed a special pride in what they considered their racial-religious propensity for freedom. Their assertions of racial superiority rested heavily on what they saw as a uniquely free religion, and they identified themselves—in simultaneously racial and religious terms—with the values and virtues of freedom, modernity, and civilization.[8]

These imperial assemblages shaped the conditions for religious freedom talk in the colonial Atlantic world. From the seventeenth century onward, novel articulations of this freedom facilitated British colonial expansion in North America. Perhaps the most obvious examples are the founding stories of Rhode Island, Maryland, and Pennsylvania, each with a distinct model of either religious freedom or religious toleration as part of its raison d'être. We will linger instead on the Fundamental Constitutions of Carolina, coauthored in 1669 by none other than John Locke, the preeminent theorist of religious toleration, then serving as secretary to the lords proprietors of the recently established Carolina colony.[9] Carolina's royal charter had allowed its proprietors the discretion to permit "Indulgences and Dispensations" for settlers who may not be able to fully "Conform" to the Church of England, as long as they did not threaten the "peace and safety" of the colony. On these grounds the new constitution liberally granted that "any Seven or more persons agreeing in any religion" could "constitute a church or profession" of their own. But it limited this toleration, as well as the status of a "freeman" and the right to own property, to those who "acknowledge a God, and that God is publicly and solemnly to be worshiped." It granted a measure of toleration even to the "natives of this place," positing that their "Idolatry, Ignorance or mistake gives us no right to expel or use them ill." These conditions revealed an implicitly Christian model for what counted as religion, in keeping with the norms of an English society in which Christianity provided the cultural and social grounding for all of public life. Within these limits, the scope of toleration it granted was unusually broad for the time. This latitude reflected the economic imperatives of a colony that desperately wanted settlers, even if some of them were not English.[10]

Two decades later, Locke's *Letter Concerning Toleration* expanded on this liberal policy of toleration and suggested that it gave the English a superior claim to empire. "Not even [the Native] Americans," he wrote, "subjected to a Christian prince, are to be punished either in Body or in Goods for not embracing our Faith and Worship" (34). Locke rejected a key Spanish rationale for colonial conquest—the claim that the Indians' lack of Christianity justified the appropriation of their lands—on the grounds that it falsely granted the civil authorities a right to rule over the conscience. In contrast, the policy of toleration evidenced a superior English standard of justice. Thus Locke positioned the English as distinctively liberal colonial rulers whose policy of religious toleration demonstrated the practical and moral superiority of their rule, in contrast to their Spanish rivals. At least in his eyes, these claims helped justify the imperial expansions of the time.[11]

Locke's *Second Treatise of Government* (1690) further grounded English imperialism on the biblical injunction to "replenish" and "subdue" the earth. America was a "vacant land" occupied only by "wild Indians" who did not follow the divine command to cultivate the land, he wrote, leaving it available for those "industrious and rational" enough to do so. This logic provided an enduring rationale for the seizure of indigenous land. Although white settlers knew very well that American Indians cultivated crops, they constantly represented the latter as "savages" who merely roamed the land and did not improve it. As Patricia Seed puts it, the acts of erecting permanent habitation, of fencing and farming the land, were the archetypal English "ceremonies of possession" that, in English eyes, conferred divinely ordained and therefore indisputable rights of ownership. Locke's ideology of religious freedom thus worked as one more dimension of a civilizational assemblage that elevated the Englishman over the "wild Indian" and so legitimized the former's appropriation of indigenous lands.[12]

The Fundamental Constitutions of Carolina also suggest how the emerging ideal of religious freedom forged conceptual distinctions between race and religion as newly separable forms of identity. Assuming the practice of slavery, this governing document outlined guidelines for its regulation.

These included the presumably benevolent guarantee that slaves too must be granted the freedom of conscience: "Since charity obliges us to wish well to the souls of men, and *religion ought to alter nothing in any man's civil estate or right*," slaves (like other residents) could join "what church or profession any of them shall think best." This freedom was a convenient legal fiction. Slavery restricted every aspect of the slaves' lives, including those practices that they or their masters might designate as religious. The very next sentence, which specified that religious affiliation had no bearing on a slave's civil status, clarified the practical effect of such a guarantee. "But yet no slave shall hereby be exempted from that civil dominion his master hath over him," Locke wrote, "but be in all things in the same state and condition he was in before."[13] Because English common law prohibited the enslavement of fellow Christians, some enterprising slaves had begun to appeal for their emancipation on the grounds that they were Christians.[14] Locke refigured religion as a matter of conscience that must remain outside the domain of the state: *religion ought to alter nothing in any man's civil estate or right*. It followed that conversion to Christianity could have no legal bearing on the "state or condition" of the slave and that slaveholders could permit missions in the slave quarters without fearing that they might jeopardize their own property rights in the process.

The Fundamental Constitutions were among the first in a series of colonial laws that worked to end the legal possibility that slaves might argue for emancipation on the basis of Christianity. These laws did not eliminate the slave owners' anxieties about the effects of Christian conversion. Nor did they end the slaves' tendencies to find a liberatory message in Christianity or claim the right to freedom as Christians.[15] But they did effectively foreground race as the legal basis for enslavement and so sharpened an emerging distinction between race and religion as separable categories of difference. Because the freedom of conscience rested on a heightened distinction between the religious and the civil, when extended to slaves it arguably worked to redefine slavery as a permanent status. In so doing, it reinforced emerging views of race as physiognomy, an immutable difference written above all on the body.

In much the same way, the category of religion became legally irrelevant to the civil status of Native Americans living in the colonies and on their borders. If the rationale for appropriating indigenous land had relied on the Indians' "heathenism," or lack of Christianity, then Indians could presumably have contested settler land seizures by becoming Christians. But as with African slaves, Locke's idea that religious conscience could not be subjected to civil authority made religion irrelevant to their civil status and privileges (or lack thereof) in the colony. It was not the Indians' "heathenism" but their failure to cultivate and "improve" the land in the English style that provided the major rationale for their dispossession. Under this model, neither enslavement nor dispossession could be justified primarily via religious status but instead through the assemblages of race and civilization. Conversion to Christianity could not erase the racialized stain of heathenism. Locke's distinction between the rights of conscience (identified as the sphere of the religious) and the regulation of the body (which belonged to the civil authority) had arguably helped define religion and race as distinguishable categories of identity. In the process, the emerging ideology of religious freedom helped support increasingly race-based systems of slavery and settler colonialism in the colonial Atlantic world.

Thus the imperial Enlightenment emphasis on the freedom of conscience created new boundaries around religion that sought to separate it not only from the civil sphere (politics, the domain of the secular nation-state) but also from other ways of categorizing human difference, most importantly race. It did not signal the disappearance or decline of religion as a meaningful category of identity and classification, as the secularization narratives that continue to frame many of our histories would suggest. The Enlightenment attempt to separate religion from other spheres of life was never realized in practice. In fact, English settlers and their Anglo-American descendants defined race in part through language associated with the category of religion. They typically associated whiteness with Christianity and identified both Indians and Africans as racially inferior through the notion of "hereditary heathenism."[16] Far from disappearing, the discourses and traditions of religion would continue to shape race across the Americas, just as race increasingly framed the terms of religious difference. In the American context, at least, race and religion were co-constituted from the start.[17] Religious freedom talk, this book contends, played a key role in their ongoing process of mutual formation.

Liberal ideologies of freedom shaped the logics of both British and American imperial expansion. It was no accident that Locke and subsequent liberal philosophers such as James Mill, John Stuart Mill, and Sir Henry Maine served simultaneously as colonial administrators and theorists of empire. Their ideals of freedom, reason, and the rights of conscience were built around contrasts between the rational, civilized white male subject who possessed these attributes and the irrational, primitive, childlike or female "other" who did not. These liberal thinkers defended empire as justifiable, even laudable and benevolent, because it provided a way to bring the values and virtues of freedom and civilization to the racialized subjects of colonial rule. Liberal universalism—the articulation of supposedly universal principles of rationality and governance—served as a rationale for empire because it explained how Europeans and white Americans, who were convinced they alone had realized these principles, were superior to other peoples and why their tutelage would ultimately benefit those they ruled.[18]

A century after Locke wrote the Fundamental Constitutions of Carolina, the events of the American Revolution turned religious freedom into a defining ideal for the new nation. There was never any consensus, however, about its meaning. What precisely did the First Amendment's clauses on religion prohibit, and what did they protect? Enlightenment-minded elites like Thomas Jefferson and more radical deists prioritized liberty for the individual conscience, Congregational elites in New England asserted a corporate right to religious freedom against a Church of England that they considered little different from Rome, and radical dissenters like the Baptists demanded the freedom to follow God's law as they understood it without interference from the state. Meanwhile, the small minorities of Catholics and Jews in the new nation invoked the revolutionary principle of religious freedom to argue against the Protestant norms and privileges that virtually everyone else, including most deists and dissenters, simply assumed.[19]

All these ambiguities and contestations only added to the cultural power of religious freedom talk in American life. Anyone seeking to defend their traditions or communities had a strong incentive to classify them as religious and to claim the protections of religious freedom as their own. Debates over this freedom thus became a crucial way to sort out what counted as religion and what did not, forging and reinforcing key distinctions between the religious and the secular, the political, and sometimes even the racial. Over the course of the nineteenth century, as Americans debated the contentious questions of Western expansion, slavery, immigration, and more, religious freedom claims and counterclaims provided a way to construct and defend—but also to challenge—the civilizational assemblages of an expanding U.S. empire.[20] This book picks up the threads of that story at the dawn of the twentieth century, as the United States exported its ideologies of religious freedom into new imperial arenas beyond the bounds of the North American continent.

Few scholars have tackled the question of how and why Americans invoked the ideal of religious freedom in the early decades of the twentieth century, before the Supreme Court became the primary agent in its definition and adjudication. Fewer still have been concerned with its implications in the politics of either race or empire.[21] It turns out that Americans of every description—and with them many unwilling subjects of U.S. empire—appealed to religious freedom for all sorts of purposes in this period. In some respects the nation's imperial expansions and the growing importance of race only intensified the role of religious freedom. The white Protestant majority construed this freedom as a key to their own successes and to the legacy they would impart to those they colonized. Because religious freedom was not yet heavily litigated, federal authorities had immense discretion in applying this principle to subjugated populations on Indian reservations and in imperial territories alike. The people they colonized turned to this freedom as one avenue of resistance, while racialized minorities within the United States deployed it to defend (and define) their own distinctive identities and traditions through the protected category of religion. In so doing, some of these minorities managed to establish credibility as patriotic Americans and to renegotiate their standing in the civilizational assemblages of empire.

This book further identifies religious freedom as a key node in the navigation of race, religion, and the American secular. There is nothing new about the idea that religious freedom is a defining element of the modern secular democracy or about American Protestant claims to a unique affinity with this freedom—and through it with the governing norms of secular modernity. But all of these assertions need to be unpacked as ideological projects, aspects of the civilizational assemblages of race and religion that have supported the systems and structures of U.S. empire. The first three chapters of this book show how imperial administrators both in the Philippines and on Native American reservations presented the freedom of religion as a simultaneously Protestant and secular national norm. They posited Protestant Christianity as part and parcel of becoming American, the only way to form subjects who could responsibly exercise freedom. When American Catholics and Jews articulated their own commitments to religious freedom and their own varieties of American secularism, they were not only challenging Protestant exclusivity but also asserting more advantageous positions for themselves within the racial-religious hierarchies of U.S. empire. If religious freedom talk is a major component of American secularism, playing a significant part in the construction of the secular, then unpacking it helps us see how contested and multifaceted the formations of secularism have always been. American secularism is not simply Protestant, and its predominantly Protestant public profile is no accident of history but an ideological project interlaced with the civilizational assemblages of empire.

As a part of the disciplinary regimes of U.S. empire, religious freedom talk helped colonial administrators navigate the rocky terrain of imperial rule: to classify subject populations and negotiate their differences, to assert the legitimacy of U.S. rule, and to support the twin civilizing missions of Christianity and the American secular. It enforced new religious-secular distinctions that effectively reorganized indigenous societies, valorized Western models of governance, and, more often than not, disempowered indigenous leaders relegated by its logic to the privatized realm of the religious.

At the same time, across the cultural landscapes of U.S. empire, minority and subjugated peoples invoked the principle of religious freedom to defend their own traditions and communities, claiming the protected status of religion in American life. I have chosen to begin this book with the debates over the Spanish-Cuban-Filipino-American War and the colonization of the Philippines, both because these were key moments in the history of U.S. empire and because religious freedom was so central to these debates. Chapter 2 describes how religious freedom talk became a tool for Filipino revolutionaries as they fought for independence against the United States. Later, it offered one way for the people of the Philippines—including the Muslim Moros of the southern Philippine Islands—to navigate within the legal regimes of U.S. empire. Chapter 3 returns to the United States, showing how Native Americans in the early twentieth century rearticulated the principle of religious freedom to resist the suppression of indigenous ceremonies. All of these efforts had their limits and perhaps inevitably reshaped the traditions they sought to protect. In each case they required shifts in indigenous practice to meet official expectations for what counted as religious. Yet within the constraints of U.S. empire, religious freedom provided a valuable tool for resistance, a meaningful way to claim protection at least for those aspects of tradition that could be successfully classified as religion and defended as such.

The cultural weight of religious freedom in the United States encouraged its invocation by a dizzying array of people, on behalf of every imaginable practice and tradition. By defining communal identity as *religious*, minority invocations of religious freedom could at times provide an avenue of escape from the defining power of race. Chapter 4 argues that American Jewish appeals to religious freedom sought to hold the nation accountable to the promise of this ideal and, in the process, worked to redefine what it meant to be Jewish in religious rather than racial terms. In most times and places around the world, Jewishness had been a complex form of peoplehood, incorporating the various dimensions of identity that had only quite recently come to be distinguished by those claiming the mantle of modernity along the lines of race, nation, and religion. Even as they battled the intensely racialized anti-Semitism of the early twentieth century, Jews would gradually and always tentatively come to be recognized as a mostly *religious* rather than racial minority in American life. (The emerging category of ethnicity, not race, would become the primary alternative for Jewish identity in America. Like religion, ethnicity helped move Jewishness away from a specifically racial category of identity.) Thus the rhetorics of religious freedom would help American Jews escape the stigma of racial minority status, easing their acceptance into the racial privileges of whiteness in American life.

Not every minority group was able to leverage the power of religious freedom in this way. As chapter 5 will describe, African Americans especially found themselves unable to escape the overdetermined classifications of race. Most had been less interested in a specifically religious freedom than they were in escaping insistently racialized forms of oppression. Yet African Americans too would increasingly invoke the freedom of religion. Among those who did so were the leaders of the historically black denominations, especially when their right to control their own churches came under direct assault. Many who moved outside the bounds of Christianity, as in the Moorish Science Temple and the Nation of Islam, also used this ideal to articulate their concerns. As with the American Jews, they used religious freedom talk in an effort to redefine their peoplehood in primarily ethno-religious rather than racial terms.[22] The larger society, however, dismissed these groups as fraudulent, inauthentic, and overly "political" rather than legitimately religious. For African Americans, religious freedom talk provided precious little escape from an oppression that the larger society defined overwhelmingly in terms of race.

The point here is not that prior arrangements and structures of power were superior, that theorists of religious freedom are to be held responsible for racism and the violence of empire, or that the ideal of religious freedom, as such, is harmful to human flourishing. Rather, it is that both religion and religious freedom are modern inventions, with complex histories and constantly shifting consequences, and that like other human constructs they are inevitably implicated in relations of power. From its beginnings, the concept of religious freedom worked to negotiate pivotal distinctions between what (or who) counted as religious and what did not. Dominant discourses of religious freedom helped forge new distinctions between the racial and the religious, and they supported civilizational assemblages of race and religion that legitimated imperial rule.

As it tracks the intersections of race, empire, and American religious freedom, this book challenges easy assumptions about religious freedom as a universally beneficent ideal. It offers a cautionary tale, a corrective to overly celebratory histories of this freedom, and a longer historical perspective on the twenty-first-century politics of religious freedom.[23] Religious freedom has often been presented as a key dimension of liberal secularism, a necessary inoculant for democratic and pluralistic societies against conflicts that either participants or observers define as religious. In the United States and elsewhere around the world, religious minorities, anticolonial movements, and other activists have found it to be a vitally useful ideal. I do not want to suggest that it should be eliminated from their cultural toolbox or that we should no longer reach for its receding horizons. Yet we need to remember that this ideal is neither timeless nor removed from the coercions of modernity.

In sum, this book asks how the discourses of religious freedom have historically intersected with American formations of race and empire. It does not argue that the ideal of religious freedom inherently or necessarily serves the interests of empire. In my view any discourse, however hegemonic, is more malleable and less predictable than that. But it does suggest that the dominant varieties of American religious freedom talk were configured, more often than not, in ways that enabled imperial forms of domination. Throughout the twentieth century, racialized minorities and imperial subjects regularly invoked and reconfigured this ideal to serve their own liberatory projects. But their efforts were invariably limited by the constraints of the larger society. As they appealed for religious freedom, these groups had little alternative but to transform their practices, traditions, and sometimes their own identities in order to fit dominant models for what counted as religion. Americans forged and reforged the ideal of religious freedom within the shifting historical contexts of empire. In turn, its diverse articulations have continually reshaped the intersecting civilizational assemblages of race and religion in the United States, across its spheres of imperial domination, and, increasingly, around the world.

CHAPTER ONE

Making the Imperial Subject

Protestants, Catholics, and Jews

In August 1898, as the United States celebrated its quick and decisive victory in what most Americans called the Spanish-American War, President William McKinley met with his cabinet to discuss the terms of the treaty that was soon to be negotiated in Paris. The public rationale for the war had been to support the Cubans in their fight for independence from Spain. (Indeed, since Cubans and Filipinos had both been fighting long before the United States entered the conflict, it is more accurately named the Spanish-Cuban-Filipino-American War.) Although some Americans had long hoped to claim the small island of Cuba as a new U.S. territory, its quest for independence resonated with America's own founding ideals and coincided easily enough with U.S. commercial interests in the region. Thus when the USS *Maine* was bombed in Havana's harbor and the United States declared war on Spain, anti-imperialists insisted on a proviso guaranteeing that the United States would recognize Cuba's independence in its wake. But soon Cuba would no longer be the only Spanish colony at issue. Within weeks U.S. forces had occupied key locations in Puerto Rico, Guam, and the vast archipelago of the Philippine Islands in Southeast Asia. Ignoring the independence movements already raging in most of these colonies, Americans now began to debate the prospect of claiming all of them as the spoils of war.[1]

The Philippines were the largest and most strategically located of these colonies and so moved immediately to the center of this American debate. When they met that August, McKinley and his cabinet reached no final consensus on whether or not they should insist that Spain cede the entire archipelago. But they did agree on a minimal set of demands that they thought essential to U.S. interests in the Pacific. The United States would at the very least take Luzon, the largest of the Philippine Islands and the site of the colony's capital, Manila. And if Spain was to retain the rest of the archipelago, McKinley would insist on three basic conditions: (1) U.S. commerce must be granted full access to all the islands; (2) Spain must guarantee "religious liberty, in the American sense of the term, in all the Philippines remaining under her control"; and (3) Spain must promise that it would not in future cede any of the islands to any power other than the United States. These demands never made it to the negotiating table, since the president soon announced his decision to claim the Philippines as a whole. But his cabinet's preliminary list reveals the importance of religious freedom as an American diplomatic priority in the immediate aftermath of the war.[2]

This chapter interrogates the American debates over the Spanish-Cuban-Filipino-American War and the subsequent colonization of the Philippines in order to understand the civilizational and imperial politics of religious freedom in the United States. Historians have amply explored the topics behind the McKinley cabinet's first and third demands. The hope of commercial profit has arguably served as the primary fuel for U.S. imperialism and indeed for most other empire-building projects around the world. And it is not a surprise that many American leaders at the end of the nineteenth century wanted to compete with the European empires that were themselves jockeying for the profits, power, and prestige that new colonies could bring. The general themes of freedom and liberty, as well, are familiar themes within the American rhetorics of war and empire. But the presence of religious freedom as one of the administration's nonnegotiables may come as a surprise. Few historians have attended to this specific freedom as anything more than window dressing, a minor aspect of the broader theme. And while scholars in the distinct field of American religious history have been very much interested in religious freedom within the United States, they too have neglected its relationship with U.S. empire in either the Philippines or elsewhere.[3]

The importance of religious freedom for these debates must be understood first of all in relation to the Protestant-Catholic tensions that had for so long structured American controversies around religion in public life. During the buildup to the war, the violent contractions of a waning Spanish Empire provided ample fodder for militantly Protestant rhetorics that identified Catholicism as the foundation for its alleged tyrannies. Those who identified themselves as Anglo-Saxon Protestants viewed their own freedoms—and the barbarism and tyranny they attributed to Catholics and Catholicism—in simultaneously racial and religious terms. They attributed America's freedoms and the American system of government to the Anglo-Saxon and Protestant character of the nation's founders. Thus they asserted an Anglo-Protestant foundation not only for religious freedom but also for the secular modernity it signified. Translating all this into a rationale for empire, imperialists claimed that U.S. rule would introduce the democratic principles of civil and religious freedom to territories that Spanish misrule had left behind in a barbaric darkness. Religious freedom talk thus strengthened Anglo-Protestant claims to racial-religious supremacy both in the United States and in its colonial possessions. It bolstered dominant civilizational assemblages of race and religion, helping many white Protestants to see the nation's imperial ascendancy as both inevitable and desirable, an essential step in the development of the modern world.

At the same time, religious freedom talk provided a way for some racial-religious minorities to assert their own civilizational credentials and thus to improve their standing in the racial-religious hierarchies of U.S. empire. In the debate over the Philippines, Catholics in particular refused to accept the Anglo-Protestant logics of religious freedom and the secular modernity that it signaled. Catholic elites rearticulated this freedom to insist on a special role for their church and at times even to assert exclusive prerogatives in what was, after all, a predominantly Catholic colony. They used religious freedom talk, in other words, to claim the right to leadership in the administration of empire. In so doing they also identified Catholicism as an all-American religion and implicitly claimed for Catholics the civilizational status of white Americans, equipped to manage the non-white subjects of imperial rule. Thus they rejected the constructs of Anglo-Protestant supremacy that had assigned the predominantly immigrant Catholic population to a simultaneously racial and religious inferiority in the United States. In this way, Catholic deployments of religious freedom enabled a new access for Catholics to the privileges of whiteness in American life.

American Jews, as well, invested in a religious freedom talk that supported the politics of war and empire. As a much smaller minority both in the United States and around the world—a group never securely located in the realm of the religious and subject at the time to increasingly racialized forms of anti-Semitism—Jews were in a more precarious position than their Catholic counterparts. As chapter 4 will show in much greater detail, Jews had embraced the constitutional principle of religious freedom as a pragmatic and symbolic resource for life in the United States. The results of that effort would be complex and fraught with ambiguity for Jews, as it was for other racial-religious minorities in the United States. The last section of this chapter dips briefly into American Jewish deployments of religious freedom in the Spanish-Cuban-Filipino-American War and the colonization of the

Philippines to illustrate the utility of this ideal for racial-religious minorities seeking to improve their status and situation in the modern world.

In very different ways, Jews as well as Catholics used religious freedom talk to assert their equality within the civilizational assemblages of U.S. empire. Emerging discourses of religious brotherhood, an ideal linked integrally to religious freedom, supported both Catholic and Jewish participation in new arenas of American society, including the administration of empire. Thus American religious freedom talk helped justify U.S. imperial expansions and in the process fostered the gradual expansion of whiteness to include Catholic and Jewish immigrants who had once been excluded from its privileges.

ANGLO-SAXON PROTESTANTS AND THE LOGICS
OF WAR AND EMPIRE

For a dominant culture shaped by Anglo-Saxon Protestant norms, religious freedom served first of all as a key marker of American superiority over Spain. During the buildup to the war in 1898, Episcopalian rector Randolph McKim of Epiphany Church in New York told his congregation that they faced a world-historical struggle between competing models of civilization. Where Spain stood for "the civilization and the government and the religious ideas of the Middle Ages," he preached, the United States stood "on the whole for the enlightenment, for the progress, for the freer thought, for the larger liberty, and especially for the religious freedom of the modern world." According to McKim, a U.S. victory in the war would have dramatic consequences for Cuba, which would "at long last" be liberated "from the rule of her oppressors." The global impact would be even more significant. America would become a great world power, McKim told his congregation, allowing it to disseminate everywhere "the principles of civil and religious liberty which we ourselves enjoy in the good providence of God." Religious freedom was at the top of McKim's list of the features that defined the United States in opposition to Spain. It was also one of the signal blessings that a benevolent U.S. empire would bestow upon the world.[4]

McKim's sermon built on civilizational assemblages that were grounded in centuries of Protestant-Catholic conflict and had developed in support of U.S. imperial expansions across the North American continent. Protestants from the Reformation onward had painted not merely the papacy but the entire Catholic approach to church authority as a system of tyranny that impeded what they viewed as the direct accountability of the individual before God. The British colonial wars against France and Spain had only strengthened Anglo-Protestant associations between Catholicism and tyranny on the one hand and Protestantism and freedom on the other. When the United States gained independence, its overwhelmingly Protestant leaders transferred these representational patterns to the new nation. By identifying free (Protestant) Christianity as the essential source of American freedoms, they identified the United States as an essentially Protestant nation. By contrast, they depicted Catholicism not merely as an outdated, foreign, and "superstitious" version of Christianity but also as an active threat to the fundamental American principles of religious and civil liberty and thus to American democracy itself.[5]

The Mexican-American War (1846–48) turned these associations into a rationale for U.S. imperial expansion. In 1844 the United States had annexed the province of Texas, then struggling to maintain the independence it had won from Mexico eight years earlier. Advocates for that annexation coined the phrase "Manifest Destiny" to encapsulate their growing conviction that God had ordained the nation's expansion across the continent. Proponents of the ensuing war with Mexico made no secret of their desire to acquire still more territory, a goal they achieved when the United States won the war and seized the vast provinces of New Mexico and California. In the months and years thereafter, religious freedom talk helped assuage the fears of many northern Protestants that these new territories and their alien peoples posed a threat to American democracy.[6] Anti-Catholic propagandist Nicholas Murray wrote in 1851 that until they had become part of the United States, "nothing in the way of religion" could "dare be lisped" in these territories "save Popish mummeries." Murray placed these conquests alongside the liberal revolutions that had swept Europe in 1848 and the British "opening of China" to commerce and missions as signs that Protestantism and freedom were advancing in concert all around the world.[7]

Writing in the 1880s, the Lutheran minister and pioneering church historian Philip Schaff credited the Protestant Reformation with recovering Christ's original emphasis on the individual conscience, thus enabling the later emergence of religious freedom as a political ideal. Where the Catholic Church claimed to be the infallible and divinely appointed guide to scripture and to the will of God, the Reformation had (at least in theory) recognized each individual's right to read and interpret the Bible and eliminated the role of the church as intercessor between the individual and the divine. According to Schaff, the Reformation had thus released adherents from the "thralldom" of "popery" and so "carried in it the modern principles of religious and civil liberty." By giving believers the right and the responsibility to interpret and follow the Word of God for themselves, he claimed, Protestantism had formed subjects uniquely capable of free moral judgment, enabling them to function as citizens of a free republic. Schaff asserted further that these principles had been fully realized only in the American system of government. The United States had transcended not just the "papal tyranny" of the Catholic world, he wrote, but also the British model of mere "toleration" for religious dissent.[8]

These associations were always open to challenge, as the rest of this book will document. From the revolutionary period onward, Catholics, Jews, and many others articulated more inclusive versions of American national identity. Nevertheless, the identification of Protestant Christianity with religious freedom and the American nation—or in other words its constitutive part in the making of the American secular—held sway far beyond the leadership of the Protestant churches. U.S. elites lived in a political culture indelibly shaped by Protestantism, and most took for granted its asserted role as the historical source and necessary grounding for American freedoms. The political tradition of Christian republicanism, invoked in one way or another by every U.S. president since the nation's founding, typically identified not just Christianity but *Protestant* Christianity in particular as an essential ingredient of American democracy. The majority cultures of Protestantism, then, shaped the underlying grammar and the day-to-day vocabulary of American secularism's dominant forms.[9]

The ideal of religious freedom perhaps inevitably intersected with race as America's most fundamental system of social classification and control. Just as they used the principle of religious freedom to equate Protestantism with America, many Protestant and secular voices assumed its association with an Anglo-Saxon racial identity. My point is not that these speakers falsely conflated race, nation, and religion—as if these were distinct and unchanging categories of identity—but that these classificatory terms mutually defined one another in American culture. Those who saw themselves as Anglo-Saxons defined their own identities not only against Africans, Asians (who were commonly called Orientals), and American Indians but also against European immigrants whose racial characteristics were constituted in large part through their Catholicism or their Jewishness. As long as whiteness was equated with the Anglo-Saxon Protestant, then neither Jews nor Catholics could be seen as entirely white.[10]

These civilizational assemblages are clearly visible in the book *Our Country*, written by the widely respected Congregationalist missionary leader and social gospel proponent Josiah Strong in 1885. Strong described emigrants from southern and eastern Europe as distinctly inferior because they lacked the vigor, independence, and clear thinking that he associated with Anglo-Saxon Protestants. The Catholicism that had formed them taught a "slavish" and superstitious submission to authority, he believed, leaving them fundamentally unprepared to live as free American citizens and destined to remain within the tyrannical grasp of Rome. Protestant triumphalists like Strong increasingly portrayed Catholics as inherently different from and clearly inferior to the superior race. In his view, the immigrants' failure to claim the freedom of religion by becoming Protestants demonstrated their permanent inferiority (and their essentially un-American nature) in simultaneously racial and religious terms.[11]

In the buildup to the war with Spain, many Protestants drew on the "Black Legend" of a distinctively Spanish imperial cruelty that was allegedly rooted in Catholicism. Proponents portrayed the Spanish Inquisition as the model for an ongoing pattern of colonial abuse. Henry van Dyke, pastor of Brick Presbyterian Church in New York, contended for example that the suffering of Cuba and the Philippines reflected the ongoing "cruelties of the Inquisition." A writer in the *Trenton Evening Times* explained that after "the fanaticism of Isabella and the zeal of Torquemada" had banished "the Jews and the Moors" in the fifteenth century, "the fires of the Inquisition" had targeted "the thinkers" of Spain. "From the days of Ferdinand to the days of [contemporary Spanish general Valeriano] Weyler," he concluded, "it has been the policy of Spain to terrorize her subjects into submission by torture and butchery." Recent historians have viewed the Inquisition as a tool for the early modern Spanish monarchy as it solidified its claims to power, sometimes in competition with papal authority, and have judged the Spanish Empire as no more violent or cruel than any other. But in their enthusiasm for war, these American Protestants drew a direct line between the Inquisition and the violence of a waning Spanish Empire. In so doing they obscured the violent imperatives of empire in the contemporary world.[12]

Van Dyke described an impending war of civilizations, with the forces of freedom arrayed against the despotic power of Spain. He equated the contemporary United States with sixteenth-century England, which in his telling had also battled Spain for the sake of freedom. "The dark and bloody tyranny of Spain then beclouded the whole world," he told his congregation. Against all odds, England had defeated "the mighty Spanish Armada, . . . strong with the pride of successful oppression and laden with the cruelties of the Inquisition." Now the United States bore the weight of the responsibility, once held by England, to defend the world from the intertwined tyrannies of Catholicism and the Spanish Empire. Van Dyke elided the geopolitical contexts for both wars—the colonial rivalries between England and Spain in the sixteenth century and between Spain and the United States at the dawn of the twentieth—by identifying the United States as England's successor in the fight for Christianity, civilization, and freedom. He asked his fellow Americans to take up the "sacred obligation" that England had once borne and to "deliver a fair portion of this continent from . . . the most obstinate barbarians who exist outside of Turkey, to bring liberty to captives, and to let the oppressed go free." In this telling, the fight for Cuba's independence was an Anglo-Protestant holy war against the cruelties of an essentially Catholic Spanish Empire.[13]

These civilizational assemblages were also deeply gendered, with freedom, vigor, and the modern all coded as male. McKim told his congregation that Americans would gain very little glory from "conquering a weak and effete nation like Spain." The glory would come instead, he said, from the "potent influence" that the United States would be able to exert around the world after winning the war. This was a manly conflict, despite the "effete" weakness and corruption of the enemy, because it was being fought to defend the Christian principles that McKim equated with freedom, democracy, and modernity itself.[14] Rev. Heber Newton of the All Souls' Episcopal Church in New York argued similarly that by accepting America's "duty" to save humanity from the "world wrongs" committed by Spain, the United States had recovered a national manhood that the "peace and quietude" of its prior isolationism had compromised. "A few months ago, what hosts of our young men seemed to be given over to the idle life of sport and pleasure," he recalled. Now, as the nation assumed its rightful place in the world, these "petted playthings of society" were "rushing to the front and asking for the post of danger."[15]

Calling for a new alliance of British and American power, Newton identified this restored manliness with the racial-religious character of the nation. Applauding the progress of the war and arguing that the United States should annex the Philippines, he concluded, "Could the English-speaking peoples stand together, the destinies of the world would be in their hands. When England and America shall say together in the presence of any wrong, 'This must stop!' it will stop. Then from the soul of the English-speaking race, which stands for peace, will be heard with the tone of an authority not likely to be slighted, the sacred words of our greatest soldier, 'Let us have peace.' "[16] According to clergymen like McKim and Newton, the "English-speaking race" had been divinely ordained to bring the blessings of peace and freedom to the world. The war was revitalizing the manliness of the United States—a manliness evidenced by its exercise of imperial authority, its inherent love of freedom, and the Christian character of its goals. At long last, the nation was ready to take on the mantle of imperial power.

Through the public debates around the Spanish-American War and empire in the Philippines, pundits and politicians who were not speaking directly as Protestants drew on representational traditions that reflected the pervasive influence of Protestantism in American public life. They pointed to Catholicism as evidence of a Spanish civilizational inferiority constituted through assemblages of race, gender, religion, and nation. "On the one hand . . . [is] the shriveled and decrepit survival of a semi-barbarous system of oppression, cruelty, inhumanity, and violence," claimed the Kansas Democratic and Populist representative Mason S. Peters at a pro-war rally, "on the other, civil and religious liberty, equality, human rights, progress."[17] In Peters's account, religious freedom appeared as a sign of modernity and progress, a key organizing principle for the secular modern state. Yet just below the surface were the rhetorics of an Anglo-Saxon Protestant triumphalism that defined itself against Catholic "barbarism" and tyranny. Religious freedom stood at the nexus of Protestantism and the secular modern and of whiteness, masculinity, and American claims to empire. For all of these reasons, this principle took center stage in the American drumbeat for war.

Debating Empire: Race, Religion, and
the Anglo-Protestant Secular

The same discourses of religious freedom that helped drive the war against Spain also worked to build the case for U.S. empire. As soon as public debate turned to the Philippines, mainstream Anglo-Protestant opinion contended that, like Cuba, these islands stood in need of liberation from Spain and the tyranny of its Catholic establishment. The activities of the Spanish friars—Dominicans, Augustinians, and Franciscans, the mendicant religious orders that administered most Catholic missions and parishes in the Philippines—had sparked some of the most serious Filipino protests against the Spanish Empire. Over the years these religious orders had accumulated a large amount of property, making them the largest landowners in much of the archipelago. They had also banned native Filipinos from their ranks, part of a series of nineteenth-century efforts to sharpen lines of racial distinction and so to reinforce imperial authority across the Spanish

Empire. And because the friars were often the only Spaniards living in local communities, they had regularly served as the primary agents of the imperial regime. As chapter 2 will detail, Filipino reformers and revolutionaries named the wealth and power of the Spanish friars and the religious orders in general as key factors behind their revolt against Spain.[18]

In the eyes of an Anglo-Protestant culture, this Spanish regime looked like a direct assault on the freedom of religion. In his 1898 book *Our New Possessions*, journalist Trumbull White narrated a long history of Filipino revolts against Spain and attributed all of them to the tyranny of the Catholic Church. One of the first uprisings in the Philippines had been sparked by the "despotism of a Jesuit priest" in the seventeenth century, White wrote, who had "ordered his parishioners arrested when they failed to attend mass." Similarly, he claimed, the "increased power" of the friars in recent years was "the first cause of the [current] insurrection."[19] Reflecting the overwhelmingly Protestant assumptions of the dominant society, such narratives attributed Filipino resentments against Spain almost entirely to Catholicism and the church-state collusions that had given it so much power. By blaming Catholicism rather than the inherent inequities of empire, Anglo-Protestant writers like White helped justify the U.S. seizure of the Philippines.

Protestant missionary leaders further accused Spain of violating the principle of religious freedom by banning missionaries and restricting evangelical activities in all of its colonies. This followed a long history of similar allegations by British and U.S. Protestants who had built a global missionary movement alongside the British Empire. As British power expanded around the world, missionaries and their supporters had challenged all sorts of restrictions on the activities of missionaries or their converts as inconsistent with the basic principles of modern civilization. During an 1855 Evangelical Alliance campaign for religious liberty in Turkey, where conversion from Islam to Christianity was then illegal, the Earl of Aberdeen wrote, for example, that "if the Porte [had] any regard for the friendship of England," it would need to "renounce absolutely . . . the barbarous practice which has called forth [this] remonstrance."[20] Evangelical missionaries and their supporters thus used religious freedom talk to define English Protestantism in opposition to both Catholicism and Islam as the religion of modernity and civilization.

During and after the war with Spain, Anglo-Protestant religious freedom talk similarly supported the imperial ambitions of the United States. Not long before the war, the Caroline Islands in the Pacific region of Micronesia, not far to the east of the Philippines, had become a new site of contention.

The American Board of Commissioners for Foreign Missions sent missionaries to the Carolines starting in the 1850s, when they were nominally under German rule, and had founded about fifteen small churches there. The board complained that the situation had become far more difficult after Spain assumed control of the islands in the late 1880s. "Neither Bibles nor books have been permitted since then to be sent to the churches founded by our countrymen," one missionary advocate explained.[21] Much to the delight of the board, the people of the Carolines were well aware of Spain's global travails and had initiated their own revolt against Spanish rule. In that context, American Protestant opinion unanimously supported the demand of the board that the treaty with Spain ensure "full religious liberty" for both the Carolines and the Philippines, whether or not either of these colonies remained in Spanish hands. "Spanish Catholicism has throttled the best life of the Carolines and Philippines long enough," opined the *New York Observer and Chronicle.* "It is the providential duty of America to see to it that priestcraft in those sections no longer rules out other sects from equal religious privileges."[22]

The situation in the Carolines joined more general Protestant attacks on Catholic despotism to help make religious liberty a pivotal issue for American public opinion regarding the Spanish-American War and the geopolitical reconfigurations that followed. If the United States should gain control of the former Spanish colonies, the *Congregationalist* commented that spring, it would bring "religious as well as political liberty" to their people for the first time. The editors stated that the only people in Manila who opposed the prospect of American rule were "the priests and friars who [had] joined with the Spanish officials in plundering and debasing the natives" and so wanted no "abolition of union between church and state."[23] According to the *Washington Post,* the "religious press" of the United States overwhelmingly favored the colonization of the Philippines "for the reason, chiefly, that the clericalism which has prevailed there, and against which the recurring native revolts were mainly directed, would give way to freedom of conscience and religious liberty."[24] In this way, evangelical religious freedom talk enabled American claims for a superior right to empire in the Philippines.

These discourses of religious freedom defined the cast of American secularism—by which I mean both its quality and its cast of characters—and in so doing reinforced the assemblages of race and religion within the United States as well as among the colonies it seized. Protestant attacks on Spanish Catholicism challenged not only Spain's right to imperial authority but also the truth of American Catholic commitments to democracy. In an 1899 book titled *Facing the Twentieth Century,* Methodist clergyman James King, general secretary of the National League for the Protection of American Institutions, celebrated the growth of American religious liberty and highlighted the purported perils of Catholicism, or in his words "the claims of Political-Ecclesiastical Romanism to universal dominion," in the United States and across its expanding empire. Thankfully, he wrote, "Christianized Anglo-Saxon blood, with its love of liberty," was "the regnant force in this country. . . . God is using the Anglo-Saxon to conquer the world for Christ by dispossessing feebler races and assimilating and molding others." For King, the polity and the theology of Catholicism had made its adherents incapable of exercising true freedom, of being truly American, or of assuming the tutelary burdens of empire. In all these ways they resembled the "feebler" races whose racial classification reflected their status as the targets and subjects of empire. A vigorous, manly, and independent people would never embrace such a tyrannical system. In this civilizational assemblage, the basic principles of American secularism—the freedom of religion and the separation of church and state—were simultaneously Anglo-Saxon and Protestant. Conversely, the value of these principles showed the Anglo-Saxon Protestant's unique fitness for democratic practice and for imperial rule.[25]

The dominant varieties of American religious freedom talk linked white Protestantism to the secular modern, structuring the racial-religious assemblages of U.S. empire. At the fall 1898 triennial conference of the Protestant Episcopal Church in Washington, D.C., Bishop Daniel Tuttle of Missouri applauded the nation's leaders for taking on the civilizing "responsibilities" of a benevolent empire. "The Anglo-Saxon race seems harnessed to the twofold work of giving the world the sweets of personal liberty and the restraints of order, without which liberty cannot be preserved," he preached. Tuttle identified his own "Anglo-Saxon church" as best equipped to support the nation in this task.[26] For others, Protestant Christianity more generally played that role. The Reverend Robert S. MacArthur, pastor of New York's Calvary Baptist Church, celebrated the racial-religious character of the Anglo-Saxons in a sermon that identified both the British and U.S. empires with the intertwined progress of freedom and Christianity around the world. "The Anglo-Saxon stands for liberty in its fullest sense—political as well as religious," he claimed. "The Anglo-Saxon is also the colonizing race . . . [and] the great missionary race. It is divinely commissioned to introduce the highest forms of Christianity in all parts of the world."[27] Repeated ad infinitum in sermons and speeches, such rhetorics identified Americans as racially Anglo-Saxon, religiously Protestant, and divinely ordained for empire.

Yet the call for empire was far from unanimous, even among Anglo-Protestant elites. Like the Whigs who had opposed Manifest Destiny and the war with Mexico half a century before, some Americans argued that the nation could neither maintain its republican institutions on such a large scale nor survive the annexation of so many alien, non-white peoples. Appalled that the McKinley administration seemed set on seizing the Philippines and Puerto Rico, a determined and growing cadre of critics argued that the defining ideals of the United States could not be reconciled with an empire. "Have we set the Cubans free, or have we lost our own faith in freedom?" Henry van Dyke asked of those who wanted to annex the Philippines. "Imperialism and democracy . . . are self-contradictory terms." Van Dyke had ardently supported the war against Spain but argued that seizing any of Spain's former colonies would directly contradict the principles for which it had been fought. The United States must not betray its founding principles for the "European ideal of colonial conquest," he wrote. Convinced that freedom and empire could not be reconciled, van Dyke was among those who formed the Anti-imperialist League to oppose the U.S. colonization of the Philippines, Puerto Rico, or any other overseas territory.[28]

Anti-imperialists occasionally invoked the principle of religious freedom as a part of these broader critiques. The realities of acquiring and managing new colonial territories, they argued, would inevitably betray rather than bestow this hallowed ideal. When the Filipinos renewed their fight for independence in 1899, this time against the imposition of U.S. rule, the Anti-imperialist League published statements from a variety of (mostly Protestant) clergymen arguing that Americans had no right to force either their government or their religion on others. "How can we hope to recommend our religion or our civilization to those who can see in it only the ally of invading strangers who appear among them, much as Spain has done, with no right of mastery but that of the iron hand?" asked Charles Ames, minister of the Church of the Disciples (Unitarian) in Boston. A religion that accompanied imperial conquest would never be accepted freely but would inevitably be resisted. The truly American religion—assumed by these divines to be Protestant and liberal, tolerant and modern—was a free religion that could not be forced. And they contended that such a religion could neither accompany nor justify the violence of imperial conquest.[29]

Some Protestant anti-imperialists feared that the entrenched Catholicism of the Philippines would make it impossible to instill the freedom of religion in that colony and that the compromises of empire could threaten it even within the United States. Congregationalist minister and Yale church historian Leonard Bacon warned that U.S. property law would not allow the government to seize the Spanish friars' landholdings despite their history as "the real tyrants of the islands." Because the treaty with Spain guaranteed that the United States would uphold the rights of existing property-holders in the islands, its unintended consequence would be "to rivet forever upon the necks of the Philippine people the intolerable yoke of this spiritual and secular tyranny." In "the name of religious liberty," Bacon wrote, America would ironically become "the bulwark of an established church in the most offensive form." The logistics of imperial rule would make America complicit in a system that was the very antithesis of religious freedom. Worse yet, the annexation of so many new Catholic subjects or citizens would likely give increased political influence to Catholic leaders in the United States as well. In this way, Bacon warned, the realities of empire would actually undermine religious freedom both in the Philippines and in the United States.[30]

Clearly the disavowal of empire implied no necessary opposition to the hierarchies of race and religion. Some critics thought freedom and empire incommensurable precisely because they could not envision incorporating non-white and non-Protestant peoples, who allegedly lacked a racial propensity for the exercise of freedom, into the fabric of American democracy. One Episcopal clergyman asserted that "eight millions of people confessedly incompetent to govern themselves" could not "be injected into our system" without destroying it.[31] The populist hero William Jennings Bryan, who assumed the anti-imperialist mantle as Democratic candidate for president in 1899, expressed much the same fear of racial pollution. The nation's earlier expansions across North America had succeeded, Bryan said, because they had involved contiguous territory that was "to be populated by homogeneous people." (Never mind the indigenous and Mexican peoples who were conquered and displaced in the process, a violent history that Bryan's account conveniently erased.) President McKinley, Bryan charged, was proposing a completely novel plan for U.S. "sovereignty over an alien race . . . a theory entirely at variance with constitutional governance."[32] As Bryan's campaign reveals, a great deal of the popular momentum against imperialism grew out of a racial vision of America as a white republic, one that could not safely incorporate any more non-white subjects, either as immigrants or through the annexation of colonized territories, and reliably maintain its free institutions.[33]

Many anti-imperialists thus shared the view of religious freedom as a distinctively white and Protestant possession. Arguing against the idea that Protestant missions could "spread among all peoples the doctrines of human rights," Senator Donelson Caffery of Louisiana insisted that "the principles of democracy could [not] be advanced by force," and indeed might not be transferrable to non-white peoples at all. "The history of the world shows that God has set the bounds where the different peoples of the earth shall abide," Caffery claimed. "I am unalterably convinced that no permanent sway can be held by the white man over the black man in the sub-tropics, except by a strong military and cruel despotism."[34] Left unspoken here were the systems of racial subordination then being institutionalized across the South, systems that placed people of color outside the bounds of equal citizenship, excluding them from meaningful access to freedom of any kind. In other words, whether they were for or against imperialism, the majority of Anglo-Protestants agreed that they were racially superior and had a unique propensity for freedom. They differed on the prospects and possibilities of empire. Where the imperialists argued optimistically that Americans could impart the principles of freedom and civilization to their racial-religious inferiors, anti-imperialists judged the civilizational divide so impassable that all such attempts would be futile. At worst, they endangered the racial-religious purity of the American nation, threatening the foundations of freedom and democracy within the United States itself.

The Case for Empire in the Philippines

As soon as the treaty with Spain was settled, American imperialists shifted their focus away from the evils of the Spanish Empire to articulate their own model of imperial rule. They had to explain why the people of the new territories—who after all had been fighting for their own independence— should instead become subjects of the United States and how exactly U.S. rule would differ from its Spanish predecessor. The British imperial poet Rudyard Kipling entered into this American debate with his characteristic brew of white supremacy and a world-weary imperial cynicism. His poem "The White Man's Burden," aimed at those Americans who were not yet convinced of the need for empire, urged the United States to take up the thankless task of civilizing its "new-caught, sullen peoples / Half-devil and half-child." This was a virulent racism that could explain any indigenous opposition, any resistance to colonial rule. Far from the freedom fighters that they claimed to be, Kipling suggested, such people simply lacked the capacity to understand the civilizing benefits of Anglo-Saxon rule.[35]

What Filipinos most needed, according to the Anglo-Protestants who dominated American public debate, was the sort of tutelage in freedom that only the United States could provide. As the social gospel leader Washington Gladden put it, the most important benefits of U.S. rule would be the introduction of "religious freedom, education, [and] the ideals of democracy." Cubans, Puerto Ricans, and Filipinos had all been kept in a "degraded" condition by Spain, he claimed. Maintained as "child races, not far removed from barbarism," they remained entirely unprepared for the exercise of freedom. And while the more "advanced" races had no right to "enslave or exterminate" their inferiors, they did have "the right to civilize them." This was a fine line indeed, since Gladden explained that such civilizing work could and should be advanced by force if the "child races" offered any resistance. Protestant Christianity and scientific racism worked together in this prescription to frame the civilizational assemblages and justify the violent impositions of U.S. empire.[36]

Gladden's rationale also demonstrates the ways in which religious freedom intersected with the commercial imperatives of empire. The freedoms bestowed on colonial subjects were not mere abstractions but would serve as engines of economic development. Making the land "productive" for commercial profit appeared in Gladden's argument as a key component of the civilizing task. And the freedom of religion, because it formed subjects capable of individual initiative and independent judgment, was essential to the development of commerce, capitalism, and free enterprise in the Philippines. For Gladden, the absence of religious freedom was the factor that most defined the racial "backwardness" of Spain's colonial subjects. Its advent under U.S. rule would do more than any other single reform to aid their progress in the values, virtues, and profits of civilization.[37]

The role of religious freedom in the formative stages of U.S. policy in the Philippines is perhaps best understood through the figure of Dean Worcester, an ambitious young scholar who would help shape and administer that policy. As a zoologist at the University of Michigan, Worcester had conducted research in the Philippines for several years prior to the war with Spain. His book *The Philippine Islands and Their People* took advantage of the political moment by providing a kaleidoscopic study of the islands along with concluding recommendations on how they should be governed. Worcester came from a family with a long history of involvement in Protestant missions and moral reform. His grandfather, the Congregationalist minister and missionary Samuel Worcester, had supported the Cherokee Indians in the losing battle against their removal west to the Indian Territory in the famous case *Worcester v. Georgia* (1832). Dean Worcester was no missionary, but he was similarly convinced of the link between Protestantism and freedom and equally committed to the civilizing goals of U.S. empire. Soon his ideas would have more than academic significance. Several months after the book appeared, President McKinley appointed him to the first Philippine Commission, charged with shaping policy for the new colony. Later he became secretary of the interior for the Philippines, responsible for various aspects of colonial rule including the management of the "non-Christian tribes" in the islands.[38]

Worcester's proposals for civilizing the predominantly Catholic population of the Philippines gave considerable prominence to the principle of religious freedom. Like most Americans grounded in the dominant Protestant milieu, he considered the Spanish Empire corrupt and despotic, mired by its Catholic establishment in the cruelties of the medieval world. Even as he praised Spain for turning its colonial subjects into the most "civilized" people of Southeast Asia, he accused the friars of the Dominican, Augustinian, and Franciscan orders of a crippling tyranny that had resulted in "the utter demoralization of many Philippine towns and villages," leaving the people subservient and childlike. The Protestant and democratic traditions of the United States made it the ideal nation to complete this failed civilizing mission. American religious freedom would open up "an active competition" between Protestants and Catholics in the archipelago, he wrote, strengthening both traditions and enabling Filipinos to exercise true freedom of conscience for the first time. In keeping with the Christian republican tradition, Worcester saw religious freedom as the key to independent judgment and thus to responsible citizenship in a modern democracy. In other words, it would elevate the Filipinos' level of civilization, eventually enabling them to gain the political independence they so greatly desired. (As always in such civilizing schema, the catch here was that Americans, not Filipinos, were to judge when this process was complete. In practice this was an ever-receding horizon, providing an ideal rationale for the indefinite maintenance of U.S. rule.)[39]

Worcester did not, however, apply this freedom evenly to all the peoples of the Philippines. Critical of simplistic reports like Gladden's that depicted all Filipinos as "savages," he followed a classificatory model created by Jesuit ethnographers to identify more than eighty tribes in the islands. These tribes could be organized into four broad categories, defined in simultaneously racial and religious terms as "Negritos, Mohammedan Malays, pagan Malays, [and] civilized Malays." Worcester condemned the "religious monopoly" of the friars among the civilized Malays—defined as such because of their conversion to Catholicism—but praised the Jesuit missions to the non-Christian Negritos and pagans as "distinctly a power for good." While Worcester

detested the friars, members of the mendicant orders that so dominated Filipino Catholic life, he generally admired the Jesuits for their universities and
widespread missions across the Philippine Islands. But Worcester's praise for
the Jesuits also reflected the distinctions he made among the peoples of the
archipelago. In his view, the relatively civilized Catholics required liberation
from the tyranny of the friars so that they could progress to the highest levels
of civilization. In contrast, the "savages" of the Philippines were so wild and
anarchic that they needed the disciplining influence of Catholicism before
their civilizing process could even begin. These racial classifications, paired
with Worcester's inability to recognize religion among those he classified as
"pagan" or "savage," would make the concept of religious freedom entirely
irrelevant to his recommendations for their futures.[40]

Worcester applied yet another set of policy recommendations to the
remaining racial-religious category of "Mohammedan Malays," better
known as Moros. The Spanish term, meaning "Moors," dated to the early
modern wars between Catholics and Muslims in the Iberian Peninsula,
and Spaniards had applied it to all the Muslims they encountered. Like the
Spanish and the British in the region before them, Americans considered all
Muslims to be fanatics who shared certain racial-religious characteristics.
The Moros were "fanatical Moslems" and "fierce warriors," Worcester wrote,
driven above all by the "bitterest hatred" toward all Christians. As a result
they would require special techniques of governance. "I consider it certain
that the nation which would have any hope of getting on peaceably with
them," he opined, "*must let their religion strictly alone*." Even as he called
for the imposition of American standards of religious freedom for Catholic
Filipinos, he believed that the Moros were not yet ready for that system. He
warned that any interference with the Moros' religion would spark a revolt
that could not be subdued without "a considerable body of troops for many
years to come." Even as he advocated an individual freedom of conscience
for the Catholic Filipinos, then, Worcester insisted that the Moros should
be permitted to maintain their own religious traditions without interference
from missionaries or anyone else. When it came to "fanatical Moslems," this
was evidently the only kind of religious freedom consistent with the maintenance of colonial rule.[41]

These American images of the Philippines were part of a global circula-
tion of imperial knowledge and power that rested on (and continually reinscribed) the intersecting civilizational assemblages of race and religion. A
typical editorial page in the ardently imperialist weekly *Outlook*, this one
from October 1899, remarked on current events including the crisis in South

Africa, where the Dutch settler-colonial society of the Boers was embarking on its revolution against British rule; the ongoing Philippine-American War, labeled an "insurrection" by the *Outlook*; the rights of corporations and their stockholders in a burgeoning economy; various hot topics in the leading Protestant denominations; and the racial and religious progress attributed to the "Negro" in the American South.[42]

Read together, the editors' remarks offer a kaleidoscopic view of the classificatory rationales of American empire at the dawn of the twentieth century. In the South African situation, many Americans found their sympathies divided between the Boers and the British, whom they viewed as allies in the global expansion of "Anglo-Saxon" principles of freedom. Yet the Boers elicited sympathy, the *Outlook* suggested, because their story so closely paralleled "the setting forth of the Pilgrims from Holland." Like the Puritans they had shown a "touching reliance upon the Supreme Being," as well as "the spirit of entire democracy in ritual," while their fight against the British echoed the themes of the American Revolution. Whatever position the editors might ultimately take on the Boer War, their frank admiration for the Boers as white Protestants settling and "civilizing" an African frontier could not have been clearer. In contrast, the *Outlook* depicted all Filipinos as racial "savages" who required the civilizing influence of white American rule.[43]

Consider also the *Outlook*'s remarks about reports of "progress" on the part of "the Negro of the New South." The editors applauded the emergence of a more "self-conscious colored man, less optimistic, less mirthful . . . and with a more acute sense of pain and suffering." Summarizing an essay by David St. Clair, who had recently returned to the region after a long sojourn in the North, they noted a trend in "the colored churches" toward "more decorous services." The editors went on to explain that the "educated colored preachers" were "now trying to teach [their] people to reason and think." White Americans had long portrayed black religiosity as excessively emotional; standard accounts of "Negro" worship mocked the "ignorance" of the preachers and depicted its "frenzy" as entirely opposed to the virtues of reason and morality. (The contrast to the journal's portrayal of the white Boers' sober religiosity, with a ritual that conveyed "the spirit of entire democracy," was stark.) According to St. Clair, "the Negro" was progressing away from such religious emotionalism and in the process developing "a nervous system like that of the white." Such apparently sympathetic reports rested on the assumption that if black or brown peoples were to progress toward civilization, they would need to adopt the racial-religious characteristics ascribed to white Protestant America.[44]

The *Outlook*'s juxtaposition of topics reveals the subtle ways in which the ideal of religious freedom helped constitute the civilizational hierarchies of empire. Commenting on current efforts to reform theological education, the editors asserted that the "manhood" of too many seminary students was being "stultified" and "threatened" by "dictated lectures" and "plagiarized platitudes." "Seminaries which will emancipate the minds of their students must themselves be free from bondage to the letter of antiquated creeds," they concluded.[45] This particular piece had no direct link to the rhetorics of empire. Situated alongside the editors' comments on South Africa, the Philippines, and the New Negro, however, it posited a simultaneously racial, religious, and gendered capacity for the free exercise of conscience as a primary factor in the presumed superiority of white (and male and Protestant) subjects.

AMERICAN CATHOLICS AND THE PROSPECTS OF EMPIRE

Far beyond the world of the Anglo-Protestant elite, religious freedom talk was a useful tool for many people who wanted to locate themselves as equal partners in the American experiment—and to transform themselves into actors rather than subjects of the imperial modern. In the Spanish-American War, whether or not they supported the call for empire that followed, Catholics, Jews, and many others outside the cultural mainstream invoked the ideal of religious freedom to resist the norms of the Protestant secular and the assumptions of Anglo-Protestant superiority that so pervaded American public life. For Catholics this was an especially urgent task because anti-Catholicism was so central to the public rationale for the war with Spain. Their deployments of religious freedom would unsettle the Protestant foundations of the American secular and, in the process, would implicate them too in the civilizational hierarchies of U.S. empire.

Many Catholics found it difficult to support a war against Spain, which they had long admired for its successes in exporting Catholicism to its colonial possessions around the globe. During the buildup to the war, Jesuit priest Thomas Hughes condemned the impulse to "tear away the last shred of [Spain's] American possessions" as motivated by a pervasive hatred of Catholicism. The revolutionaries in Cuba and the Philippines had set themselves against "Catholic principles and Catholic life," he claimed, and did not represent the vast majority of their people. Hughes offered a romantic portrait of Spanish culture as devoutly Catholic and blessedly free of the "sectarianism, infidelity, and paganism" that were so rampant in the United States. Denouncing the Black Legend of Spanish imperial cruelty, he pointed out that the indigenous populations of Latin America had remained large and relatively prosperous, even as the North American Indians had been virtually eliminated. "Anglo-American hypocrites" had single-mindedly pursued land and gold, he wrote, decimating indigenous populations rather than bringing them Christianity and civilization. "And then do you not smile when they preach liberty, felicity for the whole world," Hughes asked, "believing themselves invested with the divine mission of propagating civilization all over the earth?" In his view, any war against Spain would be driven by the irrational Anglo-Protestant hatred of Catholicism and by a pervasive greed that the rhetorics of a civilizing mission could never really mask.[46]

American Catholic opinion was never monolithic, though, and by the time the war began some Catholics were prepared to offer it their enthusiastic endorsement. Among them were the Paulists, an order founded by the American convert Isaac Hecker and known for advocating Catholicism's compatibility with American values.[47] The Paulist journal the *Catholic World* judged the conflict regrettable but necessary and applauded President McKinley's "wise, humane, and patriotic" response to what the editors recognized as Spanish imperial cruelty in Cuba. Against the flood of Protestant propaganda, however, the editors carefully exonerated the Catholic Church from responsibility for the abuses of Spain. Instead they blamed the irreligion of a Spanish aristocracy that had abandoned its salutary guidance. The Freemasons, long condemned by Rome as an enemy to religion, had become "rampant" among the "greedy officialdom" of Spain, the paper reported. More generally, the editors believed, a dangerously antireligious liberalism had gained influence among the Spanish elite. All this had left the Spanish ruling class bereft of any spiritual and ethical grounding and motivated solely by the accumulation of wealth and power. Spain had fallen into "spiritual degeneracy," one writer explained. "Her officials became venal, and some of her clergy the victims of the state." The same forces that had attempted to destroy the church in Spain had turned the Spanish Empire into a profit-making machine. If Spain had been authentically Catholic, it would have treated its colonial subjects with justice and there would have been no war.[48]

Whether or not they supported the war, Catholics invariably located their church alongside the United States as a champion of freedom. The Catholic Church should not just be absolved of responsibility for the crisis, they argued, but should actually be called upon to help resolve it. "The sentiment that burns so strongly in the American heart that Cuba must be free will so impress itself on the European nations and the Holy Father," predicted the *Catholic World*, "that they will compel Spain to yield to the demands of humanity" so that the war would be mercifully brief. Protestant pundits were predictably infuriated at such calls for papal mediation. They argued that such an appeal would compromise American principles of church-state separation and that it revealed the hidden political allegiance of American Catholics to the pope. (There could be no "settlement of the burning questions confronting us as a Nation, based upon propositions emanating from Rome," one Methodist resolution read. "American institutions will guard their own honor.")[49] Catholics disagreed. They countered Protestant outrage by presenting the pope and the church more generally as forces for "humanity," working for human dignity and freedom around the world. In other words, they positioned themselves and their church on the side of the modern values of freedom, democracy, and civilization.[50]

By participating in the war, many American Catholics sought to demonstrate their patriotism and their commitment to the United States and to its founding principles. In the process they also asserted their own right to be recognized as fully American, equal in every way to the Anglo-Protestant elite. In an obituary for one Captain John Drum, killed in action in Cuba, the *Catholic World* described the deceased as a "manly Catholic character . . . truly cultivated [and] a lover of learning . . . that type that has added new glories to the church and is daily imparting strength and beauty of character to the Republic itself." The captain, an Irish immigrant who had arrived in the United States as a teenager, was also a veteran of the Indian wars of the 1870s, when he had fought against the Kiowas and Comanches in Texas and the Apaches in Arizona. His obituary illustrates how Catholic participation in the violence of U.S. imperial expansion enabled Catholic pundits to (re)present Irish immigrants—so often despised and denigrated as racially inferior to the Anglo-Saxon model of American manhood—as true American patriots who fulfilled every requirement of the civilized and democratic ideal. Drum was "a true American, a true Catholic, a true man," the obituary concluded. In this way, the *Catholic World* used Drum's faithfulness as a Catholic and his service to the imperial project to identify him as the very model of civilized (white) American manhood. By killing Indians and Spaniards, it seemed, an Irish immigrant to America could also become white— and in so doing could push the bounds of an imperial secular beyond its Anglo-Protestant foundations.[51]

When public debate turned to the question of annexing the Philippines, the majority of American Catholics took an anti-imperialist stand. Most were longtime Democrats with an inherited suspicion of the Republicans as the party of Protestant moral reform. Now they joined in the Democratic attacks on Republican imperialism as fundamentally un-American, a misguided attempt at reforming the world. Irish and German Catholic newspapers in particular condemned the civilizing claims of the imperialists as hypocritical, driven by Anglo-Protestant greed and hatred for Catholicism. Biased colonial officials were likely to expel the Spanish friars from the Philippines, they warned, and the imposition of an unfamiliar U.S. legal system would strip the church of its accustomed privileges and perhaps even of its landholdings in the islands. The Cuban and Filipino insurgents had been "lifted out of barbarism by the Church," remarked Boston's Catholic weekly, the *Sacred Heart Review*. "It is these ungrateful people that some of our Protestant missionaries encourage in their acts of lawlessness." American Protestants with their imperial ambitions had no right, they argued, to interfere with the legacy of Catholicism in colonies that had for so long been ruled by Spain.[52]

Like their Protestant counterparts, Catholic anti-imperialists identified their cause with the American secular ideals of democracy and freedom. But they flipped the script to assert that it was the Anglo-Saxon Protestants, not the Catholics, who most threatened those principles in the current debate. George Washington himself had warned against "the development of greed for foreign territory," noted the *Sacred Heart Review*, and the "Anglo-Saxon imperialists" would do well to follow his example. According to Bryan J. Clinch, an Irish nationalist in California and a regular contributor to the *American Catholic Quarterly Review*, the United States should not compromise its republican principles to follow the shortsighted and greedy "land-grabbing" example of the British. "Would the lordship of Asia make ourselves either more free or more prosperous, or would it develop new virtues in our people?" Clinch asked. "If not, why should we attempt it at the sacrifice of our best traditions?" Such arguments had special resonance for Irish immigrants who had come to the United States to escape legal discrimination and abuse at the hands of British Protestants. The idea that Britain and America should now join together in the name of a shared Anglo-Saxon imperial mission was, in their eyes, hypocritical cant that betrayed the American principles of freedom and equality that they had embraced.

In the current drive for U.S. empire, they saw only Anglo-Protestant hubris and hypocrisy.[53]

In and through the language of religious freedom, these Catholics positioned themselves as more truly American than their Anglo-Protestant counterparts, better aligned with the nation's founding ideals. In other words, they expanded the bounds of the American secular to include or even to center themselves and the interests of their church. The *Sacred Heart Review* condemned the hypocrisy of American Bible Society missionary John Hykes, for example, whose recent report on the Philippines presented the Spanish friars as obstacles to an otherwise ripe field for "Bible work." "If we have any control of the islands, it will be as much our duty to protect the Spanish priest as the American missionary," the editors remarked, "unless we reverse our ancient policy and make of our claim of freedom of worship a barren ideality." It would have prevented many unnecessary complications, they claimed, and might have been better for all concerned, "if Dewey had sailed away after he [so] gallantly destroyed the Spanish fleet" in Manila. Unless the Anglo-Protestant bigots could be held in check and the United States held accountable to its constitutional principles, the editors argued, the prospect of U.S. rule in the Philippines posed a significant threat to Catholicism and to the freedom of religion that the Catholic people of the islands already enjoyed.[54]

Commodore George Dewey had not sailed away, of course, and as it became clear that the imperialists were on the winning side, Catholic commentators turned to the question of how to protect the church's interests in the former Spanish colonies. Protestant meddlers seemed to be at work even in Cuba, despite the U.S. promise to recognize that nation's independence. "Let the Protestant zealots do their best on their own hook," opined the *Sacred Heart Review*, "but when our government undertakes to interfere in any way to the advantage of the Protestant propaganda, we insist that it is an exercise of arbitrary, tyrannical power." Whether in Cuba or in the Philippines, the paper stated, the United States had "no right . . . to change the character of the Catholic schools and make them secular after the example of the schools in our own country, nor to suspend the salaries of the priests." Where Protestant pundits were always clamoring that Catholics posed a threat to American freedoms, Catholic writers asserted that the Protestants were actually at fault. Despite the constitutional ban on religious establishment, they had the nerve to call America a "Protestant country" and infringed on the legitimate rights and freedoms of the Catholic Church both within the United States and in the island territories it now claimed.[55]

As they laid claim to the all-American principles of freedom and democracy, Catholics were not only expanding the bounds of the American secular but also locating themselves within the hierarchies of the imperial modern. We have seen that the Anglo-Saxon majority typically classified the immigrants who made up the bulk of the U.S. Catholic population as inferior in simultaneously racial and religious terms. At times that situation inspired Catholic statements of solidarity with other racialized subjects of American rule. Especially in the Northeast, some Irish Catholics affirmed African American critiques of U.S. imperialism as the other face of the domestic racial order and identified common elements between black and Irish experiences of oppression.[56] Yet this solidarity had its limits. However critical they were of Anglo-Saxon racism and wherever they stood on the question of empire, most Catholic speakers rhetorically positioned themselves on the white side of the racial divide. When the *Sacred Heart Review* quoted African Methodist Episcopal bishop Henry McNeal Turner on the hypocrisies of empire, it did not challenge the idea that the "colored" and "oriental" races stood in need of civilization. "Wouldn't it be well for Uncle Sam to solve the race problem," the editors asked, "which [as] Bishop Turner, the colored Methodist divine says, is still far from solved in this country, before he undertakes to elevate the various oriental races that inhabit the Philippines?"[57] Such critiques rarely challenged the racial hierarchies of empire. Instead they reconfigured those hierarchies to rank (white) Catholics and (white) Protestants as equals. In other words, they pushed to replace the Anglo-Saxon at the top tier of the American racial order with the somewhat broader category of whiteness, a category that could include European immigrants who happened to be Catholics within its scope.

American Catholics as Agents of Empire

Even as popular Catholic opinion maintained a decidedly anti-imperialist tone, the American Catholic hierarchy readily identified with the prospects and possibilities of U.S. empire in the Philippines. Soon after the end of the war, Pope Leo XIII appointed Archbishop Placide Chapelle of New Orleans to serve as apostolic delegate to Cuba and Puerto Rico, and to the Philippines as well if they were to become a permanent possession of the United States. The archbishop, a personal friend of President McKinley's, traveled to Paris that October to discuss the situation with the pope. His public account of the visit promised that Rome would support the imposition of American law in all the territories taken over from Spain, including "the conditions of religious liberty" that had enabled Catholicism to prosper in the United States. "My duties will be to enable the Bishops to place the church on a footing suitable to the new political changes," he explained. Chapelle promised especially to foster "the liberty of conscience" and, in whatever ways might be appropriate to his role as a representative of the church, to support the government in ensuring "liberty and justice for all." In other words, the archbishop insisted that Catholic interests were entirely consistent with American rule and the concomitant advancement of religious freedom in the former Spanish colonies.[58]

Through such statements the Catholic hierarchy hoped to convince both Protestants and Catholics that U.S. imperial interests were seamlessly aligned with those of the Catholic Church in the Philippines. Archbishop Chapelle claimed that, although the church would no doubt have a difficult period of adjustment after it lost state support in the former Spanish colonies, its freedom from state control would prove beneficial in the long run. Catholicism had lost a degree of public esteem both in Cuba and the Philippines from the church's evident support for Spanish rule. Catholics generally denied that the church had been guilty of anything other than cooperating with legitimate civil authority. If it had been involved in any improprieties, they argued, it had done so only under pressure from Spain. Chapelle and his colleagues argued that by eliminating even the possibility of such collusion, the end of the colonial Catholic establishment could facilitate a renewal of Catholic faith wherever it may have been shaken by the corruptions of the Spanish regime. In this way they tried to convince a skeptical Protestant public that under U.S. Catholic leadership, the church in these new colonies would support the American model of religious freedom and church-state separation, as well as to reassure their Catholic flocks that the church would benefit from this change.[59]

Catholic leaders insisted that the new terms of American rule must grant certain prerogatives to the church, both to preserve the freedom of religion and to protect the interests of the colonial order. The real danger to religious freedom, they argued, came not from Catholicism but from the bigoted attitudes that threatened to violate its rightful place in the islands. Archbishop John Ireland of St. Paul, Minnesota, one of the most liberal members of the U.S. Catholic hierarchy, sparked considerable controversy when he criticized Protestant plans to send missionaries to Cuba and the Philippines. He argued that while such missionaries had every legal right to be there, their presence would be disruptive because they would offend the freely chosen faith of these historically Catholic peoples. Telling the Filipinos "that their historic faith is wrong," he said, "would be the speediest and most effective way to make the inhabitants of these islands discontented and opposed to America." Protestants had "no more occasion to send missionaries to Santiago, Havana, or Manila than to Washington, D.C.," he complained.[60] Because their people were already Catholic, Catholicism was the faith best equipped to support the transition of these former Spanish colonies into modern and democratic societies under the guidance of the United States. Properly understood, the American principle of religious freedom would protect Catholicism as the chosen religion of their people.

The real offenders against religious freedom in the Philippines, asserted the *Catholic World*, were not Catholics but the Protestants who called for the Spanish friars to be permanently banished. These "bigots" had apparently forgotten that the "constitutional prohibition against establishing a State Religion" prevented the U.S. government from "having anything to say as to who shall exercise the pastoral office among Catholics."[61] Reporting the appointment of Dean Worcester to the Philippine Commission in February 1899, the editors bemoaned the lack of any commissioner who could "establish a sympathetic relationship with the people in their most sacred interest." They warned that if the government took an "attitude of opposition to the friars, and as a consequence an appearance of antagonism to the highest aspirations of the people in their religious life," it would "require a mint of money and no end of soldiery to keep the islands in subjection." They argued that a favorable climate for the church would only aid the civilizing work of the tutelary regime. "We cannot hope to teach the natives there self-government while we are considered enemies to their religion," they concluded. Where Protestant-minded officials like Worcester were convinced that all Filipinos hated the friars and that expelling the latter would help pacify the islands, Catholic pundits asserted that such expulsions would be a travesty of justice and would only exacerbate Filipino resentments against American rule. Their critiques unmasked at least one of the exclusions of the Anglo-Protestant secular. In so doing, their religious freedom talk linked the protection of Catholic institutions to the interests of U.S. empire in the Philippines.[62]

Accounts of American troops who looted Catholic churches and colonial officials who actively favored Protestant teachers and missionaries were even more upsetting to Catholic sensibilities. Archbishop Ireland reported that some ignorant soldiers had committed the offense of stealing "Catholic vestments" from churches "as trophies from the Philippines." And when a military officer led the way in establishing Protestant churches, as one had recently done in Puerto Rico, this "was enough to make [the people] think that America was officially opposed to the Catholic religion." Americans must "assure the Filipinos without delay," the archbishop concluded, "that no churches will be looted, that Catholic churches and monasteries will be respected everywhere; [and] that what we are introducing is a civilization under which Catholics and Protestants have equal rights under equal State protection."[63] Given the freedom to manage its own affairs, a freedom it had never enjoyed under Spain, the Catholic Church would become a more powerful civilizing influence than it had ever been before. "If the United States respects the rights of conscience, [and] leaves to the church, so long fettered by connection with the state, the power to complete the work she began so well," claimed the *Catholic World*, "[then] it is beyond the limits of imagination to predict the future of the Philippines."[64] As these American Catholics saw it, they were better equipped than their Protestant counterparts to complete the civilizing work so nobly begun by the Spanish friars in the Philippines.

Such complaints were not confined to the pages of Catholic periodicals. In November 1900 fifty delegates from fourteen different laymen's organizations organized a national federation to combat anti-Catholic discrimination in the United States and its colonial possessions. Father F. H. Wall of New York City's Holy Rosary Church commented that these good Catholics were "simply demand[ing] their rights under the Constitution." The cases of discrimination he named all involved colonial administration: the U.S. government's abandonment of its pledge to support the civilizing work of Catholic schools on Indian reservations, "the looting of Catholic churches in the Philippines by the American troops," and the recent refusal by General Leonard Wood, who was then governor-general of Cuba and would later be reassigned to the Philippines, "to recognize a marriage solemnized by the rites of the Catholic Church."[65] This was a Catholic articulation of American secularism that clearly asserted a place for Catholics as agents of U.S. empire.

Catholic reviews of Dean Worcester's book *The Philippine Islands and Their People* further illustrate how Catholic religious freedom talk strengthened the position of (white) American Catholics in the civilizational hierarchies of empire.[66] In order to defend their church, Catholic writers generally ranked the Filipinos at a higher level of civilization than Protestant-minded imperialists were willing to do. The *Catholic World* commented that even Worcester had been forced to recognize the friars as Spain's most successful agents of colonial "subjugation" and to acknowledge that they had turned the Filipinos into a civilized people.[67] But by attributing all of the Filipinos' civilizational progress to the church, these American Catholics tended to demean their prior racial capacities. Like Worcester—and recall that Worcester himself had followed the lead of earlier Jesuit ethnographers—they placed non-Catholics in the islands at the very bottom of the civilizational scale. An essay by Augustinian priest W. A. Jones on the legacy of the Spanish friars featured a photograph of well-dressed Filipinos in front of a church with the caption "Barbarian Hordes Transformed into a Most Civilized People." The "pagans" remaining in the Philippines were a small minority whose inferiority, for Jones, only proved the broader successes of a church that had turned its converts into "the most civilized people of the Orient." Like their Protestant counterparts, Catholic imperialists pegged the scale of civilization to a European standard. However much the church had succeeded in civilizing the Filipinos, as formerly "barbarian" Orientals they could never quite measure up to those who had set the standard in the first place.[68]

Catholic anti-imperialists linked the civilizing successes of the church to its established status and warned that the United States with its secular system of government might not be capable of ruling such a "savage" people. The *Sacred Heart Review* asserted that the Moros and other "savage" tribes were "incorrigible pirates" and headhunters, a primitive and violent people who had not yet been tamed by Christianity or the rule of law. The Catholic Church was the only authority that had ever made progress in civilizing such people, and the United States should think twice before it interfered with its role. Under the "present regime," the editors claimed, the people "look up to the missionary as a father, and he treats them as children." If the United States destroyed that system, they wrote, "a state of anarchy seems certain to follow." If the civil authority of the church and the friars were eliminated, as they inevitably would be under U.S. law, the once-civilized people of the islands would likely sink back into the "anarchy" of their "savage" counterparts. "Do We Want These Citizens?" the headline asked. In this piece the *Sacred Heart Review* questioned the civilizing abilities of a secular empire. In so doing it positioned American Catholics—in contrast to the non-white Filipinos whose modernity would always be in question—as modern, civilized subjects who did not require the guiding hand of an established church.[69]

The U.S. Catholic hierarchy generally rejected the pessimism of this anti-imperialist position and rearticulated the principle of religious freedom to locate Catholicism as a truly American religion, squarely in the mold of the American secular and working in the interests of U.S. empire.

When Protestant pundits attacked the work of the Spanish friars, the *Catholic World* replied that despite the structural challenges they faced, the friars had proven themselves far more effective than the Protestant missionaries in that other new U.S. territory of Hawai'i. These missionaries had utterly failed to "make anything out of the natives," one Catholic visitor to Hawai'i commented. Their "principal work" had been "to convert the earth to their own inheritance." With the islands under U.S. rule, Catholic priests had now embarked on the "good work" that needed to be done on the Hawai'ian Islands.[70] In this way both the imperialists and the anti-imperialists among American Catholics positioned themselves and their church as the agents of civilization. They became fully American, fully modern, and racially white by contrasting themselves not only to Anglo-Protestant avarice but also to the "natives" of Hawai'i and the Philippines, portrayed as racial inferiors whose conversion to Catholicism and the civilization it brought was inevitably incomplete.

A growing editorial sympathy for these Catholic claims from leading American newspapers suggests that these repositioning tactics succeeded. The outbreak of war between the United States and the newly declared Republic of the Philippines facilitated this shift. As chapter 2 will detail, Filipino revolutionary leaders considered themselves rightfully independent and resented the imposition of U.S. rule. Suddenly most Americans started to see the Filipinos not as hapless victims of Spanish tyranny but as racial savages and potential tyrants themselves. This shift enabled many non-Catholics to find a new credibility in the Spanish friars' accounts of the Filipinos' revolt against Spain. Reporting on the arrival of thirteen Augustinians in San Francisco, the *New York Times* described their "story . . . of persecution, rapine, and revolting cruelty" at the hands of Filipino revolutionary forces as "the best-authenticated bit of history on that subject" that the world had yet heard.[71]

The *New York Times* now saw the Filipino revolutionaries rather than the Spanish friars as the most significant threat to religious freedom in the islands. In this interview and elsewhere, exiled friars accused Filipino troops of unspeakable "barbarism" and "inhumanity" against the religious orders, and thus against religion itself. Their only hope was that peace would someday be restored, they said, so that they could "go back to their parishes . . . and resume their work there among the natives." With Spanish authority irrevocably gone, they saw the United States as their only salvation. "We all look for tolerance from the Stars and Stripes," one of the friars explained, "and nothing but protracted persecution" from the "sham and nominal republican form of government" that the Filipinos had recently announced. Appealing to the good graces of U.S. empire, these Spanish friars and the growing ranks of their American supporters deployed the freedom of religion as a sign and symbol of American modernity, of democratic freedoms that the purportedly savage Filipinos could simply not be trusted to manage.[72]

In the fall of 1898 and the early months of 1899, as tensions in the Philippines escalated and the war began, many Americans concluded that Filipinos were not racially equipped to handle the full scope of democratic freedoms. Some argued that even the freedom of religion should be introduced only gradually so as not to disrupt the moral authority of Catholicism in the islands. "The Roman Catholic Church must [somehow] be maintained in full efficiency in Cuba, Puerto Rico, and the Philippines," the *Times* opined that September. In order to govern effectively, the editors argued, the U.S. government must find some way to support this church without violating the First Amendment. Noting the long history of the Catholic Church in the islands, and building on lingering associations of Catholicism with the superstitious and the primitive, they asserted that only it could "reach, influence, and restrain" such a people. Without it, they feared, "we should find it a hard task to prevent a progressive degradation and relapse toward savagery."[73] Well beyond Catholic ranks, the church now appeared to many Americans as a valuable tool for imperial management and control.

In the civilizational assemblages of empire, the idea that Filipinos were racially unprepared for complete religious freedom would help explain the variety of prophetic movements that joined in the revolt against American rule. In 1900 the *New York Times* ridiculed the messianic teachings and what it called the "weird shriekings" of the Gabinists, a heterodox religious movement with a history of several decades in central Luzon, whose leader had just been arrested by American officials for "banditry" and insurrection. "With the advent of the Americans and their proclaimed intention to give everybody the right to have whatever religion best suited him," the writer commented, "the flame [of the Gabinists] was fanned into fresh life" and now nurtured violent revolt. This piece figured the revolutionary involvements of the Gabinists as precisely the kind of irrational "savagery" that the *Times* had warned against two years earlier: the product of what the editors saw as more religious freedom than Filipinos could handle. Revolutionary violence could be attributed not to the condition of colonial subjugation but instead to a "savage" or "primitive" religion whose persistence defined the Filipinos as racially incapable of handling the full freedoms of American democracy, let alone their own affairs as an independent nation. Along the way, American Catholicism had been successfully repositioned as the ideal civilizing force, a church that had adapted itself to American democracy but maintained the claims of a singular Truth and was already embedded as a moral authority in the Philippines. Catholicism, in other words, now played a key role in the imperial secular.[74]

AMERICAN JEWS, RELIGIOUS BROTHERHOOD, AND THE IMPERIAL MODERN

Catholics were not the only racial-religious minority to reframe the principle of religious freedom to challenge Anglo-Protestant supremacy in the quest for empire. American Jews, too, overwhelmingly joined in the praise for the war and the imperial expansions that followed as triumphs for "civil and religious liberty." With no immediate need to distinguish their rhetorics of freedom from those of the Protestant majority, Jews tended to join that majority in blaming Spanish colonial cruelties at least in part on the Catholic Church. The *American Israelite*, published in Cincinnati, attributed the "cruelty of Spain" and "the inferiority of her army" to the "overwhelming power" of a church that controlled every aspect of Spanish life.[75] But this critique did not simply echo Anglo-Protestant rhetorics. Instead it reflected a long history of Spanish restrictions on Jewish mobility and livelihoods, beginning with the formal expulsion of Jews (and Muslims) from Spain in 1492. Jews had generally attributed all such restrictions both in Spain and in its imperial possessions to the established Catholic Church. Fervently supporting America's claim to the Philippines, for example, Reform rabbi Gustav Gottheil claimed that Spanish Catholic leaders had mandated the exclusion of "Jews, infidels, and married women" from any sort of legal protection in the Philippines. This oppressive reality would finally end with the religious freedom that would accompany American rule.[76]

This kind of enthusiasm for U.S. empire reflected a general conviction among American Jews that they enjoyed much better conditions than their counterparts around the world. The *Israelite* explained that in contrast to Spain, the United States had "permitted no Church in any form to interfere with the State; emancipated the people from all authority of any Church; [and] started out with civil and religious liberty for all alike." In contrast to the cruelties and cultural stagnation of Spain, the policy of religious freedom had forged in Americans the traits of "free individuality, energy, wealth, power, profound peace, satisfaction and loyalty." Religious freedom had thus built the national character that enabled victory over Spain and demonstrated America's fitness for empire.[77] It would also be one of the most important results of American rule. The *Israelite* commented several years after the war that the discrimination against Jews in the Philippines under Spain had caused American Jews to "[hail] with joy the announcement that the American flag was to fly forever over the Philippines, and that in consequence religious liberty would prevail there." Through their enthusiasm for American religious freedom, then, Jews too implicated themselves in the justificatory rhetorics of U.S. empire.[78]

A few Jews rejected such sugarcoated images of American freedoms, pointing instead to the inequalities they had experienced in order to expose the hypocrisies of U.S. empire. Americans must first realize their own ideals, they argued, before attempting to impose them anywhere else. After conceding that "all the charges against Spain" in the pro-war *Journal of Commerce* were "perfectly true," one anonymous letter-writer challenged the celebratory narratives of religious freedom that supported America's claims to the Philippines. "The author must have had his rose-colored spectacles on when he speaks . . . of religious liberty [in America]," he wrote, "when a poor peddler cannot sell a pair of shoestrings on the 'Holy Sabbath' without being fined or sent to jail." Perhaps drawing on personal experience, this letter-writer judged the idea that America could bestow religious freedom on the Philippines to be laughable when that freedom did not even exist in the United States.[79] His perspective remained very much in the minority, however, as most American Jews celebrated the victory over Spain and the acquisition of its former island colonies as a triumph for the mutually aligned interests of the United States, global Jewry, and the ideals of "civil and religious liberty."[80]

Given the racial politics of the United States and the growth in global anti-Semitic violence in this period, Jewish religious freedom talk served as an important positioning tactic for a group whose status was always more tentative than its members wanted to acknowledge. As the peddler's story suggests, subtle and not-so-subtle forms of discrimination against Jews were very much a reality in the United States. This pattern of discrimination resulted not only from explicit anti-Semitism but also (and more pervasively) from a taken-for-granted deference to Christian norms across the public sphere. A new generation of scholars in American Jewish history have undermined the exceptionalist narratives that long dominated that field. By tracking a more significant history of restrictions and violence against Jews in the United States—and by recognizing a broader range of possibilities for

Jews than an older historiography recognized in Europe and elsewhere—recent historians have challenged familiar accounts of American Jewish life as exceptionally free.[81] American Jews in the nineteenth and early twentieth centuries, however much they celebrated the United States as the land of opportunity, saw a need for constant vigilance to hold the nation accountable to its promise of equality. Jewish celebrations of religious freedom provided a standard of accountability for the nation that everyone recognized as profoundly American—and in the process also helped position Jews alongside Protestants as truly committed to the nation's founding ideals.

Jewish religious freedom talk also helped establish the credentials of American Jews as civilized moderns, in contrast to the racialized subjects of imperial rule. "America must grow," opined the *American Israelite* with some ambivalence as the United States negotiated its treaty with Spain. "We must carry liberty throughout the world—[but] alas! To do that just now it will have to take its departure from America." These expansions, the editors cautioned, came with perils that had "already engulfed other Powers." "Not only are new races to be reckoned with, but a civilization whose barbarism may react upon our own," they warned. "In our haste to export Yankee notions we may import the implements of savagery to our own fireside." Such accounts made imperial hierarchies of race and religion appear natural and even benevolent, entirely obscuring the Filipino subjectivities and struggles for freedom that chapter 2 will describe. The racial "savagery" of the Philippines seemed to threaten an American civilization that the *Israelite* defined in large part by the promise of religious freedom for Jews. The editors subtly reassembled the racial-religious hierarchies of empire to condemn all restrictions on Jewish freedom as savage and to place Jews themselves on the civilized side of the ledger, within the racialized category of the imperial modern.[82]

Such narratives positioned Jews not only as fully modern and wholeheartedly American but also as racially white. This was a racial status that could in no way be taken for granted and indeed was increasingly under siege. As chapter 4 will describe in more detail, Jewishness had never been an exclusively religious identity. Rather, it had continued to reflect the complex forms of peoplehood that post-Enlightenment modernity had tried to sunder into the distinct categories of race, religion, and nation. In other words, Jews and Gentiles alike had long seen Jewish identity as simultaneously racial, national, and religious. But by the turn of the twentieth century, anti-Semitism was becoming a more and more explicitly racial phenomenon. As part of a society organized by race, American Jews had powerful motivations to present themselves as white. Their participation in the imperial discourses of religious freedom would help them do just that.

Despite their differences, both Catholics and Jews in the United States used the principle of religious freedom to challenge the public privileges of Protestantism and to claim full equality within the civilizational hierarchies of U.S. empire. In so doing, they were pushing the boundaries of Christian republicanism to identify their own traditions as equally foundational sources for American freedoms. Both groups gained support in this endeavor from sympathetic Protestants and perhaps even more importantly from politicians who sought a broader constituency than the exclusive rhetorics of Protestantism could provide. Together they articulated a pluralist discourse that leavened and moderated the more oppositional Protestant and Catholic articulations of religious freedom and helped expand the boundaries of whiteness from the more limited category of the Anglo-Saxon Protestant to include both Catholics and Jews. Their inclusion as equal partners in American freedom provided a compelling alternative to the Anglo-Saxon triumphalism that so clearly privileged Protestantism as the foundation of American identity.[83] Religious freedom talk thus supported a reconfigured assemblage of race, nation, and religion—a newly expansive but still racialized imperial secular—that located Catholic and Jewish immigrants alongside Anglo-Saxon Protestants as racially white.

The logics of this civilizational assemblage operated in at least two ways. First, when prominent political leaders identified American freedoms with religious equality for Jews and Catholics, they affirmed Jewish and Catholic appeals for equal status and implicitly for whiteness in American life. Second, such religious freedom talk clearly located Jews and Catholics as *religious* groups and in so doing worked against the countervailing identification of European immigrant populations in racially derogatory ways. By categorizing the terms of their difference as religious rather than racial, religious freedom talk enabled their movement into whiteness. Whiteness would gradually come to be associated with Protestant, Catholic, *and* Jewish religious identities. Thus the reformulation of American religion as tri-faith rather than exclusively Protestant—a shift that would not be complete until after the Second World War, when it would be encapsulated in Will Herberg's famous title *Protestant, Catholic, Jew*—also helped enable the expansion of whiteness to a variety of European immigrants who in the early twentieth century were still viewed by the dominant society as racially distinct. When the United States fought Spain and colonized the Philippines, this process was very much in flux.

As chapter 4 will describe, over the next few decades Jews in particular would find whiteness even more difficult to claim. But at this moment of aggressive U.S. imperial expansion, religious freedom talk enabled both Catholics and Jews to claimed a contested (and always unstable) place in the racialized ranks of the imperial modern.

The racial impact of this pluralist vision coincided with the particular turn-of-the-century moment, a time of growing racial violence and discrimination that is often described as the "nadir" of African American history. The nation's political classes had long since abandoned the political project of Reconstruction, which had attempted to address African American inequality after the Civil War, and in its place were rapidly implementing the Jim Crow model of legalized segregation. Historian Edward J. Blum has argued that the Spanish-American War helped finalize a race-based reconciliation between the white North and the white South. This was a reconciliation built on a shared repudiation of African American interests, he argues, and increasingly defined America as a "white republic."[84] It was no accident that this process also facilitated the claims of Catholics and Jews to full inclusion in the body politic. As the Reverend Dr. George Duncan opined at his Presbyterian church in Washington, D.C., the salutary results of the war with Spain would include "a closer unity" for the nation: "The white heat of patriotism will serve to fuse together North and South, East and West," he preached. "Sectional lines are forgotten, religious differences are put aside, unhappy divisions of long ago are obliterated in the one desire to serve the nation in this time of need."[85] The pluralist ideal of brotherhood between Protestants, Catholics, and Jews—whatever its virtues in other respects—worked in tandem with this sectional reconciliation to reconfigure the American racial order through the racial binary of black and white.

Religious freedom talk helped to challenge Anglo-Saxon exclusivity by installing whiteness as the assumed racial referent for the American. Discussing a very different historical moment, Matthew Frye Jacobson has argued that the discovery of white ethnic "roots" in the late twentieth century facilitated the development of a newly inclusive definition of whiteness, secured through historical narratives of immigrant arrival through the iconic portal of Ellis Island. Jacobson argues that these narratives simultaneously worked to exclude African Americans and other people of color—most of whose ancestors came to the United States not via Ellis Island but through various forms of colonization and enslavement—from new configurations of American identity.[86] I am suggesting that the rhet-orics of religious freedom and interreligious brotherhood facilitated an earlier stage of this process, so that whiteness would come to be defined in part through images of Protestants, Catholics, and Jews as the tri-faith exemplars of American identity. Catholics and Jews helped secure that definition by asserting their allegiance to the ideal of religious freedom in the service of empire.

Several examples will clarify the point. Consider the congressional debate in 1898 over a set of proposals to improve conditions for Ameri-can troops during the war. One of the bills under discussion granted "any church or religious sect" the right, with permission from the secretary of war, to "erect a house of worship" at the military academy of West Point. The single existing "non-sectarian" chapel was in reality a Protestant facil-ity, one supporter explained, and as "a believer in religious freedom" he felt that Catholics should have the same right to a place of worship there. Several congressmen objected that they could not support any measure designed to benefit any single religious group, and that this one would make the Catholics the only denomination with a dedicated chapel at West Point. But as the *Washington Post* reported, Texas Democrat and House minority leader Joseph Bailey countered with a rousing speech in favor of the measure, featuring "a superb tribute to the Christian soldiers of the country, notably the Confederate leader Stonewall Jackson, and to the spirit of the fathers of the republic which moved them in incorporating in the Constitution the safeguard of religious liberty." Bailey was just one of several congressmen that day to jointly invoke the heroes of the Union and the Confederacy, hinting at how much of the political discourse of the time involved efforts to resolve the lingering sectional tensions of the Civil War. The same vision of interreligious brotherhood that brought Catholics and Jews under the protective umbrella of American religious freedom also worked to incorporate them into the racial classification of whiteness—a process that neatly coincided with a sectional reconciliation between white northerners and southerners at the expense of African Americans throughout the country.[87]

At the end of the Spanish-American War, the leaven of an emerging tri-faith pluralism enabled otherwise competing rhetorics of religious freedom to work together as a layered rationale for U.S. empire. Theodore Roosevelt, immensely popular after his exploits as commander of the "Rough Riders" regiment in Cuba, announced in August 1898 that he would "report for promotion four of his command for special gallantry in service—one was a Catholic, one a Jew, one a Protestant, and the religion of the fourth he did not know." According to the *Jewish Messenger*, Roosevelt's gesture illustrated "the rallying of the creeds under one banner" that America had shown in the war with Spain. This genial "fraternization" had helped realize America's ideal of "civil and religious freedom to all," the editors claimed, and served as the country's most important "lesson to other nations" in the war. "American brotherhood is thus ranging the sects as partners in the great task which our Republic [now] has to accomplish," the *Messenger* concluded. Signaling its emphatic approval, the *New York Times* immediately reprinted this piece without further comment. For many Americans, religious freedom served as a signal national ideal, exemplified by the interreligious "brotherhood" that Roosevelt honored. That ideal had become a message to the world, one that simultaneously enabled and justified the new imperial ventures upon which the nation had now embarked. In this episode, occurring shortly before his election to the vice presidency and at the peak of his popularity as a war hero, Roosevelt helped shape newly pluralist rhetorics of religious freedom as one more rationale for the expansion of U.S. empire across the Pacific.[88]

The future president was far from alone in making this case. An interreligious conference, "Brotherhood and the Golden Rule," held in New York in March 1901, brought together a variety of Protestants, Jews, and at least one "representative of Confucianism" to call for a "Universal Golden Rule Brotherhood" that could advance the principles of peace, religious liberty, and interfaith harmony around the world. Funding for the conference and for the monument that participants hoped to erect came from the Baron and Baroness de Hirsch Monument Association, established by the German Jewish philanthropists Maurice and Clara de Hirsch. At that event the Reverend Robert S. MacArthur of Calvary Baptist Church in New York, mentioned earlier as a champion of Anglo-Saxon expansion, celebrated America's movement from "continental isolation into universal recognition and power" as an opportunity to disseminate these ideals. While he did not refer directly to the Philippines in this speech, MacArthur had this new U.S. possession very much in mind. After recalling the history of Spanish cruelty toward the Jews, he concluded, "The eastern sky is even now resplendent with the crimson and gold of the dawn of a bright day."[89] Such pluralist visions could not entirely displace the anti-Catholicism and anti-Semitism that were so embedded in American public discourse. But they provided an alternative framework that symbolized the potential unity of (white) American Protestants, Catholics, and Jews at a time of war and empire-building abroad.

ASSEMBLING EMPIRE: RELIGIOUS FREEDOM
AS A RATIONALE FOR U.S. RULE

The treaty between Spain and the United States, negotiated in Paris in December 1898, reflected McKinley's conviction that America could indeed bring liberty and civilization to its imperial subjects and reiterated the centrality of religious freedom within that vision. One of its articles recognized the continued sovereignty of Spain over the Caroline Islands on the condition that its inhabitants would henceforth enjoy the freedom of religion. Another on the rights of Spanish subjects in the ceded colonies of Puerto Rico, Guam, and the Philippines gave Congress the right and the responsibility to determine the "civil rights and political status" of these islands' "native inhabitants." The only right specifically guaranteed to the people of the Philippines, one that for quite different reasons both Protestants and Catholics found reassuring, was that they would be "secured in the free exercise of their religion."[90]

Protestant missionaries, Catholic leaders, and U.S. government agents would never quite agree on the meaning of that freedom. Yet all of them were convinced that the United States was uniquely destined (or even divinely ordained) to bring the principles of freedom and democracy to the Philippines. Together, they set out to create a tutelary regime that would, they hoped, do just that. On the ground in the Philippines, in part because it had been such a critical part of the case for empire, religious freedom became a vital component of this new tutelary regime. Its importance to the Americans gave it a new relevance to the peoples of the Philippines. The next chapter turns to their stories.

CHAPTER TWO

Making Empire in the Philippines

Filipinos, Moros, and the Ambivalence
of Religious Freedom

In October 1903, the American political monthly the *Independent*
treated its readers to a novel perspective: an essay by Archbishop Gregorio
Aglipay of the newly created Iglesia Filipina Independiente, the Philippine
Independent Church of the Philippines. Starting with the "unpunished
crimes" of the Spanish friars, Aglipay framed his story in the language of
religious freedom. "Now the day of reckoning has come," he wrote, "and with
the assurance of liberty of conscience we have cast off the oppressive yoke
of the friars forever." Readers who had followed the recent U.S. war in the
Philippines knew of Aglipay as a priest who had served as vicar general for
the briefly independent Republic of the Philippines and as a military commander in the Filipino revolutionary forces. Aglipay wrote that he no longer
wanted to resist U.S. rule and now believed that it offered the best hope for
his people. He explained further that he had not originally intended to separate from the Catholic Church but rather had wanted to secure positions
of authority for Filipino priests who had for so long been marginalized. But
when the pope ignored his pleas and appointed American archbishops to
replace the Spanish hierarchy in the Philippines, he and his supporters had
concluded that the only way forward was to declare their independence
from Rome. "This movement . . . has been watered by the blood of the mar-
tyrs," he wrote, "[and] has continued under fierce opposition for thirty years;
why should it not continue now under religious liberty?" Religious freedom
talk would make the claims of Aglipay's new church plausible and perhaps
even laudable to American audiences. In so doing, it enabled a degree of
Filipino cultural and religious autonomy under the constraints of U.S. rule.[1]

Aglipay and other Filipino intellectuals found the principle of religious
freedom useful in large part because it was so important to their American

54

interlocutors. As I argued in chapter 1, the significance of this ideal for U.S. debates over war and empire made it immediately relevant to the terms of American rule in the Philippines. The architects of U.S. colonial policy defined this freedom as a matter of individual conscience and the separation of church and state. But its meanings and implications were always contested in the Philippines, just as they were in the United States. Colonial officials found themselves mediating between American Protestant missionaries, Catholic bishops, and Filipino nationalists like Aglipay. All of these groups advanced different versions of religious freedom as they debated the role of the Spanish friars, clergy appointments, and the ownership of church properties in the Philippines. Despite their differences in other respects, American Protestants and Catholics articulated similar hierarchies of race and religion that located Filipinos as semicivilized and thus in need of American tutelage—and themselves as white Americans with the values and virtues of modernity.

In this context, religious freedom talk became an ambivalent resource for some Filipinos in their struggles to resist and then to navigate the imposition of U.S. rule. Invoking this ideal became one way, however limited and circumscribed, to create cultural space in resistance to empire. The leaders of the nascent Philippine Republic came from the class known as *ilustrados*, the wealthy intelligentsia that had emerged in the late nineteenth century under Spanish rule. Before the U.S. occupation of Manila, these Filipino elites had not articulated their protests, even those directed against the Catholic Church, in the language of religious freedom. But with the arrival of the Americans, invoking this ideal became one way to demonstrate their civilizational credentials and so to make the case for their independence. Still later, after their defeat and eventual surrender to U.S. forces, Filipino elites would rearticulate religious freedom both to assert a degree of autonomy under U.S. rule and to support their ongoing case for an independent Philippines.

The imperial politics of religious freedom could hardly have been more different in the Moro provinces of the southern Philippines, discussed at the end of this chapter. While U.S. colonial officials considered the Catholic Filipinos to be relatively civilized, they classified the predominantly Muslim Moros as "barbarians" and "fanatics" who could not yet be trusted with the individual freedoms and responsibilities of democracy. Initially, to prevent the Moros from joining in the Filipinos' war for independence, American officials promised that there would be no outside interference in the Moros' traditions or modes of government. All this changed when the war ended in the north and the newly emboldened Americans initiated more ambitious civilizing projects in the region. Against the backdrop of a new Moro revolt, Americans rearticulated the principle of religious freedom to impose a new separation of church and state in the Moro provinces. By consigning traditional Moro leaders to a strictly "religious" sphere, Americans asserted their own exclusive right to civil power. Moros attempted in response to articulate their own visions of religious freedom but were ultimately forced to accept a delineated and privatized sphere for Islam in Moro life. In this way, the dominant articulations of religious freedom supported the civilizational assemblages of U.S. empire.

Across the Philippines, the assemblages of empire identified Christianity with the civilized modern. Many U.S. officials overtly favored Christianity, and sometimes Protestant Christianity in particular, because they viewed it as the ideal grounding for democratic freedoms. Others drew on anthropological theories that identified religion in general as inherently primitive, a superstitious relic that must inevitably give way to the purportedly rational and scientific spirit of modernity. Yet even for them, Christianity was the most rational and advanced religion, a civilizing agent and the way to become modern. (Protestant) Christianity was simultaneously the high mark of the religious and the pathway to its transcendence. Deployed in the contexts of empire, the American secular privileged Christianity and delegitimized non-Christian traditions by labeling them as exclusively "religious." This designation relegated them simultaneously to the realms of the primitive and the nonpolitical, making them doubly irrelevant to secular modernity's governing norms. In this way, Americans claimed a civilizational superiority grounded both in the asserted virtues and legacies of "Christian civilization" and in the supposedly universal norms of the secular modern.[2]

RELIGIOUS FREEDOM AND THE PHILIPPINE REPUBLIC

For several months after the Battle of Manila Bay, U.S. intentions in the Philippines remained unclear. Until the treaty with Spain could be finalized in Paris, nobody was sure whether the Americans would claim all of the Philippines, the island of Luzon alone, or just a military outpost in the capital city of Manila. Filipinos had been fighting against Spain for more than two years and had already declared an independent Republic of the Philippines with the revolutionary general Emilio Aguinaldo as its president. But American troops were now occupying Manila, and even in the initial euphoria of victory against Spain they refused to allow Filipino forces to enter the city. Anticipating conflict, Aguinaldo moved the seat of his government to the strategically located town of Malolos and began to extend its authority across the archipelago. For about a year this nascent republic exercised effective control over most of the Philippines, with the notable exception of the Moro-majority islands of Mindanao and Sulu in the southern Philippines. But its leaders were very much aware of how precarious their situation was. Fearing that the United States would claim the entire archipelago, Aguinaldo demanded the immediate withdrawal of all U.S. troops. It was in this context that Filipinos first began to invoke the language of religious freedom.[3]

Before the arrival of the Americans, Filipinos had not articulated their concerns in quite this way. The broader ideals of freedom and democracy were in no way new. The *ilustrados* had been well educated in the Spanish colonial system. Shaped by indigenous cultural systems and by Spanish Catholicism, they had involved themselves in global circulations of knowledge and engaged with the republican and revolutionary trends of nineteenth-century Europe long before the arrival of the Americans.[4] For decades they had been calling for equality in every sphere of colonial life, including the church. The growing ranks of Filipino priests were especially frustrated at their exclusion from the Spanish religious orders and at their generally low status as parish assistants rather than as full-fledged priests. But they understood their marginalization in primarily *racial* terms, not religious, and initially they demanded equality rather than freedom. These grievances became flashpoints for Filipino revolutionary sentiment. In the words of Filipino reformer Marcelo H. del Pilar, it was time for the church to replace the Spanish friars with native Filipino clergymen, "lovers of Spain and of religion," who could better serve Spain, the church, and the Filipino people. Thus the Filipino priests and their supporters did not frame their cause in the language of religious freedom. Rather, they called for a full equality of rights and status within the church.[5]

Nor did Filipino revolutionaries mention this ideal in their initial encounters with U.S. officials as the war with Spain began. Hoping that the United States would become an ally in the cause of an independent Philippines, Aguinaldo reportedly promised the U.S. consul in Singapore that his government would ensure free trade, the freedom of the press, the freedom of assembly, and "general religious toleration." His next sentences reiterated the need to expel the Spanish friars and to secure leadership positions for the Filipino priests within the Catholic Church. Given the preceding list of freedoms, this shift to the language of "toleration" is telling. Even in a conversation aimed at securing American aid, Aguinaldo did not articulate his goals in the language of religious freedom.[6]

Religious freedom talk gained currency among Filipino leaders almost as soon as the United States seized control in Manila. In the year it took for Americans to enforce their sovereignty across the Philippines, this ideal performed two kinds of cultural work in support of an independent republic. It would ultimately prove inadequate on both counts. First, Filipino *ilustrados* and revolutionary leaders highlighted their adherence to religious freedom as one way to demonstrate their status as civilized moderns. But set against the civilizational assemblages of race and empire, their appeals could not convince the outside world that the Philippines were ready for independence. Second, hoping that they could join together the archipelago's diverse peoples under the banner of the Philippine Republic, Filipino leaders used the language of religious freedom to promise equal status and freedom for the Muslim Moros and so-called pagan tribes alongside the majority Catholic population. But like the Americans, they viewed the Moros and "pagans" as uncivilized and very much in need of their tutelage in freedom and democracy. Rather than transcending these civilizational hierarchies, the promise of religious freedom only reinforced them. In the unsettled negotiations of war and empire, such guarantees had little power to forge a unified nation.[7]

The Imperial Secular and the Quest for Legitimacy

As the U.S. occupation of Manila began, Aguinaldo and his government began what turned out to be a formidable quest for legitimacy in the eyes of the world, the United States in particular. They clung to the hope that if they could demonstrate success in governing and adherence to Euro-American standards of civilization and modernity, then the world would accept their bid for independence. In an address to the Philippine Congress assembled in Malolos in September 1898, Aguinaldo articulated an already familiar comparison to the American Revolution. "In the same manner as God helped weak America in the last century, when she fought against powerful Albion, to regain her liberty and independence," he said, "He will also help us today in the identical undertaking."[8] Knowing that Christianity served as an assumed foundation for European civilization, Filipino leaders pointed first to their Catholicism as evidence that they belonged within that communion. "The Filipinos can justly boast of a social status on par with cultured peoples and are fit to co-mingle and live on an equality with civilized nations," Secretary of Foreign Affairs Felipe Buencamino told the U.S. Congress in August 1899. In his summary of their many achievements,

Buencamino gave particular emphasis to Christianity. "We have accepted an enlightened religion—the Roman Catholic faith," he concluded. "Strict morality which emanates from christianizing influences governs our manners and customs." Buencamino presented his nation's Christian foundations as evidence that the Filipinos were a civilized people whose claims to independence must be recognized.[9]

However, Christianity had increasingly been joined in imperial visions of modernity with the ideal of the secular state. In keeping with Anglo-American ideologies of secularism, Filipino leaders soon began to articulate the ideals of disestablishment and religious freedom as another way to demonstrate their civilizational credentials. The political philosopher Apolinario Mabini, Aguinaldo's chief adviser, offered a draft constitution for the new republic that made these commitments clear. "The Republic as a collective entity does not profess any determined religion," he wrote, "leaving to individual consciences full liberty of selecting that one which may appear most worthy and reasonable."[10] After a great deal of debate, the fifth article of the constitution finally ratified by the Philippine Congress assembled at Malolos in December 1898 would read simply, "The state recognizes the equality of all religious worships and the separation of Church and State." The prominent placement of this article just after the constitution's opening declaration of a republican system of government—rather than alongside the subsequent enumeration of guaranteed rights and freedoms—suggests that many Filipino leaders had come to think of religious freedom not merely as one freedom among others but as a defining principle for their new republic.

Filipino diplomats presented these constitutional provisions as evidence that they were already civilized and entirely capable of governing themselves. In a letter to the U.S. secretary of state, written in February 1899 just after formal hostilities between American and Filipino troops began, Sixto López of the foreign secretary's office reviewed the relevant history. "This government has preserved civil and religious liberty and protected private property," he concluded, "and has with such humanity exercised its offices that the Filipinos feel that, as their representative, it should be welcomed to the family of independent nations."[11] Felipe Agoncillo, Aguinaldo's personal representative to the United States, assured an audience of Protestant missionary leaders assembled in Montreal that his government "was determined to give religious freedom and toleration to all." Facing a barrage of questions on the prospects for religion in an independent Philippines, he repeated several times that the "fixed purpose" of the republic was to ensure "that every man must be protected in his freedom of conscience." Agoncillo thus wielded the principle of religious freedom in hopes of establishing the credibility of an independent Philippines in North American eyes.[12]

As they embarked on their new war for independence against the United States, Filipinos accused the Americans of abandoning their democratic ideals, invoking them merely as a cloak for imperial ambitions. The Spanish archbishop Bernardino Nozaleda of Manila had warned them even before the Battle of Manila Bay that an alliance with the United States would result in a more onerous imperial burden than Spain had ever imposed. If the Americans seized control of the Philippines, he had claimed, Filipinos would see "the demolition of your temples of worship, or their conversion into chapels of Protestantism where God of the Eucharist shall be furnished no throne."[13] Now Governor Vicente Lukban of Samar Province echoed that warning as he denounced the "unprincipled [American] imposters" who had promised liberty under U.S. rule. If they had really come to bring freedom, he asked, then "why profane our temples and the images of our saints" and "rob and sack sacred edifices," as some of the American troops had done? "Open your eyes, my beloved people," Lukban concluded, "to the fact that the Yankees do not respect the religious beliefs of the people." He argued that the United States had betrayed its promise of religious freedom by imposing Protestantism on the Catholics of the Philippines.[14]

As the war progressed, some Filipinos worried that the United States would instead bring back the Spanish friars and so reverse the freedoms gained under the Philippine Republic. Filipino nationalists in Hong Kong alleged that the Americans had betrayed their own principle of church-state separation by forming an alliance with Archbishop Nozaleda, who had now accepted the imperial claims of the United States. These critics accused the U.S. military of burning the village of Pandacan to the ground merely because the archbishop had condemned it as a center of Freemasonry in the province of Luzon. The United States, they fumed, was guilty of a rank hypocrisy. Apparently, "religious freedom" under American rule meant that the archbishop had the power to direct the course of imperial retribution and violence. Filipino revolutionaries thus positioned themselves as the real guardians of religious freedom and human dignity, better equipped than their imperial overlords to advance the banner of modernity in the Philippines.[15]

These Filipino leaders demanded that the world honor their freedom as a people and their right to exist as an independent nation. At this juncture they were not asking the United States to grant them freedom of religion or any other constitutional freedom. Such an appeal made no sense when they did not recognize U.S. sovereignty and when the United States did not exercise control over Filipino affairs on the ground. Rather, Filipino revolutionaries asserted their own commitment to the principle of religious freedom as a way to defend their political sovereignty, the right to manage their own affairs as an independent nation. In this modern age of empire, religious freedom talk served as one way to support that claim, one way to resist the racial and civilizational assemblages of empire.

From the beginning, however, the standards of civilization that they hoped to satisfy were hopelessly stacked against them. As Talal Asad and others have shown, nineteenth- and twentieth-century imperial powers disseminated ideologies of modernity that turned an idealized vision of their own cultural and political systems into a universally applicable standard.[16] Racialized colonial subjects and those who aspired to a postcolonial independence were effectively forced to marginalize indigenous systems that, measured against this standard, appeared retrogressive and "primitive." Europe and the United States had already defined civilizational legitimacy in ways that made them the model for what counted as modern, the ideal against which all others inevitably fell short. The established status of the Church of England reveals that complete disestablishment has never been essential for acceptance as a modern secular state; instead, the British Empire served as a model and arbiter of the imperial modern. Throughout the Spanish-American War, Protestants in the United States had decried Spain's Catholic establishment as evidence of its premodern and barbaric character and located Spaniards far below Anglo-Saxons on the racial-religious scales of civilization. Yet the status of Spain as an imperial power and its place within the circle of European Christendom meant that it could not be summarily dismissed from the bargaining table. The Filipinos, racialized as the objects of colonial subjugation, could not succeed in placing themselves at that table whether they believed they met the posited standards of civilization or not.

Forging a Republic: The Grounds of Filipino Nationalism

Within the nascent Republic of the Philippines, religious freedom talk signified far more than a quest for civilizational legitimacy. As Filipino leaders struggled to create new institutions of governance in a time of war, they wrestled with the meanings and implications of this freedom on the ground. Many members of the congress assembled at Malolos were devout Catholics who were not convinced that this freedom was desirable or, if so, that it meant an end to the Catholic establishment they had always known. Many argued against any radical change in the system of government, particularly in the midst of war. Thus the draft constitution presented in the fall of 1898 assumed a continued church establishment even as it guaranteed complete "freedom of religion" to all non-Catholics in the Philippines. Its author, lawyer Felipe Calderon, was a political moderate who considered it far too disruptive to cut ties with the church at such an unsettled time. Any such action would discount the central role the Filipino priests had played in the revolution, he warned, and so risked losing their allegiance along with that of their devoutly Catholic supporters. More generally, Filipino conservatives saw the church as an essential source of cohesion for the fragile new republic.[17]

On the other side of the debate, the advocates of disestablishment named the system of "feudal theocracy" as a major flaw in the Spanish colonial system. Why would Filipinos want to replicate that system in their own independent republic? They pointed to the United States, and other more recent examples, for evidence that a system of equality for all religious groups not only was effective but also would actually benefit the Catholic Church. "In the United States, where there has been religious freedom for more than a hundred years, the Catholic Church is most flourishing," said delegate Arcadio del Rosario, while "the decline of the Spanish is principally due to the denial of religious liberty and the existence of a powerful clergy." Liberal delegates like del Rosario argued that a thoroughgoing religious freedom, enabled by the complete separation of church and state, was the only way to eliminate the abusive power of the Spanish religious orders in the archipelago and to prevent such problems from developing again within an independent Philippines. They approved the revised fifth article by the slimmest of margins and only after two consecutive votes had tied. They did so because many had come to believe that this freedom supported their cause against the Spanish religious orders and facilitated the work of governing the Philippines.[18]

Barely present in the Philippines just a year before, the discourses of disestablishment and religious freedom also grounded a new plea for unity across the ethnic, religious, and cultural diversities of the archipelago. The proponents of disestablishment saw it as a balm to unify the diverse peoples of the Philippines. In the city of Manila, where the new republic was struggling to secure the loyalty of an occupied population, this strategy seemed especially promising. Manila had long had its share of skeptics and freethinkers, and the U.S. occupation brought an assortment of Protestant military chaplains and missionaries as well. Protestant preaching and the missionaries' demands for religious freedom added new tensions to an already unsettled city. Thus when Filipino revolutionaries organized a "Popular Committee" in the city in the autumn of 1898, four of its fourteen operating principles aimed at transcending differences that they classified as religious. The committee planned a "propaganda" campaign to "inform the people of all the rights of man," first among them the "liberty of thought," the "liberty of expression," and the "liberty of conscience," and "to teach the people that no one must be molested by reason of his political and religious opinions." They pronounced "any discussion of religious matters" strictly forbidden "in order not to cause antagonism among the members." On the verge of open warfare with the United States—and given the revolutionary propaganda against U.S. imperial hypocrisy—at least some members of Aguinaldo's government believed that the principle of religious freedom could help unify the people of Manila in support of an independent Philippines.[19]

The Philippine Republic also deployed the principle of religious freedom in an effort to gain the allegiance of the Moros, who were both culturally and geographically distant from the capital. The differences between (Catholic) Filipinos and (Muslim) Moros were in many ways products of Spanish colonialism, and the Moros' reputation for fanaticism and violence reflected their centuries-long struggle to remain independent from Spain.[20] But their warfare and raiding had disproportionately impacted their Filipino neighbors, who (like the Spanish) came to view the Moros as uncivilized and inherently violent. The Moros were "our mortal enemies since time immemorial on account of their religious fanaticism . . . and their objection to leading a civilized life," as the Filipino governor of a province adjacent to the Moros on Mindanao Island put it to Aguinaldo. He did not think they could be trusted to honor a recent agreement for "peace and good harmony." As they struggled to make the case for their own status as a civilized people, Filipino leaders thus assumed a posture of racial-religious superiority over and against the Moros and other non-Christian peoples of the archipelago.[21]

At the same time, the Philippine Republic desperately needed the allegiance of the Moros and indeed of all the peoples living in the archipelago. Tomas del Rosario, vice president of the Philippine Congress, proposed the final wording of the constitutional article on religious freedom in part to gain the allegiance of non-Catholics, the Moros in particular. Del Rosario argued that the Philippine Republic must act carefully if it wanted to incorporate the Moros. "The imposition of a religion" across the Philippines could even "provoke civil war," he warned, "and the mere granting of a privilege to one religion may lead to serious conflicts."[22] The prospect of armed conflict was very real. The Moros had never entirely been subjugated by Spain, had until quite recently continued to raid Filipino towns, and had never agreed to ally with Filipinos in the fight against Spain. They had their own patterns of governance and did not recognize the authority of the newly announced government of the Philippines. Del Rosario's claim that a Catholic establishment could provoke a "civil war" thus projected a national unity that did not exist on the ground.[23]

Filipino leaders hoped that the promise of religious freedom could bring the Moros into an alliance against the Americans and ultimately secure their allegiance to the new republic. In a message to Congress in January 1899, Aguinaldo urged negotiation "with the Moros . . . for purposes of establishing national solidarity upon the basis of a real federation, with absolute respect for their beliefs and traditions."[24] A few days letter, one of his cabinet members asked the governor of Iloilo Province in the Visayan Islands, just north of the predominantly Moro island of Mindanao, to ensure that all the people "guard with watchfulness and solicitude the maintenance of a national unity" and that "legal representatives" be sent from each province to "agree upon a fundamental law for all." The Visayan governor was to offer the Moros of Mindanao and the Sulu Archipelago the promise of full equality in "a true federation" and assure them that the republic would "absolutely respect their faith and traditions."[25] The fact that this message had to be sent through the governor of a neighboring province suggests the difficulty of such communications and the tenuous quality of the relationship between the Moros and the nascent republic.

As their situation became more desperate, Filipino leaders supplemented such promises of constitutional equality with the claim that racial-religious bonds predating the Spanish conquest could unite all the peoples of the archipelago. Even though the Spaniards had turned brothers to fight against brothers, one letter contended, the Filipinos and Moros were truly "brothers and sons of the same race" who should now join together "in the aspirations of independence and liberty." Filipino nationalist Mariano Trías began another missive by praising the Moros for the "legendary valor" that had kept the Spaniards at bay for centuries. "The Yankee with criminal ambition [now] wishes to violate" the hard-won independence of the Philippines. "Now, more than ever," he wrote, "since the same God has created us, since the same blood runs through our veins, since we are inspired by the same ideal, Liberty and Independence; let us unite to hate and drive back this invasion, even if we die."[26] Rather than stressing the promise of religious freedom, Trías posited a precolonial unity that was simultaneously racial and religious. At the deepest level, he suggested, Catholic Filipinos and Muslim Moros were one. Unfortunately for the republic, however, the Moros did not seem to have found any of these arguments persuasive. Not long after Trías's message, U.S. general John Bates announced that he had negotiated a peace treaty with the most prominent Moro leader, the sultan of Sulu. Neither the principle of religious freedom nor the articulation of a common racial-religious identity could turn the tides of the war.[27]

The Vicar General and the Republic at War

The many challenges that faced the new republic made it difficult for its leaders either to sustain their claims to secular modernity or to unify the far-flung peoples of the Philippines. As their situation in the war grew more and more dire, the conservatives in the Malolos Congress rallied against the recent constitutional articulations of religious freedom. Leading the charge against disestablishment was none other than Gregorio Aglipay, future archbishop of the Philippine Independent Church. Aglipay was the only priest serving in the Malolos Congress, and he presented a petition on the clergy's behalf for Article 5 to be revoked. This petition grounded its claims in the papal encyclicals that had denounced the liberal principle of religious freedom as a threat to the social order. "Neither society nor good government can exist without morality, order, and authority . . . and therefore without religion," the clergy contended. "To permit the liberty of all religions is to concede liberty to both error and impiety." At this point in Aglipay's career, on the basis of his Catholic theological commitments and for the good of the republic as he understood it, he and his fellow Filipino priests stood directly opposed to the freedom of religion.[28]

They gained support in this endeavor from Apolinario Mabini, the philosopher of the revolution, now serving as prime minister. Even though his own draft constitution had specified that the republic would "not profess any determined religion," Mabini had become convinced that the more radical features of the new constitution could not be implemented during a war. Now he contended that it was "not advisable to openly establish the separation of the Church from the State at these critical times."[29] Writing privately to Aguinaldo, he proposed setting aside the "religious question" entirely. If Article 5 were implemented, he worried, "the supporters of the religion of the State" would be likely to withdraw from the government. Mabini saw the war with the United States as a crisis that made it impossible for the Philippines to function as a democracy or to protect the individual liberties guaranteed in the constitution. It was even less practicable to implement the drastic and contentious change of separating church and state. Following the advice of Mabini and Aglipay, Aguinaldo suspended the fifth article and directed his government to do whatever it could to support the work of the loyal Filipino priests.[30]

It was in this context that Aguinaldo named Aglipay to the position of vicar general for the Philippine Republic. This appointment sought both to harness the moral authority of the church for the revolution and to address an urgent logistical problem. The absence of the Spanish friars—virtually all of them now in exile or in Filipino prisons, charged with supporting Spain against an independent Philippines—had created a vacuum of religious authority and a lack of priestly ministrations across the islands. Aglipay addressed this situation by appointing Filipino priests to the vacant parishes. He asked the clergy in each province to elect a lieutenant military vicar who could coordinate local church affairs and delegates for a council that would coordinate decision-making in the absence of a regularly appointed hierarchy. Knowing that he lacked ecclesial authority for this role, Aglipay convinced the imprisoned bishop José Hevía y Campomanes of the Diocese of Nueva Segovia to appoint him as diocesan administrator, responsible for diocesan affairs in Bishop Hevía's absence. Although this appointment conferred only a limited administrative authority, Aglipay leveraged it as far as possible. His installation was a grand affair, complete with parades and a public oath of allegiance before the cathedral in Vigan, that highlighted the continuing importance of the church for the success of the revolution. He held out hope that the Vatican would elevate Filipino priests to the episcopacy and so legitimate the steps they were taking along with the independent status of the Philippines.[31]

These activities brought Aglipay into direct conflict with the existing church hierarchy in the Philippines. Archbishop Nozaleda in Manila had made it very clear that he considered Filipinos incapable of self-governance and had forbidden his priests from supporting the revolution. Now he denied the legitimacy of the Philippine Republic and insisted that the Spanish friars must be returned to their parishes. Nozaleda summoned Aglipay to a disciplinary hearing before an ecclesiastical tribunal under charges of usurping episcopal authority and summarily excommunicated him after he refused to appear.[32] In response the vicar general accused Nozaleda of supporting an unjust colonial regime and imposing racial distinctions that were entirely contrary to Catholic teachings. Now that the Americans had taken over Manila, Aglipay charged, the archbishop was working with them against an independent Philippines and opposed Filipino leadership in the church even though he knew that "an independent nation is entitled to have one of its sons given the supreme ecclesiastical seat within its territory." In his most dramatic act of defiance, Aglipay pronounced the archbishop's excommunication on charges that he had betrayed Christianity itself through his abuses of the Filipino people.[33]

Despite these acts of insubordination, Aglipay was not at this juncture attempting to separate from the Catholic Church and did not yet appeal to the principle of religious freedom. From his perspective, the church in the Philippines would not be legitimately constituted until it had an indigenous clergy under the authority of the pope. As soon as it became possible to send a delegation to Rome, he informed the Filipino priests when they met in October 1898, they would "go in haste to the Vicar of Jesus Christ to offer our humble and respectful homage . . . and to obtain from him after all the graces and privileges that we need for government and administration of the Filipino Church."[34] But the pope was not likely to grant this kind of recognition until the American invaders were defeated and the independence of the Philippine Republic secured. With Aglipay at the head of the Filipino clergy, the leaders of the struggling republic had shifted away from their initial enthusiasm for the freedom of religion in the hope that they could achieve these goals. Talking less and less about this freedom, they stressed instead the need for moral authority and the kind of spiritual grounding that a national church could provide.

The Imposition of U.S. Empire

As the U.S. military destroyed Filipino forces and seized control of more and more of the islands, the operations of Aguinaldo's government became more and more limited. Filipino nationalists now focused entirely on the urgent task of defending their nascent republic from military conquest. Aglipay became a guerrilla commander in the war, feared by Americans as one of the Filipinos' most skillful military tacticians. In American eyes, Aglipay's combination of roles demonstrated a racial inability to keep religion in its proper sphere, apart from the worlds of politics and war. Imperial propagandists represented the Filipinos as naturally ignorant, incapable of practicing the principles of democracy. "By his fiendish religion," one military commander wrote, "[Aglipay] struck terror into the hearts of the ignorant natives." Once again, Americans assembled the intersecting hierarchies of race and religion to support their claims to empire.[35]

Filipino hopes for an indigenous Catholic leadership fell with the republic. Although a handful of exiles had attempted to advocate for Aglipay in Rome, the conditions of the war made it impossible for the planned delegation of priests to visit the Vatican. In the meantime Pope Leo XIII had been in regular communication with the U.S. Catholic hierarchy. As soon as the Spanish-American War ended, he had begun the process of transferring episcopal responsibility to the American church, displaying an imperial disdain for the capacities of colonial subjects. Archbishop Placide Chapelle of New Orleans, appointed in October 1898 as apostolic delegate to the Philippines, had begun his ministry in the racially segregated worlds of Baltimore and Washington, D.C., and brought with him the racial sensibilities of the American South. Much like Nozaleda, he believed Filipinos incapable of managing their own parishes, let alone a diocese or a nation. Chapelle convinced U.S. governor-general E. S. Otis that the Spanish friars should be permitted to return to their former parishes, at least until American priests could be appointed to replace them. Filipino Catholics thus found themselves under the ecclesial authority of an archbishop who came to them from yet another imperial power and considered them racially incapable of governing themselves.[36]

American military commanders were committed to the ideal of a benevolent tutelary empire—as we saw in chapter 1, they thought it their responsibility to instill the principles of democracy in the Philippines—and so they did their best to honor the principle of religious freedom on the ground. Despite the collaborations between Chapelle and Otis, military policies and procedures around religious conflicts often imposed an implicitly Protestant sensibility. Even though Otis had endorsed the return of the friars, for example, directives from his office granted local people the right to choose their own priests. "It is apparent that congregations by [their own] action may reject any clergyman who is not acceptable to the majority," one circular stated. The U.S. military should not interfere with that process, "provided that any action in the premises be not accomplished by application of violence."[37] According to this policy, religious freedom meant that no outside authority, even Rome, had the right to remove a priest who enjoyed the support of his parish. This was a congregational model of church governance that characterized many Protestant denominations but directly contradicted the hierarchical polity of the Catholic Church. U.S. military policy thus reflected the generally Protestant assumptions of the American secular. In this case (though not always), these assumptions worked to the advantage of the Filipino priests.

By the end of 1900, more and more Filipino elites, including some members of Aguinaldo's government, were ready to concede that they had lost their war for independence. Desperate to end the violence, some of them began to accept the promises of the tutelary regime and to proclaim religious freedom as a signal benefit of American rule. The platform of the Federal Party, organized that December, called for an end to hostilities and "the absolute application of the American constitution, with all the rights possessed by every citizen of the Great Republic," including "individual rights, liberties, and guarantees of person, property, and domicile, with freedom of worship and complete separation of church and state." Among the leading figures in this new party was Tomas del Rosario, who as vice president of the Malolos Congress had proposed the constitutional amendment guaranteeing the same freedoms in an independent Philippines. The Federalists represented an attempt on one hand to build a new Filipino consensus for surrender and on the other to prove to American colonial authorities that Filipinos were civilized moderns, conversant with the principles of democracy, who should be granted the right of a representative government under American rule. Abandoning their hopes for independence, they grounded new appeals for individual liberty in the U.S. Constitution.[38]

The revolutionaries who had not yet surrendered to the United States were enraged at this betrayal. Governor Vicente Lukban of Samar Province condemned the Federalists as "disciples of Judas" who would only "lead us into an abyss of dishonor." He urged Filipinos not "to be deceived by the lavish display of individual liberties so alluringly set forth in their platform." Such promises depended on the beneficence of a U.S. government that had never once honored its word. Although the Americans had promised not to "meddle with religious affairs," Lukban wrote, "there they are in Dagupan, Jaro, and elsewhere, forcing us to submit to our ancient tyrants, the Friars, whom we hate." Instead of freedom, the Americans would bring only "the repugnant filth of servility and subjection." Lukban would be among the last of the Filipino commanders to surrender, remaining at the head of guerrilla forces in Samar after Aguinaldo himself had been captured. In his eyes, the evident hypocrisy of American religious freedom talk only proved the need to maintain the fight for an independent Philippines.[39]

In the end, the overwhelming force of the U.S. military made it impossible for even the most committed revolutionaries to continue that struggle. Mariano Trías and Victor Celis, *principales* and revolutionary leaders in the province of Cavite, issued a statement in March 1901 explaining their decision to surrender.[40] They had observed with horror, they wrote, the deteriorating situation in the Philippines: "plantations destroyed, estates abandoned, tears of women and children, homes abandoned, everything due to a disastrous war." There was no longer any hope of success, and the people were demanding an end to the suffering. Trías and Celis were now convinced that the United States had "no other purpose in view" than "the intellectual and commercial progress of the Filipino people." These former revolutionaries linked the Filipinos' quest for freedom from the "yoke" of the Spanish friars to the American promises for free exercise in industry, commerce, and religion. The United States wanted "to save us from the covetousness of the friars," they wrote, "and to win us over with its innumerable plans for the construction of railways and the digging of canals." Aguinaldo himself surrendered in April 1901, proclaiming that he could no longer "refuse the voice of a people longing for peace . . . yearning to see their dear ones in the enjoyment of the liberty promised by the generosity of the great American nation." Whether by conviction or coercion, American promises of freedom—including the freedom of religion—had emerged as an irresistible alternative to the suffering and violence of the war.[41]

The ideal of religious freedom served U.S. imperial authority not only because it posited a contrast between American freedoms and the specter of Spanish (Catholic) tyranny but also because under U.S. law this was above all an individual freedom, guaranteed and protected by the authority of the United States. In July 1902 President Theodore Roosevelt declared "the insurrection against the authority and sovereignty of the United States . . . now at an end" and "peace . . . established in all parts of the archipelago except in the country inhabited by the Moro tribes." The secretary of war issued a statement of gratitude for the "courage and fortitude" of an army that had, "utilizing the lessons of the Indian wars[,] . . . relentlessly pursued the guerilla bands to their fastness in mountain and jungle, and crushed them." In the logics of the benevolent empire, American officials justified the violence of this war as a regretful necessity that ultimately benefited the Filipinos.[42] They assured "the people of the Philippines the blessings of peace and prosperity" with "individual liberty, the protection of personal rights, civil order, public instruction, and religious liberty" that came with American rule.[43] This was a freedom for Filipino individuals under the enforced sovereignty of the United States, resting on the violent imposition of American rule. It stood in direct opposition to the Filipino revolutionary cause, a nationalist project of freedom and independence from colonial rule.

ARCHBISHOP AGLIPAY AND THE IMPERIAL POLITICS
OF RELIGIOUS FREEDOM

As the people of the Philippines struggled to accept the reality of American rule, religious freedom talk would help them accommodate to their new situation. Exhausted and embittered by the war, some Filipinos had already come to accept American assertions of religious freedom as a way to legitimate the imposition of U.S. rule. As they gained familiarity with the new imperial context, others began to rearticulate this freedom to facilitate a degree of autonomy within the constraints of the new system. Over time, still others would cite it to support the ongoing struggle for an independent Republic of the Philippines. Invoked for all these purposes, religious freedom had ambivalent and sometimes unintended consequences for the people of the Philippines.

For Gregorio Aglipay, the former vicar general of the Philippines, religious freedom talk in this new context facilitated an ecclesial autonomy that intersected closely with the desire for national sovereignty. Like Aguinaldo, Aglipay had surrendered to U.S. forces in the spring of 1901. His excommunication by Archbishop Nozaleda meant that he could no longer serve as a priest in the Catholic Church, and with the destruction of the Philippine Republic he was left without a position. Among his most important conversation partners at this time was Isabelo de los Reyes, an *ilustrado* journalist and labor leader who had been in Europe during most of the war and became disillusioned with Catholicism after he attempted to advocate at the Vatican on Aglipay's behalf. De los Reyes now pushed for a complete break from Rome. At a Manila labor rally in August 1901, it was he who announced the formation of an independent church for the Philippines. Soon thereafter Aglipay agreed to assume the role of Obispo Máximo de Filipines, archbishop of the newly created church.[44]

From the beginning, the principle of religious freedom helped Aglipay and his followers assert their independence from Rome. To mark the public announcement of the church's formation in October 1902, the new archbishop celebrated an open-air Mass in Manila with several thousand people in attendance.[45] Hoping to counter the comfortable relationships between Catholic authorities and American officials in Manila, he immediately linked his cause to the principles most celebrated by the American tutelary regime. Although he had opposed the move toward disestablishment in the Malolos Congress, his new circumstances reshaped these convictions. "The separation of Church and State is easily the best move yet instituted by the

American authorities," he told reporters, "and will do more for the permanent peace than any one thing undertaken." Noting that Catholic authorities had always opposed this separation, he argued that their opposition to the Philippine Independent Church reflected their desire to maintain exclusive privileges, if not a formal establishment, in the Philippines. The survival of the new church would be secured by the American guarantee of religious freedom and an equal status for every church in the archipelago.[46]

Aglipay's articulations of religious freedom gained him the support of the Federal Party, which had embraced the promise of individual liberties under American rule. The party's newspaper *La Democracia* offered this assessment of the new archbishop: "The die is cast! Padre Aglipay has crossed the Rubicon of intransigency and absolutism, with the decision and energy of a Roman captain. . . . It is the assertion of the dignity of the people," the editors concluded, "the last consequence of the revolution, which in order to be complete requires religious liberty." Or as the same paper put it several months later, the Aglipayan church proved that "freedom of worship, freedom of conscience, and liberty of action" had finally come to the Philippines. At long last the Catholic Church was seeing "the political and religious effects" of its former abuses. For the Federalists, the new church signaled the final end of the Catholic monopoly under Spain and the dawn of true democracy and religious freedom in the Philippines.[47]

Filipino priests and lay Catholics alike faced the difficult decision of whether to remain loyal to the Catholic Church or to affiliate themselves with Aglipay and the nationalist sensibilities he represented. Aglipay's appeal grew as the Vatican insisted first on reinstating the Spanish friars and then on the appointment of new American bishops in the Philippines. In the spring of 1902, the new governor-general of the Philippines, future U.S. president William H. Taft, went to the Vatican to conduct negotiations over the future of the Spanish friars and of the friar lands, the vast estates that the religious orders had claimed. He returned with assurances from the pope that the friars would refrain from "political intermeddling," that the church would work toward a native priesthood through improved "ecclesiastical education," and that American priests and bishops would soon be appointed to serve the Philippines.[48]

Soon thereafter, a new apostolic delegate, the Italian archbishop Giovanni Battista Guidi, brought instructions from Rome that solidified the control of the American hierarchy. The papal constitution *Quae mari Sinico* (September 1902) provided new guidelines for church administration and clergy education. At the same time it warned the clergy against any "participation in politics" and "exhort[ed] them to holiness." In other words, it identified the proper concerns of the clergy as purely spiritual, delegitimizing the desire for indigenous leadership. In patronizing terms, it promised that Filipinos would be given authority in the church in due time, when they had been adequately prepared. In fact the Vatican had already consulted with the White House and with Governor Taft on prospects for a new archbishop of Manila and in April 1903 announced the appointment of Jeremiah Harty, formerly a priest in St. Louis. Joining him were three new American prelates: Frederick Rooker as bishop of Jaro, Dennis Dougherty as bishop of Nueva Segovia, and Thomas Hendrick as bishop of Cebu. In the eyes of many Filipinos, these appointments mocked their aspirations and dismissed the capabilities of the native priests.[49]

All of this only strengthened the appeal of the Philippine Independent Church. In his "Fifth Fundamental Epistle," Archbishop Aglipay fumed that the pope would give the friars "all the ecclesiastical honors" and addressed the Filipinos "as if dealing with savages." "Instead of pacifying us," he wrote, "this Constitution will make the Filipino clergy shake off the Roman yoke."[50] As he predicted, many priests who had been wavering now joined the new church and often brought their congregations with them. As the movement grew, at least a tenth of the Filipino priests across the archipelago withdrew from the Catholic Church. The size of the Aglipayan movement in its early years is difficult to determine. Estimates range from two to three million members in 1905 and 1906, when the movement reached its largest size and momentum. The new church was particularly strong in provinces where the Philippine Republic had been well established, especially in Aglipay's own home province of Ilocos Norte, where twenty-four out of twenty-five former Catholic priests participated in the consecration of Father Pedro Brillantes of Bacarra as a bishop in the new church.[51]

As in many such schisms around the world, the creation of the Philippine Independent Church sparked an immediate controversy over the ownership of church properties. On one hand, Aglipay argued to both Nozaleda and Taft that because the people of the archipelago no longer accepted the religious authority of the Catholic Church, the Manila Cathedral and all other church buildings in the islands should at once be transferred to the Philippine Independent Church. He claimed that under Spanish colonial law these properties had belonged not to the church but to the crown and that the United States had now inherited them as Spain's imperial successor. Now the United States should turn them over to the church of the people. Returning them to the Catholic Church would amount to an unconstitutional establishment, he argued, denying the principles of the U.S. Constitution and the freedoms that the United States had promised to the Filipino people. But the Catholic hierarchy insisted in response that the Manila Cathedral and all the church buildings in the Philippines belonged the Catholic Church. As places of worship, all of these properties belonged to the church for which they had been built.[52]

These disputes could sometimes be violent, and colonial officials who wanted to be fair faced an immense challenge. In one case where a loyal Catholic priest had criticized Archbishop Aglipay, a mob of women threw the priest to the ground, tore off his cassock, and invited Aglipay himself to say Mass in their church. During the next few weeks, the women actually slept in the churchyard to prevent the offending priest's return.[53] Governor Taft faced urgent queries from his subordinates on how to manage such disputes, and he announced that for the time being his administration would consider all local parish buildings the property of the group that currently held possession of them. This "Doctrine of Peaceable Possession" meant that the local priest, who normally held the keys, most often determined whether a church was Catholic or Aglipayan. But this was never intended to be a final settlement. The Philippine Commission had assigned jurisdiction over such matters to the newly constituted Supreme Court of the Philippines. Commenting that such "religious disputes . . . are always bitter and productive of disorders and breaches of the peace," the commission urged the court to decide the question as quickly as possible.[54]

In the midst of these conflicts, Catholic authorities mobilized the principle of religious freedom to discredit the Aglipayan movement. The Reverend Edward Vattman, senior Catholic chaplain in the U.S. Army, claimed that Aglipay had been legitimately "silenced by the church authorities on ecclesiastical grounds." This renegade, perhaps misled by American "bigots," had now effectively "declared that Americanism meant Protestantism" and was leading the Filipinos to believe that the United States stood against the Catholic Church. The exile of so many Spanish friars had resulted in a relative scarcity of Catholic priests in the Philippines, Vattman explained, leaving the field wide open for Aglipay to disseminate his heretical and dangerous ideas. Now he was "creating so-called priests and making converts at a dangerous rate." This situation showed how desperately the Philippines needed "American Bishops and American clergy . . . in order to prove to the natives that the United States is not a Protestant country." By arguing that the Aglipayan movement directly threatened the principles of the First Amendment, Vattman leveraged the power of religious freedom for the

Catholic Church in the Philippines. His account so powerfully bolstered the American archbishops' position that they commissioned him to report to the Vatican on their behalf.[55]

Catholic propagandists aimed to discredit the new church by identifying it as a *political* rather than a religious movement. They claimed that the Aglipayan movement concealed an anti-American and even seditious spirit under the cloak of religion. Aglipay had "instilled a spirit entirely foreign to submission to American rule," Vattman wrote, and his movement was "not only full of danger to the Church, but to the State as well."[56] Some writers accused Aglipay—a guerrilla commander in the recent war—of using his church as a front for anti-American activities. "Under the guise of religious zeal," wrote the Paulist priest Ambrose Coleman, "it conceals the elements of revolution." This supposed church had "the active support of professed atheists and freethinkers, of revolutionists who never enter a church or think about religion," he wrote, "who are pledged to extirpate Christianity" and were "utilizing the revolt of Aglipay for a common end."[57] Colonial officials even outside of the Catholic Church sometimes harbored this suspicion. According to the Philippine Commission in 1904, most Americans in the Philippines considered the new church "political rather than religious" and thought that its real "motive [was] another insurrection."[58]

To name a church as political was to deny it status as a religion and so to delegitimize its claims to religious freedom. As a scholar concerned with the historical formation of religion as a category and its implications in the civilizational assemblages of empire, I see such religious-political distinctions as themselves the data for analysis. As I argued in the introduction to this book, the assumed clarity of distinction between the political and the religious had emerged out of a distinctively Euro-American trajectory. It was now part of the ideological and institutional apparatus of U.S. empire: a marker of the civilized modern and a measure that the colonized could never quite seem to reach. The attacks on Aglipay were one place in which these civilizational assemblages became explicit. In a colony that had only just been subjugated by the force of the U.S. military, Americans interpreted a church that called for indigenous leadership as "seditious" and anti-American. In other words, the demand that Filipino Christians restrict their concerns to the purely religious was in itself deeply political, because by delegitimizing a potential avenue for Filipino protest, it worked to bolster U.S. colonial rule.

Once again, the civilizational assemblages of empire identified these religious-secular distinctions with the hierarchies of race. Coleman explained the allegedly political nature of the Aglipayan church as a Filipino racial characteristic. Reflecting on the "real import and tendencies" of the Philippine Independent Church, he wrote that in the broadest sense this was "simply a phase of the revolt of the yellow against the white man." Describing the Aglipayan movement as a "form of Oriental fanaticism," he rendered the Filipino desire for independence as inexplicable racial hatred: "At heart they are all fanatically opposed to the white man, be he Spanish or American," he wrote. The alleged inability to distinguish between the religious and the political appears here as a distinctly racial trait. Isabelo de los Reyes's book *Religion of the Katipunan,* which sought a pre-Christian religious source for archipelagic unity, was for Coleman ample evidence of the Aglipayans' "political" and "fiendish" nature. Wherever they gained a foothold, he wrote, they were using civil authority to "persecute Catholics" and foment rebellion. "The introduction of Aglipayanism into a parish is often the signal for [anti-American] disturbances," he claimed, "caused by a few influential men who have never shown any signs of religion, getting up a faction in its favor and terrorizing the majority of the people." Coleman described Filipinos as "Orientals" who were inclined toward "despotism," incapable of democratic practice, and unwilling to accept their place in the racial-imperial order. Like images of the Moros as violent "fanatics," such accounts obscured the context of the Filipinos' resistance to empire.[59]

The principle of religious freedom provided Archbishop Aglipay and his church with an imperially sanctioned response. When a Catholic attorney in Manila claimed that he had the evidence to prosecute Aglipay and de los Reyes for the crime of sedition, Aglipay responded, "I am greatly surprised that the said attorney (a Catholic) confuses the authority of the pope with that of the American government." The attorney, he argued, had conflated the rejection of papal authority with a rebellion against U.S. colonial rule.[60] According to Aglipay it was not his church but its critics who had confused the religious and the political. When Catholics called on government authority to crush a church whose only crime was to break free from the pope, they (and not the Aglipayans) violated the American principles of religious freedom and the separation of church and state. In this rendering the real civilized moderns, those who truly represented the principles of freedom and democracy, were the people of the Philippines and especially the members of the Philippine Independent Church.

Aglipayans regularly invoked the U.S. Constitution to defend themselves against Catholic attacks. "The Filipino national Catholic church is a fact," asserted the Aglipayan newspaper *La Verdad.* "Under the constitution of the United States there is absolute liberty of conscience and religious equality for all. . . . We will insist on all that is due each law abiding citizen of whatever creed." The editors went even further by locating the new church firmly within the American revolutionary tradition. "The authority of the English state church in America" had ended with the Revolution, they noted. "The Church of England in America was transformed into the Protestant Episcopal Church of America," and in the same way "the Roman Catholic Church of the Philippines has developed into the independent Catholic Church of the Philippines."[61] The end of Spanish rule meant that Spain's established church could no longer assert legal privileges or priority in the Philippines. Instead, with the religious freedom guaranteed by the United States, the Philippine Independent Church had equal standing with every other church in the islands.

The principle of religious freedom soon entered into the formally articulated theology of the new church. Aglipay wrote his "Sixth Fundamental Epistle" in August 1903 to clarify church policy against a group of priests who announced that although they rejected the pope's authority in matters of discipline, they would continue to follow him in doctrine. The Independent Church had been formed not only to address "the human question of curates and bishops," he wrote, but also to re-establish "the purity of the sacred doctrines of Jesus Christ contained in the New Testament, redeeming consciences . . . from all exaggeration and [from] anti-scientific scruple against the laws of nature and against sane, free judgment." Here Aglipay affirmed the right of his church and its members to read and interpret the Bible for themselves—and signaled his growing interest in harmonizing that biblical revelation with the discoveries of modern science and "the light of reason which God has given us." The epistle ended with a prayer of gratitude: "Holy, Holy, Holy, thou art the Eternal Trinity to whom we owe our religious liberty. Heaven and Earth are full of thy glory." God had given the gift of this freedom, and the Philippine Independent Church now claimed it as a divinely ordained right for all.[62]

American Protestant missionaries reacted to the new church as an indigenous Filipino Reformation, at least potentially in line with its sixteenth-century counterpart. Even before the announcement of the new church, some missionaries had hoped that the Filipinos' liberation from Spanish rule would spark a Filipino movement away from Rome. But with a racialized condescension toward the subjects of empire, they had anticipated that such a movement would require their guidance. The "peace-speaking guns of Admiral Dewey" had "opened the gates" to millions who had been "fettered by bonds almost worst than heathenism," declared the Presbyterian foreign missions chairman George Pentecost in 1898. "The very guns of our battleships"—and here the interests of American empire and Protestant missions cannot be distinguished—"summoned us to go up and possess the land."[63] Initially the missionaries seem to have believed that mass conversions into the Protestant churches were imminent. "Their readiness to accept a pure gospel is astonishing and gratifying," wrote the Presbyterian missionary Arthur Judson Brown. "The fields are more than white; they are dead ripe."[64] The Methodist Homer Stuntz was less sanguine. The people were "hungry" for the Word of God, he claimed, and had come to hate the Catholic Church. Protestant missions were urgent if they were to be saved from the rampant varieties of "unbelief or misbelief" that were circulating in the islands.[65] Through such accounts American missionaries depicted Filipinos not as independent agents but as hapless targets of a religious-imperial competition for their bodies and souls.

Protestant missionaries were not entirely pleased with the announcement of an independent Filipino church, therefore, especially one that initially maintained allegiance to the doctrines and practices of Catholicism. Like other Americans, many of them suspected Aglipay and his followers of concealing nationalist, anti-American, or even violent revolutionary designs. Most considered the Aglipayans theologically confused, far too attached to the "superstitions" and rituals of Rome to have embraced, as yet, the (Protestant) purity of the Christian gospel. "Whether the movement is based on those vital principles of religious life on which a church can be permanently established remains to be seen," wrote Brown.[66] The best thing about the new movement, Stuntz explained in 1904, was that it had thrown off "the yoke of the pope" and encouraged the people to read the Bible. Aglipayans had purchased 25,000 copies of the Bible, he reported, and were now distributing them around the Philippines. "Aglipay loosens this fruit from the tree," he concluded, "and we [will] gather it." These missionaries approved of the Philippine Independent Church only if they could lead it into the complacent and imperially complicit mainstream of the Protestant world.[67]

Aglipay's essay in the *Independent* pushed back against these American Protestant missionaries, who wanted to reshape the new church to fit their own mold, and against a Catholic hierarchy that denied its claims to church property or even to the status of a church at all. The Philippine Independent Church would maintain the theology and ritual practices of Catholicism, Aglipay explained, but would do so under indigenous leadership. "We have capable Filipino priests of our own, to govern our Church," he wrote, "and in the same manner as the American Civil Commission recognizes the ability of Filipinos to sit on the Supreme Court, be Governors of provinces, and even Commissioners, we demand recognition, and having been refused by the Church of the Italian Cardinals, we have established our Filipino Independent Catholic Church." The rapid growth of the new church demonstrated that it was meeting the religious needs of the people. Aglipay went on to reassure his American (and mostly Protestant) readers that this church was both progressive and biblically grounded. "The liberalizing influences at work among us make it certain that our religious progress will be upward," he wrote, "largely influenced by the Bible, and will be permanent." In this way he rearticulated the principle of religious freedom to protect a church formed in and through Filipino resistance against American as well as Spanish colonial rule.[68]

Aglipay concluded his essay with the still unresolved question of church property. Indeed, the entire piece can be read as an extended argument to support the Aglipayan position in this dispute. Demonstrating a savvy knowledge of the *Independent*'s likely readers, he invoked long-standing Protestant fears of the pope as a foreign power. "There is not a human being in possession of his senses," he wrote, "who would suggest that because the Roman Catholic priests were servants of the state, that therefore state property belongs to an Italian in Rome." The churches had been built for the people by the colonial state, he explained, using public money collected from the people in the form of taxes. Because the Treaty of Paris had transferred all public properties from Spain to the United States, these church buildings now belonged "to the United States . . . in trust for the people." And because American law did not permit state ownership of churches, or favoritism to any one church, they should now be granted to whatever church the majority of the people in each community favored, whether that be the Philippine Independent Church, the Roman Catholic Church, or anything else. Note the change here from Aglipay's initial, more radical claim that *all* church buildings belonged by rights to the Philippine Independent Church. The new argument was more realistic and more likely to succeed in the courts. It moved away from any suggestion that Aglipayanism was the church for all Filipinos and toward a more even-handed framework for the separation of church and state.[69]

Once again Aglipay's hopes would be dashed. After a long battle in the courts, the Catholic Church eventually reclaimed all the disputed church buildings. The Supreme Court of the Philippines ruled in *Barlin v. Ramirez*

(1906) that the Catholic Church held legal title to the properties originally built for its services. Aglipayan priests all over the Philippines had to abandon the old colonial churches, turning over the keys to Catholic bishops or priests. Finding themselves suddenly without places of worship, Aglipayans scrambled to construct whatever new buildings they could afford. Many parishioners did not make the move with their priests, choosing instead to continue attending services in the old parish buildings that had been their places of worship for so many generations. Unsure that the movement could survive, a number of Aglipayan priests returned to the Catholic fold. At the same time, Archbishop Harty had been sensitive to the desire for indigenous leadership in the church, and by 1920 he had consecrated so many Filipino bishops that they found themselves in the majority. As the fervor of the revolution faded, these accommodations helped smooth the way for many Filipinos back into the Catholic Church. The Philippine Independent Church would regain some ground over the next decade and then stabilized at around 1.4 million members within a rapidly expanding population.[70]

Archbishop Aglipay maintained his commitment to religious freedom for the rest of his life. Indeed, in the 1910s and 1920s he embraced an increasingly liberal theology and built ties with the Unitarian churches in the United States and Europe. This connection provided external validation and a certain amount of financial support for the Philippine Independent Church. But because most Unitarians discussed religious freedom primarily in terms of the individual conscience—as a question of individual belief or unbelief, rather than communal or national self-determination—this affiliation also signaled the archbishop's declining radicalism and his willingness to back away from claims that might be interpreted as political. Meanwhile, most rank-and-file members of the Aglipayan church maintained a largely Catholic theology and style of worship, and after Aglipay's death in 1940 they splintered into several denominations. The largest of these affiliated with the American Episcopal Church, while two smaller groups retained their Unitarian affiliations.[71] Religious freedom talk had in a very real way made the Philippine Independent Church possible. At the same time it had served as a disciplinary force, remolding the Aglipayan movement to fit an American model of distinctions between the religious and the political. In so doing it reinforced the structures of imperial power.

All of these developments had strengthened the cultural authority of Catholicism in the United States as well as in the Philippines. When the former apostolic delegate Archbishop Chapelle died in New Orleans in 1905, his obituary praised his contributions both to the church and to the interests of American empire. At the peace conference in 1898, the *Washington Post* reported, the archbishop had "rendered signal service both to the Holy See and to the U.S. . . . He was the means through which the clause guaranteeing religious liberty and the rights of ecclesiastical property was inserted in the Treaty of Paris." The properties in question were not only the parish buildings reclaimed from the Aglipayans but also the friar lands, the vast estates once owned by the religious orders and confiscated by Aguinaldo's government, which the United States had finally purchased from the church in order to settle the question of their rightful ownership.[72] In Cuba, Puerto Rico, and the Philippines, the obituary concluded, Archbishop Chapelle had "outlined the work" needed to successfully reorient the church in these new American colonial possessions. In his obituary, the archbishop appeared as the champion of a church seamlessly aligned with the recent expansions of U.S. empire.[73]

The *Washington Post* presented the Catholic victories in the property disputes in the Philippines as self-evidently consistent with the principle of religious freedom. Only a few years earlier, Protestants in the United States had sharply contested that view along with the Aglipayans. That the *Washington Post* would so readily describe the protection of "ecclesiastical property" as a triumph for religious freedom reveals how successful the church had already been in reframing these disputes. The editors may well have taken the language of the obituary directly from a Catholic press release, thus presenting a distinctly Catholic articulation of religious freedom as entirely uncontroversial. In the newspaper of record in the nation's capital, the taken-for-granted meanings of religious freedom now encompassed what had been a distinctly Catholic position in a heated sectarian debate. In the eyes of American Catholics, the all-American principle of religious freedom very clearly supported the interests of their church in the Philippines— and their church just as clearly supported the interests of U.S. empire. This congruence of interests had helped American Catholics secure the future of Catholicism in the Philippines. By locating Catholicism as part and parcel of the imperial project, allied with the imperial rhetorics of freedom and democracy, it also helped build the stature of Catholics and Catholicism in American life.

Over the next few decades, Filipino nationalists would continue to assert the principle of religious freedom to support the cause of independence from the United States. Speaking to the U.S. Congress in 1911, Nationalist Party leader Manuel Quezon argued that during its brief period of effective independence, the Philippine Republic had amply demonstrated the ability of the Filipino people to govern themselves. The constitution endorsed at Malolos had enshrined the principles of liberty that characterized a modern republic, including "the separation of the church and the state and the liberty and equality of all religions." Its leaders had governed effectively, establishing public order and organizing all the necessary public services even under the difficult conditions of war. Quezon acknowledged that there were inherited rivalries between Christians and non-Christians in the Philippines—particularly between Filipinos and Moros—but he denied the idea advanced by some American authorities that independence would only create the conditions for violent conflict between them. Instead, he insisted that "religious intolerance" had largely disappeared and a Filipino government was best equipped to unite the archipelago.[74]

Quezon gained considerable sympathy for his position in the United States. Yet even the generally anti-imperialist Democratic Party had become convinced that Filipinos could be granted their independence only gradually, after they had proven their abilities through still more American tutelage in democratic self-government. Once again Filipino leaders invoked religious freedom to demonstrate their belonging in the communion of civilized nations, and once again the United States refused to recognize their claims. Religious freedom talk would play a similarly ambivalent role in the U.S. conquest of the Moro provinces of the southern Philippines, where it worked subtly to distinguish Moro religion from a governing process that American officials now designated as secular.

GOVERNING THE MOROS: SOVEREIGNTY AND SECULARISM IN THE PHILIPPINES

From the time the United States concluded its peace treaty with Spain, American colonial officials had applied very different policy prescriptions to the Moros of the south than to the Catholic Filipinos who made up the majority elsewhere in the archipelago. Because the Moros were Muslims, Americans expressed a great deal of anxiety about them as troubling new subjects for U.S. imperial rule. "Thus for the first time is the Mohammedan religion brought under the protection of the Stars and Stripes," commented the *Washington Post*. The paper warned that even the most determined Jesuit attempts to Christianize these "turbulent" and "piratical Moslems" had failed, most often ending with "the missionaries . . . put to death."[75] Such accounts drew both on the representational legacy of colonial violence and on long-standing American images of Islam as a bad religion, one that inspired "fanatical" devotion and refused to honor modern distinctions between the religious and the political.[76] In this context, American religious freedom talk would serve to rationalize empire and to manage imperial subjects by defining the limits of the religious, a category implicated here and elsewhere in imperial techniques of classification and control.[77]

Slavery, Polygamy, and the Racial Logics of Religious Freedom

For ideas on governing a Muslim people, Americans turned to both Spanish and British precedents in the region. Spain had only recently consolidated its authority over the Moros by promising them the benefits of trade and military protection from any external threats and pledging not to interfere with their practice of Islam. The treaties they made reflected the pressures facing both Moros and Spaniards in an increasingly competitive imperial world. The Moro sultans were very much aware of the British policy of indirect rule in neighboring Malaysia, which allowed full rein for local "religion and customs," and they insisted that Spain must grant them the same privileges. In return they had claimed the protection of the Spanish Armada from the aggressions of the British or any other imperial power. Thus the Spanish presence in the Moro territories had remained minimal, and the Moros maintained a considerable degree of autonomy despite their formal recognition of Spanish sovereignty.[78]

The United States had both ideological and pragmatic reasons to follow this example. The Philippine Commission judged the model of indirect rule inapplicable elsewhere in the Philippines, arguing that Spain had long since destroyed the native leadership and that the Catholic Filipinos were ready for direct tutelage in democracy. In contrast, conditions in the Moro territories were more like those in the Malay Peninsula, where the British had been able to govern through the native chiefs and sultans. This analysis fit neatly with the strategic goal of preventing the Moros from either joining the Filipino revolt against U.S. rule or initiating their own resistance movement. The commission concluded that indirect rule was the only way to secure the Moros' allegiance and so to advance the strategic imperatives of U.S. empire in the Philippines. In keeping with that recommendation, General John C. Bates negotiated a treaty with the Moro leader Jamalul Kiram II, better known as the sultan of Sulu. It guaranteed that the United States would respect "all the religious customs" along with "the rights and dignities of the Sultan and his *Datus*," the chieftains who governed local Moro communities.[79]

Back in the United States, the most controversial feature of this treaty was its implicit recognition of slavery and polygamy as ongoing Moro practices. While it did not mention polygamy directly, its promise not to interfere with Moro "religious customs" implicitly included this institution. Its only reference to slavery was an article granting any slave "the right to purchase freedom by paying to the master the usual market value," a provision that assumed the practice would continue. In response to his critics, General Bates later explained that he had seen this provision as a route to freedom for individual slaves and an opening wedge for a more general emancipation in the future. But the only question in the treaty negotiations had been whether or not a specific price should be named; the phrase "market value" had been inserted because the sultan thought the figure in Bates's first proposal too low. Slavery thus appeared in the treaty not in connection with Islam but as an economic and social reality in the southern Philippines.[80]

The Moro practices of slavery and polygamy were embedded in complex social hierarchies that bore little resemblance to their American counterparts. In the United States, the introduction of plural marriage among the Latter-day Saints (Mormons) had initially been controversial even among the Mormons themselves. In contrast, most Southeast Asian societies had long accepted polygyny (marriage to multiple wives) as a sign of wealth and status for local leaders. The Qur'anic permission for this practice under some conditions and its prevalence in many Muslim societies had given it even more legitimacy among the Moros. Spanish rule had ended polygamy among the Catholic Filipinos, but it remained culturally legible throughout the Philippines, not at all the public scandal that it had been in the United States. Moro models of slavery were similarly distant from the racially defined and plantation-based institution that Americans remembered from the antebellum South. The Spanish word *esclavo* collapsed a wide variety of indigenous categories of bondage, and the conditions of those it designated varied a great deal depending on where they had come from, how they had been enslaved, and the status of their masters. As with polygamy, most forms of slavery had been eliminated in the northern Philippines under Spanish rule but remained as a recognizable cultural norm across the archipelago.[81]

Disregarding the complexity of these social relations, the advocates of imperial expansion had initially described both slavery and polygamy as evidence that the Philippines required the benevolent hand of American rule. "President McKinley Will Be a Second Emancipator," proclaimed the *Los Angeles Times* some months before the Bates Treaty was announced.[82] Thus when the terms of the Bates Treaty became public, a firestorm of controversy ensued. Critics attacked the McKinley administration for endorsing the same practices that the president's own Republican Party had so valiantly opposed in the past. "The inclusion of this picturesque barbarian, with his harem, slaves, and despotic rule, under the 'banner of freedom,'" commented the *Washington Post* regarding the sultan of Sulu, "marks the utmost limit of the incongruous in our expansion of the 'home of the free.'"[83] As the campaign season of 1900 moved into full swing, the presumptive Democratic presidential nominee William Jennings Bryan charged McKinley with betraying the Thirteenth Amendment and the integrity of the Constitution simply to benefit his capitalist cronies. For anti-imperialists, the treaty's acceptance of Moro slavery and polygamy demonstrated the corrosive tendencies of empire and dramatized McKinley's betrayal of America's must treasured principles.[84]

The vision of a Republican administration endorsing slavery was by no means the only irony in this situation. Some of the same Democrats who expressed such qualms about the Philippines had ardently defended slavery in the United States and were now advancing the politics of racial segregation across the South. Most were far more offended by what they saw as Republican hypocrisy than by the institution of slavery itself. The same flag that McKinley described as a symbol of "liberty, opportunity, and humanity," remarked the *Baltimore Sun*, had brought the South "four years of war and destruction of a species of property [then] recognized by the Constitution."[85] Representative John Sharp Williams of Mississippi warned that the "brown man and the yellow man from the Orient" were simply unfit to participate alongside the "Anglo-Saxon in governing a free republic." American freedoms, he believed, relied on the maintenance of white racial control.[86]

Faced with a massive public controversy, the McKinley administration mobilized the principle of religious freedom to defend the treaty and its overall policies in the colony. Philippine Commission chair Jacob Gould Schurman explained to the press that the United States had inherited the Spanish policy of limited sovereignty over the Moros, including the promise "not to interfere with the religion or customs of the islands," and could not immediately change it.[87] As a sympathetic journalist put it: "If any attempt is made to appease the sentimental portion of the press and the American people by interfering with the religious liberty of the Moros in Mindanao, which is Mohammedan, or with their slaves, which they hold as a part of their religion, we shall have a savage, bloody, and quite unnecessary war."[88] Portraying abolitionist sentiment as misguided and naive, these imperialists deployed the civilizational assemblages of race and religion to argue that slavery and polygamy were to be expected among "Orientals" and other civilizational inferiors—and that a "barbaric" religion such as Islam would naturally sanction them. The Moros were simply not yet civilized enough to give up this practice and would require a long period of American tutelage before they could be expected to make such a change.

On both sides of this debate, as historian Michael Salman has explained, the persistence of slavery provided further evidence of the barbarity of non-Western peoples and the civilizing influences of imperial rule. Whether or not Americans supported the annexation of the Philippines, they defined their own identities over and against the image of the "Mohammedan fanatic." Despite how recently slavery had been eliminated in the United States and its frequently rosy depictions in popular culture at the time, many Americans figured its abolition as a defining accomplishment of Western modernity. Like the principle of religious freedom, the absence (or abolition) of slavery could demonstrate a nation's belonging in the ranks of the civilized. And one of the civilizing tasks of a benevolent American imperialism would be to abolish the institution of slavery among the allegedly barbaric colonial subjects who still practiced it. Thus the humanitarian impulse of abolitionism worked as a further rationale for imperial conquest, and ardent abolitionists would continue to agitate for direct intervention to halt all practices of slavery in the Philippines. This political pressure would in the long run work to undermine the Bates Treaty and the premise of Moro self-governance that went along with it.[89]

The public controversy over the Bates Treaty also coincided with a new flurry of protest against Mormon political power and the legacy of polygamy in the United States. Utah had become a state in January 1896, a step very much opposed by Protestant reformers who were convinced that the Mormons were still secretly practicing polygamy and would use the status of statehood to legalize it. Controversy erupted when a Utah district elected B. H. Roberts, a member of the Latter-day Saints church hierarchy who had served five months in prison for the crime of bigamy, to the House of Representatives in 1898.[90] Anti-polygamy activists presented seven million signatures imploring Congress not to seat him. Mounting a spirited defense, Roberts's supporters argued that barring him from Congress imposed an unconstitutional religious test for public office, violated his First Amendment right to the freedom of religion, and denied the right of Utah's people to elect their own representative to Congress. But judging by the petitions to Congress and the overwhelming House vote against him, most Americans felt that seating Roberts would mean accepting the

Mormons and their practice of polygamy back into the fold, endangering the very fabric of American democracy and civilization. Roberts would never enter the U.S. Congress.[91]

The most ardent anti-polygamy reformers applied the same logic to the Moros. Building on a long tradition of comparing Mormons and Muslims, they placed the Roberts case alongside the Bates Treaty to make the case for an anti-polygamy amendment to the U.S. Constitution. Alarmed by Roberts's election and the rumored persistence of polygamy in Utah, activists pointed to the administration's willingness to tolerate the same practice in the Philippines to argue that the existing legal strictures against polygamy were entirely inadequate. In one missive against Roberts, reformer Melusina Fay Peirce asked McKinley to explain how his administration could even consider allowing a convicted polygamist to enter Congress and how at the same time it "happen[ed] to be subsidizing a Mohammedan Sultan with a harem." The conscience of the nation would not be clean, she concluded, "until the United States flag . . . floats in protection over no polygamist in any part of the world." Peirce did not make it clear whether or not she favored U.S. rule in the Philippines. Either way, she considered polygamy a threat to the fabric of American civilization and could not countenance its presence in any territory controlled by the United States.[92]

Most Americans, however, considered the Mormons a far greater threat to American civilization than the Moros could ever be. Mormons not only had brought polygamy within the bounds of the continental United States but also, as the descendants of New England Puritans, posed an existential threat to the civilizational identity of white American Protestants. Anti-polygamy reformers in the nineteenth century had undermined the Mormons' claims to whiteness by associating them with the frontier "savagery" of Indians and the foreign "barbarism" of Islam.[93] Similar rhetorics reappeared in the campaign against Roberts. One letter to the *Washington Post* opined that a "self-respecting people" would "shudder with outraged indignation to think of the leprous buttocks of a polygamous monster befouling a seat in our national Congressional halls." "The adherents of such abandoned heathenism," the writer concluded, "must stand back and not profane our national councils."[94] The practice of polygamy, activists implied, had reversed the Mormons' status as a civilized and Christian people. As the Supreme Court had said in the *Reynolds v. United States* decision of 1879, quoted now by the House committee reviewing Roberts's case, "Polygamy has always been odious among the northern and western nations of Europe, and until the establishment of the Mormon Church, was almost exclusively a feature of the life of Asiatic and African peoples." Most Americans simply could not tolerate such practices among a people who continued to claim the privileges of whiteness and lived within the continental United States.[95]

In contrast, such behavior was expected among the unequivocally non-white and non-Christian subjects of imperial rule. Eschewing the moralism of the anti-polygamy reformers, the *Washington Post* advocated for a tolerant policy both in the case of Roberts and toward the Moros. The editors did not suggest that the Latter-day Saints should have been permitted to continue their practice of polygamy. Congress and the courts had long since decided that question. But they did argue that Roberts should not be penalized for having "contracted plural marriages at a time when they were tolerated by law" and should not be excluded from Congress simply for his religion. The distinctions of geography, race, and religion enabled the editors to construe religious freedom even more expansively in the case of the Moros. "If civilization is to be extended into those portions of the islands which Spain has never mastered, it must be understood that the law and the faith are one with both Moslems and Hindus," they wrote. "If the Koran says a man may have four wives and as many concubines as he can afford to support, there is no earthly use in the government telling him that he is naughty, or in the missionaries threatening him with a sultry hereafter." For constitutional reasons too, the *Post* advised, Americans would need to recognize the Moros' right to maintain polygamy as a religious practice: "As the United States guarantees religious freedom to all its citizens, is it proposed to draw the line at Mahometanism?" The editors offered no explanation for why the same freedom should not have applied to the Mormons.[96]

Journalistic images of Moro polygamy worked to support this racialized ideology of religious freedom and the philosophy of indirect rule that it supported. Journalists and travel writers offered colorful narratives of the sultan of Sulu and his "harems" of wives and concubines. In contrast to the female moral reformers who had decried the oppression of women under Mormon polygamy, they spun Orientalist tales of an alien, timeless, and exotic people whose lives Americans could not hope to comprehend. While dominant images of Mormon women had emphasized their need for protection, American reporters had few such concerns on behalf of Moro women. According to reporter Anna Northend Benjamin, the sultana Inchi Jamela, mother of the current sultan, was a scheming woman who had poisoned her first two husbands to become the true "power behind the throne at Maybun."[97] The sultan's first wife was "of blood royal," reported J. N. Taylor in the *Boston Daily Globe*, but she had left him because she was "jealous of a pretty concubine" and "doesn't like his mother a bit." He had no shortage of wives and could "round up and run in any girl or woman in the island" if he so desired.[98] Given a different set of ideological interests, these reporters could have chosen to emphasize the plight of the young girls whom they briefly mentioned as the sultan's concubines. Instead they focused on accounts of his wife and mother as powerful but petty women, manipulating the men in their lives in order to achieve their own ends. Rather than appearing as a threat to female purity and to civilization itself, polygamy in these accounts was an expected and even amusing foible of the "barbarous" Mohammedan.

These racialized depictions of Moro women supported quite different deployments of religious freedom in U.S. government policy toward the Mormons on one hand and the Moros on the other. Mormon polygamy had been utterly unacceptable and possible to eliminate because the Mormons were uncomfortably close, both racially and geographically, to the white Protestant majority. Reporters' snide remarks—"It makes one smile to think of 'blood royal' among these black toothed betel chewers," wrote Taylor—betrayed their utter disdain for the Moros, whom they depicted as racial inferiors far beyond the pale of civilization.[99] The Moros were non-white, non-Christian, exotic and faraway colonial subjects; virtually all Americans agreed that they were unprepared for the full measure of civilization. The ideal of religious freedom would in their case need to be adapted to include a broader range of practices, even those as odious to the sensibilities of the American public as slavery and polygamy.

Political rhetorics on both sides of the aisle reinforced the self-image of white Americans as civilized moderns, racially superior to people of color at home and to their colonial subjects abroad. Whatever their position on the Bates Treaty or the colonization of the Philippines, both Republicans and Democrats attributed the difficulty of eradicating these Moro institutions to the alleged "Mohammedan fanaticism" that defined Moro racial identity in American eyes. Thus in the controversy that flared around the treaty and over U.S. imperial expansion in general, both Republicans and Democrats assumed the superiority of an American civilization that for the most part they described as both Christian and white. Despite their differences on other points, they could define themselves as civilized moderns over and against the Moros, whose "fanatical" religious practices of polygamy and slavery seemed to demonstrate their civilizational inferiority in simultaneously racial and religious terms.

Enforcing the Imperial Secular

On the ground in the Philippines, American religious freedom talk supported the shifting operations of imperial rule. From the time of their initial negotiations with the Moros, American colonial officials invoked this freedom as a governing principle. But its meaning changed significantly over time. Initially, as I have already described, the administration used this principle to justify the policy of indirect rule. Within just a few years, though, officials would redeploy it to impose new religious-secular distinctions on the Moro people. More specifically, they limited the sultan of Sulu and the Moro *datus* to an explicitly religious sphere of influence. Thus the rhetorics of religious freedom delegitimized Moro claims to political authority, now identified as the exclusive realm of the colonial power—a power that despite clear preferences for Christianity proclaimed itself secular, untainted by the particularity of the religious.

Religious freedom played an ambivalent role in the early U.S. negotiations with the Moros. Cornell University president Jacob Gould Schurman, chair of the Philippine Commission, immediately foregrounded this freedom when he held preliminary conversations with the sultan of Sulu, Kiram II, in June 1899. Schurman assured the sultan that the United States "had no wish to subjugate the population or to interfere with their customs or religion." Not unlike Emilio Aguinaldo in his early encounters with American officials, Kiram II initially showed little interest in protecting this specific freedom. According to the commission's records, he did not respond to this point but emphasized instead that "he earnestly desired peace and was anxious to continue the existing treaties" as he had negotiated them with Spain. Focusing on the question of sovereignty, the sultan raised questions about which flags the Moro ships would fly and which government would have jurisdiction over crimes committed in Moro territories. Above all he expressed the desire to maintain the region's fragile balance of power, reflected in the mostly peaceful accommodations and the networks of trade that he and his predecessors had managed to forge.[100]

Schurman's approach to religious freedom for the Moros—his promise that the United States would not interfere with their religion—was entirely different from the American insistence that Protestants and Catholics must enjoy equal privileges elsewhere in the Philippines. Along with Dean Worcester and other colonial officials, Schurman assumed that as Muslims the Moros were violent fanatics motivated entirely by their religion. Any attempt "to interfere with the religion of these people," he wrote, "would precipitate one of the bloodiest wars in which this country has ever been engaged."[101] General Bates maintained the same position during the final treaty negotiations several months later. Bates began by demanding that the Moros acknowledge "the sovereignty of the United States over the whole group" of islands and promised that in exchange "we certainly will not interfere with their religion or customs."[102] Religious freedom appeared here as a compensatory promise, a guarantee that American rule would not touch the Moros' "religious customs." Both Schurman and Bates assumed that the sphere of religion was easily distinguishable from that of political sovereignty and that its protection was the Moros' most important concern.

Sultan Kiram II shared none of these assumptions. His draft of the treaty would have allowed him to maintain much the same level of authority he had always enjoyed, checked mainly by the traditional prerogatives of the *datus* within his domain. Divining the importance of religious freedom to his American interlocutors, he made a point of addressing this topic. But his approach to the category of religion and the protections it required was subtly different from the general's. The relevant article in his draft read: "The Americans will respect the dignity of the Sultan and the *datos* [sic] and his advisors; and above all, will respect the Mohammedan religion; they will not change or oppose any execution of the same." In contrast to Bates, Kiram II embedded the idea of respect for religion within a broader provision for "the dignity of the Sultan and the *datos* [sic]." Rather than separating "religion and customs" from the structures of governance, he assumed that they were necessarily intertwined. His vision of religious freedom provided leverage to defend these integrated systems of authority.[103]

The competing visions of religious freedom articulated by the general and the sultan sat side by side rather uncomfortably in Article 3 of the final treaty. Located just after a declaration of U.S. sovereignty and a guarantee that Moro ships would fly the Stars and Stripes, this article gave religious freedom pride of place but a rather ambiguous definition: "The rights and dignities of His Highness the Sultan and his *Datos* [sic] shall be fully respected, the Moros shall not be interfered with on account of their religion: all their religious customs shall be respected, and no one shall be persecuted on account of his religion." The transcript of the negotiations reveals that the sultan and his advisers had inserted the phrase "all their religious customs shall be respected," which is absent from both of the initial proposals. This clause could be read very expansively to protect any number of "customs," including the traditional authority of the sultan himself. The final clause—"no one shall be persecuted on account of his religion"—came from Bates's first draft. It introduced a very different vision of religious freedom as an individual liberty from religious persecution. Although the sultan may not have realized it at the time, this clause opened up the possibility of U.S. intervention to protect that right for individuals (even non-Muslims) within the Moro territories. Thus it hinted at a different balance of power in which ultimate sovereignty and the legitimate use of force resided in the United States alone. A great deal rested on the question of what precisely fell within the domain of religion and who had the power to shape its limits.[104]

Convinced of the need to keep the Moros pacified during the Philippine-American War, President McKinley announced his conditional approval of the Bates Treaty in the fall of 1899. He had serious reservations on the question of slavery. Stung by the criticisms in the press and worried about the constitutional implications of a treaty that tacitly endorsed slavery, he directed the secretary of war to tell General Bates that the tenth article could not be approved. Bates dutifully informed the sultan that this article must be suspended, that nothing in their agreement implied U.S. approval for the practice of slavery, and that the entire subject would need to be discussed further in the future. For the time being, however, the treaty effectively left the Moros in control of their own internal affairs. In truth, American military officials simply did not have the ability to eliminate slavery, polygamy, or any other practice in the predominantly Moro provinces of the southern Philippines.[105]

The question of sovereignty, meanwhile, remained unresolved. In their attempts at political damage control, the administration's spokesmen insisted that because the United States was already sovereign over the Philippines, this was not a "treaty" contracted between two sovereign powers but simply an "agreement" that could be amended by the U.S. government at will.[106] But in the sultan's eyes it was a binding treaty, one that maintained the delicate balance of power he had previously negotiated with Spain. That balance had enabled him and other Moro leaders to maintain their existing social institutions and patterns of governance. He had little reason to think that this would be any different now that the United States had replaced Spain as the imperial power involved. As it read in the Sulu language of Tao Sug, the treaty actually left the balance of power in the sultan's hands. Rather than clearly asserting U.S. sovereignty, as the English translation did, the Tao Sug version simply placed "the support, aid, and protection of the Jolo Island and Archipelago . . . in the American nation." Thus the sultan had not agreed to cede his sovereignty to the United States. Instead he had accepted the far more ambivalent promise of American "support, aid, and protection." Schurman and Bates had achieved a temporary modus vivendi with the Moros, but these differences on the question of sovereignty would lead to further conflicts in the years to come.[107]

As the Philippine-American War began to wind down in the north, U.S. colonial officials started to envision more ambitious civilizing projects for the Moros. President McKinley's charge to the second Philippine Commission in the fall of 1900 noted the "inviolable principles" of American government, including the guarantee "that no law shall be made respecting the establishment of religion, or prohibiting the free exercise thereof, and that the free exercise and enjoyment of religious profession and worship without discrimination or preference shall forever be allowed." But McKinley went on to specify that when it came to establishing colonial policy for the Moros and other "uncivilized tribes" in the Philippines, the commission should follow the model set by U.S. policy toward "the tribes of our North American Indians." As with the Indians, he continued, officials should permit these tribes "to maintain their tribal organization and government" while also providing "wise and firm regulation . . . to prevent barbarous practices and introduce civilized customs." Suddenly the Moros were to be classified alongside the uncivilized "wild tribes" of the Philippines, in need of firm direction and colonial control.[108]

McKinley was hardly the first to compare the so-called uncivilized tribes of the Philippines with American Indians, or to turn to the federal Bureau of Indian Affairs as a model for governing them. But in the initial phase of colonizing the Philippines, such comparisons were just as likely to be applied to the Filipino revolutionaries in the north or to designate all the people of the archipelago as an undifferentiated mass of "savages." McKinley's new instructions celebrated the "civilized" qualities of the Catholic Filipinos while identifying the "wild tribes" and the Moros as requiring distinct tactics of colonial control. These instructions initiated a shift in colonial policy that also followed recent trends in U.S. Indian policy. In both cases colonial authorities moved from an initial stress on conquest and pacification to the more ambitious goal of imparting civilization. The Bates Treaty—still formally in effect—had served to forestall conflict with the Moros through the principle of indirect rule. As a U.S. victory in the Philippine-American War became imminent, the generals charged with managing what had been designated the Military Department of Mindanao and Jolo found themselves less and less satisfied with the ambiguities of sovereignty that had accompanied that policy. Commanding officers complained that the treaty had given the sultan of Sulu and the Moro *datus* a "supreme and arbitrary power" that impeded progress among their people and abdicated the rightful sovereignty of the United States.[109]

The "Mohammedan fanaticism" that Americans attributed to the Moros had initially served as an argument for indirect rule. Now U.S. officials began to invoke this same characteristic to justify direct and even forcible models of colonial control. Even Schurman, one of the architects of indirect rule, argued in 1902 that the "Mohammedan (Moro) and heathen tribes" required "a strong external sovereignty" and must be more forcefully managed in future.[110] Secretary of War Elihu Root summed up the situation through the familiar hierarchies of a settler-colonial state. "Such measures of force as are necessary to control the various Moro tribes have no more relation to the recent Philippine insurrection," he wrote, "than our troubles with the Sioux or the Apaches had to do with the suppression of the Southern rebellion." Root saw the Christian Filipinos as comparable to the Confederates in the American Civil War: recognizably modern subjects, despite their rebellion, and at least potentially within the circle of the civilized. In contrast he equated the Muslims and "wild tribes" with American Indians: racial-religious savages whose "reduction" to a civilized status might ultimately need to be accomplished against their will.[111]

These vocabularies of racial-religious denigration also reflected an interplay of Christian and secular norms in the U.S. administration of Moro affairs. President McKinley's instructions to the Philippine Commission avoided explicitly religious models of classification. In contrast to Schurman's emphasis on the terms "heathen," "pagan," and "Mohammedan"—words grounded in centuries of Christian polemics—the president preferred the anthropological (though equally pejorative) categories of "uncivilized" and "barbaric." But the apparent absence of religion from the president's directives should not blind us to its constitutive role in his administration's systems of classification. When the new commission created an agency to study and recommend policy for the people they considered "uncivilized," they named it the Bureau of Non-Christian Tribes. The bureau's secular locus of authority did not obscure its continued use of a system that classified Filipinos in simultaneously racial and religious terms, identifying only those who had converted to Christianity as "civilized." Both its title and its mandate continued to follow the Jesuit mapping of Filipino peoples according to the presence or absence of Christianity.

Reinforcing the secular-anthropological locus of authority for imperial rule, the bureau's first director was David Prescott Barrows, an anthropologist whose doctoral research had focused on the Coahuila Indians of Southern California. His appointment reflected the assumption that the "wild tribes" of the Philippines were essentially similar to American Indians, making academic or administrative expertise in one field easily applicable to the other. The "practical duties . . . of investigating the material conditions of these wild peoples, and of assisting in the measures adopted for their material progress," the new director wrote, "affiliate its efforts with those of the U.S. Bureau of Indian Affairs."[112] Hoping to gain insights relevant to his new position, Barrows immediately embarked on a tour of Indian reservations in the American West. These ties to Native American affairs were not unusual. Through the decades of U.S. rule in the Philippines, federal agents often moved from positions on Indian reservations to work with the Moros in the Philippines, and vice versa, forging regular comparisons and exchanges in the colonial management of peoples they called uncivilized and wild.

In some ways, the replacement of overtly Christian language with a more secular discourse actually made it easier for colonial administrators to attack indigenous traditions without any suspicion that they might be violating the treasured American principle of religious freedom. McKinley's category of "barbarous practices," those that must be eliminated in the name of civilization, included aspects of indigenous life that the Moros themselves described as religious. Barrows would continue to assume the need for Christian influence in order to civilize an Islamic people. After his tour of Indian reservations in the United States, Barrows argued that indirect rule in the Moros' case had been a mistake. He claimed that allowing the Moros to govern themselves, as Indians did on their reservations, only prevented them from interacting with the Christian Filipinos and so inhibited their "progress" toward civilization. While that system might be effective for Native Americans, whom he called "thoroughly democratic," Barrows could not countenance it when dealing with a Muslim society that he considered "oppressively aristocratic." The bureau's mission was upheld by official claims of secularity. But it reflected a continuing conviction that Christianity was a necessary precondition for the development of civilization among any "savage" or "barbaric" people.[113]

After their initial effort to discourage Christian missions under the Bates Treaty, colonial administrators would begin to welcome missionaries as their allies in the work of civilizing the Moros. Charles Brent, the influential Episcopalian bishop of the Philippines, developed a particular interest in the "pagans" and Moros and cultivated close friendships with the successive American governors of the Moro territories. With funding from philanthropist J. Pierpont Morgan, also an Episcopalian, the bishop soon established a medical mission on the island of Mindanao.[114] Governor-General Leonard Wood helped raise funds for these missions and described them as the best way to pacify the Moros. Missionaries, he wrote, "would have a dominant influence over the people and nip incipient rebellion in the bud." Wood defended American imperialism as a way to bring Christianity, civilization, and capitalism to the Muslim world. Converting the Philippines would be the key to a regional and even global mission, giving U.S. imperial rule an eternal significance. "We are a stone, if not the keystone, of the arch of Christian civilization in the Pacific," he explained in a 1925 interview. Wood saw no conflict between the principles of religious freedom and church-state separation on the one hand, which he championed as essential for the rule of law in the Philippines, and, on the other, the role he saw for Christianity in the civilizing tasks of American empire.[115]

The Philippine Commission Act, passed by Congress in June 1903, formalized the shift toward direct colonial rule in the territories it renamed the Moro Province. Intended as a step toward civilian governance, this act granted the American governor-general absolute authority as chief executive and gave him the power to appoint the five executives who served on the Moro Council. This structural change signaled a far more intensive regime of colonial surveillance and control. Among the council's first acts was to abolish slavery, which the Bates Treaty had tacitly allowed. Soon thereafter the council imposed a new system of taxation that restricted the *datus'* traditional methods of collecting fees and fines, requiring the Moros to pay taxes directly to the colonial state instead. Both of these changes significantly undercut the traditional authority of the Moro leaders and threatened the existing economic systems of the islands. Finally, following the advice of the U.S. military officials on site, President Theodore Roosevelt formally abrogated the Bates Treaty in March 1904.[116]

These changes in American policy sparked a cycle of Moro revolts and American disciplinary violence. The sultan of Sulu, by all accounts a pragmatic man, deplored the abrogation of the Bates Treaty but did his best to keep the peace. In his judgment, further negotiation rather than conflict with the Americans would best serve the interests of his people. But his efforts could not stem the anger of other Moro leaders who found their authority and their sources of livelihood suddenly curtailed. The violence of what came to be known as the Moro War peaked in 1906, when troops under Governor-General Wood's command surrounded a group of rebels and then proceeded to massacre nearly a thousand men, women, and children at Bud Dajo (Mount Dajo) on Mindanao Island. Once imagined as willing subjects of U.S. rule, the Moros had now become its most intractable enemies.[117]

Religious freedom talk played a crucial role in the negotiations of power between Americans and Moros during these years. Informed by his initial negotiations with General Bates, the sultan of Sulu invoked this freedom to assert the widest scope of authority he could muster under the growing constraints of American rule. In 1904, two years before the massacre at Bud Dajo, his chief political adviser, Hadji Butu, insisted in negotiations with General Wood that the sultan's sources of revenue and authority should be maintained because the people of Sulu wanted him to "continue in a position of dignity . . . as the head of their church and an example of all there is good in their religion." But unlike Bates five years earlier, General Wood would have nothing of it. When the sultan asked whether he would continue to be recognized as "ruler of Jolo" under the new arrangements, Wood answered that although the sultan "would always be religious head," he could not assume the position of governor unless he came to understand "our way of governing" and could demonstrate the capacity for that role.[118]

For years to come, the sultan of Sulu would use the principle of religious freedom to ground his demands for a greater scope of authority under U.S. rule. In 1905 he asked General Luke Wright, then governor of the Philippines, for a guarantee that the office of the sultanate would continue "for ever and ever . . . because the Sultan is head of the Mohammedan religion." He wrote that he had honored the Bates Treaty in every respect, even fighting against his own subjects when they rebelled against American authority, and that he regretted the Americans' unwillingness to do the same. Under the circumstances he was willing to make some concessions. His people would end the practice of slavery, for example, as long as the slave owners were compensated for their losses. But whatever else might change, he insisted that the Americans honor their promise not to "make us do what is against our religion." The sultan asserted his traditional ownership of all "pearls and tortoise shells of a certain size and weight," on the grounds that these supported the needs of his office. He also defended his right to judge in "four matters which are part of the Mohammedan religion," specifically the approval of marriages, the adjudication of marital quarrels, the inheritance of property, and the appointment of all "religious" leaders. "You may take my temporal power and rights if you pay for them according to law and justice," he concluded. "But I beg to be left to my rights as religious head of the Moros, with the dignities pertaining to that office, and the contributions due me as such." By this time the sultan had been forced to concede ultimate sovereignty to the United States. But here we can see him invoking the idea of religious freedom to defend an ambitious vision of his scope of authority under American rule.[119]

By this time American colonial officials had decisively rejected the principle of indirect rule in the Moro Province, and they would continue to whittle away at the sultan's authority. Frank Carpenter, the first civilian governor of the Moro Province, made an agreement with the sultan in 1915 under the heading "Being the Renunciation by the Latter of his Pretensions of Sovereignty and a Definition of his Status." Once again American negotiators felt the need to specify that the sultan's authority was to be limited to "spiritual" matters alone. The agreement stipulated that the sultan was to maintain "all the rights and privileges which under the government of the USA may be exercised by such an ecclesiastical authority." In exchange he agreed "without any reservation or limitation whatsoever" to recognize the full "sovereignty of the USA," including its jurisdiction over "all civil and criminal cases falling within the laws and orders of the government."[120]

Forced to accept his reclassification as a purely religious leader, the sultan of Sulu had attempted to negotiate an expansive vision for what counted as his religious authority. But ultimately that effort failed. By insisting on a distinction between "ecclesiastical" and "governmental" power, the 1915 agreement undercut the sultan's continued claims to a broad scope of authority as the "religious head" of the Moros. "The Sultan of Sulu and his adherents and people of the Mohammedan faith shall have the same religious freedom had by the adherents of all other religious creeds," the agreement concluded, "the practice of which is not in violation of the basic principles of the laws of the U.S.A."[121] Thus American colonial officials deployed religious freedom to solidify the sultan's assignment to the delimited sphere of religion, rejecting his earlier assertions of sovereignty over matters they placed in the domain of the state. By separating out religion as a distinct sphere to be protected, the ideal of religious freedom served to rationalize the sultan's loss of political power and the Americans' claim to imperial authority over Moro affairs. In this way religious freedom demarcated the boundaries of religion and the secular, categories deeply implicated (here and elsewhere) in imperial techniques of classification and control.[122]

As the Philippines moved toward independence from the United States during the 1920s and 1930s, religious freedom talk would continue to play a part
in the classificatory hierarchies of empire, the rhetorics of resistance, and
the negotiations of sovereignty on all sides of the archipelago's racial and
religious divides. For as long as Americans denied Filipino claims to independence, they presented religious freedom as a signature gift of a benevolent empire. The *Los Angeles Times* claimed in 1927 that the Filipinos' rapid
"progress" did not demonstrate their readiness for independence but rather
reflected the good governance of the United States, which had granted them
"religious freedom and equal standing of all persons before the law."[123]

Filipino nationalists continued to invoke their commitment to religious
freedom to prove that they were a modern people, fully equipped to govern
themselves. Condemning legislation proposed in 1926 to make Moro Province a separate colony—an effort that he noted had gained the support of
American businessmen and investors, who wanted to expand the rubber
industry in the archipelago and resented the restrictions imposed by the
Philippine Legislature in Manila—Pedro Quevara denied the idea "that the
Mohammedan Moros would not live in amity with the Christian Filipinos"
or that the old conflicts between Filipinos and Moros presented any barrier
to national unity. "Religious liberty exists in the islands and is guaranteed by
laws enacted by the Philippine Legislature," he said. Like his revolutionary
predecessors, Quevara denied the presence of "religious prejudice" among
modern Filipinos in order to defend the idea of the Philippines as a single
nation and to champion its ultimate independence.[124]

Many Moros supported the proposal for a separate colony, however,
revealing the limits of Quevara's nationalist vision. Datu Mohammad
Maulanz explained in a letter to a U.S. congressman who had recently visited his province in Sulu that his people were concerned about the recent
news "that independence will be given to the Christian Filipinos" and
hoped that Moro Province would not be included. Instead they wanted to
be kept "separate . . . for the following reasons: We have different religions,
we do not understand one another, and lastly, Mindanao and Sulu had
been separated from Luzon since our ancestors. We have been independent for five centuries," Maulanz continued, "ruled by our Sultan and never
since had been ruled by the Christian Filipinos."[125] The Philippines would
finally achieve complete independence in 1946, after a transitional decade

as a commonwealth under the protection of the United States and after the trauma of Japanese occupation during the Second World War. Throughout these events the Moros opposed their subordination to the Christian-dominated government in Manila, and the chasms that divided them have continued to simmer and sometimes erupt into violence ever since.[126]

The American colonial officials' disparate policies toward Catholic Filipinos on one hand and the Moros on the other had exacerbated the Moros' self-understanding as set apart, different from their counterparts in the rest of the Philippines.[127] The discourses of religious freedom had helped mediate the colonial redefinition of the sultans' authority, enabling Christian Filipinos to assert their own cultural and political authority over a putatively unified nation. At the same time, this principle provided a language for Moro resistance in the early colonial period, a way for Moros to assert their own identity as an Islamic people against the constraints of both American and Filipino rule. And the American identification of the Moro sultans and *datus* as strictly *religious* leaders had facilitated a Moro sense of communal identity centered primarily in adherence to Islam.[128]

Within the disciplinary regimes of U.S. empire, religious freedom talk helped colonial administrators navigate the rocky terrain of imperial rule: to classify subject populations and negotiate their differences, to assert the legitimacy of U.S. rule, and to support the twin civilizing missions of Christianity and the American secular. It enforced new religious-secular distinctions that effectively reorganized indigenous societies, valorized Western models of governance, and, more often than not, disempowered indigenous leaders relegated by its logic to the privatized realm of the religious.

At the same time, across the cultural landscapes of U.S. empire, minority and subjugated peoples invoked the principle of religious freedom to defend their own traditions and communities by claiming the protected status of religion in American life. The principle of religious freedom provided an ambivalent tool for resistance, a way for colonized peoples to mark out a degree of autonomy under the constraints of American rule. The next chapter shifts our attention to the utility and the limits of religious freedom for a very different colonized people: the Native Americans whose dispossession had marked the very formation of the United States as a settler-colonial society.

CHAPTER THREE

Making Religion on the Reservation

Native Americans and the Settler Secular

In August 1914, forty "chiefs, headmen and members of the Pawnee tribe" wrote U.S. Commissioner of Indian Affairs Cato Sells to contest allegations that what a Methodist missionary had called "heathen rites" presented a "menace to the morals" of their children. After answering each of the missionary's charges in detail, these Pawnee leaders provided their own positive statement of the history, significance, and benefits of the Ghost Dance ceremony. "Our Messiah or Ghost Dance is a religion that we think a great deal of," they wrote, "for through it, we found the white man's Christ, and the Book of Revelation of the New Testament furnishes us much of our ceremony whereby we worship the great spirit in Heaven." This Pawnee statement identified the Ghost Dance as an aid, not a detriment, to the civilizing goals of the Bureau of Indian Affairs (BIA). Theirs was a religion completely consistent with the practice of Christianity, they argued, and it would bring about "the reformation of the Indian . . . in the Indian's own way." The statement concluded by appealing to the commissioner's authority and discretion to honor the principle of religious freedom. "We come to you as our protector and guardian," they wrote, "and ask to be allowed to worship in our own good way."[1]

Like these Pawnee tribal leaders, many Native Americans in the early twentieth century invoked the principle of religious freedom to defend indigenous practices and traditions against the forceful civilizing policies of the settler-colonial tutelary regime. In contrast to the people of the Philippines, the indigenous people of North America had experienced wave after wave of Euro-American settlement and settler violence that left them at a distinct demographic disadvantage. In the decades after the Civil War, the last independent Native nations in the American West had been defeated by the U.S. military and forced onto government-designated reservations. There they faced poverty, dislocation, a barrage of daily humiliations, and the threat of cultural genocide. In the name of progress and civilization, the federal government created a vast bureaucracy, the Bureau of Indian Affairs, aimed explicitly at the destruction of Native traditions and ways of life. In this situation the principle of religious freedom provided Native people with an important strategic tool. If they could convince government officials that their ceremonial practices and traditions were religious in nature and merited the protections of the First Amendment, they possessed a critical defense against their suppression.

The principle of religious freedom, like the category of religion upon which it relied, did not have deep roots in the Native societies of North America. Indigenous cultures did not distinguish certain beliefs and practices as *religious*, set apart from other (secular or profane) aspects of life, and Native American languages generally had no words that could be translated directly as "religion."[2] Nor did they have an exact equivalent for the concept of religious freedom. This is not to say that indigenous traditions or "doings" left no space for individuality and personal expression.[3] Native American societies generally encouraged the individual pursuit of dreams and visionary revelations, incorporated new ritual practices based on such experiences, and in many ways facilitated individual access to spiritual power.[4] But for the most part indigenous doings were not conceived as matters of belief or conscience, to be accepted or rejected by the individual. Rather, they were practical ways of harnessing other-than-human power for the benefit of the community, of all living beings, and of the earth itself. Prior to the colonial period, then, religious freedom was not a meaningful part of indigenous cultural vocabularies.

Some Indians had begun to use the language of religious freedom almost as soon as they encountered Christianity and the liberal ideals of the settler-colonial society. Christian missionaries were not welcome in the Wyoming Valley of western Pennsylvania, one Lenape chief explained in the 1760s, because "the white people were contriving a method to deprive [the Indians] of their country." However, the chief hastened to add, any Indian Christians who came to the valley would enjoy complete freedom to "practice their faith." Here religious freedom talk served to identify the Lenapes as a civilized people—indeed, as more committed to the ideals of civilization than were the settlers who threatened to dispossess them—and in so doing supported their right to exist as a sovereign nation.[5] In contrast to the Lenapes, most of the Indian people who converted to Christianity had already been overwhelmed by the settler-colonial society. For them, the principle of religious freedom supported the autonomy of indigenous congregations that helped them maintain tribal identities and sometimes protect tribal lands.[6] Other Native Americans, such as the Cherokees, invoked religious freedom to support their quest for recognition as modern peoples and sovereign nations. In the Cherokee Constitution, religious freedom served both to moderate internal tribal conflicts and to ground Cherokee claims to political sovereignty within the geographical boundaries of the United States. Like the Filipinos profiled in chapter 2, these Native people invoked religious freedom to resist the impositions of U.S. empire and claim the status of sovereign nations.[7]

This freedom took on different implications for Indians in the late nineteenth and early twentieth centuries, when indigenous nations across the West faced a new barrage of settler-colonial violence and recent federal policies that aimed to eradicate their tribal identities and traditions. In this context, religious freedom served as a means of defense against the colonial regime. One dilemma was that in making such appeals, Native leaders were also acknowledging the governing authority of the United States. Many had opposed reforms aimed at assimilating them into the settler society, such as U.S. citizenship for Native Americans or the application of state and federal laws on reservation land, because these reforms threatened the integrity and governing authority of Native nations. But as citizenship became a reality for more and more Indians, they would increasingly invoke the U.S. Constitution to argue for their rights to the freedoms of speech, assembly, and religion. Confounding the expectations of the tutelary regime, they invoked these citizens' rights as a way to defend indigenous practices and traditions. In contrast to the Lenape chief, their appeals implicitly recognized the U.S. government as the final arbiter and so acknowledged the loss of tribal sovereignty in the management of Indian affairs.

Just as it did in the Philippines, the loss of sovereignty transformed the context for and the implications of Native American religious freedom talk. During their months of effective independence from either Spanish or U.S. rule, Filipino leaders publicized their commitment to religious freedom as one way to demonstrate their status as civilized moderns. After they were forced to accept U.S. sovereignty, the language of religious freedom helped them negotiate a degree of autonomy under the American tutelary regime. In much the same way, the loss of sovereignty changed the ways in which Native Americans invoked this ideal. Hoping to fend off settler encroachments, many indigenous leaders in the eighteenth and nineteenth centuries had invoked the freedom of religion as one way to make the case for cultural and political self-determination. Once forced to accept settler-colonial rule, Native Americans used the principle of religious freedom to defend particular practices and traditions from suppression by the agents of the tutelary regime.

Such invocations of religious freedom subtly changed the traditions they aimed to protect. If their claims were to succeed, Native Americans had to convince government agents that their doings were legitimately religious. But these agents overwhelmingly assumed a Christian model for what counted as religion and condemned what they called "heathenism" or "savagery" as a major impediment to their civilizing goals. In order to convince them, Native leaders had to make their indigenous practices appear as much like Christianity as possible or even subordinate them to Christianity entirely. When they avoided this conundrum by defending tribal dances not as religion but as "social dances," they effectively redefined these practices as secular forms of entertainment and so relocated them outside the bounds of the religious. Thus under the conditions of a racialized secular colonial rule, Native American articulations of religious freedom not only worked to (re)make indigenous religions but also forged the very distinction between the religious and the secular in Native American societies.

In the face of colonial mechanisms designed for management and control, the persistence of Native American resistance suggests how important indigenous practices and traditions were for the human dignity and ultimately the survival of Indian people under settler-colonial rule. But no matter how persistent they were, no matter how much they adapted their traditions to fit a white Christian mold, Native American appeals to religious freedom almost always fell short, limited by the cultural biases and the coercive structures of a settler-colonial tutelary regime. Like the people of the Philippines, Native Americans found the principle of religious freedom useful in many respects, a promising and sometimes valuable tool in the struggle to maintain their lives and identities under colonial rule. But they too found the promise of this freedom circumscribed by the imperial assemblages of race and religion that structured and supported that regime.

THE LOGICS OF SUPPRESSION

When Indians asserted the right to religious freedom on behalf of indigenous practices and traditions, they pushed back against settler assumptions about what counted or did not count as religion in the first place. Popular narratives of the Western frontier defined indigenous practices not as religion but as cruel and violent forms of "savagery" or "heathenism" that impeded any real progress in civilization. Federal Indian agent N. A. Conroyer reported in 1873 that the Umatilla Indians along the Columbia River in Oregon were "still wedded to their old superstitions, and are opposed to any religion whatever." Here Conroyer distinguished what he called the Indians' "superstitions" from the category of religion. He went on to describe their "medicine-men" as outright frauds who "keep their followers in subjugation" and simply impeded the progress of their people.[8] Like Conroyer, the array of missionaries, anthropologists, policy makers, and other imperial knowledge producers associated the Indian with a set of overlapping terms—heathen, pagan, savage, barbaric, tribal, and primitive—that inscribed a simultaneously racial and religious inferiority. Indigenous practices were by definition savage, superstitious, and coercive, not religion in any legitimate sense of the word.[9]

Through the late nineteenth and early twentieth centuries, an ever more elaborate program of assimilationist reforms sought to civilize the Indians by eradicating indigenous practices and identities. In 1882 Commissioner of Indian Affairs Hiram Price called for increased federal support for both Protestant and Catholic mission schools. He did not see these programs as a violation of Indian religious freedom. Instead, in his eyes, they were an essential step in the Indians' liberation from the savagery that enslaved them. "In no other manner and by no other means," he wrote, "can our Indian population be so speedily and permanently reclaimed from barbarism, idolatry, and savage life, as by the educational and missionary operations of the Christian people of our country."[10] A year later the BIA announced a new "Religious Crimes Code," which banned a variety of indigenous practices including the "practices of medicine men" along with "the sun dance, scalp dance, war dance, or other similar feast." As codified in 1892, the penalties for violating this code included fines, forced labor, the loss of rations, and up to six months in prison for any Native person who used "the arts of a conjurer to prevent Indians from abandoning their barbarous rites and customs."[11] In this way the federal government classified Native American traditions not as religions that must be granted First Amendment rights but instead as impediments to the Indians' proper exercise of freedom and to their civilizing progress more generally.

The principle of wardship provided legal sanction for these authoritarian measures. By the 1870s Congress had abandoned the policy of making treaties with tribes as sovereign nations and began to manage Indians as colonial subjects instead. Although Indians would continue to insist on the principle of tribal sovereignty—and court decisions occasionally reaffirmed its validity, at least in theory—the BIA now claimed the right to manage every aspect of Indian life. Presumed incompetent to manage their own affairs, Indians were defined as wards who required a more or less extensive period of tutelage before they could assume the full rights and responsibilities of citizenship. Native people were thus denied almost all the rights held by citizens. On most reservations they could not freely assemble, were not considered competent to make their own contracts, and did not have the right to their choice of legal counsel. As a policy statement from the 1890 census put it, "The Indian not being considered a citizen of the United States, but a ward of the nation, . . . cannot even leave the reservation without permission." Even though the First Amendment applied in theory to all persons within the United States and not just to citizens, the government's assumption of authority over those it labeled wards had entirely voided its protections.[12]

Ironically, while these policies effectively excluded Indians from the protections of the Constitution, they were at least officially intended to instruct them in the skills of citizenship in a free republic. In the flush of optimism that had accompanied the early assimilationist era, reformers argued that, given the proper opportunities, most Indians would soon be prepared for full citizenship. The Dawes Allotment Act of 1887 reflected that vision. It assumed that private property would civilize Indians by breaking up tribal relations and giving individuals responsibility for their own livelihoods, and it granted Indians citizenship along with their individual land allotments.[13] Advocating for this legislation, Commissioner Price claimed that for Indians to take land in severalty would almost immediately "awaken [their] spirit of personal independence and manhood[,] . . . create a desire for possessing property," and instill in them "a knowledge of its advantages and rights." Price warned, however, that "the Indian" could not simply be granted citizenship without adequate preparation. "He must be brought up to that standard where he can understand the white man's law," he wrote, "its benefits to him if he obeys it, and its penalties if he violates it."[14] In short, before they could take up the rights and responsibilities of citizenship—and be considered fully civilized—Indians required a careful education and a period of guidance from the colonial tutelary regime. The only real question up for debate was the length of time that this process would require.

By the turn of the century, many policy makers had lost confidence in the premise that Indians had any racial capacity for civilization in the first place. This shift corresponded with increasingly sharp lines of racial distinction and racial violence in many arenas of American life. Among other things, these years witnessed increased rates of lynching and the codification of segregationist Jim Crow laws in the South, mob violence against immigrants and nativist political organizing in many parts of the country, and an Anglo-Saxon racial triumphalism that supported the nation's imperial aggressions during these years. As I noted in chapter 2, the racial and colonial logics of federal Indian policy had provided much of the framework for U.S. policy in the Philippines. In the early twentieth century, the civilizational assemblages (re)formed in the Philippines rebounded to influence U.S. policies toward Native Americans as well. Abandoning the early optimism of assimilationist reform, white reformers in Indian affairs increasingly saw indigenous traditions and identities as stubbornly racial characteristics that Native Americans would not (or could not) easily leave behind. Reflecting this pessimistic view, Congress amended the Dawes Act in 1906 to provide a long period of federal guardianship over Indian land allotments and to postpone citizenship for Indians until they were deemed "competent and capable of managing [their] own affairs," or up to twenty-five years after they had received their allotments. Even for Indians who became citizens, a series of administrative and legal decisions would effectively redefine that status so that they remained wards of the government, unable to exercise many of the rights that other U.S. citizens enjoyed.[15]

In keeping with these trends, more and more of the BIA's agents in the field began to think that the goal of civilizing Indians might ultimately be impossible. Reporting on recent "disturbances" among the Hopi Indians of Arizona, Agent Leo Crane argued that the government must soon "show its strong hand" against the Hopi "Hostiles," who were known for their "extreme opposition to the intrusion of white civilization." Their chief was a "usurper," Crane wrote, who kept his people "bound in superstitious ignorance" through "dreams and omens and prophecies." Crane's views about the so-called Friendlies were not much better. This faction wanted only to curry favors against their rivals, he believed; he harbored "no illusions" about their "professions of good will." "Down deep in their hearts," he wrote, the Friendlies as well as the Hostiles were "Indians still." Even when they expressed the desire for civilization, all Indians in Crane's view remained racially bound to savagery, in need of the strong hand of colonial control.[16]

Federal Indian agents in this period proudly defined their roles in terms of imperial command and at times drew direct comparisons to the tactics of empire in the Philippines. "Young man! You have an empire to control," Crane remembered an army colonel instructing him after a "show of force" against the Hopi Hostiles in 1911. "Either rule it, or pack your trunk!"[17] In his correspondence with BIA officials in the mid-1920s, C. J. Crandall of the Northern Pueblos Agency would invoke the precedent of U.S. military violence against the Moros to support his argument for stronger authority over the Pueblo Indians. "If the Moros become hostile in the distant Philippines," he wrote, "we generally find a way to settle them. The question in my mind is, if we must submit to the pagan demands of these Indians here at home."[18] Agents like Crane and Crandall saw Indians as "savages" and "pagans" who could be managed only through the same methods of violent suppression that the U.S. military was using in the Philippines. It is worth noting again that the channels of influence flowed both ways: these were tactics that had first been tested in the nineteenth-century wars of conquest against the indigenous nations of the American West.

Imperial assemblages of race and religion enabled this model of colonial control. Writing for the ecumenical Protestant Home Missions Council in 1923, Gustavus Elmer Emanuel Lindquist offered what was for him the positive assessment that "the religious instinct" was "of the very fiber of the [Indian] race." Lindquist's book was the product of six months of coordinated research on the conditions of Indian life across the country. An enthusiastic foreword from Commissioner of Indian Affairs Charles Burke reminds us just how closely connected the BIA and the missionaries still were at the time. Both men believed that this racial instinct for religion could be taken in either productive or destructive ways. "The crude Messianic beliefs prevalent among many of the Indian tribes responded readily to the teachings of the early missionaries," Lindquist wrote, "and the Indian of to-day continues to respond by 'outward and visible signs' to the 'inward and spiritual grace' bestowed upon him through increasing knowledge of the word of the 'Great Spirit.'" The "racial weaknesses" he saw in the Indians, however, meant that the missionaries could not yet relax their vigilance. While "the old superstitions" and "the medicine man" were disappearing, he warned, "the new and insidious cult of peyote" was now spreading so rapidly that it threatened to "rival [their] malign influence."[19]

At the dawn of the twentieth century, then, no matter what strategies Native Americans used to defend indigenous practices and traditions, BIA officials tended to view them as racially inclined to superstition, perpetually in need of guidance at the controlling hand of the tutelary regime. Faced with this overwhelming set of ideological and institutional barriers, Native leaders had little reason to expect that the principle of religious freedom would provide them with any effective means of defense.

In the face of all this settler-colonial violence, Native Americans insisted that their practices and traditions were *religious* and must be granted the same rights and freedoms that other religions enjoyed. They did so first and most forcefully to defend the new prophetic movements—the Ghost Dance, the Shaker religion of the Pacific Northwest, and the widely practiced Peyote religion—that spread rapidly across Indian country near the turn of the century. These movements provided ways for Native people to make sense of the dislocation and suffering they were experiencing. They reconfigured indigenous traditions in order to move forward, to shape meaningful lives under difficult conditions. All three movements already reflected the influence of Christianity and of the larger society's concepts of religion. Even when they did not succeed, their appeals to religious freedom required further accommodations to those norms. The forceful suppression of the Ghost Dance on one hand and the gradual but always limited acceptance of the Shaker and Peyote movements on the other reveal a great deal about the racial barriers to religious freedom under a white settler-colonial regime.

The Ghost Dance: Wounded Knee and
the Limits of Religious Freedom

The movement that came to be known as the Ghost Dance began in Nevada with the prophetic revelations of a Paiute prophet named Wovoka. Wovoka built on the legacy of an earlier Paiute prophet; his new message resonated with the existential crises that so many Native people were facing at the time. He offered strict moral guidelines and instructed his followers to remain at peace with their white neighbors. Wovoka's religious views had been influenced by close contact with both Catholics and Mormons; his prophecy that God was about to usher in a new world of peace and harmony echoed millennial themes that were familiar across Christian traditions. Many of those who traveled over the western mountains and plains to hear him returned home with the message that if their people performed the new dance and remained faithful to Wovoka's instructions, God would usher in a new world and restore their dead relatives and the buffalo of the plains to life.[20]

These hopes for indigenous revival terrified many white Americans. This was especially the case in South Dakota, where memories of Indian wars were still quite fresh and some Lakota Indians had openly expressed their anger at the poverty, mismanagement, and indignities of reservation life. When Lakotas began to gather in large numbers to perform the Ghost Dance, sensation-seeking newspapers began to spread rumors that the "bloodthirsty braves" were preparing to go on the warpath. The Ghost Dancers refused to obey their agents' orders to halt the dance; tensions heightened on both sides when the army sent in troops. The crisis culminated on the banks of Wounded Knee Creek with the massacre of several hundred Minneconjou and Hunkpapa Lakotas. Their only crime had been to participate in a ceremony that local whites and military officials viewed as a sign of revolt against settler-colonial rule. The massacre at Wounded Knee did not stop the Ghost Dance, or "spirit dance" as some called it, among other Native peoples who had embraced it. The BIA had made it very clear that this dance would no longer be tolerated, however, and Ghost Dancers across Indian country immediately moved their practice underground.

The BIA was entirely unwilling to accept the Native insistence that the Ghost Dance was religious and must be granted the right to religious freedom. Ghost Dancers invoked this freedom both before and after Wounded Knee. "This is our way of worshipping the Great Spirit," a Lakota chief explained to one Jesuit missionary who, hoping to avert tragedy, was trying to convince the Lakota people to abandon the dance. "You white folks have different prayers, and you quarrel saying each that the other is not right. Let us alone; let us worship the Great Spirit in our own way."[21] Why should Indians change their way of worshipping, he asked, when white Christians could not agree themselves on which of their own conflicting traditions were correct? This chief implicitly located the Ghost Dance within the denominational structure of American religion and, in so doing, asserted its right to the same status as any of the white churches.

The case for religious freedom relied on convincing officials that Native American doings were legitimately religious. In effect this meant showing their similarities to Christianity, or better yet their compatibility with Christianity as a civilizing and positive moral influence. "This dance was like religion; it was religious," said the Lakota Ghost Dance leader Big Road shortly after the massacre at Wounded Knee. "Those who brought the dance here from the West said that to dance was the same as going to Church. . . . The Messiah [Wovoka] told us to send our children to school, to work our farms all the time, and to do the best we could. We and our children could dance and go to church too; that would be like going to two churches."[22] Devastated at the deaths of so many Ghost Dancers, Big Road expressed a sense of confusion and betrayal at the movement's violent suppression. Wovoka's message, he was certain, had been completely compatible with the government's program of progress and civilization. He defined the Ghost Dance as a religion in full harmony with Christianity: a religion that had inculcated moral virtues and helped Native people move forward in the modern world. While Big Road was in no way dissembling, there is no doubt that the structures of power in this situation *required* him and other Ghost Dancers to present their practices in this way. If they were to have any hope of maintaining them, they would need to ensure that their ceremonies took a more or less Christian shape.

At least a few non-Indian officials were convinced by these claims. One army lieutenant who investigated the Ghost Dance in 1891 concluded that the Arapaho Ghost Dance prophet Sitting Bull had "given these people a better religion than they ever had before, taught them precepts which if faithfully carried out will bring them into better accord with their white neighbors, and has prepared the way for their final Christianization." While he clearly considered Christianity superior, this lieutenant offered a social evolutionary analysis that identified the Ghost Dance as a step in the right direction. On that basis he repudiated its violent suppression and advocated for the Indians' right to what he judged a valid religion.[23]

The anthropologist James Mooney, who began his research shortly before the massacre at Wounded Knee, also defended the religious legitimacy of the Ghost Dance. He did so in part by comparing it to millennial movements across the history of Christianity. In the face of their oppression as a race, he wrote, the Ghost Dancers' hopes for messianic renewal represented "a hope and longing common to all humanity." Mooney developed other comparisons to Christianity as well, especially around the system of ethics in the Ghost Dance movement. For him, even the movement's diversity across tribal lines provided evidence of its basic similarity to Christianity. The many tribal versions of the Ghost Dance were "differences of interpretation . . . precisely such as we find in Christianity," he wrote, "with its hundreds of sects and innumerable shades of individual opinion." Yet even Mooney misjudged the particular Lakota version of the Ghost Dance as a turn to violence that distorted the prophet's message. Even though he found their grievances entirely comprehensible, his account allowed readers to conclude that the Lakota people had to some extent brought the massacre upon themselves. Like most writers on the topic, he left the distinct impression that this movement was a sort of last gasp, a tragic ending to indigenous ways of life.[24]

Official channels of government authority granted no religious legitimacy to the Ghost Dance at all. John Wesley Powell, the influential director of the

Bureau of American Ethnology and Mooney's immediate superior, publicly repudiated Mooney's analysis. Congress had funded the bureau with the explicit goal of studying the Native population in order to more effectively manage it. Powell's program of research thus took for granted the interests of the settler-colonial regime. As a leading proponent of social evolutionary theory, he placed Native American societies quite low on the civilizational scale and assumed the federal government's obligation to civilize them. While he personally was a religious skeptic rather than a committed Christian, he nonetheless assumed the utility of Christianity as a civilizing force. Thus he could not stomach Mooney's portrayal of Christianity and the Ghost Dance as basically similar religious forms. Powell allowed Mooney to publish the work, but his introduction to the first edition instructed readers to exercise "caution . . . in comparing or contrasting religious movements among civilized peoples with such fantasies as that described in the memoir." Whatever "interesting and suggestive analogies" Mooney may have identified, he wrote, "the essential features of the movements are not homologous."[25]

Many Native Americans would continue to practice the Ghost Dance despite the federal government's concerted efforts to suppress it. In some communities this ceremony seems to have helped reinvigorate other tribal traditions—the hand game among the Pawnees, for example—that became locally associated with its practice.[26] But it is not surprising, given the constant threat of violence, that whenever possible Native people would hold such ceremonies under the radar and far away from the prying eyes of the missionaries and BIA agents. One agent at the Wind River Reservation in Wyoming told Mooney that the Arapaho Indians had "abandoned" the Ghost Dance because he had convinced them of its futility. But when he traveled into the mountains, Mooney heard "ghost songs" in the distance and learned from his half-Arapaho interpreter that the dance was indeed taking place. "That's something I have never reported, and I never will," the interpreter explained. "It is their religion, and they have a right to it."[27] This BIA employee justified his refusal to report Ghost Dancers on religious freedom grounds, demonstrating how First Amendment ideals could provide some protection even where outside authorities did not believe them applicable. Like this interpreter, many Native people who had been educated according to Euro-American standards used their knowledge of U.S. cultural and political ideals to defend indigenous traditions. In so doing, they confounded the expectations of assimilationists who had convinced themselves that educated Indians would unequivocally reject tribal identities and ways of life.

Making the Shaker Church: The Accommodations
of Religious Freedom

As far as I can determine, the Indian Shakers of the Pacific Northwest were the first pan-Indian religious movement to develop an organized and successful campaign for religious freedom. The founding prophet of the Shakers was John Slocum, a forty-year-old Sahewamish Indian who lived near the Squaxon Reservation on the Puget Sound near Tacoma, Washington. Believed dead after a logging accident in the fall of 1882, Slocum returned to life and began to tell his family and friends about the angels who had healed and instructed him. Soon he had gathered a small group of followers, whom he advised to lead moral lives and to believe in Jesus Christ. A year later Slocum's wife, Mary Thompson, healed him of another severe illness through a ceremony involving bodily shaking, which she identified as medicine from God. Thompson initiated the characteristic Shaker healing practices of ringing bells and shaking, and she served alongside Slocum as a significant leader in the movement's early years. These practices resonated with the region's indigenous healing traditions and opened up the role of healer to many people who lacked the traditional qualifications for medicine men and women.[28] Despite considerable opposition from the BIA, the new movement spread quickly across Oregon and northwestern California and then north into Washington and the Canadian province of British Columbia.[29]

Government agents and missionaries were immediately disturbed by what they saw as the Shakers' "heathenism" and by their tendency to combine Christian and indigenous practices. Writing in 1884, just as the Shakers were emerging as a distinct movement, Congregationalist missionary Myron Eells described Slocum as a part of an indigenous "Catholic element" that blended "superstition, their old heathenish rites, their own imaginations, and a little religion" into such an unholy mixture that "the real Catholics hardly recognize them."[30] BIA agent Edwin Eells, the missionary's brother, shared this discomfort with indigenous hybridity. As long as the Indians were worshipping as Catholics he "felt he had no right to interfere"—again, the right of religious freedom applied only to competing varieties of Christianity—but when he determined that "the Catholic ceremonies were . . . merely like a thin spread of butter over something else," he felt no qualms about ordering the Shaker meetings stopped and locking up their leaders.[31]

Within a few years the Shakers began to argue for religious freedom based on their rights as U.S. citizens. Many Native people in the region had become citizens in the late 1880s under the Dawes Act, and soon they began to realize the possibilities citizenship offered for "freedom from agency control," as one of their frustrated agents put it.[32] In 1892 Shaker leaders learned of a district court case in which charges of selling liquor to a Puyallup Indian had been dismissed because the Indian in question "owned land in severalty" and so was identified as a "free and independent" citizen of the United States. This decision challenged the idea that Indian citizens were still wards, under the tutelary control of the federal government. Lawyer and county judge James Wickersham assured the Shakers that as citizens "they were as free as the [BIA] agent." They had the right to make their own decisions "both in religious and worldly matters," he assured them, just as "other citizens of the United States could." The Shakers immediately saw the possibilities in this claim. The missionary Myron Eells, who had convinced himself that the Shaker movement had run its course, fretted that the movement had "revived quite strongly" after its leaders "learned that the freedom of citizenship allowed them this religion as much as they wished."[33]

The Shakers gained non-Indian support for these citizenship claims by establishing their religious legitimacy as Christians. In order to do this they carefully distanced themselves from indigenous prophetic movements. They had "no sympathy with [the Ghost Dance] ceremony or any other founded on the Dreamer religion," they explained to Wickersham.[34] When Eells and other missionaries accused them of using Christianity as a cover for "barbarism," they insisted that they had abandoned the indigenous "*tamahnous* practices" and that their healing methods were quite different from that "old fashioned form of Indian doctoring."[35] Instead they highlighted their similarities with other Christian churches: "We believe in God, and in Jesus Christ as the Son of God, and we believe in a hell," they explained. "In these matters we believe the same as the Presbyterians." At the same time they insisted on their right to a distinctively Indian form of Christianity. "They say that they do not need to read the Bible," Wickersham reported, "for do they not have better and more recent testimony of the existence of heaven and the way to that celestial home than is contained in the Bible?" To defend what might seem like unacceptable heterodoxy they appealed to the model of denominationalism: "The Bible says there are many roads; the Catholics have one, the Presbyterians another, and the Congregationalists a third; but John Slocum gives them a short, straight road—and they choose that." Their movement was simply an Indian way of being Christian, they argued, one better suited to them because it offered them direct access to the divine.[36]

These claims convinced many non-Indians that the Shakers were legit-imately religious and a benefit to their communities. After his discussions with Slocum and other leading members of the church, Wickersham had come to see them as a force for morality and civilization even though he thought much of their theology false: "I feel that their church is a grand suc-cess in that it prevents idleness and vice, drunkenness and disorder, and tends to produce quiet, peaceable citizens, and good Christian people." Within a few years local Presbyterians too had come to see the Shakers as a positive if not entirely orthodox influence and tried for a time to bring the whole movement into their church. Shaker leader Louis Yowaluch, for example, served simultaneously as a Presbyterian elder for part of his career.[37] Some BIA agents also came to accept the Shakers' claim that theirs was a legitimate form of Christianity that could speak uniquely to Indians. In 1901 Agent Samuel Morse at Neah Bay actually invited Shaker evangelists to the reservations he supervised in hopes that they could "do something along the Christian line for our poor people."[38]

By the first decade of the twentieth century, the Shakers were organizing in ways that strengthened their religious freedom claims. Moving beyond simple assertions of Christian identity, they began to create the formal insti-tutional structures of a church. Yowaluch, who replaced John Slocum as the movement's primary leader, drew from his experience as a Presbyterian elder to create an ordained Shaker ministry. In written instructions sent to ministers, he exhorted them to follow the high moral standards of the church, to "love one another as Christians, and lead pure, clean lives." Then he reminded them of their legal rights, should they encounter any opposi-tion from authorities. "The Government at Washington allows Indians to worship God according to his own conscience," he wrote, "so long as we are law abiding and live good lives." BIA field matron Lida Quimby, report-ing on these developments, claimed that she had persuaded the Shakers to eliminate "Indian doctoring by Tamahnous." Now that they had dropped "the obnoxious practices," she "recognized their inalienable rights to their own belief and particular forms."[39] Yowaluch's success in articulating a Christian identity and the new organizational structures he was creating were beginning to convince the BIA that the Shakers were part of a legiti-mate religion that had the constitutional right to exist.

The movement's troubles were by no means over. In 1906, Agent Charles Buchanan condemned the Shakers on the Tulalip Reservation as "drunken with fanaticism" and banned their services. Even though he noted that the Shakers made up only a small fraction of the Indians under his supervision,

Buchanan echoed the alarmist rhetorics that had been directed against the Ghost Dance nearly two decades earlier:

> At Tulalip they have, upon occasion, made threats of shaking away law, order, the courts, the agency, all control or supervision, the Government itself, all whites, and have promised to restore olden times and conditions existent before the advent of the white man. On the surface they assume an appearance of a crude Christianity in order to cover their real beliefs and practices, which latter are at heart unprogressive, barbarous, and antagonistic. . . . I have seen little if any good ever come from this practice at Tulalip, and I do not believe that there is a scintilla of sense or real religion in it. What little benefit may have been imagined to flow from it is more than counterbalanced by the highly unnatural, excited, frenzied state of mind which its practice induces and maintains in its devotees.[40]

Buchanan's depiction of the Shakers as barbarians possessed of an uncontrollable "frenzy" recalls not only white settler fears of the Ghost Dance but also U.S. colonial authorities' contemporaneous descriptions of the Moros in the Philippines as "fanatical Mohammedans." His report illustrates once again the imperial assemblages of race and religion that reinforced and enabled the racial order of the settler-colonial state.

The Shakers needed still more ammunition, and soon they strengthened their claim to religious legitimacy through the legal process of incorporation. Shakers on the Warm Springs Reservation began this process in 1907 when another BIA agent moved to shut down their services. After a lawyer informed them that their faith in John Slocum could not serve as the basis for incorporation, they decided to list the Bible instead as the foundation for their church. Their statement of purpose also stressed their adherence to moral strictures such as temperance and the Golden Rule. Three years later when they renewed their lapsed incorporation, the Warm Springs Shakers pledged to elevate "the Indian race" and asserted the right to "the worship of God in our own way." The Shakers of Washington State also incorporated in 1910, and other Shaker groups followed over the course of the next few decades. All listed similar purposes. By claiming the legal status of an incorporated church—and by asserting their commitments to religious freedom, Christianity, and "civilized" standards of morality—the Shakers sought to definitively establish their religious legitimacy in the eyes of the outside world and to hold the U.S. government accountable to its own constitutional ideals.[41]

The move to organize and incorporate Shaker churches would change certain aspects of Shaker practice. Mary Thompson, John Slocum's widow, opposed these changes from the start because she argued that they would destroy the spontaneity and the spirit-based foundations of the tradition. Thompson claimed that matters of the spirit must be lived and experienced. Putting them in writing interfered with the spirit's movement, channeling its action into predetermined streams. Along the same lines, the licensed ministry that had come with incorporation lessened the significance of visions as the source of spiritual authority. Shakers were now committed to paying regular salaries to their ministers; this in turn required a more formal system of ordination along with documents of employment for the Shaker ministry. Local Shaker elders now felt the need to ask church leaders about the proper procedures for holding meetings along with a multitude of other questions. Thompson and other critics argued that all this formality hampered the original Shaker way of seeking and bestowing spiritual power.[42]

Thompson's complaints also reveal how the new structure of Shaker ministry limited women's leadership in the movement. Her role as a visionary innovator and prophetic healer reflected an openness to women's leadership in the early Shaker movement, echoing the role of women as spiritual leaders and healers in the region's indigenous traditions. By lessening the importance of visionary authority, the Shakers' new denominational structure had undermined the only real basis for women's leadership in the movement. This process was in no way unique to the Shakers. The roles of prophet and visionary, and claims to direct inspiration from the Holy Spirit, had worked to enable women's preaching and religious leadership in a wide variety of Christian movements. The Shakers' shift toward bureaucracy can be described in Weberian terms as the routinization of charisma, a process that frequently had gendered dimensions.[43] In the case of the Shakers, this change also meant the loss of indigenous patterns of leadership and an accommodation to the dominant society's expectations for an organized church. The incorporation papers of the Indian Shaker Church had stressed a commitment to "the worship of God in our own way." In the process the Shakers also defined and delimited their tradition in ways designed to please the outside society, to fit into white Christian models for what counted as religion. An exclusively male ordained ministry was a part of that model.

Despite all these accommodations, the Shakers faced a constant struggle to convince authorities that theirs was a legitimate religion that should be permitted on Indian reservations. Yakama evangelist John Johnson explained to Commissioner Cato Sells in 1915 that the songs and "bell ringing" of the Shakers were their equivalent to the "singing, pipe organs, different stringed instruments and in some cases brass bands . . . of the different denominations," such as the Salvation Army. Through these comparisons Johnson positioned the Shaker church as a Christian denomination like any other. This church could more effectively reach Indian people, he explained, because it spoke directly to them. As an Indian he understood the "customs" as well as the "vices" of his people, he wrote, and so "they will listen to me and believe in my teachings, when they would not listen to a white man." He complained that despite his many documented healings and all the people he had helped in his twenty-nine years of ministry, some BIA agents continued to ban his meetings and expel him from the reservations they supervised. Enclosing letters of support from several "influential business men," Johnson asked the commissioner for a letter he could carry with him that would instruct "the Government Agents . . . not [to] interfere with me, or prohibit my preaching, or place restrictions on my holding meetings as I see fit." Shaker leaders like Johnson not only claimed the status of religion in general but specifically identified themselves as Christians and located themselves within the denominational structure of Christianity in American life.[44]

The commissioner's reply immediately conceded the principle of religious freedom and even recognized the Shaker movement as legitimately religious. The decades of Shaker organizing had forced the BIA to grant participants that much. "It is not my purpose to interfere with any religious faiths or forms of worship which make men and women better," Sells wrote Johnson, or to interfere with "the content of the Shaker creed in which you believe." The government, he claimed, "seeks no abridgement of the religious liberty guaranteed by the Constitution." Yet the assemblages of race, religion, and civilization that he mobilized set clear limits to that liberty. "The Indians are the wards of the government," he wrote, and so the government had the right and even the "duty" to "direct their affairs." The government, and not the Indians themselves, had the right to determine what practices were legitimately religious and therefore permissible. Sells invoked the precedent of federal restrictions on Mormon polygamy—restrictions that the Supreme Court had approved on the grounds of morality and civilization. "If certain things plainly detrimental to the well-being of the Indians socially, physically, or morally, and repulsive to the accepted conventions of civilized life are done in the name of religion," he insisted, "the Government should and will restrain those things just as it did the practice of polygamy in one of its Territories," even though "that act was regarded by many whom it affected as a curtailment of religious freedom." Even as the commissioner commended Johnson for his "sobriety, honesty, thrift and industry," he remained unwilling to grant the Shakers' right "to conduct your meetings as you see fit, irrespective of any oversight by the agents of the Government." Settler-colonial structures of authority simply could not accommodate such an outcome. While he acknowledged the Indians' right to practice their religion, Sells insisted on his right to deter-mine what it could and could not include.[45]

The struggles of the Shakers on Oregon's Klamath reservation in the mid-1910s reveal the implications of this policy in practice. Even as he insisted that the Klamath people enjoyed complete religious freedom, Agent William Freer implemented rigorous restrictions on what he called the "barbaric" and "harmful practices" of their "cults."[46] He limited Shaker meetings to one per month, ending before midnight; forbade the practice of "incantations" or the "ringing of bells" over the sick; and banned all payments to Shaker ministers or healers. Convinced that all physical contact was potentially sexual, he further specified that the Shaker practice of conferring spiritual "power" through touch must be practiced "upon men by men only, and upon women by women only." The colonial structure of the tutelary regime gave its officials the power to set the boundaries of what counted as religion and to impose strict limits on all that lay beyond those bounds.[47]

The Klamath Shakers refused to follow these regulations. Instead they insisted on their right to define the contents and contours of their own tra-dition. The Shakers had already restructured their movement as a church in order to fit the denominational model for religion in America. From the beginning they had stressed their credentials as Christians and even shifted their practice to make it recognizable as Christian to the missionaries and BIA agents in charge. The Klamath protests reveal frustration and anger that all of these accommodations had still not been enough. Far from hurting their people, they insisted, their religion had "helped and healed" them. "This religion has brought many a man and woman from destruction and it teaches the Word of God," wrote Klamath elder Esther Silvers Anderson.[48] The Klamath Shakers argued that their agent's restrictions violated "the rules of this religion," which they had received directly from God. "The White man's medicine has been tried but failed," said church member Charlie Brown. "The power has been given to those parties of Shakers to heal and to help and that is the reason that we do so." Brown's testimony reflected an indig-enous emphasis on accessing and managing sources of other-than-human power. The Klamath Shakers were not willing to abandon these practices.

One Shaker minister explained that he was "willing to be punished" if he violated Freer's orders. "When we joined this religion we confessed to our Christ that we have to follow the rules of the Shaker religion," he said. "If I die and don't follow my religion I will be punished by God." Caught between earthly and heavenly authorities, he preferred to take the consequences in this world rather than in the next.[49]

Faced with this defiance, Freer ordered the agency police to close the Shakers' meeting hall and to expel all non-Klamath Shaker ministers, including the Yakama minister John Johnson, from the reservation.[50] His superiors in Washington fully supported his right to do so. "The superintendent in charge of the reservation has full authority to make regulations for its government and any such rules must be obeyed," wrote Assistant Secretary of the Interior E. C. Bradley. If the Shakers did not cooperate, "the government may close the Church or take such further action as it may deem appropriate under the circumstances." Both officials insisted that they had not violated the Shakers' freedom of religion. Bradley's rationale reveals the racial contours of what BIA agents recognized as religion: "It is not the custom for White persons to conduct their church meetings later than ten o'clock," he wrote, and for the Indians to do so "would materially interfere with [their] health and welfare." Although the BIA had "no intention to interfere with the Indians' mode of worship," he concluded, "all well-governed churches [must] comply with the civil laws of the country." As the Shakers well knew, however, they were being forced to comply not just with generally applicable "civil laws"—laws that already reflected the Anglo-Protestant norms of the dominant society— but also with regulations that had been designed specifically to eliminate all traces of their indigenous practices and ways of life.[51]

The Shakers' story illustrates the marginal status of indigenous religious movements under the racial order of the settler-colonial state. In order to resist the collusion of missionaries and government officials in suppressing their ceremonies, Shaker leaders had no choice but to shift their strategies of self-representation, and then to formally organize themselves as a church, in order to conform to white Protestant models for religion. Cultural and political pressures essentially forced them to marginalize any aspects of the movement that could be attacked as too indigenous. Their appeal for religious freedom had no hope of succeeding without laying claim to the cultural status of a Christian church in these ways. Yet even with all of these accommodations, they found that the BIA had the power to rule on the religious legitimacy of every detail of their practice. And invariably, whatever the BIA associated with indigeneity—anything that departed from the model of white Christianity—was labeled "harmful" or "demoralizing" and singled out for elimination. Even for Indians who claimed citizenship rights, religious freedom could not encompass indigenous traditions that did not fit into dominant ideas about what counted as religion.

From Peyote Cult to Native American Church:
The Coercions of Religion

The Peyote movement that swept across the Great Plains and Mountain West at the end of the nineteenth century followed a similar trajectory, but on a much larger scale. Faced with official suppression, the movement's leaders initiated a campaign for religious freedom that would continue through the twentieth century in every branch and level of government. In some cases this included tribal governments, pitting the principle of religious freedom against that of tribal sovereignty. Often the Peyotists succeeded. Much like the Shakers, however, if they tried to gain any traction in this campaign they found that they had to foreground those aspects of their tradition that fit into white American ideas of what counted as religion. For them, too, there were limits both to the adjustments they would make and to the freedoms that government officials were willing to grant them.

The indigenous people of southern Texas and northern Mexico had ingested small amounts of the peyote cactus as a part of tribal ceremonies for centuries, finding spiritual and physical healing in its mildly hallucinogenic effects. As the ceremonial use of peyote spread among the Kiowa, Comanche, and neighboring Native nations in the late nineteenth century, it increasingly blended Protestant norms with the indigenous traditions of the region. Moving like wildfire across Indian country, this emerging new religious movement linked Plains-style visionary enthusiasm with an evangelical Protestant model of missionary outreach. All-night ceremonies, led by a ritual specialist known as the Roadman, included prayer, singing, and periods of quiet meditation along with the consumption of the "sacred herb." The Peyote movement linked Protestant themes of individual salvation and morality with a more indigenous emphasis on healing and communal well-being. Adherents viewed peyote as a medicine, as a teacher that provided them with an ethical way of life, and as a "gift of God" or even as God's flesh ingested as a holy sacrament. Many people credited "Grandfather Peyote" with healing powers against alcoholism, disease, and despair.[52]

From the beginning, the major streams of the new Peyote religion reflected a degree of Christian influence and included Christian elements as part of their ritual practice. The Comanche chief Quanah Parker, among the most important leaders in the movement's early history, described a vision in which Jesus Christ had instructed him to take this new medicine to all Indians. Parker's Half Moon Way incorporated Jesus as a culture hero and spiritual guide. Roadman John Wilson, a Caddo, whose Big Moon Way became the second major strand of the Peyote religion, incorporated even more Christian references, including a crucifix prominently displayed on the Peyote altar. These Peyote leaders understood their ceremonies as a distinctively Indian way to communicate with the divine, a communicative channel more powerful than anything available in mainstream white Christianity. Both of them maintained a degree of distance from a white Christianity that they found inadequate for Indian needs. As Parker put it, "The White Man goes into his church and talks about Jesus," while "the Indian goes into his tipi and talks *with* Jesus." Peyote gave its adherents direct access to the divine. They had no need, then, of a written Bible or other accretions of a Christian tradition that, as far as they could see, had been shaped by and for Europeans.[53]

The Bureau of Indian Affairs found the so-called peyote cult far more alarming than they did the Shakers. Authorities believed that both movements impeded the Indians' civilizational progress, perpetuated Native "superstitions," and endangered the lives of sick people who were deceived by their healing claims. The Peyote movement was far more widespread, however, and it sparked fears among officials and reformers of a drug epidemic in Indian country. Alarmist reports misidentified the mildly hallucinogenic peyote as a "dangerous narcotic" and claimed that it permanently damaged the "mental and physical vigor" of its users, perhaps even leading to death.[54] This movement, critics alleged, used the forms of indigenous ritualism to draw a demoralized Indian population into a new and dangerous addiction. On these grounds the BIA placed the use of peyote on its list of punishable "Indian Offenses" and lobbied for an array of state and federal laws to prohibit its transport and use. Oklahoma Territory enacted the first law suppressing peyote in 1899, and thirteen other states would follow suit over the next three decades.[55]

While most government agents granted the Shakers a modicum of religious legitimacy, they condemned the Peyote religion as a complete fraud, no more than a cover for drug dealers and profiteers. S. M. Brosius of the Indian Rights Association told a congressional subcommittee during its hearings on peyote in 1918 that the claims that it was being used in "a religious ceremony" were "a very flimsy pretense" that "might be made for the use of any other intoxicant or any drug that is now prohibited by law."[56] The campaign against peyote intersected with a crusade, reignited by the national Prohibition movement, to enforce alcohol bans on Indian reservations. In 1906 Commissioner Francis Leupp hired the outspoken prohibitionist William "Pussyfoot" Johnson as chief special officer charged with eliminating the alcohol trade across Indian country.[57] Soon Johnson assumed responsibility for the eradication of peyote as well, and Leupp touted his methods as evidence that the BIA was acting decisively in the Indians' best interests. "In May [1909] Chief Special Officer Johnson visited Laredo, Tex., the source of the supply of peyote," the commissioner reported, "bought up the entire supply in the market, destroyed it, and obtained from the wholesale dealers agreements that they would no longer continue in the traffic."[58] Convinced that they knew what was best for Native people—but realizing that they lacked secure legal footing for their crusade—anti-peyote reformers and government officials kept pushing for federal legislation to definitively outlaw its use.[59]

Across Indian country, Peyote leaders appealed directly to the U.S. Constitution to defend their cause. Theirs was a religion that had virtually eliminated drunkenness among its adherents, they contended, bringing them healing and "moral uplift" and advancing the cause of Christianity in Native communities. As the Peyote Roadman and Arapaho tribal council member Jack Bull Bear explained in an Oklahoma newspaper, "We feel we are guaranteed freedom of religious worship under the Constitution of the United States. We are living uprightly under the United States flag, and helping to improve the condition of our Indian race, to make them better Christians, and to live the real civilized life." In statement after statement, Bull Bear and other Peyote leaders emphasized their rights as citizens under the U.S. Constitution and their allegiance to its principles. Like other colonized and subaltern peoples, they invoked religious freedom to make space for indigenous forms of cultural and religious expression. In so doing, they implicitly accepted the framework of U.S. sovereignty and the terms set by the settler-colonial state.[60]

Like the Shakers, Peyote leaders had little choice but to adapt themselves to the larger society's standards for what counted as religion. When the U.S. House Committee on Indian Affairs held hearings in 1918 on proposed legislation to ban peyote, Osage chief Fred Lookout testified that his people used "this medicine that is known as peyote . . . in the worship of God." This was their way of "praying to God," he said. "We use it like people going to church." Representative John Tillman of Arkansas challenged Lookout to show where "the Bible [gave] authority" for this practice. "Is this a Christian religion," Tillman asked, "or is it a mere worship of peyote, or the drug itself?"[61] These questions illustrate the overwhelmingly Christian bias for what the U.S. government recognized as religion. Like Tillman, many members of Congress assumed that only something sanctioned in the Christian scriptures could be legitimately religious. The Peyotists' religious freedom claims could not succeed without persuading authorities that their practices were compatible with Christianity—or better yet were actually Christian, an Indian form of Christian worship.

The Peyote movement achieved a great deal of success with these claims, convincing a growing number of non-Indian scholars and legislators that this was a legitimate religion. When the state of Oklahoma formed in 1907, Quanah Parker and other Peyotists successfully deployed the principle of religious freedom to persuade the new legislature to omit the anti-peyote measure.[62] The ethnologist James Mooney, who had turned his attentions to the Peyote religion after his work on the Ghost Dance, testified in its favor at the 1918 congressional hearings. Responding to a question from Representative Tillman about whether this was "a Christian religion," Mooney noted the Peyotists' hymn singing and prayers to Jesus and called it "as close an approximation to Christianity and as efficient a leading up to Christianity as the Indian, speaking generally, is now capable of." Mooney portrayed the Peyote movement as a beneficial influence, "an essential uplift, as compared with the original tribal religion." This stand had real consequences for Mooney: his superiors at the Bureau of American Ethnology were so appalled that they refused to renew his position or to support publication of his scholarship on peyote. Neither Mooney nor the Native Peyotists who testified managed to convince the House, which voted for the anti-peyote legislation. However, the Senate rejected the measure on First Amendment grounds, thus granting a hard-won success to the religious freedom campaign.[63]

For the Peyote movement, this struggle involved not merely representational politics but also some concrete changes in practice. Albert Hensley, who helped shape the Cross Fire tradition among the Ho-Chunk (Winnebago) people of Nebraska, repeatedly tried to convince the BIA that the Peyote religion was legitimately Christian. Hensley explicitly identified peyote as the Indian form of the Christian sacrament. "Our favorite term is medicine," he informed Commissioner Leupp in 1908, "and to us it is a portion of the body of Christ even as the communion bread is believed to be a portion of Christ's body." Hensley taught that peyote provided the key to understanding the Bible and identified its persecutors with the "Scribes and Pharisees" who had doubted and abused "the Son of God." This persecution, he said, proved that "the peyote is fulfilling the work of God and the Son of God." The Cross Fire movement soon incorporated Bible reading and hymn singing into what they began to call their worship services.[64] A suggestive anecdote comes from one of the movement's opponents, Gertrude Bonnin, who quoted a former Winnebago Roadman as saying that only after they were "interrupted by the police because they were on drunks" had he and other Peyotists "bought a Bible, and then . . . began to read out of it to make it a religion."[65] This episode illuminates the cultural bias and constant threat of repression that led many Peyotists to make their practice recognizably Christian, so that authorities would grant them the status of religion. It casts no doubt on the sincerity of their convictions to point out that the need for outside approval pushed the movement to embrace a more overtly Christian identity.

Following the example of the Shakers, several branches of the Peyote movement filed for incorporation as churches. The largest of them was the Native American Church of Oklahoma, which with Mooney's encouragement filed for incorporation in 1918 soon after the House hearings on peyote that year.[66] Its stated aim was to promote "the Christian religion with the practice of the Peyote Sacrament as commonly understood and used among the adherents of this religion." Most of the newly incorporated Peyote groups adopted versions of the name "Native American Church," thus omitting the controversial word "peyote" from their formal title and, like the Shakers, locating themselves as one more church on the denominational landscape of American religious life.[67]

An exchange between Commissioner Charles Burke and Agent C. H. Ziebach on the Fort Hall Reservation reveals how helpful this strategy could be on the ground. Ziebach was convinced that peyote caused insanity and undermined the "progress" of the Bannock and Shoshone Indians on the reservation. As soon as he announced a ban on its use, however, Peyote leaders showed him the "charter issued to the Native American Church by the Secretary of State at Boise, Idaho that they had incorporated under the laws of this state" and demanded their right to religious freedom. Ziebach described these claims as "the same old excuses" and did everything he could to stop them. He fired one of the judges in the reservation's court system for using peyote, a decision he had the authority to make because the judge was a BIA employee. But without state or federal legislation banning peyote, there was little more that he could do. Ziebach wrote to Burke that

South Dakota's law against peyote had been quite useful "in wiping out the evil in that state," and he could only hope that Idaho would do the same. Emboldened by their status as a legally incorporated church and by the constitutional principle of religious freedom, the Bannock and Shoshone Peyotists had simply refused to accept his authority to forbid their ceremonies on the reservation.[68]

Where states had passed legislation banning Peyote, Native assertions of religious freedom and tribal sovereignty were far less successful. In *State v. Big Sheep* (1926), the Montana Supreme Court affirmed one such law and refused to take the Indian defendant's religious freedom argument seriously. Like Representative Tillman in the 1918 hearings, the Montana justices entirely rejected Native American Church members' claims to Christian identity—along with any sort of religious legitimacy for peyote—by reasoning that peyote was mentioned nowhere in the Bible. Evidently the Montana Supreme Court had not yet been touched by the secularizing trends in legal institutions that on a national level had already made openly Christian claims less acceptable as the basis of legislative reasoning.[69]

Native American leaders struggled to balance assertions of a prior indigenous sovereignty with more pragmatic appeals to the First Amendment. One Osage petition in 1921 began by "respectfully ask[ing] Congress, the Secretary of the Interior, and the Commissioner of Indian Affairs to continue to allow us to use peyote in our religious worship." Rather than taking the Constitution for granted, the Osage petitioners went on to outline the circumstances in which it had been created. The white people who "came to this country from Europe" had "adopted a Constitution" that gave "any human race of citizen who lives upon this American continent . . . the full right to worship God in their own way," they explained. "Whereas, this country once belonged to the Redman alone, God erected the Indian upon this land and gave us certain ways to live upon this land." Thus they reminded lawmakers and federal officials that the Osage people had been on the continent long before the United States came into being. None of the treaties they had made were still in effect, they wrote; all had been "abolished." The one thing they asked was "to be given the important thing, to be free in our religious worship." Those who now had "power over the country and the people and their property," they wrote, should not forget to "respect . . . the Redman" by granting them this basic right. Poignantly, this Osage petition reminded lawmakers of their people's prior sovereignty only to renounce it, accepting their subordination on the sole condition that the United States live up to its own constitutional guarantees.[70]

The questions around religious freedom and tribal sovereignty became even more complicated in the 1930s when the BIA reversed its policy on peyote. The new Commissioner of Indian Affairs was John Collier, a former critic of the BIA tapped by Franklin Delano Roosevelt to administer his "New Deal for the Indians." Collier was a longtime advocate of religious freedom for indigenous traditions, including the Peyote religion. But when several tribal governments made the decision to ban peyote, which they saw as a detriment to tribal traditions and a potentially dangerous drug, the principle of tribal sovereignty came into conflict with the Peyotists' religious freedom appeals. Secretary of the Interior Harold Ickes warned the Taos Pueblo tribal council in 1934 that if it continued its program of "religious persecution" against the Native American Church, the Department of the Interior would do whatever it could "to protect the religious liberties of the minority." Given that threat, the tribal council eventually conceded the Peyotists' right to religious freedom.[71]

A similar conflict played out differently on the Navajo reservation, where the Navajo tribal council maintained its ban on peyote for many years on tribal sovereignty grounds. As Collier explained in a 1944 congressional hearing, he had reluctantly approved the council's anti-peyote ordinance, even though he could not reconcile it with the principle of religious freedom, "because I thought the tribal council had a right to its own decision." In both of these cases, tribal assertions of sovereignty conflicted with religious freedom claims from the Native American Church. Having taken on various Protestant characteristics, including a conscious accommodation to Protestant denominational patterns, the Peyote religion found American legal guidelines on religion to be a relatively comfortable fit. From the perspective of tribal leaders, however, the principle of religious freedom as adjudicated by the federal government could seem not an advance for Indian rights but a threat to tribal sovereignty.[72]

For most of the twentieth century, the Native American Church continued to face an array of regulations and restrictions and so had little option but to continue its religious freedom campaign. These efforts had a mixed record of success in the courts. In the long run, both state and federal laws would grant religious exemptions to drug laws for church members, tacitly granting the religious legitimacy of the movement. In the meantime, the struggle forged significant changes within the Peyote movement. For most of the twentieth century, any hope of success with these claims required not merely an identification of the Peyote movement as *religion* but also a whole set of supporting arguments and organizational strategies to make that case in terms acceptable to the dominant society. In other words, the Peyote movement had to represent itself as Christian, and in order to do so it had to adjust itself to fit into white settler models for what counted as Christianity. Even with these adjustments, a patchwork of state laws and government regulations had continued to restrict the use of peyote and to make life difficult for Native American Church members throughout the country.

INDIAN DANCES AND THE RELIGIOUS-SECULAR DIVIDE

However difficult their appeals, both Shakers and Peyotists understood the principle of religious freedom as their best recourse against government suppression. Christianity had influenced both of these movements at their origins, and their styles of outreach across tribal lines reflected the model of evangelical Protestantism. Indeed, their increasingly pan-Indian identities were arguably possible precisely because these movements identified themselves as *religions*, separable from the identity and practices of any specific tribe. None of this was the case for the practitioners of Native American ceremonial dances. Simply as a matter of form—communal dancing as opposed to a group of seated worshippers—tribal dances were more difficult to fit into the dominant society's model for what counted as religion. These practices were also far more grounded in particular tribal traditions. After Wounded Knee, even the Ghost Dancers had largely ended their evangelizing and blended the new dance into each community's characteristic round of ceremonies. Given the BIA's concerted attacks on what it called "heathenism" and "barbarism," Native American dance leaders had little reason to believe that religious freedom talk would, for them, provide an effective means of defense.[73]

Much like the Shakers and the Peyotists, Native American tribal dance leaders often insisted that their ceremonies were religious activities that must be granted recognition and protection as such. Especially in Oklahoma, where both the Ghost Dance and the Peyote religion had taken root in many Native communities, the organized advocacy of the Peyote movement provided an instructive example.[74] In 1916 a Kiowa leader named Big Tree protested a ban on the Ghost Dance by explaining that this was a "Worshiping Dance" that was performed "for good and not evil" and concluded that "it would [not] be right for you to stop our way of worshiping." In the same letter, Big Tree also defended the "good medicine" of peyote.[75] If it had not already occurred to dance leaders that they could appeal to the constitutional principle of religious freedom, the Peyote movement helped inspire some of them to do just that. They too grounded such claims in their rights as U.S. citizens. Responding to an inquiry from Kiowa dance leader Red Buffalo, an Oklahoma lawyer confirmed that as citizens the Kiowas "had the same rights of citizenship as any white person, and [were] permitted to worship as [they] deem fit," even though the BIA agents might try to make them believe otherwise.[76]

To strengthen their religious freedom claims, dance leaders identified parallels between tribal ceremonies and conventionally Christian practices of worship. When Commissioner Cato Sells insisted that the Blackfeet Indians of Montana limit their Fourth of July celebration to only one day, tribal representative Wolf Tail petitioned for at least three days by comparing the "Medicine Dance" of the Blackfeet—identified in earlier correspondence as another term for the tribe's Sun Dance—to the Holy Week in the Christian tradition. "These gatherings are to us as Easter is to white people," he wrote. "We pray, and baptize our babies only instead of water we paint them."[77] And on the Cheyenne River Reservation, a committee of Lakota Indians led by John Lastman offered a biblical rationale for dancing. They petitioned for permission to hold their Omaha Dance on the grounds that it was a "fast disappearing form of worship" that fit the biblical model of dance "as symbolic of rejoicing."[78]

Like the Shakers and the Peyotists again, dance leaders who appealed to religious freedom tended to shift their practices to look more like Christianity, fitting them into white Christian models for what counted as religion. After their requests to hold a Ghost Dance had been repeatedly rebuffed, Pawnee tribal leaders asked for permission to "hold a two days' religious meeting," assuring their agent that they were not attempting "to oppose the lately issued edict" against the Ghost Dance. This event, they wrote, would allow "Methodist and Baptist minister[s] of the gospel . . . to address the assembled tribe."[79] The agent recognized that the "proposed ceremonial" would be "of a similar nature" to the Ghost Dance, but he approved the request on the grounds that this gathering would facilitate Christian missions on the reservation. The Pawnees had always insisted that their Ghost Dance was compatible with Christianity. Yet it was only after they had entirely subordinated its practice to the goal of Christian missions that the BIA allowed them to hold any event they identified as religious.[80]

Another case comes from the Ojibwe people of the Red Lake Reservation in Minnesota, who sent a series of letters in 1916 and 1917 to protest the prohibition of their Medewiwin Society ceremonies. The Medewiwin, an important part of Ojibwe life at least since the eighteenth century, was a tightly organized society of initiated religious specialists who conducted two major annual ceremonies of prayer and healing.[81] The local BIA agent advocated a complete ban on what he called a "so-called religious ceremony" on the grounds that the Ojibwes were no longer sincere in its practice and that it was "broadly detrimental" to their progress as a people.[82] In a petition signed by more than sixty-five people, the Ojibwes responded by distancing their "gathering" from the nonreligious connotations of its English-language appellation: "The so-called 'Grand Medicine Dance' is not a dance in any sense of the term." Instead they stressed the ceremony's parallels with Christian worship. "It is . . . for the purpose of giving praise to the Great Spirit," they explained. "The beating of the Drum is simply an accompaniment to the songs of praise uttered by the congregation," just as "in every Church of the White man a Piano or Organ is found for the same purpose." The petition concluded with a reminder that the government guaranteed all Americans "the freedom of worshipping God, and we cannot understand why we are deprived of this privilege."[83]

If they were to make such arguments credible, tribal leaders had to make subtle adjustments in their traditions. That winter the Ojibwes sent a delegation to Washington demanding the freedom to practice "the Chippewa religion . . . based upon what are known among the religions of the whites as 'The Ten Commandments.' "[84] Dan Perkins, an Ojibwe who wrote fluently in English, enclosed another tribal petition with his own cover letter explaining that the Medewiwin was completely consistent with Christianity, a "form of worshipping God" that was "not against any church denomination whatever" since a participant could "continue his membership with any church, so long as he is of good moral character."[85] An Ojibwe petition to the governor of Minnesota classified the Medewiwin as a Christian denomination: "This dance is one of the many religions, same as the Catholic and Methodist Episcopal Church," the petitioners wrote. "Can you tell us if an American citizen can be stopped from dancing?" they asked. "Can you tell us if any church or religion can be stopped?"[86] Although the Medewiwin had generally been associated with traditionalist Ojibwes, who resisted conversion to Christianity, its teachings and practices already reflected some Christian influences. Repeatedly attacked by the government, its defenders attempted to associate it more and more closely with Christianity as their only hope of achieving recognition as a legitimate religion.

Ceremonies defended in religious terms tended to conform more and more closely to what counted as religion in mainstream America. Those who practiced them would increasingly emphasize (or adopt) characteristics generally associated with Christianity, because these were most likely to support the designation of religion in the eyes of the outside world. In the process I would suggest that these ceremonies were also *becoming* religion and in the process forged new distinctions between the religious and the secular in Native American life.

At the height of the assimilationist era, however, such efforts often failed. BIA officials rarely accepted tribal dance leaders' assertions of religious legitimacy because they understood the term "religion" to be essentially synonymous with Christianity. Assistant Commissioner E. B. Meritt explicitly rejected the Ojibwes' religious freedom claim. "While it is not the purpose to interfere in any manner with religious ceremonies," he wrote, "the old and harmful practices of the Indians, which are clearly detrimental to their progress and welfare, cannot be tolerated even under the guise of a religious ceremony."[87] The Ojibwes had insisted that their Grand Medicine Dance deserved to be designated a religion and had already adjusted it as much as they could to fit the Christian norms for religion in America. Yet still they could not escape the racialized limits of religious freedom in the settler-colonial state.

Many government officials continued to view "heathenism" as the most significant obstacle to their civilizing projects. Meritt regularly reminded his subordinates that "the sun dance and all similar dances and so-called religious ceremonies" were specifically prohibited. In keeping with this directive, many agents were far more concerned about those dances they classified as religious than those they saw as purely "social."[88] Agent Jewell Martin wrote that the "Sun-dance, [which] consists of a sort of admixture of religious ceremonies and side-show features," was the biggest challenge he faced among the Uintah and Ouray Indians. If he could not ban this dance entirely, Martin hoped to move it from the Fourth of July to the "agricultural fair" held at the agency each September. There it could "be supervised and later modified into what the Indians will appreciate as only a relic of the past," he wrote, and so divested of its "religious significance." From Martin's perspective, any claim that a dance might have religious significance revealed a dangerous categorical error, one that he saw as an Indian racial characteristic. Its associations with the body, with sensual and potentially ecstatic experiences, made dance a particularly dangerous type of "primitive" religiosity. True religion underwrote the virtues of morality, rationality, and civilization, and it was by definition divorced from such extravagant bodily practices. Placing dance in its proper sphere—as a form of recreation and entertainment, not religion—was among the civilizing obligations of the colonial tutelary regime.[89]

Even the most sympathetic officials assumed their own right to determine what counted as religion and excluded from this category any Native practice that did not conform to that standard. Whether they recognized it or not, their models for religion reflected the Christian norms of the dominant society. On the Kiowa reservation, Agent Ernest Stecker advised that the Washington office provide a "strong suggestion that [the Indians] give up the Ghost Dance with all their old-time dances and join with their Christian brothers in religious worship." This, he hoped, would "encourage the church faction and deplete the ranks of the dancers."[90] Here Stecker equated "religious worship" with Christianity. Layered alongside the racial and civilizational hierarchies that so denigrated indigenous peoples and traditions under settler-colonial rule, this usage reinforced the categorical exclusions that left so many government officials unable to see the First Amendment as applicable to Native American dances in the first place. The following year, the newly appointed superintendent C. V. Stinchecum reported on his efforts to suppress the Kiowa Ghost Dance this way: "I advised them that if they would . . . promise me that no dance of any description would be held, that they would be permitted to worship God in such manner as they saw fit."[91] The fact that dancing was itself their preferred manner of worship was an irony that entirely escaped him.

Given these ideological and institutional barriers, Native Americans sometimes found it more effective to defend their dance ceremonies in nonreligious terms. They distanced their dances from charges of "savagery" and "paganism" by arguing that they were simply harmless social affairs, no different from the recreational dances held in white communities around the country. On some reservations, Christmas, Thanksgiving, New Year's Day, George Washington's birthday, Independence Day, and Armistice Day all became occasions for Indian dances. Most important for this purpose was the Fourth of July, which tribes as widespread as the Uintah and Ouray in Utah, the Bannock and Shoshone in Idaho, the Shoshone and Arapaho in Wyoming, the Kiowa in Oklahoma, the Lakota and Dakota in South Dakota, and the Blackfeet in Montana all celebrated with dances. Agents could hardly object to Native Americans wanting to observe this holiday, especially when small towns across the country held festivities that also included dances. The Fourth of July became especially prominent on Indian reservations in the years following World War I, when it became a way to honor tribal members who had served in the armed forces. Despite their agents' hopes that military experience would facilitate assimilation, Indian veterans claimed the right to dance on the grounds that, like other Americans, they deserved to enjoy the liberties they had fought to defend.[92]

A related strategy made dances an occasion for charitable giving, either to the Red Cross or to the war effort more generally. Agent Henry Tidwell reported in 1918 that, although he had forbidden any more dances on the Pine Ridge Reservation that summer, "practically every community on this reservation" had continued to hold them "under first one guise and then another, and more under the guise of a Red Cross meeting to raise funds than anything else."[93] Especially for Lakota and Dakota Indians, such collections provided a useful rationale for gatherings where dances, along with a modified version of the otherwise forbidden giveaway tradition, could then be held. This practice also enabled dance leaders to position themselves as more patriotic than their critics. "If we had given [the churches] all the money that we had donated to the World War," wrote Lakota dance leaders, "we believe that [the missionaries] would not say anything against our dancing."[94]

Indians who asserted their rights as citizens did not necessarily invoke the principle of religious freedom. A group of Cheyenne River Lakotas argued in 1920 that their inherent rights to "life, liberty, and the pursuit of happiness" included the right to dance. While promising to abandon any "objectionable parts," such as "the Giving Away of money and property," they insisted that "the dance alone is not harmful to us." Some of their sons had "made the supreme sacrifice" in the late war, they noted, and had believed that "the war would not be fought in vain." These Lakotas further reassured their agent that these dances presented no conflict with Christianity. "All Indians are faithfull [sic] Christians, especially the old Indians," they wrote, "and we are helping the different church missionaries in their religious work." While they invoked the "laws made separating the church from the state" to challenge the influence of the missionaries within the BIA, they did not argue for their dances on religious freedom grounds. Presenting these practices as religious would potentially have placed them in competition with Christianity. Instead they described their tribal dances simply as "entertainment," a source of "enjoyment" that the missionaries should approve if they really wanted to further "the spiritual welfare of the Indians."[95]

Many local agents found that if they wanted to maintain good relations with the people they had been assigned to supervise, they had little choice but to grant permission for at least some of their dances. Despite the missionaries' continued objections, Agent C. D. Munro concluded that "an arbitrary order to discontinue all dances" would be likely to create a backlash of resentment that he simply could not afford and would in any case be impossible to enforce. The Indians' strategic rights talk and the dogged persistence of their demands had convinced him that it was both impracticable and unjust to forbid these practices.[96] As they learned to know the people and practices on the reservations they supervised, agents sometimes found it harder to condemn them. Dana Kelsey, agent to the Creek (Muscogee) Indians in Oklahoma, reported that the Muscogee "busk" or Green Corn Dances were nothing like "the fatiguing or fanatical dances of certain of the reservation tribes . . . such as I take it the office is attempting to prohibit."[97] Even BIA officials in Washington acknowledged that it would be impossible to prohibit all Indian dances and that an outright ban "would not be productive of the best results."[98]

Indian dance leaders gained sympathy from some of their white neighbors as well by presenting their dances as purely social and thus no different from other popular dances of the time. One editorial in Wyoming's *Lander Eagle* criticized the BIA's order to cancel a planned Fourth of July Sun Dance on the nearby Wind River Reservation for this reason. The contemporary Sun Dance as practiced by the Arapaho and Shoshone people was "merely an imitation of the traditional torture dance," the editors opined, and included "no more barbarism than . . . rag-time contortions." Misguided official condemnations could not and should not stop the Indians from this pastime: "While Lo! the Poor Indian buried his worship of the glorious orb of day and bowed to the mandate of the Great Father at Washington, a two-step that resembles a cross between the 'Turkey Trot' and the fantastic wiggles of the Sun Dance was in progress on the reservation."[99] The editors considered this dance unobjectionable because they believed it had been stripped of the "heathen" elements of "torture" and sun worship to become an innocent form of entertainment. In this way, Native dance leaders who managed to avoid the classification of their dances as religion—primitive or false religion—could sometimes gain support from white observers and opinion makers.

This was never simply a matter of representation. Native American dance traditions were changing for a variety of reasons, and some dances were losing ceremonial significance. Seeking the historical roots of modern powwow culture, Clyde Ellis has charted the emergence of dance complexes that were increasingly shared across the Great Plains. Among the most significant of these was the Omaha Dance, also called the Grass Dance, which had developed out of the ceremonial dances held in previous decades by "medicine societies" across many Plains tribes. The Omaha Dance had already become "more social in form and function" by the late nineteenth century, Ellis suggests, mostly because the way of life that had sustained the older ceremonies no longer existed. This process of secularization was never complete, and Native people continued to attribute sacred significance to the powwow dances. But as time went on, many Indians found that they had the most freedom to perform dances in intertribal and apparently secular settings like fairs and exhibitions, where officials found it more difficult to accuse them of immorality or of preserving tribal "savagery."[100] In this way, the dynamics of government suppression pushed Indians to minimize the ceremonial significance of their dances. If Native American dance cultures became increasingly secular in the early twentieth century, such changes were at least to some extent a product of their need to escape attacks that had been framed in specifically religious terms.

Whether Native Americans classified their dances in religious or non-religious terms, the struggle against government suppression partially remolded the traditions they sought to protect. Those ceremonies most often defended in the language of religion emphasized (or adopted) those characteristics that supported the designation of religion in the eyes of the outside world. Meanwhile, ceremonies that were classified as social lost, at least to some extent, those attributes commonly marked as religious and for that reason are often said to have been secularized.[101] The point here is not only that some dances were secularized while others became more religious but also that the very distinction between religion and the secular in Native American traditions must be understood as a product of government suppression. Although these distinctions had a real impact on the ceremonies they named, they were never absolute. Many Native people have insisted, for example, that putatively social dances also have sacred significance that cannot be separated out from the entirety of Indian life—an insistence that reflects the continued inadequacy and instability of religious-secular distinctions within Native societies.[102]

INDIAN SOVEREIGNTY AND THE ASSAULTS
OF THE IMPERIAL SECULAR

"This dance is a custom which we inherited from our fathers," wrote Bannock Indian dance leader Jacob Browning to Commissioner Charles Burke in 1925, "and one which we feel we cannot in justice to them abandon."[103] Browning's letter protested the recent suppression of the annual Bannock and Shoshone Sun Dance by a new BIA agent, C. H. Ziebach. After tribal leaders on the Fort Hall Reservation had flouted Ziebach's orders not to hold the dance that year, the agent sent policemen to break up the ceremony and to imprison the "ringleaders" in the agency guardhouse.[104] In response, Browning employed a number of the strategies that Native dance leaders had used throughout the assimilationist era: comparisons between Indian and non-Indian dances, a defense of the moral standards and positive impact of dancing within Native societies, and the reminder that Native Americans held a prior claim to the land. More directly than most, he challenged the underlying legitimacy of U.S. rule, the very foundations of the tutelary regime: "The White man has taken our lands from us, and at the rate they have continued to make encroachments upon our rights, the time will not be long distant when they will deny us and begrudge us six feet of our ground for a final resting place. . . . We dance both for the good of our bodies, and for the good of our souls. For the White man to take this right from us, after he has taken everything else, seems to us a gross injustice."[105] While Browning described the dance as "good [for] our souls" and a "custom . . . inherited from our fathers," he did not directly articulate a religious freedom appeal. He was certainly familiar with the concept, as he had been active as a dance leader, a critic of BIA policies, and an advocate for citizens' rights including religious freedom for more than a decade.[106] The absence of this theme in his 1925 letter suggests that he had not found it to be the most useful approach. With the benefit of experience, Browning simply preferred to defend the Sun Dance in less explicitly religious terms.

Where the Shakers and the Peyotists had moved decisively to identify themselves and their movements as religious—and in the process had gradually changed their practices to conform more closely to the Christian model for what counted as religion—many tribal dance leaders like Browning had found that strategy impracticable and impossible to sustain. Making indigenous dances recognizable to white authorities as religion may have required more adjustments than the Bannock and Shoshone people were willing to make. Browning called instead for a self-determination that did not require such adjustments: "I do not understand how one people can say what is good for another people and what is bad for them," he wrote. The Indians did not try to tell white people whether or how they should dance; why then should white people presume to impose their own standards on the Indians?[107]

In an exceptional flourish for a Native leader in this period, one that prefigured future directions for global anticolonial and indigenous organizing movements, Browning concluded his letter by identifying Native Americans with the subjects of empire around the world. "In case you have never read Mark Twain's 'Following the Equator,'" he advised Burke, "permit me to suggest that you do so." Written in Twain's characteristically biting style, *Following the Equator* (1899) poked equal-opportunity fun at the whites and "savages" encountered in a year traveling across most of the British Empire. Although the book reinscribed many racial stereotypes, Twain's final message was that the "civilization" touted so highly by the "white man" was just as arbitrary and as ludicrous as any other. The circumstance of their imperial power gave Americans and Europeans no right to impose it on anyone else. By invoking Twain, Browning appealed to the cultural authority of one of the nation's most widely admired writers and deftly linked his people to the travails of colonized peoples everywhere. Rather than invoking the right to religious freedom under the U.S. Constitution, he issued a far broader demand for self-determination and the sovereignty of indigenous peoples.[108]

Browning wrote at the cusp of significant changes in federal Indian policy, changes that in some respects facilitated Native American appeals to religious freedom. As we have seen, Native leaders around the country had been insisting for many years that the freedom of religion must apply not only to Christianity but also to their indigenous ceremonies and traditions. The persistence of their demands had already forced government officials to concede, at least in principle, that some Native traditions were legitimately religious and so must be granted the right to religious freedom.

By the 1920s, such appeals were becoming culturally legible within the dominant society. Several years before Browning wrote his letter, a coalition of non-Indian artists, writers, and anthropologists—modernists who tended to romanticize what they saw as "primitive religion"—had spoken out against Commissioner Burke's renewed restrictions on Indian dances. With their support, as part of a national debate among missionaries, reformers, and government officials, the Pueblo Indians of New Mexico had successfully wielded the principle of religious freedom against the threat of government suppression. In so doing they managed to position their ceremonial dances as indigenous *religion*, distinct from yet compatible with the Catholicism that most of the Pueblos also practiced. The BIA was no longer able to take for granted its right to suppress indigenous ceremonies that it defined as "heathen" without taking into account Native assertions of religious freedom.[109]

This limited recognition of Native American religion was part of a broader transformation in the BIA's approach to the subject of religion. In the late nineteenth century most agents had considered it part of their responsibility to Christianize as well as civilize the Indians and justified their suppression of "heathen" dances on explicitly Christian grounds. By the 1910s and 1920s, much of this was changing. While officials like Burke and Ziebach continued to believe that Christianity and civilization went hand in hand, they saw their own work as distinct from that of the missionaries. If they acknowledged that they favored Christianity, they explained that preference on the grounds that Christianity provided a more positive influence for civilization and morality. And when they attempted to suppress a ceremony like the Sun Dance, they did not justify their actions by labeling the ceremony "heathen" or opposed to Christianity but instead as an impediment to the Indians' civilizing progress. As Ziebach put it, "I believe this dance to be harmful with our efforts for better citizenship and progress, and [that it] has a demoralizing effect with the younger element of the reservation."[110]

Similarly, as we have seen, the BIA explained its effort to suppress the Native American Church primarily on the grounds that peyote was a dangerous drug with "demoralizing" effects. While some in Congress continued to condemn Peyotism because it was not Christian, the more common line of attack was that it could not be considered religion at all. Peyote's opponents moved away from Christian condemnations of Indian "heathenism" to more secular rationales. Modern Peyotism was not based in any "ancient" or "primitive" Native religion, these critics charged. Instead it was a complete fraud, merely a "cloak" for the drug trade. All of these critics wanted peyote banned. But they were being forced to recognize at least the theoretical possibility that Native Americans might have religious traditions that were distinct from Christianity—and that the category of heathenism provided no logical or constitutional reason for banning them. These changes in assimilationist rhetoric reflected what I have described elsewhere as a secularization of federal Indian policy: a shift from explicitly Christian and toward more secular rationales and sources of authority in Indian affairs.[111]

None of this meant that indigenous traditions were gaining equal status within the larger society or under U.S. law. This increasingly secularized administration maintained an overwhelming bias toward Christianity, if only because Christianity continued to set the standard for what counted as religion. As we have seen, Shakers, Peyotists, and tribal dance leaders who demanded their right to religious freedom had little choice but to adjust to a Christian mold. Looking like a church—through the legal process of incorporation, by adopting a denominational structure, and in a myriad of other ways—continued to be virtually indispensable for Native American movements that hoped to succeed in their religious freedom claims. The very distinction between religion and the secular, I have argued, represented a necessary accommodation to the norms of the dominant society. All this remained the case even after authorities no longer explicitly favored Christianity or believed they had any legal right to do so. No wonder Jacob Browning had lost all interest in religious freedom as the way to frame his appeals.

Federal Indian policy would become even more strongly secularized under Commissioner John Collier and his Indian New Deal in the 1930s. A longtime critic of assimilationist policies, Collier sought to replace them with a new respect for indigenous practices and traditions. His most ambitious initiative was the wide-ranging Indian Reorganization Act, enacted in June 1934, which ended any further allotment of Indian lands and outlined plans for economic development on the reservations. The bill also sought to strengthen tribal sovereignty by encouraging each tribe to apply for a charter, which would provide them with the legal authority to purchase land and conduct business as a corporate body, and to develop a formal tribal constitution. This legislation, he assured Native American leaders, would at long last restore tribal self-government, protect indigenous land and traditions, and ensure the freedom of religion for tribal communities as well as for the individuals within them.[112]

Advocates for the old assimilationist order were outraged. Elaine Goodale Eastman, who had emerged as a leading critic of the Native American Church, published a scathing attack on Commissioner Collier for encouraging the revival of "repugnant," "degrading," and "primitive" practices. Would the "degrading" cult of peyote, outlawed in many states, be "introduced into tax-supported schools, under the present regime?" she asked. "If not, why not?" Eastman was certain that the better-educated Indians would not be led astray; surely they could no longer be "spiritually satisfied" by such "primitive rites" and "bastard religions." But "some such pseudo-native institutions as the 'peyote church,' or a new 'messiah craze' invented by self-seeking fakirs," she warned, "may serve to drug the Indian masses into forgetfulness of the fact that the present Indian policy tends not to the promised full enfranchisement, but rather to a perpetual twilight of insincere praise and actual inferiority."[113] Eastman's piece, appearing in the *Christian Century*, demonstrated how prevalent the link between civilization and Christianity still was. In her view, indigenous traditions were by definition degrading and could claim no legitimate title to the protections of the First Amendment.

The commissioner was a practiced polemicist, and his spirited rebuttal illuminates the shifting tides of the imperial secular. He began by positioning his policies as entirely mainstream. Both Catholic and Protestant missionary agencies, he wrote, had readily approved the new regulations, which simply granted "any representative of an Indian religion" the same right to provide religious instruction in the BIA boarding schools that the Christian churches had long enjoyed. Under earlier administrations, he explained, without any debate whatsoever on the question of religious liberty, "Indian religions were treated as being simply a part of the tribal and cultural complex which it was the government's business to eliminate." Collier aimed to rectify these mistakes. He defended the Peyote movement in particular as a legitimate religion and rejected Eastman's claim that Indian tribes had "commercialized their religious rituals." In short, he identified "native Indian religions" as legitimate *religions*, complete with all the elements of "mystical experience," codes of conduct, and spiritual disciplines that he named as characteristic of any religion. Under his administration, religion would be understood to be an anthropological category that could describe indigenous traditions as readily as Christianity. Christianity could no longer define its limits, at least not explicitly, or claim exclusive privileges under the U.S. Constitution.[114]

Collier's magnanimous intentions could not eliminate the structural reality that Native Americans existed as the subaltern subjects of a white supremacist settler state. As we saw in the case of the conflicts over peyote on the Taos and Navajo reservations, Collier's long-belated recognition of a Native American right to religious freedom continued to assume the final authority of the federal government and its right to adjudicate Native American appeals. The commissioner recognized, too, that his actions could always be reversed by future administrations. "I do assure you that your traditions and form of government will be retained and respected by me so long as your people wish to retain them," he wrote to Sotero Ortiz of the All-Pueblo Indian Council. "You must know, however, that the Secretary of the Interior, the President, or the Congress may change this at any time." Collier urged Ortiz and other Native American leaders to organize their tribal governments according to the provisions of the Indian Reorganization Act, which encouraged and enabled the development of formal tribal constitutions. This, the commissioner told them, would provide the greatest degree of tribal sovereignty and the most expansive protection possible under U.S. law.[115]

Collier's sincerity notwithstanding, the cultural and structural pressures that U.S. rule exerted upon Native American societies remained very much in place. Even the commissioner's emphasis on preserving and protecting "Indian religion" worked to separate out a differentiated *religion* from other aspects of Native American life. This was not merely a matter of language and representation. The new constitutions developed under the Indian Reorganization Act brought a variety of changes in tribal systems of governance, including new distinctions between religious and political authority within the tribe. In some Native communities this was a welcome change, because it offered a structural solution to long-standing conflicts around tribal leadership and the presence of competing religious movements. Especially where they were in the minority, for example, members of the Native American Church welcomed constitutional provisions that granted individual tribal members the right to religious freedom and distinguished the leadership of tribal chiefs or governors from that of the priests, shamans, or "caciques," who could now be cordoned off as exclusively religious leaders.[116]

THE CONCEITS OF EMPIRE AND THE MAKING OF INDIAN RELIGION

In some Native American communities, these constitutional provisions simply confirmed and codified changes that were already well underway. In part through the religious freedom appeals that this chapter has documented—appeals always formulated under the structural conditions of settler-colonial rule—Native Americans had increasingly come to identify their own traditions as *religious*. With that identification, and given the need to satisfy government officials' criteria for what counted as religious, they had also begun to separate this newly identified religion out from other aspects of their lives. The new tribal constitutions furthered these changes, helping to solidify the emerging distinction between religion and the secular within many Native American societies. Under the circumstances, such changes may well have been essential to the survival of indigenous traditions and ways of life. Native American societies are no exception to the processes of change, over time and through encounters with others, that all human cultures experience. The development of an increasingly differentiated sphere of religion is perhaps best understood as a Native American adaptation to the impositions of settler colonialism. These adaptations enabled Native American traditions and tribal identities to survive.

At the same time, it is essential to expose the systems of power—the civilizational assemblages of race and empire—that constrained Native American options and made such changes necessary in the first place. As I argued in chapter 2, among the conceits of U.S. empire was the claim that America's model of religious freedom set the standard for modernity, supposedly qualifying the United States to uplift those societies still mired in their primitive or premodern traditions. White settler celebrations of American religious freedom, set in contrast to portrayals of Native American traditions as "tyrannical" and "theocratic," provided ideological justification for the seizure of Native American lands and the violent imposition of settler-colonial rule. It made little practical difference whether BIA officials identified Native American traditions as insufficiently Christian or as insufficiently secular. Either way, Native people were deemed racially inferior and their cultures barbaric, in need of uplift and modernizing reform.

Precisely because the dominant society valued it so highly, the principle of religious freedom provided one way for Native Americans to defend indigenous practices and traditions. In the process, however, Native people found their practices and traditions transformed. In order to meet the demands of BIA officials and lawmakers for what counted as a legitimate religion, they had little choice but to restructure their traditions to fit the model set by Christianity. At an even deeper level, their appeals had the effect of forging new distinctions between the religious and the secular in their own societies. Despite all their accommodations, Native Americans met with ongoing barriers to their appeals for religious freedom. The civilizational assemblages of race, religion, and empire had clearly identified white settlers with Christianity and the progress of freedom. As long as U.S. law maintained the structural biases that privileged white settler Christianity, the limits of religious freedom would continue to be set along these lines. As long as religious freedom talk assumed the prior condition of U.S. rule, it was no substitute for the more radical Native American demands for sovereignty as indigenous nations.

Native Americans were hardly the only people caught in the interstices of U.S. empire who invoked religious freedom as a way to protect their communal traditions or whose religious freedom talk transformed them in the process. In many ways the same could be said of every people group discussed in this book. Chapter 2 described how both Catholic Filipinos and Muslim Moros found the principle of religious freedom useful in their efforts to navigate the impositions of U.S. empire and how their traditions were transformed by the religious-secular distinctions of the colonial administration. The next chapter returns to the American Jews, discussed briefly in chapter 1. As with Native Americans, the terms of Jewish peoplehood had never fit neatly into the categories of race, religion, or nation. Jews too invoked the principle of religious freedom to defend traditions and identities that would in the process be (re)defined as religious. In contrast to the indigenous experience, however, Jewish deployments of religious freedom proved quite effective as a way to navigate the civilizational assemblages of American life.

CHAPTER FOUR

Making American Whiteness

Jewish Identity and the Tri-faith Movement

"Let us tarry a moment in Rhode Island, the land where the banner of religious liberty was first unfurled," wrote American Jewish historian and diplomat Oscar Straus in his book *Religious Liberty in the United States.* "The time, let us hope, is not far off, when the civilized people, in the remotest corners of the world, will recognize the truth and power of the principles which throw around the name of Roger Williams a halo of imperishable glory and fame."[1] Straus had a long-standing admiration for Williams, the dissenting Puritan turned Baptist, founder of Rhode Island, and early proponent of religious liberty. Several years earlier he had published a biography of this colonial pioneer, and in 1891 he and his wife had named their son after him.[2] Straus celebrated Williams as the champion of a freedom that he considered essential to Jewish life. But he did not see Williams or indeed any Christian as the originator of this ideal. Rather, he argued in *The Origin of Republican Form of Government* that the ancient Hebrews were the source of the republican system of government and its ideals of civil and religious liberty. Through their influence on the Puritans, he argued, they had shaped the political institutions of the United States.[3] Straus was deeply invested in the discipline of American Jewish history, mentoring younger colleagues and presiding over countless sessions during a long tenure as president of the Jewish Historical Society in New York.[4]

Alongside his historical scholarship, Straus was a respected diplomat who considered the history he studied immediately relevant to the most pressing challenges of the contemporary world. His diplomatic career included terms as U.S. minister to Constantinople, Theodore Roosevelt's secretary of labor and commerce, and U.S. minister to the International Court of Arbitration at The Hague. (In that role after the First World War, he helped ensure that the newly negotiated Covenant for the League of Nations would be included in the Treaty of Versailles.) Throughout this career, Straus highlighted the principle of religious freedom as a model for the world and worked to hold the United States accountable to this ideal. "The so-called American policy which is invoked against immigrants from the Old World," he wrote in conclusion to his Williams biography, "is a libel upon the immortal fame of the patriarchs of our freedom. . . . Let us take care that we do not, in the years of our prosperity . . . violate the universal principles of justice and liberty underlying our American institutions."[5] Among the groups targeted by the exclusionary immigration proposals of the time were eastern European Jews, fleeing pogroms and persecution in Russia, Romania, and elsewhere in the region. Straus's historical work on American religious freedom thus situated the cause of the Jews in both Europe and the United States as an all-American, deeply patriotic concern.

Roger Williams Straus, who became a successful businessman in New York, followed in his father's footsteps as another dedicated champion for religious freedom. For three decades the younger Straus would assume a leading role in the National Conference of Christians and Jews (NCCJ), which worked against religious bias and bigotry by bringing Protestants, Catholics, and Jews together. Straus is especially remembered as a cochair of the NCCJ's 1932 Conference on Religious Liberty, which aimed to counter the rising tides of anti-Catholicism and anti-Semitism of that time. As Nazi armies moved across Europe, his book *Religious Liberty and Democracy* issued a desperate plea for unity against the antireligious totalitarianisms of the world. None were immune, he warned: the first attack of the Nazis had been "directed against the Jew, the next against the Catholic and finally the last one against the Evangelical Protestant." Totalitarianism would destroy not only the Jews but all religion and along with it the core values of the Western world. "It is essential for the preservation of Judeo-Christian principles . . . that the forces of religion" unite to defend human freedom, he wrote, which was "the foundation of all religion as well as of what we call democracy."[6]

For American Jewish intellectuals and civic leaders like the Strauses to place so much stress on religious freedom signified, among other things, their tendency to define Jewishness and Jewish communal identity in the language of religion. This approach was associated with the Reform movement and competed with images of the Jews as a distinct race or nation. Reform Judaism had emerged first in Germany as part of the intellectual ferment of the Enlightenment. Its leaders argued that to emphasize the distinctly religious dimensions of being Jewish was to purify Judaism of nonessentials— and that by giving up any assertions of a distinct racial or national identity, Jews would be accepted as loyal citizens of the countries in which they lived.

In staking out these claims, the Reform movement was not simply or even primarily following a Protestant model. Despite their minority status and the discrimination they faced, these Jews were very much a part of the multiple upheavals of modernity. They adopted these redefinitions to meet the needs of their communities and in keeping with their understanding of the world. The Strauses' celebration of religious freedom helped enable their successes in the worlds of politics and business by working against potential suspicions of their Jewishness as a threatening form of difference. If the Jews could be defined not as a race or a nation but solely as a religious group—a difference to be protected and even celebrated on the all-American grounds of religious freedom—then perhaps the lingering barriers to full Jewish participation in the cultural and civic life of the nation could finally be removed.[7]

This emphasis on religious freedom had clear benefits, but it also had its limits and its pitfalls. Many Jews outside the Reform movement (and some within it) did not accept the classification of Jewishness simply as a religion. In their eyes, the category of religion alone simply could not account for the complexity of Jewish communal life and experience. Such reservations would become stronger with the resurgence of an increasingly racialized anti-Semitism in the early twentieth century. The Zionist movement, which argued for a Jewish homeland and so encouraged the idea of a Jewish nation, gained momentum as the limits of religious freedom in addressing anti-Semitic dis-crimination and violence grew more and more clear. Many Jews chafed at the model of religion that religious freedom seemed to impose. As with the Native American traditions described in chapter 3, the defense of Judaism as a religion required highlighting those aspects of Jewish tradition that the white Protestant majority could easily recognize as such. When that strategy was successful, it worked against other models for being Jewish, such as the emerging framework of ethnicity. Religious freedom was a double-edged sword: while it promised expanded rights for minorities, it also required that they reshape themselves and their traditions according to its demands.

Yet American Jewish appeals to religious freedom remained pragmati-cally useful. I argue in this chapter that Jewish religious freedom talk, how-ever unevenly and incompletely, shifted mainstream American views of what it meant to be Jewish away from the racial and toward the religious. In and through their battles against the intensely racialized anti-Semitism of the early twentieth century, Jews gradually and always tentatively came to be recognized as a primarily religious rather than racial minority in American life. For many Americans, the idea that the Jews were a separate race would become more and more difficult to sustain as Nazi racism was publicly condemned, especially after the horrors of Auschwitz, Buchenwald, and the broader Nazi agenda were widely acknowledged. In the wake of the Second World War, Jews in the United States would largely escape the racial stigma that had previously haunted them and would gain general acceptance as racially white—a category into which they had never been fully admitted before. Religious freedom talk, employed for its practical utility even by those Jews who resisted the limits of religion for communal identification, served along the way as a mechanism for this reclassification. The rhetorics of religious freedom thus helped Jews escape the stigma of racial minority status and eased their acceptance into the racial privileges of whiteness in American life.[8]

As Oscar Straus's diplomatic career reminds us, these discourses of religious freedom took shape in the context of an expanding U.S. empire. Molded by their own history as the scapegoats of an imperial Christendom, Jews could sometimes be sharp critics of U.S. empire and the assemblages of race and religion that sustained it. But as we saw in chapter 1, they more often served as eager participants in and advocates for that empire. During his tenure as minister to the Ottoman Empire, Straus was the American diplomat behind the scenes who convinced the sultan of Turkey to intervene in the Philippines, encouraging the mostly Muslim Moros to accept the imposition of U.S. rule. Just as the history of anti-Semitic persecution in Spain and its empire helped drive American Jewish enthusiasm for the war against Spain and the subsequent U.S. imperial expansions, the pogroms and official discrimination that targeted Jews in Russia and the Ottoman Empire shaped American Jewish perspectives in the First World War and the reconfigurations of empire that followed. The ambitions of the Zionist movement for a Jewish state in Palestine, which gained momentum after the British took control of Palestine, are a case in point. The ideal of religious freedom and the secular credentials it secured would also help American Jewish leaders navigate the terrors of the Second World War and framed the creation of Israel as a secular yet officially Jewish state.

My point is not just that American Jews, like many other people, have been at once victims and accomplices of disparate racial and imperial projects. It is also that American assemblages of race and religion, including the modern formation of Judaism as religion, were forged in and through a rhetoric of religious freedom that must be understood as part of the discursive apparatus of U.S. empire. When early twentieth-century Reform leaders insisted that Jewish identity must be defined as solely religious, argued that the religion of Judaism was the original source for American ideals of democracy and religious freedom, and contested Christian triumphalism by identifying Judaism rather than Christianity as the highest and most ethical development of the world's religions, they were speaking in the register of empire. When Zionists and nationalists contested these notions of Judaism, they were a part of that same discursive world. It should be readily apparent that religious traditions, including Judaism, have simultaneously provided resources for resistance to empire and facilitated the processes of imperial conquest and control. This chapter suggests as well that our ideas about what counts as religion in the first place, Jewish and otherwise, have been inexorably shaped through the racialized assemblages of empire.

DEFINING JEWISHNESS: REFORMERS, ZIONISTS, AND THE FIRST WORLD WAR

The revolutionary promise of religious freedom, enshrined in the First Amendment to the U.S. Constitution, had long encouraged Jews to present themselves as a primarily religious minority in American life. This classification was always unstable and contested, and it would be fundamentally challenged at the turn of the twentieth century. Race was becoming more and more important as an organizing mechanism for the hierarchies of U.S. empire, not only in the Jim Crow South, in the Philippines, and on Indian reservations but also throughout American society. Like other minorities in this environment, Jews found themselves defined and sometimes defined themselves as a race. But perhaps even more important as a means of Jewish self-definition was the idea of nationhood, advanced above all by Zionists who considered the category of religion utterly inadequate for the task of defending Jewish lives. By the time of the First World War, the global forces of anti-Semitism, immigration, and empire strengthened the hand of the Zionists so that even within American Jewish communities the concepts of race and nation seemed just as significant as religion in defining what it meant to be a Jew.

Claiming Religion: American Jews in the Late Nineteenth Century

Throughout the nineteenth century, religious freedom talk had provided a practical way for Jews to protest the legal privileges that Christianity enjoyed in the public sphere. In the decades after the Civil War, many states had responded to lobbying from evangelical Christian organizations by expanding the "blue laws" that limited business and entertainment activities on

Sundays. Jewish businessmen pointed out that they were forced either to remain closed on both Saturdays and Sundays or to violate their own Sabbath by opening on Saturdays. Around the country they made common cause with Seventh-day Adventists and Seventh Day Baptists who faced the same dilemma. As one letter writer put it, the Seventh Day Baptist W. B. Capps, imprisoned for working on a Sunday, was "a martyr to the cause of religious liberty in the bigoted State of Tennessee." Small donations from Jews around the country paid Capps's fine and helped him re-establish his ruined business.[9] The journal's editors commented on a series of such cases that as long as "the highest courts of more than one of the States of the Union declare officially that this is a Christian country, and that therefore all work must cease on the Christian Sabbath," and as long as "a Jew who observes the seventh day is subject to arrest and imprisonment for laboring on Sundays even if he does not annoy his neighbors," then "in the interest of truth and honesty . . . the first amendment, which, it is alleged, guarantees us the freedom of religion," should simply be eliminated. Whether or not these writers were committed to the Reform vision of Judaism as religion, religious freedom talk worked to defend Jewish interests by presenting the Jews as more loyal to American ideals than those who would privilege Christianity at their expense.[10]

These articulations of religious freedom must be understood in the context of a rising tide of racialized anti-Semitism at the turn of the century, both in the United States and around the world. In one publication typical of the genre, Missouri lawyer and Methodist layman Orville Jones contended that the Jews had brought on whatever persecution they experienced through their "persistent determination . . . to practice fraud, extortion, and especially usury." Jones warned that the Jew was now recruiting "the nations of Christendom" to join "his crime against civilization." This conspiracy was visible in America not just in the wealth of certain Jewish bankers and merchants, he claimed, but also through the rising power of an Episcopalian "political-religious oligarchy" that had allied with them to take over the banking system and, ultimately, the entire U.S. government. Jones went on to blame the Jews for virtually all the systemic evils of the modern world, not just for the ills of capitalism, the oppression of the poor, and the mountains of debt that had trapped both individuals and nations but also for the failures of democracy and the despotic cruelties of monarchies and empires everywhere. His work illustrates how the idea of religious freedom could be mobilized against the Jews as well as in their defense. "Again the Sons of the Republic are called upon to fight the initial battle of the world's hope for civil and religious liberty," he wrote, a battle that in his telling had to be waged against the "sneaking cowardly cruel indirect power" of the Jew.[11]

Although his rhetoric was extreme, Jones represented a growing swath of American public opinion. The United States was never the exceptional haven that many Jews believed it to be. While American Jews never faced large-scale pogroms like those that devastated Russian Jewry in the late nineteenth century, the pogroms were hardly the norm in Russia, let alone elsewhere in eastern Europe, and cannot stand in for the entirety of Jewish experience even there. And Jews faced episodes of racialized discrimination and violence in the United States as well. A series of brutal assaults targeted Jewish merchants in Mississippi during the mid-1890s, and Jews were lynched on several occasions over the next few decades in attacks that suggested the structural similarities between anti-Jewish and anti-black discrimination. Across the country, universities, businesses, and social institutions would increasingly limit Jewish enrollment or ban Jews altogether. In short, American Jews faced far more discrimination and violence than their traditionally celebratory histories would suggest. It is not surprising that, in the age of scientific racism and Jim Crow, these barriers were increasingly framed in the language of race.[12]

The thousands of immigrants that poured annually into the United States in the 1880s and 1890s, many of them Jewish refugees from Russia, helped fuel this newly racialized anti-Semitism. Several of the major trade unions, fearing that the arrival of so many new workers would destabilize the labor market, called for new restrictions on Jewish immigration and at times depicted even the existing Jewish population as a threat. Union leaders accused the Jewish Colonization Society—founded by the Baron Maurice de Hirsch of Paris to support the movement of persecuted Jews to "various parts of North and South America" and supported by many American Jews—of leading immigrants to choose the United States over other possible destinations.[13] Commenting on the controversy, the *New York Herald* ultimately supported the rights of the immigrants but noted that there was "some show of reason" in the critics' claim that persecution had given them "a spirit of rebellion against all existing forms of government," leaving them unfit to participate in the "free institutions . . . of this Republic." In other words, even a generally sympathetic newspaper considered the Russian Jews to be potentially dangerous, a foreign element that could not be trusted to uphold the principles of American democracy. Over time, Congress and the Bureau of Immigration would respond to these fears with various new measures designed to limit the influx of immigrants belonging to the "Hebrew race."[14]

Barriers of class, culture, and tradition stood between the new immigrants and the more established Jewish communities in America. Most of the latter were from middle-class German immigrant families that had largely assimilated into American society and embraced the Reform approach to Jewish tradition. In contrast, the new immigrants were generally quite poor, with traditions and worldviews shaped by the distinct experiences of Jewish life in eastern Europe. The modern rabbinic and Hasidic movements that accompanied them could not have been more different than the Reform approach to Judaism. They brought visibly Jewish modes of dress and ritual practice that the Reform movement had deliberately abandoned, along with a distinctive Yiddish culture that marked their Jewishness in ways that more acculturated Jews found profoundly uncomfortable. Many immigrants had embraced socialism, anarchism, and other radical political commitments that alarmed middle-class American Jews. In all these ways they exceeded cultural standards for acceptable difference and threatened the tentative level of assimilation that Jews had thus far managed to achieve. The better-established American Jews found such immigrants profoundly alien and feared (and soon saw evidence) that their arrival in such large numbers would spark an anti-Semitic backlash against all Jews in the United States.[15]

American Jewish organizations rallied to help the refugees not only out of compassion but also to guard against such a backlash. For some, this crisis made the need to position Jewishness as a *religious* identity feel all the more urgent. When Jewish leaders appealed to Protestants and Catholics on behalf of the Russian Jews—and especially when they invoked the language of religious freedom—they not only gained allies for the cause but also positioned Judaism as a religion alongside Protestantism and Catholicism in American life. Highlighting incidents of persecution against Protestants or Catholics in Russia, as well as against Jews, was particularly effective for this purpose. Thus the *American Hebrew* reported in 1889 that Russian authorities had denied Lutherans in the Baltics the "rights of conscience as to the choice of religious belief," commenting that this episode would enable all Protestants to more fully "understand what it is that the Jews have to suffer in Russia." The editors strategically placed themselves as part of an alliance of all religions against the forces of atheism and infidelity. Infidels in the United States were eager to use "every exhibition of bigotry" from one religion against another, they wrote, as "an invincible argument against [all] religion." In order to defeat them, "the exponents of religion" would need to demonstrate that "people of various religious creeds" could dwell in harmony together. By asserting that all religion would stand or fall together at the hands of unbelievers, the *American Hebrew* identified the cause of the Jews as a crucial ingredient in the survival of all religion. In the process the editors reinforced their sense of being Jewish as a religious classification— and of Judaism as a religion that stood at the heart of America's commitments to both faith and freedom.[16]

Such advocacy efforts on behalf of the Russian Jews gained significant support across political and religious lines. In the election year of 1892, both the Republicans and the Democrats emphasized their commitment to religious freedom for the Jews of Russia. As the Democratic Party platform put it, "This country has always been the refuge of the oppressed for conscience' sake, and in the spirit of the founders of our Government we condemn the oppression practiced by the Russian government upon its Russian and Jewish subjects."[17] The issue gained even broader attention a decade later when news broke of pogroms that killed hundreds of Jews in the Russian city of Kishineff, with the apparent complicity of the local police. Protest meetings around the United States called for diplomatic action against Russia for its failure to prevent these atrocities. One such "mass meeting" in Richmond, Virginia, was standing room only and reportedly attracted "more Christians than Jews." Speakers included the mayor, the governor and lieutenant governor, and Episcopal and Baptist clergymen, along with Richmond's leading rabbi and other Jewish leaders. "The keynote of Gov. Montague's speech was religious freedom," reported the *Washington Post*. "He said this was an age of religious freedom, and the principle was recognized in all lands." These Americans all agreed that the persecution of the Russian Jews must be condemned as a violation of the sacred principle of religious freedom.[18]

These expressions of concern for the Russian Jews were no doubt sincere. At the same time, they conveniently enabled America's assumption of a moral high ground in international affairs. Some of those who joined in the protests were far more concerned about preventing Jewish immigration into the United States than they were about the fate of the Russian Jews themselves. They hoped that diplomatic pressure on Russia would stop the flow of immigrants by solving the problem at its source. By criticizing Russian anti-Semitism in the language of religious freedom, Americans could highlight a freedom that they believed their nation had long since achieved. By ignoring the racial lens through which Russians themselves viewed the anti-Semitic pogroms and by foregrounding the principle of religious free-dom instead, they could also ignore the rising tides of racial discrimination and violence in the United States.

Russian diplomats at the time were quick to challenge the hypocrisy they saw in this campaign. After the Kishineff massacres in 1903, President Theodore Roosevelt agreed to forward a petition to the czar with signatures from thousands of U.S. citizens. They named the victims as "Jews assaulted because of racial and religious prejudices" and demanded that every Rus-sian subject be granted the right to "worship according to the dictates of his own conscience."[19] But the Russian government refused to accept this petition. A statement from its Foreign Office denounced the appeal as inter-ference in Russia's internal affairs and commented that the United States would for the same reason "resent an anti-lynching petition" from Russia. By locating a parallel with America's own regimes of racial violence, this response defined Jews in racial terms. This too was a self-serving way to frame the conflict, since it deflected attention back to the United States. But it effectively exposed the hypocrisy of white Americans who advocated reli-gious freedom for Jews in Russia without addressing the racial injustices in their own society. As this example suggests, Jewish efforts to be recognized as a religious rather than a racial minority meshed easily with celebrations of religious freedom that, in effect, worked to obscure the most egregious lines of racial discrimination in American life.[20]

Advocacy for persecuted Jews abroad may seem disconnected from the horrors of American racism. But by condemning Russian anti-Semitism as a violation of religious freedom, white Americans could celebrate their own nation as the land of liberty and so masked the reality of racial oppression against people of color inside the United States. Baltimore's *Afro-American* offered much the same diagnosis when, after applauding the crusade for "civil and religious liberty . . . on behalf of the downtrodden Jew on Rus-sian soil," its editors opined that those who were so concerned with liberty should "ring down the curtain on Russia for only five minutes" to consider the plight of the "colored Americans" in their own country. "While the battle of civil liberty is going on for those who are thousands of miles away," they wrote, "let us have at least one word in behalf of the downtrodden at home." While the *Afro-American* affirmed the reformers' attention to the problem of religious freedom abroad, this editorial suggested that a single-minded focus on this concern allowed white Americans to ignore racial oppression in their own communities and to celebrate America, the home of religious freedom, as uniquely free.[21]

Jewish Nationhood and the Zionist Movement

Over the course of the nineteenth century, the cultural and legal value of religious freedom in the United States had encouraged American Jews to define their communal interests in the language of religion. In so doing, even those Jews who remained outside the Reform movement came to understand what it meant to be Jewish in primarily religious terms. The events of the early twentieth century would challenge this communal self-definition. In response to the growth of a racialized anti-Semitism and with the arrival of so many Jewish migrants from eastern Europe, American Jews increasingly found themselves attracted to the Zionist movement and its campaign for Jewish nationhood. As more and more Jews understood their identities through the lens of race and nation, rather than of religion, the role of religious freedom talk would temporarily decline.

The Zionist movement had first taken shape in western Europe, where its leaders were disillusioned by the failed promises of political emancipation and the growth of anti-Semitism across the continent. Zionists argued that the only way to secure Jewish safety was to create an independent Jewish nation, either in Palestine or wherever an independent polity could be formed. In contrast to the Reform movement, Zionists insisted that it was the survival of the Jews as a race or nation that counted most. The early Zionist leaders had little or no concern about Judaism as a religion. And while they certainly supported the idea of religious freedom for Jews around the world, the movement's basic priorities made this principle relatively unimportant to its public appeals.[22]

Across the global Jewish diaspora, Zionism was far from the only alternative to the Reform model of what it meant to be Jewish. Particularly in eastern Europe, Zionism coexisted and competed with a homegrown Jewish nationalism that advocated political autonomy for the Jews, along with other national minorities, in the countries where they already lived. The nationalist movement envisioned self-governing Jewish nations that could be geographically located within states conceived as confederations of such people-groups. Like some Zionists, they went so far as to dismiss the Enlightenment goals of Jewish emancipation, citizenship, and assimilation within the existing European nation-states. Observing resurgent tides of anti-Semitism even in France and Germany, they argued that the vaunted achievements of emancipation were destroying the richness of Jewish communal traditions without solving the problem of Jewish difference. In contrast to the Zionists, they argued that these goals were not just unattainable but actually undesirable for Jews. Even if the promise of individual rights and freedoms could be realized, nationalists viewed them as ultimately homogenizing, their eventual consequence the erasure of any distinctly Jewish way of life.

The new immigrants brought other formations of Jewishness, too, that were distinct from the Reform, Zionist, or nationalist alternatives. Marxists diagnosed the ills of capitalism, viewing themselves as part of a global working class or as the intelligentsia that would help support the coming socialist revolution; some of these abandoned their attachments to any distinctly Jewish identity at all. Others came as members of a proliferating number of Hasidic sects, each focused on the leadership of a charismatic rebbe and emphasizing a joyful piety and ardent devotion. But perhaps the largest number had been shaped by the orthodox rabbinic tradition, with its focus on the study of Torah and Talmud in the yeshivas that had become so central to eastern European Jewish life. The overwhelming majority of Hasidic and Orthodox Jewish leaders saw the secular orientation of Zionism as a threat to observant Judaism and taught that the Jews were to return to Israel only upon the coming of the Messiah. All of these groups had adjusted to transformed conditions in eastern Europe and no longer assumed the all-encompassing, self-governing Jewish communities that had once been the eastern European norm. Nevertheless, they did not conceive of Jewish difference in singularly religious terms. In other words, they did not see their Jewishness exclusively or even primarily as a religious issue that could be separated from the other aspects of their lives and identities.[23]

The Reform leaders who made up the American Jewish old guard unequivocally condemned the Zionist movement. They considered the goal of a Jewish nation or even of a Jewish homeland, whether in Palestine or anywhere else, to be deeply flawed for both pragmatic and theological reasons. In an 1897 resolution, the Central Conference of American Rabbis (CCAR) denounced "political Zionism" on the grounds that Jews were "not a nation, but a religious community," and that the "mission of Judaism is spiritual not political." These Reform leaders saw Zionism as a real threat to the integrity of Judaism. It distracted Jews from the spiritual concerns that religion should properly address, they argued, and advocated an improperly political sense of what it meant to be Jewish. They feared, as well, that Zionism could further endanger their always-tentative acceptance as equal participants in American life. By presenting Jews as a national as well as a religious group, they argued, Zionists would cast suspicion on the patriotic loyalties of all Jews. The attempt to create a Jewish state would only "harm our Jewish brethren where they are still persecuted," the CCAR resolution explained, "by confirming the assertion of their enemies that the Jews are foreigners in the countries in which they are at home."[24]

Through the early twentieth century, many Reform leaders would continue to insist that political emancipation and its framework of citizenship and individual liberties were the only realistic solutions, whether in Europe or in the United States. Abram Isaacs, a rabbi and professor of Semitics at New York University, described Zionism in the *North American Review* as dysfunctionally myopic, a product of the immigrants' experiences of violence and isolation. "While not primarily responsible for the medieval Ghetto into which he was cast like a hunted criminal," he wrote, "[the Jew] is at fault if in lands that assure him civil and religious freedom he retains a trace of the Ghetto spirit." Isaacs went on to define Judaism as rational, ethical, and focused on human betterment, a "necessary religion" for the modern world. Zionist demonstrations waving "the flag of Judah" were, he wrote several years later, "utterly foreign to Judaism." Isaacs and other critics worried that Zionism would corrupt Judaism's spiritual purity and call Jewish patriotism into question even in the countries that had been most welcoming to them. They countered this movement by trying to build public awareness among both Jews and Gentiles of Judaism as a religion.[25]

Yet as the barrage of violence against Jews in eastern Europe continued and the problem of anti-Semitism grew even in France and Germany, Zionism attracted more and more converts from every sector of American Jewish life. Many of the new Zionists were recent immigrants, eastern European Jews who had never been convinced by the Reform vision of Jewishness as an exclusively religious classification. But the Zionist movement also claimed some prominent leaders from within the Reform movement, such as Columbia University professor Richard Gottheil, future Supreme Court justice Louis Brandeis, and the indefatigable Rabbi Stephen S. Wise of New York. From a practical and economic standpoint, Gottheil argued in 1899, something had to be done for "the millions of Jews in Russia who want[ed] to leave" and were not wanted in England, America, or anywhere else in the world. Establishing a new homeland for them in Palestine, the land of their ancestors, was in Gottheil's view an elegant solution. Among other things, it would avoid the difficulty of dealing with such Jews as immigrants to the United States.[26]

Zionists saw no conflict between the principle of religious freedom and the creation of a Jewish state. On the contrary, they argued that such a state would finally secure this freedom. Gottheil was a Zionist for reasons that he categorized as both political and religious. Once the Jews became a majority in Palestine, they could finally observe their own Sabbath without disturbance, he explained, and in that land of their origin the Jewish festivals would be seasonally appropriate once again. "Palestine is the place where we can live that Jewish life we are called upon to live," he wrote, "and only there can we take up the greater work for preparing for the Messianic time."[27] Zionists even outside the United States linked their movement to the American ideal of religious freedom. Max Nordau, who like many other French Jews had become a Zionist after the blatant anti-Semitism of the Dreyfus affair, suggested in 1900 that the United States would inevitably support the movement because the "Zionistic Jews, looking for a harbor of safety where they may follow their faith," had so much in common with the "Pilgrim Fathers." Zionism, like America, was founded "on the basis of liberty, fraternity, and respect for human rights."[28]

Yet when Zionists advocated for Jews abroad, they gave far less priority than did the Reform-minded American Jewish establishment to the principle of religious freedom. After the horrendous Kishineff massacres of 1903, the Zionists of Baltimore presented a Jewish "national flag" to President Roosevelt to thank him for his efforts on behalf of the Jews in Russia. Their statement to the president countered the specter of dual loyalties, which critics saw as a fatal weakness in Zionism, by positioning themselves as wholehearted American patriots. "As loyal American citizens," they wrote, "with a loyal love for the history of not only the American Nation, but the noble claims of our race as well, we beg to present to a most loyal American President the sacred flag of Zion." These Zionists identified themselves, as Jews, in both racial and national terms. Their commitment to the anticipated Jewish nation was a racial obligation, fully consistent with and, at least in this presentation, subordinate to their dedication to the United States. Nowhere in this presentation did the Baltimore Zionists mention religion or the freedom of religion. They did stress their faith in "the prophecy of God" and "the indisputable lessons taught us in the Holy Book," thus demonstrating that they were observant Jews. But instead of religion they foregrounded race and nation as the most useful ways to frame Jewish identity. In so doing, the Zionist movement signaled a turn away from religious freedom as the primary method to articulate and defend Jewish interests in the modern world.[29]

Within a decade after they began to organize in the United States, Zionists had gained so much ground that those who maintained the classic Reform position had already been placed on the defensive. At a 1909 meeting of the Board of Delegates on Civil and Religious Rights, chairman Simon Wolf complained of Zionist interference in his efforts to ensure the equal treatment of Jewish immigrants. Wolf had long battled the classification of these immigrants according to either race or religion. He told the commissioner of immigration in 1899 that identifying them by religion would be better than the racial alternative, as long as all immigrants were treated the same way, but that the method most in keeping with the Constitution would be not to classify them at all. Now he reported that the Immigration Commission of the U.S. Senate had sent out questionnaires that treated "the Jew . . . as belonging to a nationality" and advised that the Board of Delegates request a hearing to explain their objections to that policy. Unfortunately, he reported, "the Zionists had [already] appeared before the commission, approving the distinction, making it the more important that this matter should receive early attention at our hands." Much to Wolf's dismay, Zionists had become influential enough to present themselves before the U.S. Senate as the representatives of American Judaism—and had come out in favor of the classification of the Jews as a national group rather than a religious one.[30]

Minority Rights and the Problem of Religious Freedom

The changing balance of power within American Judaism was evident through the First World War and its aftermath, when the Zionists and their opponents offered distinctly different visions for the future of the Jews both in Europe and in Palestine. The American Jewish Committee, founded in 1906 to coordinate Jewish advocacy efforts, represented an elite and mostly Reform-oriented constituency. Its leaders generally celebrated America and its traditions of religious freedom, advanced the classic Reform understanding of Jewishness as religion, and normally preferred to work behind the scenes through their own contacts in the centers of power. When they began to formulate recommendations for the postwar status of Jews in the European war zones, they called for treaties that would secure for Jews "those elementary rights denied to no other people," most especially "to worship God according to the dictates of their conscience."[31] In support of this position, immigration lawyer Max Kohler wrote a history of minority rights as formulated at major international congresses. Surveying the major peace conferences and treaties of the prior century, Kohler concluded that they had forged "an almost unbroken chain of precedents" for "liberty of conscience and equality of rights, regardless of creed."[32] For Reform-minded leaders like Kohler, the freedom of religion was quite clearly the most important right to secure for the future of the Jews in Europe and around the world.

Advancing a very different position was the American Jewish Congress, formed in 1916 in hopes of providing a representative voice for all sectors of American Jewry. That goal had considerable appeal within the growing immigrant community, which felt almost entirely disconnected from either the American Jewish Committee or any other established Jewish organization in the United States. Immediately the question of Zionism came to the forefront. While the congress's stated goals were not necessarily Zionist, its leading lights sympathized with that movement, and it was soon clear that most of their constituents agreed. As articulated by its new executive committee that fall, the organization's goals were to secure "full rights for the Jews of all lands, including group rights wherever such are desired by the Jews themselves," and "the securing and protection of Jewish rights in Palestine." While voicing support for "civil, religious, and political rights," this statement placed little emphasis on the idea of religious freedom. Rather, it stressed "group rights" as a more practical solution for Jews in much of the world than any guarantee of individual freedoms could be. In other words, the American Jewish Congress assumed a more comprehensive sense of Jewish peoplehood than an exclusive focus on religion would allow. In a compromise designed to secure the widest possible support across the American Jewish community, it called not for a Jewish state as such but simply for a guarantee of "Jewish rights in Palestine."[33]

The first major political victory for Zionism came with the Balfour Declaration of November 1917, when the British foreign secretary announced his government's support for "the establishment in Palestine of a national home for the Jewish people," with the caveat that "nothing shall be done to prejudice the civil and religious rights of existing non-Jewish communities in Palestine, or the rights and political status enjoyed by Jews in any other country." Like the American Jewish Congress statement, this wording neatly finessed the question of exactly what kind of polity would exist in postwar Palestine. It promised a "national home" for Jews without mentioning the idea of a Jewish state. On the other hand, it guaranteed "civil and religious" but not national rights for the Palestinians. The statement had no immediate consequences on the ground, since at the time Palestine remained under the control of the Ottoman Empire. But it was a moderate statement of support for Zionism that also signaled the British imperial goal of claiming Palestine after the war. And when British forces occupied Jerusalem soon thereafter, British rule and a favorable policy for Jewish settlement in postwar Palestine suddenly seemed like a likely prospect.[34]

The Balfour Declaration and the British occupation of Palestine noticeably shifted the terms of American Jewish debate, adding further momentum to the Zionists and their view of what it meant to be Jewish. For many Jews, these events sparked an unexpectedly emotional response and gave Zionism a sense of imminent success that was difficult to resist. "Now at last, after nineteen hundred years of national incoherence, and homelessness, we are assured of a national rehabilitation in Palestine," wrote Sephardic rabbi David de Sola Pool of New York. These developments also reveal how intimately tied the trajectories of Jewish history were to the imperial expansions of the time. "Britain understands colonization as no other imperial power has ever understood it," Pool enthused. "Her promised cooperation in the Jewish national development of Palestine is, therefore, an invaluable asset to our Jewish national aspirations."[35]

Immediately, the American Jewish Committee backed away from any open opposition to Zionism and issued a rather circumspect statement of its "profound appreciation" for this British expression of support for the Jews. The committee clearly affirmed the right of those Jews who sought a home in Palestine, either as refugees or for reasons of "traditional sentiment," to do so. At the same time, its statement emphasized the "essential importance" of the British promise to protect the rights of the "non-Jewish communities in Palestine," along with the "rights and political status enjoyed by Jews in any other country." The committee went on to insist that most Jews would remain loyal citizens of their own countries, "where they enjoy full civil and religious liberty, and where, as loyal and patriotic citizens, they will maintain and develop the principles and institutions of Judaism." While affirming the legitimacy of Jewish settlement in Palestine, then, the American Jewish Committee restated the classic Reform idea that being Jewish was a matter of religion and not a national identity of any kind.[36]

President Woodrow Wilson's support for the Balfour Declaration added still more credibility and momentum to the Zionist cause. In August 1918 Wilson congratulated Rabbi Stephen S. Wise, then president of the American Jewish Congress, on "the progress of the Zionist movement" toward "a national home for the Jewish people." Wilson had come to see the goals of Zionism in terms of national self-determination, one of the principles advanced in his Fourteen Points for the postwar world order. Despite the Reform movement's long efforts to reclassify the Jews as a purely religious group, the president's letter to Wise suggested that he too viewed them as a race or a nation with the right to a national identity of their own.[37]

In this climate, those Reform leaders who continued to speak out against Zionism encountered more and more opposition. According to Rabbi Louis Wolsey of Cleveland, Ohio, Cincinnati's "fanatical" Yiddish daily had "been able to whip its group into a fanatic furor." Even though he had not directly mentioned Zionism in his recent address in that city, he reported, his opponents had held a "mass meeting" to attack him for "giving vent to anti-Zionistic propaganda."[38] Controversy flared, especially in the Zionist stronghold of New York, after Rabbi Abram Frisch of New York, secretary of the CCAR, telegrammed President Wilson that "thousands of Jews" considered nationalism "a menace to Judaism" both because it threatened to "eclipse . . . our religious interests by political concerns" and because "a Jewish state would tend to distract our coreligionists here from a full and perfect allegiance to American citizenship."[39] Frisch was roundly condemned for sending this telegram without the executive committee's express approval. In one agonizing letter, Rabbi Samuel Schulman of New York's Temple Beth-El resigned from the CCAR, of which he had once been president, because, he explained, the Zionists were now "portraying [that organization] as anti-Semitic, pro-German, as if they were not happy that Palestine is going to the Allies." Schulman could no longer be part of any organization in which Frisch held a leadership role.[40]

Only the most firmly committed anti-Zionists would join the new League of American Judaism, organized by Frisch and Rabbi David Philipson with the goal of advancing the traditional Reform conception of Judaism. None other than Oscar Straus, the biographer of Roger Williams and champion of religious freedom, sent his regrets. Straus wrote that although he continued to oppose the idea of a Jewish state, he considered anti-Zionist agitation at the present time to be "distinctively unwise and harmful" to Jewish interests around the world.[41] Still the league persevered. Its petition to the postwar Paris Peace Conference attacked Zionism as a violation of modern ideals and a threat to the interests of racial and religious minorities everywhere: "Whether the Jews be regarded as a 'race' or a 'religion,' it is contrary to the democratic principle for which the world war was waged to found a nation on either or both of these bases. America, England, France, Italy, Switzerland, and all the most advanced nations of the world are composed of representatives of many races and religions. Their glory lies in that freedom of conscience and worship . . . that binds the followers of many faiths and varied civilizations in the common bonds of political union."[42] According to the stalwarts of the league, Zionism stood against the principle of religious freedom, the highest ideals of secular modernity, and the religion of Judaism itself.

Whatever their stand on Zionism, American Jews agreed that the peace conference offered an opportunity to improve conditions for the world's Jews, especially in eastern Europe. The question of religious freedom would be hotly debated in Paris, first of all in the negotiations over a covenant for the new League of Nations. All the American Jewish delegates favored a clause that would require member nations to guarantee religious freedom to their citizens, but they disagreed about its relative importance. Where the Reform-minded CCAR and the American Jewish Committee clearly prioritized this issue, the American Jewish Congress called first for "a Jewish Palestine" and then for a more general clause ensuring that the "subjects and citizens" of all countries would be treated "without distinction of creed, race or language, on a footing of perfect equality." When it became clear that the final covenant would not specifically protect religious freedom, some blamed the Zionists. Rabbi Isaac Landman, representing the CCAR in Paris, publicly accused the American Jewish Congress of having ignored the "religious liberty clause," focusing solely on Palestine and so failing to secure "protection for all the Jews of all the world." One of the Zionists in Paris, he claimed, had actually advised a member of the U.S. delegation that the clause on religious liberty "would prove detrimental" to Zionism.[43]

As many observers noted at the time, the main reason that negotiators omitted the religious freedom clause from the covenant was that the United States and other world powers refused to accept any challenge to their own racial orders, a concern they phrased in the language of internal sovereignty. Despite modernity's attempts to separate them, the classifications of race and religion were tightly bound up in these negotiations. In the words of the *Boston Daily Globe*, the issue of religious freedom had become "entangled" with a "racial equality" clause proposed by the Japanese that prohibited discrimination against the citizens of fellow member states. "If there is any possibility that Japan is trying to pry open the League of Nations covenant and to insert provisions that the yellow races shall be received everywhere among the League of Nations as freely as Caucasians—in other words, if the Asiatic exclusion rule is lifted," reported the *Los Angeles Times*, then "the Roman Catholics and the Jews intend to fight for incorporation in the League Covenant of an article providing for religious freedom for inhabitants of all countries which are members of the League."[44] Because the United States and Australia did not want their restrictions on Asian immigration challenged, they rejected Japan's proposal as an infringement on national sovereignty. The nations of eastern Europe rejected any provision on religious freedom on the same grounds. Since any measure needed unanimous approval, neither the racial equality nor religious freedom provisions ultimately made it into the covenant.[45]

Once again, American Jewish advocacy efforts could not be separated from the global assemblages of race and empire. Taking imperial hierarchies for granted, Jewish leaders placed the Jews on the civilized side of the ledger. Isaac Landman's article on the League of Nation's failure to protect Jewish rights was subtitled "Religious Liberty for African Savages—But Not for Jews." Landman described how the world powers had rejected the religious freedom guarantee along with the ban on racial discrimination. He then explained that the covenant's articles on governing those peoples judged "not yet able to stand by themselves under the strenuous conditions of the modern world" mandated that they be granted "freedom of conscience or religion, subject only to the maintenance of public order and morals." Landman thought it a profound irony that "the savages of Central Africa," whom he took for granted were "incapable of self-government," would enjoy this protection while Jews, who had "demonstrated every capacity for citizenship" and had experienced centuries of persecution "on account of their religion," were not. In this way Landman used religious freedom talk to depict the Jews, in contrast to the racialized "savages" of Africa, as civilized and implicitly white.[46]

Having lost the battle for religious freedom in the League of Nations covenant, American Jewish leaders turned their attention to the treaty negotiations that would shape postwar Europe. Far more was at stake in Paris than just the conditions of peace between the existing powers. The dismemberment of the Austro-Hungarian, Russian, and Ottoman Empires meant that the victors would gain new territories and that a variety of new states would be formed. The shape of these reorganized polities was to be negotiated at the conference and the conditions of their existence secured by treaty. The status of their "national minorities," including the Jews, was a key topic in these negotiations.[47] Several of the nascent nation-states, most prominently Poland and Romania, objected to any provision on minority group rights as both counterproductive for the minorities and an infringement on their internal sovereignty. As a key figure in these negotiations, President Wilson supported minority rights in principle but agreed that any language granting them "national rights" would only mark minorities as permanently separate populations and so render them "liable to jealousy and attack." Instead Wilson advocated for religious freedom guarantees in every treaty, thus construing the Jews as a *religious* minority more than a racial or a national grouping.[48] But Romania's premier objected even to this idea, contending that since the Great Powers had already refused to incorporate a religious freedom clause in the covenant for the League of Nations, it was both hypocritical and unfair for them to impose such requirements on other states.[49]

In the end, to the delight of the American Jews active in the negotiations, the postwar treaties protected both a limited version of minority group rights and individual civil liberties, including the freedom of religion. The Polish Minorities Treaty, finalized in June 1919, became a model for those that followed. It guaranteed "the protection of life and liberty, and religious freedom," for all inhabitants of Poland "without distinction of birth, nationality, language, race or religion." At the same time it authorized all "racial, religious, or linguistic minorities" to establish and control their own educational, religious, and social institutions "with the right to use their own language and exercise their religion freely therein." The treaty also promised specific protection to Jewish Sabbath observances. Thus the postwar European order guaranteed civil liberties to every individual, regardless of identity. It also granted minority groups the right to maintain their own religious practices and cultural institutions. These treaties presented religious freedom as both an individual and a collective right. But they stopped short of the more politically oriented national rights for which the Jewish nationalists of eastern Europe had advocated and provided no clear mechanism to enforce the rights they had guaranteed.[50]

This history reveals some of the limits of religious freedom for Jews and by extension other racial-religious minorities in Europe. As we have seen, religious freedom had historically been the primary frame for Jewish advocacy efforts within the United States. But Jewish identity as socially and legally constituted in most other parts of the world could not be contained by this approach. For that reason, the Zionists and Jewish nationalists sought more expansive solutions, attempting to place Judaism within the equally modern framework of the nation rather than (or in addition to) identifying it as religion. As the debates over the Minorities Treaties suggest, states like Poland and Romania saw such proposals as a far greater threat than was the freedom of religion alone to their national sovereignty. Religious freedom thus became a fallback solution in these treaties, a minimal guarantee that could be easily accepted because its demands were relatively circumscribed. The tragedies of Jewish history in the decades that followed would only confirm these limits.

FROM RACIAL BROTHERHOOD TO TRI-FAITH AMERICA: PROTESTANTS, CATHOLICS, AND JEWS IN THE ROARING TWENTIES

In contrast to the situation in eastern Europe, the ideal of religious freedom remained as a fundamental cultural and political ideal in the postwar United States. Whatever their position on Zionism, most American Jews in the 1920s and 1930s would continue to invoke this principle. They highlighted the language of religion to build a sense of common cause with Protestants and Catholics and to combat a rising tide of anti-Semitism in the United States. Catholics and Protestants had their own reasons to articulate their concerns through the lens of religious freedom, as we will see. As these interests converged, the emerging tri-faith movement of the early 1930s would more and more successfully advance a new model of American religion as Protestant, Catholic, and Jewish. In so doing, this movement collectively recategorized the Jews as a religious rather than a racial minority in American life. Religious freedom talk thus supported the American Jewish struggle for religious equality against a racially defined anti-Semitism and ultimately for a position of relative racial privilege within the United States.

Redefining the Jew: Race, Religion, and the Ku Klux Klan

As the trauma of the First World War receded, the decade of the 1920s emerged as a time of remarkable cultural vitality but also of racial conflict and ideological extremes. The disjuncture between President Wilson's wartime rhetorics of freedom and democracy on the one hand and his reaffirmation of white supremacy on the other sparked new movements for civil rights and civil liberties that continued to develop after the war.[51] Meanwhile, unprecedented levels of immigration and urbanization were fundamentally transforming the country's cultural and demographic landscape. By 1920, as historian David Kennedy writes, these twin forces had "turned urban America into a kind of polyglot archipelago in the predominantly Anglo-Protestant American sea." All these changes helped spark a vibrant burst of new cultural production—the movements of artistic and literary modernism, the Harlem Renaissance, a flourishing jazz scene, flapper culture, and the emergence of first-wave feminism—that collectively inspired the moniker "Roaring Twenties."[52]

At the same time, the nation's shifting demographics stimulated new tensions. Some members of the Anglo-Protestant majority responded to the cultural moment with a sense of dislocation and an anxiety that fueled new xenophobic movements around the country. Recreated in 1915, the Ku Klux Klan became the most prominent such group, its white robes and burning crosses emerging as the signature public theatrics of white Protestant nativism. The assemblages of race and religion were inseparable in its calculations. The "Nordic race" had a "spiritual independence" that "found its chief expression in Protestantism," wrote Imperial Wizard Hiram Evans. "The future of progress and civilization depends," he asserted, "on the continued supremacy of the white race . . . not only in America but in the world." The KKK of the 1920s directed as much of its venom against Catholic and Jewish immigrants as it did against black Americans, whose subordination in the nation's racial order already seemed well secured. Evans wanted to convince his fellow Americans that, like the Negro, the new Jewish and Catholic immigrants were *racially* incapable of the "Nordic . . . independence, self-reliance, and freedom" that made America great. Evans called on "the children of the Pioneers" to take America back from those who were bent on its destruction.[53]

In no way did the Klan represent all white Protestants. Yet in the mid-1920s it was strong enough to swing elections in a number of states, most notably Oregon and Indiana. And many white Protestants who found its extremes distasteful nevertheless shared its basic view of Jews, Catholics, African Americans, and any other racial-religious minorities as outside the definitional bounds of the true American. These xenophobic impulses facilitated the passage of the National Origins Act of 1924, which imposed strict quotas on immigration into the United States based on race and nation of origin. America's freedoms, nativists were convinced, depended on protecting its Anglo-Protestant essence from the sinister designs and the sullying presence of non-white and non-Protestant others.[54]

American Jewish leaders responded to this climate by circling the wagons, projecting as much as they could an image of patriotism, consensus, and moderation. The domestic climate was especially alarming in an era of resurgent global anti-Semitism. Jews in Latvia, Russia, Romania, Hungary, and elsewhere were suffering renewed legal discriminations and new episodes of mob violence. The hard-won protections of the Minorities Treaties seemed to make precious little difference on the ground; the League of Nations appeared either uninterested or powerless to intervene.[55] The conflicts between Jewish organizations had in no way been resolved, but they generally avoided criticizing one another in public. Only occasionally did they attempt to challenge practices such as Bible reading and prayers in the public schools or the blue laws that forced the observance of a Sunday

Sabbath. They reasoned that such standards and practices were not intentionally discriminatory but aimed to support the religious convictions of the majority population. Opposing them with too much vehemence could spark a backlash, they feared, further fueling the anti-Semitic fire.[56]

An essay by Rabbi David Philipson, "Henry Ford's Campaign of Hatred," expressed the sense of alarm that many Jews were feeling. Philipson accused the automaker, well known for his virulent attacks on Jews, of recycling a host of "old weary anti-Semitic charges." "If a group of international Jewish bankers really form such an invisible super empire as is charged in these and similar screeds," he asked, "is it conceivable that such a mighty power would permit their coreligionists to suffer all the indescribable tortures that millions of hapless Jews have undergone and are still undergoing in various countries of Eastern Europe?" The only Jewish "conspiracy" that actually existed, the rabbi wrote in frustration, was the effort to aid "the suffering myriads . . . in Eastern Europe." Ford's campaign was completely opposed to the "American ideals of true freedom and brotherhood," he concluded, behind which all true Americans would need to unite "against the barriers erected by hatred and prejudice."[57]

Jewish organizations focused their efforts during this period on overt instances of discrimination, and once again they emphasized the all-American principle of religious freedom. Max Kohler of the American Jewish Committee framed his protests against discriminatory quotas in college admissions squarely through the patriotic values of democracy and liberty. Quoting Thomas Jefferson on religious freedom and the rights of the Jews, Kohler wrote that most Americans had believed that the "American policy of opposition to all race and creed discrimination along educational lines had been safely established soon after our government was organized."[58] No longer could "a few religio-political conspirators" plot in secret for "restrictive and repressive measures," commented the *American Israelite* when the U.S. Supreme Court ruled an Oregon statute banning parochial schools unconstitutional. Openly backed by the KKK, this law had joined proposals around the country to make Bible reading compulsory in the public schools, enforce the observance of Sunday as a day of rest, and in various ways mandate public observances of Protestant Christianity. The well-intentioned Protestant majority, the paper hoped, would now join together against "the imposition of the ecclesiastical mob."[59]

The growing restrictions on Jewish immigration into the United States presented another challenge, one that pivoted on the problem of classification. Kohler commented in 1921 that in keeping with "the whole trend of the Reform movement . . . towards regarding the Jews as a religious sect merely," he and other Jewish leaders had fought long and hard against the Immigration Bureau's persistent efforts to classify Jews "as 'Hebrews,' where that classification was not on religious lines." This problem intersected with the ability of Jewish immigrants to gain citizenship, Kohler pointed out, since U.S. law allowed for the naturalization only of "free white persons" or "African persons and persons of African descent," and several federal judges had interpreted "free white persons" as "synonymous with 'European Aryans.' " If the government racially categorized the Jews as Hebrews or Semites, he noted, then the Jews along with anyone else judged non-Aryan would according to these rulings be ineligible.[60]

In fact the majority of American Jewish leaders opposed any government program that would count or categorize Jews either as a race or a religion, arguing that any such classification opened the door for discrimination. If the Immigration Bureau was not tracking the number of Baptists, Lutherans, or Catholics coming into the country, they asked, then why should the Jews be singled out? "There is no religious qualification for the citizens of this country," commented the *American Israelite*, "and none should be set up to bar or to favor any particular religionist at our gateway."[61] Yet it turned out that in some cases, a separate classification for Jews could be helpful. In 1921 Simon Wolf of the Union of American Hebrew Congregations took advantage of that policy for several Turkish Jews who had been denied entry to the United States because "the Turkish quota [was] filled." "Since [the Immigration Bureau] classified Jews by their religion and not by nationality," he argued, "these women do not come within the quota, although they are Turks." Naming them as Jews proved advantageous, even though it contradicted Wolf's prior insistence that Jewish immigrants should be identified, like anyone else, only by their country of origin. And although he described this classification as religious and not racial, most officials in the Immigration Bureau clearly understood it in racial terms.[62]

With a racialized anti-Semitism on the rise in the 1920s, American Jews had been placed on the defensive. Focusing on the problems that seemed most urgent, they cast about for any strategy that would defend their communities against the rising tides of xenophobia and discrimination. Particularly for the Reform-minded leaders who continued to dominate the worlds of Jewish advocacy and reform, this often meant a return to religious freedom. At other times, it meant pragmatically accepting the classifications of race and nation. Even in America, religious freedom did not always have the power to transcend the racializing assemblages of an imperial world.

Religious freedom had its limits, to be sure. But given the racial inequities of American society and the cultural status and legal protections granted to religion in the United States, there were some definite advantages to religious freedom talk and the communal self-definition that it implied. As the global situation for Jews grew ever more alarming, American Jewish leaders sought alliances with likeminded Protestants and Catholics whose support, they hoped, could reverse the tides of anti-Semitism in the United States and around the world. The question of classification—were the Jews to be understood primarily as a race, a nation, or a religion?—proved crucial in that endeavor.

The challenge was that just about everyone else at the time, even the liberal Protestant ecumenists who were inclined to support Jewish rights, tended to see Jews as a race. When the executive committee of the Federal Council of Churches (FCC) issued a resolution against anti-Semitism in 1920, it assumed that classification when it called on American Christians to repudiate all "publications tending to create race prejudice . . . against our Jewish fellow-citizens."[63] The parallel structure of the FCC's outreach efforts to Jews and to black churches confirmed this model. Lamenting the rise of mob violence against African Americans in northern cities, the FCC charged its Commission on Negro Churches and Race Relations in 1922 with "bringing about a greater spirit of brotherhood between the white and colored people in our country."[64] At the same time, the new FCC Committee on Goodwill between Jews and Christians took on the problem of anti-Semitism with the goal of ending "racial antipathies" and creating a new "spirit of brotherhood" in American life. The identical language used to describe the work of these committees reflected the FCC's categorization of both Jews and African Americans primarily through the lens of race.[65]

The categories of race and religion were, as always, intertwined, and the question of Jewish identity was particularly complex. Liberal Protestants slipped easily between them, especially when it came to the thorny topic of evangelizing the Jews. It turns out that the impetus for the new Committee on Goodwill between Jews and Christians had as much to do with evangelical Protestant desires as it did with ecumenical concerns about anti-Semitism. According to the FCC *Bulletin*, the idea for the committee had emerged out of "several informal conferences between a group of Christian ministers who are especially interested in the work of the Home Missions Council, and a group of Jewish rabbis." Jews held special significance in

Christian theology as the divinely "chosen people," giving them a special place in most renderings of salvation history and making them the targets of persistent evangelical fascination.[66] Yet because Protestant home missionaries typically targeted groups they considered problematic in one way or another—new immigrants, racial minorities, and the urban poor—this evangelical impulse did not necessarily undermine the dominant classification of the Jews as a race. "Our loyalty to Jesus," noted Goodwill Committee chair Rev. Alfred Williams Anthony regretfully, often "causes us to hesitate about closer cooperation with the race of Jesus." Even as Anthony celebrated the achievement of "interreligious" gatherings in recognizing at last the "spiritual kinship" of Jews and Christians, his first impulse was to speak of the Jews first and foremost as a race.[67]

The FCC's focus on racial brotherhood had developed in part out of the organization's global sense of mission. In the wake of the war and in keeping with President Wilson's call to "make the world safe for democracy," these ecumenical Protestant leaders advocated a global "brotherhood of man" to replace the hatreds of the past. The problem they diagnosed was essentially one of racial hatred, and their proposed solutions reflected a Wilsonian view of America's benevolent role in the world.[68] In the words of Arthur Judson Brown, general secretary of the Presbyterian Board of Foreign Missions and chair of the FCC's Commission on Relief for Protestant Churches in France and Belgium, the task of the churches was to bring Christian principles to bear on the problems of the world. They alone could transcend the ancient racial or "tribal" conflicts that had caused the Great War.[69] (Earlier in his career Brown had taken special interest in the Philippines, interpreting American rule and Protestant missions as twin forces for democracy and "religious liberty" in the islands, an involvement that illustrates once again the close intersections of Protestant religious freedom talk with U.S. imperial expansions.)[70] As the United States positioned itself for a new level of global authority in the postwar world, ecumenical leaders viewed the domestic problems of racial intolerance and discrimination as a serious embarrassment, undermining America's claim to moral leadership around the world. At home as well as abroad, racial intolerance and racial hatred were the problems; the Christian spirit of brotherhood was the solution.

American Jewish leaders immediately challenged the Goodwill Committee's emphasis on race. Rabbi David Philipson of Cincinnati, a former president of the CCAR, praised the goodwill movement as "the logical outcome of the pioneer planting of the seed of religious liberty by the founders of our government." Philipson, as we have seen, had always supported the classic

Reform view of Jewish identity as exclusively a matter of religion. When he applauded the goodwill movement for supporting "the rights of free thought, free speech, and free worship" and the rights of "Protestantism, Catholicism, Judaism or any other ism" to be freely practiced, he implicitly redefined the new movement as one centered not on racial brotherhood but on interreligious dialogue and religious freedom.[71]

In contrast to Philipson, the rabbis who were on the receiving end of the FCC's initial outreach efforts in the New York area were well aware of their interlocutors' missionary agenda. Rabbi Samuel Schulman, another former CCAR president, explained to Philipson in 1924 that when Rev. Alfred Williams Anthony had initiated the first round of conversations two years earlier, he had also been serving as president of the interdenominational Protestant Home Missions Council. Schulman recalled the revulsion he and other rabbis had experienced at Anthony's comment in one meeting that "we [Protestants] want to help our Jewish brethren to find their Messiah." Alongside his reading of Protestant missionary literature, this incident led Schulman to warn his fellow rabbis that in the minds of most Christians, assurances of "goodwill" were in no way incompatible with "missionary work to the Jews." Although he ultimately judged the FCC's efforts at dialogue to be salutary, with the potential for good results, he advised that those Jews who participated must be well prepared and always on their guard.[72]

Schulman's concerns hinted at the inadequacy of religious freedom and the category of religion as the sole strategies for defending Jewish communal integrity. He saw danger not just in Protestant evangelism but also in liberal religious idealism, including the principle of religious freedom itself. "Anthony contends . . . that Judaism should be taken out of what he calls its national form," Schulman mused to Philipson, while "[John Henry] Holmes contends that liberal Jews and liberal Christians should unite, merge themselves into a theistic Church." Holmes was a celebrated Unitarian minister who had successfully branded his Community Church in New York as the home of free religion and the free conscience. In Schulman's analysis, this only made his position more insidious. The results of both Anthony's and Holmes's proposals were that "the individual should be left free to choose his religion" and that religious affiliation was not to be "a matter of birth or race." Distinguishing so cleanly between race and religion, Schulman argued, undercut any sense of Jewishness as an inherited identity. And this made it far too easy for Protestants to justify their missions to Jews or for those Jews who wanted to escape the stigma of Jewishness to exercise their vaunted freedom of religion by rejecting Judaism and with it their Jewish identity. Like many other Jewish leaders in these years, Schulman had concluded that restricting Jewish identity to religion alone could not address the realities of anti-Semitism or the needs of Jewish communities in the modern world. If pursued in isolation, the idea of religious freedom was not merely insufficient but potentially dangerous as well.[73]

Whether or not they harbored such reservations, Jewish leaders found religious freedom talk indispensable as a way to contend with the threats of anti-Semitism and the vagaries of Protestant outreach. Philadelphia's *Jewish Exponent* commented in 1924 that even those "who profess to be advocates of religious liberty often seek by indirection to interfere with the freedom of conscience of others . . . sometimes by specious efforts to 'convert' the latter, or more frequently to convert their children by various devices that are neither ethical nor fair."[74] At a goodwill dinner between Protestants and Jews in New York, Jewish Theological Seminary president Cyrus Adler argued in a similar vein that although anyone had the right to attempt the conversion of adults, the right of parents "to bring up the children under their care" within the embrace of their own tradition must be respected on both ethical and constitutional grounds. The right of Jewish parents to shape the religious formation of their children had to be protected from evangelical intrusions. Adler defended this position as a matter of both parental rights and religious freedom.[75]

Jewish religious freedom talk and its implicit identification of the Jews as a religious minority had some impact within the early goodwill movement. The *American Israelite* reported in the spring of 1925 that a joint commission of the FCC and the CCAR, representing their respective Committees on Goodwill between Jews and Christians, had just issued a formal "Declaration of Good-Will" with the goal of promoting "mutual understanding . . . in the place of suspicion and ill-will in the entire range of our inter-religious and social relationships." This document disclaimed a "proselytizing purpose" on the part of either Goodwill Committee and affirmed a recent FCC statement denouncing secret societies "whose activities have the effect of arousing religious prejudices and racial antipathies." In a set of accompanying statements, both Protestant ministers and Jewish rabbis emphasized the language of religious freedom. "The forefathers came to this land for religious liberty," said the Reverend L. E. Deer of the Dayton, Ohio, Council of Churches, "and they determined that this freedom of conscience should be not only for themselves but for those who come after them." These statements clearly used the language of religious freedom to denounce any proselytizing aims. In so doing they advanced a subtle shift in framing away from race and toward religion.[76]

The change was tentative and gradual, to be sure. In December 1927 the FCC and the CCAR jointly created the National Conference of Jews and Christians for the Advancement of Justice, Amity and Peace—soon renamed the National Conference of Christians and Jews—to replace their separate Goodwill Committees. From the beginning, the new organization articulated its goals in relation to both race and religion and noted the need to work for brotherhood wherever "religious and racial group lines are sharply defined." Its first public statement of aims clearly prioritized the question of race, with an initial statement of purpose that sought to improve group relations not only between Jews and Christians but more broadly among "Jewish, Protestant, Catholic, Park Avenue, Long Island City, whites, negroes, Italians, Irish, Russian, [and] Chinese." Speakers at the first NCCJ events similarly defined their concerns in racial terms. "We hear much about the Nordic race," said Dr. S. Parkes Cadman at a fund-raising dinner for the new organization. "But I venture to say that there is no Nordic race and never has been. Every person here tonight is a glorious mongrel. Let us rejoice in that. It is the mixture of our blood which goes to make up the human race in all its diversities." Such statements suggest the degree to which the early NCCJ understood its task as one of racial goodwill as much as or even more than one of religious harmony. Yet its outreach to the range of racial minorities named in that early mission statement remained virtually nonexistent. Instead, NCCJ activities would attend almost entirely to the problem of Christian-Jewish relations.[77]

Forging Alliances: The Dawn of the Tri-faith Movement

By the early 1930s the NCCJ would shift its rhetorical emphasis from race to religion and became the leading organizational manifestation of a growing movement for tri-faith cooperation. Although it maintained an interest in "intergroup relations" of all kinds, the NCCJ would focus above all on the issue of religious freedom and the task of improving relations among Protestants, Catholics, and Jews. Because it had emerged out of goodwill initiatives between Protestants and Jews, this embrace of a tri-faith identity required not just a change in emphasis from race to religion but also the incorporation of Catholics into its activities. In fact these two developments were closely intertwined. Without the growing involvement of Catholics, the Protestants in the organization may never have clearly defined religion rather than race as the key issue for Christian-Jewish relations. In other words, NCCJ leaders did not consistently speak of the Jews as a *religious* group until after a degree of Catholic participation reframed the organization's primary goal as one of goodwill between Protestants, Catholics, and Jews. The already accepted status of Catholics as a religious minority, not a racial one, subtly changed ecumenical Protestant ways of viewing the Jews as well.

The history of conflict between Protestants and Catholics presented a significant barrier to the tri-faith movement. Tensions simmered and occasionally erupted into open warfare over a host of issues, the most important being the role of religion in public education.[78] Couched on all sides in the language of freedom, these battles would structure the fault lines of American religious life through the middle of the twentieth century. Making matters even more difficult, the Catholic hierarchy had significant doctrinal concerns about the idea of interfaith dialogue. As we will see, the Catholic bishops generally maintained a careful distance from the NCCJ. Yet for most Americans, whatever their religious affiliation, the events of the late 1920s and early 1930s placed another set of concerns at the forefront. Alarmed at the crisis of the Great Depression in the United States and the rise of totalitarian governments around the world, a growing number of Protestants, Catholics, and Jews sought common cause in the shared defense of *all* religion against the forces that seemed poised to destroy it. In so doing, both Protestants and Catholics implicitly affirmed the definition of the Jews as a religious group on the American cultural landscape.

Despite their reservations, Catholics had their own reasons to participate in this movement. Fundamental to Catholic religious freedom talk in this period was the fear of communism as a threat to Christianity and to civilization itself. It can be hard to recall in the wake of the Cold War that initial American assessments of the Russian Revolution were actually quite diverse. Jews and ecumenical Protestants were among those inclined to view it with sympathy. One opinion piece in the *New York Times* argued that after the persecution of Jews, Baptists, Muslims, and other minorities under the czars, the revolution would elevate "the religious spirit of Russia" and usher in true religious freedom through "the final separation of Church and State."[79] This analysis rang true to many Jews, who associated czarist Russia with anti-Semitic pogroms.[80] It also resonated with historically free-church Protestant conceptions of religious liberty. Sympathetic analysts frequently equated the historic role of the Russian Orthodox Church with the Catholic establishments that Protestants customarily attacked and explained early Soviet restrictions on religious practice as a simple repudiation of the Orthodox establishment.[81] In contrast, from the beginning the Catholic Church identified the

USSR as a threat not simply to orthodoxy or to Christianity in general but to all religion. And when more and more reports emerged of Soviet propaganda that mocked Christianity, of church properties confiscated, of restrictions imposed on church activities, and of clergy imprisoned if they dared to resist or speak out against such policies, most Protestants and Jews alike joined in denouncing the Soviet Union as dangerously antireligious.[82]

Closer to home in Mexico, a different crisis of church and state proved to be a more intractable source of Protestant-Catholic conflict. To many Catholics, Mexico's left-wing government seemed just as severe a threat to Christianity as the Soviet Union. During the nineteenth century the Catholic Church in Mexico had lost most of its establishment privileges, and during the Mexican Revolution (circa 1910–20) it was targeted for its collusions with the autocratic president Porfirio Díaz. When American Catholics learned of church properties confiscated, religious orders expelled, and priests attacked by Mexican revolutionary forces, they organized mass protests under the banner of religious freedom.[83] In the 1920s, when President Plutarco Elías Calles began to enforce the anticlerical measures already present in the Mexican constitution, the U.S. Catholic hierarchy condemned his government as a "Red Menace" on the doorstep of the United States, a serious threat to the American inheritance of democracy and religious freedom.[84] But where Catholics saw persecution, many Protestants and secular liberals romanticized the Mexican revolutionaries as freedom fighters against an autocratic regime and insisted that the people of Mexico were simply gaining the religious freedom they had for so long been denied. In their view, this revolution followed the pattern of Europe's slow and uneven struggle for liberation from Catholic power.[85]

Against the backdrop of these events in the Soviet Union and Mexico, Catholic religious freedom talk laid the groundwork for a truly tri-faith movement. Consider the work of the Calvert Associates, a lay Catholic organization founded in 1923 as the fund-raising arm for the new opinion journal *Commonweal*. The first stated goal for the Calvert Associates was to combat "the rising tide of irreligion, communism, and Bolshevism in America."[86] Members did not need to be Catholics, *Commonweal* explained, but they were "firmly united in the belief . . . that religion is at once the foundation and the only sure guarantee of the highest forms of civilization and culture." This was the shared heritage of all Americans, "from the nobly stern Puritans of New England . . . to the fervent Catholic founders of Maryland who first wrote religious liberty into a colonial charter, from the God-fearing and loyal Jew, to the childlike faith of the black." This infantilization of black religiosity—set against the maturity attributed to presumably white Protestants, Catholics, and Jews—reveals once again the tight weave of racial and religious hierarchies in American culture. But the important point for *Commonweal* was that attacks on Catholicism, whether in the Soviet Union, Mexico, or the United States, were an opening gambit against all religion. Here the rhetorics of religious freedom served both to establish the all-American credentials of Catholicism and to make the case for "religion" in general as an essential safeguard against the inroads of communism.[87]

The NCCJ and the Calvert Associates had distinct origins but a great deal in common, and their interests converged in the 1928 presidential campaign. The candidacy of former New York governor Alfred E. Smith, the first Catholic to be nominated by a major party, unleashed anew the demons of anti-Catholicism in American public life. In what observers called a "whispering campaign," countless pamphlets, editorials, and sermons circulated all over the country to warn that a Catholic president would inevitably attempt to install a Catholic establishment and place his loyalty to Rome over the United States. The very ferocity of that propaganda sparked a new coalition in Smith's defense. Many moderate-to-liberal Protestants and Jews who remained otherwise suspicious of Catholicism were appalled at the vitriol and became convinced that the most serious threat to American religious freedom lay not in the Catholic Church but in the smear campaign against it. The 1928 election season thus engendered a new sympathy among many Protestants and Jews for Catholics in American public life. This sympathy facilitated new collaborations with Catholics who were engaged in the campaign or who simply wanted to defend their church from the onslaught. Smith's candidacy thus helped incorporate Catholics into the goodwill movement and so to reformulate it along tri-faith lines.

American Jews were especially invested in defending a Catholic's right to run for president. For one thing, they had long-standing ties with Smith and with the Democratic Party. As governor of New York, Smith had skillfully cultivated Jewish support. His annual Rosh Hashanah messages praised their ongoing commitments to religious faith and to "the time-honored principles of toleration and religious freedom." As a Catholic speaking to Jews, he invoked the classic Christian republican themes of faith and freedom in a way that refused any exclusive Protestant claim to these all-American ideals.[88] Recognizing the KKK as a common enemy, many Jews saw Smith's campaign as a crucial battle against Protestant hegemony in American life. At a December 1927 "tolerance dinner" sponsored by the newly formed NCCJ, the first to raise the issue was Rabbi Nathan Krass of

Temple Emanu-El in New York. At a time of extensive public debate over Smith's potential nomination, Krass asked whether the Protestants present would extend their interest in "good-will" and "toleration" to voting for a Catholic as president. Although the announced goals of the event had been "racial amity," Krass and other speakers framed the dialogue as one between Protestants, Catholics, and Jews and in so doing shifted its emphasis away from racial and toward religious modes of classification.[89]

Religious freedom talk framed a tri-faith defense of Smith's campaign. "Freedom of conscience is the greatest thing at stake in this campaign," wrote the Presbyterian minister and retired Princeton professor Henry Van Dyke in a statement released by the Democratic National Committee that summer. For the election to be decided on the basis of Smith's religious affiliation, he argued, "would dishonor the pledged faith of America and cast away her most precious heritage."[90] In a widely praised radio address given just weeks before the election, Rabbi Stephen S. Wise blasted a "combination Klan-Pro-Hoover-Anti-Smith meeting" recently held in North Carolina as fundamentally un-American. No true American, he said, could "vote as Jew or Christian, as Protestant or Roman Catholic, for a man or against a man because of his religious affiliation, which is another way of saying because of the manner of his soul's approach to the God he loves and worships."[91] Revulsion at the anti-Catholicism on display in the campaign season encouraged many Americans to see religion rather than race as the most pertinent category of difference in American life and to classify contemporary problems of bias and discrimination in primarily religious terms.

The 1928 election facilitated new connections between like-minded Protestants, Catholics, and Jews. One emerging tri-faith leader was Michael Williams, who had started his career as a correspondent for the National Catholic War Council, helped establish the NCWC (National Catholic Welfare Conference) News Service, and then became founding editor of *Commonweal* and the first president of the Calvert Associates.[92] During the Smith campaign, Williams also worked for the Democratic National Committee, managing its efforts to collect and rebut the anti-Catholic material that seemed to be appearing everywhere. Citing his dialogues with a wide variety of religious leaders, Williams identified a shared conviction that the only way to "avert the doom" of religious hatred was "the rallying together of all men and women of all political creeds and parties, of all forms of religious faith, or of no religious faith," who valued America and what it stood for.[93] Williams would build on the connections forged in the campaign to become an active leader in the emerging tri-faith movement.

The anti-Catholic vitriol that surfaced against Smith's candidacy helped convince the ecumenical Protestants active in the NCCJ that the "Christian" in its name could no longer signify Protestants alone. Inviting the full participation of Catholics, alongside Protestants and Jews, tended to reframe the organization's concerns as a quest above all for *religious* toleration and *religious* freedom. As part of the planning process for a seminar on Protestant, Catholic, and Jewish relations—held at Columbia University just two months after the election in January 1929—Columbia University historian and *Commonweal* editorial consultant Carlton J. H. Hayes became the Catholic cochair for the organization. Joining him as a key Catholic voice at the seminar was Father J. Elliot Ross, a Paulist priest, chaplain at Columbia University, and a regular contributor to *Commonweal* magazine.[94] The conversations at Columbia sparked the idea of a national conference on religious freedom. Held in Washington, D.C., in March 1932, this event gained significant media attention through a high-profile "national committee of sponsors" that included former presidential candidate Alfred E. Smith.[95] At the same time, the NCCJ encouraged religious leaders around the country to plan their own events with the goal of building "good feeling among Protestants, Catholics, and Jews" at the local level. Local seminars took place that year in cities including Cambridge, Boston, New Haven, New York, Louisville, St. Louis, St. Paul, and Berkeley.[96]

The fact that the Catholic representatives at the Columbia seminar in 1929 were a university chaplain and a history professor, rather than members of the hierarchy, suggests the distance between the tri-faith movement and the leadership of the Catholic Church. Applying papal strictures that dated to the World's Parliament of Religions in 1893, Catholic bishops generally viewed any sort of interfaith gatherings as dangerous, potentially even heretical. They warned that participants could slide into the heresy of indifferentism, viewing all religions as equally good or as pathways toward the same larger truths. Even if Catholic participants never implied such a thing, uninformed observers could conclude from the very fact of such an event that there were no substantive differences between the religions. Thus, when Father Ross sought permission to hold NCCJ events in dioceses around the country, many bishops expressed reservations about the whole endeavor. And when individual Catholics asked for advice on the organization, the NCWC—which had come to represent the collective voice of the bishops on social questions—generally advised caution. Invited to serve as consultant for an NCCJ conference in 1932, one NCWC staff member decided, after consulting with his superiors, that he should not participate. "I feel there is danger in too much isolation," he wrote to NCWC director Father John J. Burke, "and yet such conferences are apt to want to discuss topics not properly open to discussion by men and women lacking adequate equipment for such a purpose."[97]

Given the global climate, however, some Catholic leaders thought the opportunities for positive dialogue and public relations well worth the risks. "There can be, of course, no compromise in the realm of fundamental belief," commented San Francisco's Archbishop Edward J. Hanna at a meeting of the Oakland-Berkeley Fellowship, "but respect and generous feeling there may be." What the country needed more than anything, Hanna said, was "a meeting place where men of all Faiths may gather." The archbishop had the woes of the Depression and the worldwide growth of fascism and communism very much in mind. "Our country must be rooted and grounded in the spiritual," he said. "May God here raise a race of men which can carry to a later generation the realized ideals of our beloved country."[98] Making common cause with Jews and Protestants need not undermine the faith of the Catholics who participated, he and other NCCJ supporters argued, or challenge their view of the church as the sole conduit of religious authority and truth. Rather, for those Catholics who supported it, the tri-faith movement provided a source of valuable allies in the urgent task of resisting the enemies of religion and democracy around the world.

However uneven it may have been, the involvement of Catholics had transformed the NCCJ from its initial goals of Christian-Jewish dialogue, in which issues of race and religion were virtually indistinguishable, to a tri-faith model that focused almost entirely on religion. Immediately after the 1932 conference on religious liberty, the NCCJ announced plans for "a discussion tour of the country by a priest, a rabbi, and a minister." The goal, NCCJ director Everett Clinchy told reporters, was "to moderate and finally to eliminate a system of prejudices which disfigures and distorts our business, social, and political relations." This purpose was "of deep significance to the United States, where tolerance and religious freedom are ideals cherished since the founding of the colonies," he explained, which would help avert "in this country such disastrous results as have attended . . . recent outbreaks of intolerance against Jews in Germany and Catholics in Spain."[99] Here, the newly ascendant tri-faith framework became the primary lens for interpreting the growth of anti-Semitism in Germany. The project of dialogue with (white) Protestants and (white) Catholics situated Jews as a religious rather than a racial minority in American life. And placed alongside the travails of Catholicism in countries like Mexico and Spain, the persecution of the German Jews looked to NCCJ leaders like a religious problem far more than a racial one.

By celebrating a common allegiance to faith and freedom, the tri-faith movement placed Judaism and Catholicism alongside Protestant Christianity as full-fledged American religions and identified both Jews and Catholics as equal partners in the American experiment. These tri-faith rhetorics had an impact not only on how Americans understood religion but also on the racial formations with which it intersected. By locating the Jews as a religious rather than a racial minority—a classification that would not become fully normative in American public discourse until after the Second World War—tri-faith rhetorics subtly enabled the gradual acceptance of the Jews as fully white. Let me be clear that this acceptance took place within the dominant social imaginary and not always on the ground. While Catholicism as such no longer cast a shadow of racial suspicion, there were always some Catholics (such as African Americans, Native Americans, and Latinos) who remained outside the bounds of whiteness. Jewish incorporation into American whiteness would remain even more ambivalent and arguably always incomplete.[100] Yet by the mid-twentieth century, at the level of cultural representation, the ascribed or assumed racial identity of both Jews and Catholics in the United States would for the most part be white.

NAZI GERMANY, TRI-FAITH AMERICA, AND THE AMBIVALENCE OF RELIGIOUS FREEDOM

The tri-faith movement grew stronger in the 1930s because, at a time of economic depression and political upheaval both at home and abroad, it addressed the felt anxieties of a liberal American elite. Through its definition of Americans as a people of faith—whether Protestant, Catholic, or Jewish—tri-faith leaders encouraged a sense of national unity against communism and fascism abroad and just as urgently against political radicalism and totalitarian movements at home. Thus the movement served as a moderating influence, poised between the extremes of Left and Right. Its leaders worked to ensure that, in the midst of the Great Depression and the political reconfigurations of the New Deal, American democracy did not lose what they saw as its essential religious moorings and fall prey to the antireligious totalitarianisms that were spreading so rapidly around the world. All this made legible the concept of an essentially unified "Judeo-Christian tradition" as the cornerstone for American democracy. As Jewish leaders and their allies grew more and more alarmed at the virulently racialized anti-Semitism of Nazi Germany, they built on these foundations in an effort to mobilize tri-faith action on behalf of the German Jews. Yet the tri-faith movement was powerless to change the course of the war and could not anticipate the horrors of the Holocaust. Even the effort to open up U.S. immigration policies and procedures to admit more Jews would prove to be beyond its abilities. In the context of the United States, however, the tri-faith campaign against Hitler worked to support the reclassification of Jews as a religious minority in American life.

In the early 1930s, the economic crisis of the Depression would help build momentum for the tri-faith movement as a moderating, consensus-building influence for a reeling society. At the time Franklin Delano Roosevelt was elected to the presidency, unemployment and poverty had risen to alarming levels, and public expressions of hopelessness and anger were everywhere. Tri-faith leaders affirmed the economic and political reforms of the New Deal as the best way to heal the nation's collective wounds. A statement signed by 160 Protestant, Catholic, and Jewish leaders explained that the "heart-rending suffering" plaguing the nation could not be reconciled with the "principles of justice and brotherhood which our religious teachings share in common." "We ask this in joint accord," they concluded, "in the spirit of religious social justice as expressed by the Quadresigimo Anno Encyclical of Pope Pius XI, and the National Catholic Welfare Council; by the American Synagogue in the declarations of orthodox, conservative and reform organizations; and by Protestant denominations and the Federal Council of the Churches of Christ in America."[101] The Catholic, Jewish, and Protestant bodies mentioned here held entirely different roles in their respective worlds. Yet by invoking them as the representative bodies of the nation's three major religions, this statement presented the New Deal as a moral imperative for all Americans and advanced the tri-faith model as the prevailing way to map religion in the United States.

When they stressed the *religious* foundations for American democracy, tri-faith leaders were also advocating a moderate route through the crises of the times, guarding against the irreligious and antireligious totalitarianisms that they found so problematic abroad. Their approach stood in contrast to more conservative Protestants and Catholics whose strident anticommunism often led them to oppose the New Deal.[102] The moderates of the tri-faith movement wanted instead to provide a religious foundation for New Deal reforms, hoping to ameliorate the poverty and suffering of the Depression while preventing any radical (and radically irreligious) revolutionary change. In March 1933, as the Calvert Associates planned its annual celebration of Maryland's founding and the "first establishment . . . of religious liberty in America," an editorial in *Commonweal* announced that the event this time around would be "purely spiritual." Given the "critical state of both public and private affairs," the journal explained, the "time and energies of all our leaders of State and Church should not be diverted from their efforts to solve our pressing social problems." *Commonweal* championed the contemporary significance of the history it was charting. The global "tide of tyranny" and the "repression of religious rights actively proceeding against Christians and Jews in many parts of the world," the editors wrote, had made "the maintenance of the principle and the unfettered practice of religious liberty in the United States . . . a matter of paramount importance."[103] Thus tri-faith leaders supported the New Deal as a relatively moderate program for a more just social order, a way to prevent the kind of radical disruptions and assaults on religion that were occurring elsewhere in the world.

Far more than the Depression, the persecution of the Jews under Hitler's rule became a defining issue for the tri-faith movement. American Jewish leaders had been alarmed by the anti-Semitic policies outlined by the Nazi Party even before the Führer's rise to power. In January 1932, at a rare joint meeting between the American Jewish Committee and the American Jewish Congress, the latter maintained that it was essential to take a strong and vocal stand before the Nazis had gained the power to implement their program. Speaking for a largely immigrant and Zionist-leaning constituency, the American Jewish Congress argued for public protests, diplomatic interventions, economic boycotts, and assistance for any German Jews who wished to emigrate. The American Jewish Committee, which represented a wealthier and more established sector of the Jewish population, argued that such public tactics were likely to backfire. Lewis Strauss noted that the current "temper" of Germany was "not only anti-Jewish and nationalist, but also anti-American." Vocal protests from American Jews would add credibility to the Nazi slanders against "international Jewry," he feared, fueling the global flames of anti-Semitism and actually enabling Hitler to succeed. Without resolving these tactical differences, both groups agreed to consult with contacts in Germany and to follow their guidance on the best way to handle the situation.[104]

Despite these differences and despite the Nazi deployment of an overwhelmingly racialized anti-Semitism, all of these Jewish leaders framed their protests against the Nazis in the language of religious freedom. Several weeks after Hitler's appointment as German chancellor, his regime passed a series of new discriminatory legislation against Jews, encouraged boycotts against Jewish-owned businesses, and initiated various forms of anti-Semitic propaganda. Against the tactical preferences of the American Jewish Committee, the American Jewish Congress organized a protest meeting at Carnegie Hall on the "menace of Hitlerism." Honorary president and cofounder Stephen S. Wise made full use of his tri-faith connections to bring in the well-known Congregationalist minister and NCCJ cofounder S. Parkes Cadman as the headlined Protestant speaker. Attorney Martin Conboy, director of the National Council of Catholic Men and president of New York's Catholic Club, appeared as the representative Catholic. American Jewish Congress president Bernard Deutsch introduced the event by denouncing the Nazis as a danger to democracy, to "the cause of religious liberty," and to the lives of Germany's six hundred thousand Jews. The speakers at this event referred to the perils of racial as well as religious persecution. Yet by naming religious liberty as the first principle at stake, and by highlighting a tri-faith roster of speakers, this protest and many others like it identified *religion*—religious freedom, mutual respect, and the affirmation of religious values—as the key issue in the struggle against the Nazis.[105]

On this point, the American Jewish Committee could absolutely agree. Its leaders were drawn mostly from the ranks of the Reform Jews who had long worked to redefine Jewishness as a strictly religious identity. A month after the Carnegie Hall protest, the committee and the B'nai B'rith issued a joint statement condemning the Nazis' "anti-Jewish action" and "pseudo-scientific race theories" as fundamentally opposed "to the traditions of American freedom of conscience, religion and liberty." Implicitly repudiating the tactics of mass protest, they emphasized the need for an "intelligent and reasonable" response that avoided escalating "appeals to passion and resentment." In this way they hoped to rouse the "enlightened opinion of the German people," whom they hoped would then restore "civilized standards in their own great nation." Committed to the promise of the Enlightenment and to the standards of civilized modernity that it had forged, the committee's spokesmen placed even greater emphasis on the freedom of religion than did their counterparts in the American Jewish Congress.[106]

American Jewish leaders could also agree on the importance of the tri-faith movement as a way to guard against the Nazi peril. At the NCCJ National Seminar focusing on religious liberty in March 1932, Cyrus Adler warned against the growth of "bigotry and illiberalism." He urged all Americans to honor the legacy of George Washington by supporting "not only in thought but in deed the first President's dream of religious understanding and freedom of worship." The "religious stock-taking" conducted at this NCCJ seminar, opined Philadelphia's *Jewish Exponent*, seemed likely to aid the cause of religious minorities and was undoubtedly "good for the soul of the nation."[107] Then came the alarming news of Hitler's appointment and the new anti-Semitic measures of his administration. At a joint meeting of Jewish organizations in June 1933, participants debated whether to appeal further to the president (decision postponed); when and how to appeal to the League of Nations (also postponed); and whether to call a boycott against Germany (declined on grounds that this could spark further anti-Semitism in America, without materially aiding German Jews). However, all those present affirmed the need to cultivate support from the NCCJ as one of the most effective ways to educate "Christian public opinion in America." By framing their task in the language of religious freedom, American Jewish leaders hoped to secure the tri-faith support they so desperately needed.[108]

The language of religious freedom linked the distinct challenges that Jews and Christians faced in Nazi Germany. In the fall of 1933 the FCC applauded the dissenting German churches' resistance to the "worship of the State." Three thousand German evangelical pastors had informed Bishop Ludwig Mueller of the newly formed national "Reichschurch" that they would not accept Nazi edits to the Bible, add a paragraph on racial purity to their statements of faith, or otherwise "submit to curbs on their activities." The FCC defended its policy of continued cooperation with the German churches, even those that had acceded to the Reichschurch, as a way to support any continued dissent within the system. All Christians in Germany faced "the danger that worship of the State will be placed above every other loyalty," the FCC declared, and stood together against the Nazi extremists' idea "that Christianity should be entirely swept aside to be replaced by a revival of the old Teutonic pagan deities." In order to encourage their efforts at resistance, however inadequate these might seem to others, German Christians desperately needed open channels of communication with Christians around the world.[109]

Despite the initial ambivalence of the Catholic hierarchy, which considered Europe's Fascist regimes much friendlier to Christianity than the Communist alternative, many Catholics were also concerned about the situation in Germany. Among them was *Commonweal* editor and tri-faith activist Michael Williams, who took a fact-finding trip to Europe in June 1933 for the American Committee on Religious Rights and Minorities. Williams knew very well that the Jews had the most to fear from Hitler. Before his trip, in a letter to his old friend Bernard Richards of the American Jewish Congress, he had offered to deliver a petition to the pope asking him to intervene on behalf of the German Jews.[110] "No amount of official denials," he wrote in a *Commonweal* editorial, "can conceal the fact that Jews as Jews have been subjected to a bigoted discrimination and a persecution wholly unjust and abhorrent to all believers in the human rights of personal liberty, equal justice under the protection of law, and cultural and religious freedom."[111] After his return to the United States that summer, Williams wrote a series of articles that decried the "Messianic cult of Hitlerism," a new religion of the German folk, with the Jew as the symbol "of all those things which the young German wishes to wipe off the slate."[112] All of these pieces clearly defined the threat to the Jews of Germany as an assault on the principle of religious freedom.

Williams also worried about the situation of Catholicism in Germany. He decried the transformation of "German Christians" into "Christian Germans" who had abandoned the historic principles of their faith by deifying the "German folk" and called attention to the plight of those who had resisted Nazi decrees. In a radio address sponsored by the NCCJ, Williams contended that some Protestants and Catholics as well as Jews were suffering "from bigotry and intolerance" in Germany and urged his audience "to prevent alien sentiment" from similarly "jeopardizing religious freedom" in the United States.[113] Behind the scenes he fought the all-American and devoutly Catholic anti-Semitism of the influential radio personality Father Charles Coughlin and tried to convince his fellow Catholics to speak out on the situation in Germany. "I have reason to believe that my views concerning the evil nature and the deadly menace of Hitlerism, so far as its effects on personal and religious liberty are concerned, are shared by the great majority of Catholics," he said at a Madison Square Garden rally in 1934, "but I speak solely for myself." He argued for an alliance between Jews and Christians on the grounds that Christianity in Germany was "being crushed out of existence by the power of a State religion of paganism."[114] With a healthy dose of optimism, he advised Joseph Proskauer of the American Jewish Committee that he would soon be able to inform President Roosevelt "that the Catholics were in absolute accord with the Jews on the need for decisive action against the Nazis."[115] Through the 1930s, Williams remained at the forefront of a tri-faith effort to combat Hitler on religious freedom grounds.

The tri-faith movement thus became the primary locus for an anti-Nazi activism organized around the principle of religious freedom. Consider an assortment of news reports from the spring of 1933. In Cincinnati, Ohio, a "mass meeting to protest against violation of civil and religious liberty in Germany" featured statements from an Episcopal priest, the city's popular Democratic mayor, and a Reform rabbi from the city.[116] Little more than a week later, Rabbi David Philipson told a local chapter of the Knights of Columbus that "the voice of Christendom, both Catholic and Protestant, in behalf of the persecuted Jews of Germany is like a refreshing breath in a foul miasmatic atmosphere." Speaking as a Jew to an audience of Catholics, the rabbi celebrated the growing support he felt from Protestants and Catholics alike.[117] And at a Washington, D.C., protest meeting, Maryland's governor Albert Ritchie claimed that in the face of Nazi atrocities "we are not Catholic, Protestant, or Jew." The governor, a Catholic who had also used tri-faith rhetorics to support Al Smith's presidential campaign, said that those gathered in protest against the Nazis "symbolize the protest of humanity against forces which menace the economic, the civic, or the religious freedom of any race or any people anywhere."[118] By identifying Nazi anti-Semitism as above all an assault on *religion*, such tri-faith rhetorics of religious freedom attracted support from a range of (white) Protestants and (white) Catholics who were generally less interested in hearing about the problem of race.

However useful it might have been in garnering tri-faith support, the concept of religious freedom could not adequately capture the breadth and depth of the attacks on Germany's Jews. That same spring in New York, the NCCJ published the names of twelve hundred "prominent Christian clergymen" who had signed a protest against the "relentless hatred" of Hitler's message and the "ruthless persecution of the Jews" under his rule. While acknowledging the continued existence of "racial and religious prejudice" in America, this NCCJ petition denounced the systematic persecution occurring in Germany as a "return of medieval barbarity" that endangered the entire world. In the name of religious freedom, as Protestants, Catholics, and Jews united in common conviction, these petitioners identified a Nazi assault not simply on religious freedom but on "human rights" in general, on the basic principles of Christianity, and on the ethical standards of the "civilized world." The language of religious freedom had become central to the NCCJ's evolving tri-faith identity. But like so many others at the time, this statement spilled over into a kind of classificatory excess, reassembling the intertwined languages of race, religion, and civilization in an effort to capture the problem at hand. As its terminological conundrums reveal, the category of religion alone could not adequately encompass the discrimination and the horrors that were all too rapidly unfolding in Nazi Germany.[119]

INTENSIFYING THE RACIAL BINARY: JEWISH RELIGION AND AMERICAN WHITENESS

Within the United States, the tri-faith movement had added significantly to the forces undermining older visions of American democracy as intrinsically Protestant. It articulated an expanded definition of America and the true American as essentially *religious* and democratic, in contrast to an atheistic and totalitarian other. Celebrating the virtues of faith and freedom pushed both race and class into the background, encouraging Americans to foreground the category of religion both in their own self-definition and in their mapping of the world. Because the tri-faith movement so aptly represented the concerns of U.S. elites, it succeeded in shaping midcentury public discourse toward a redefinition of American diversity as primarily a matter of religion and of the barriers to intergroup harmony as above all products of religious rather than racial difference. During the Second World War, the U.S. government embraced tri-faith rhetorics and organizing schemes both in its military chaplaincy operations and in a public relations campaign that celebrated American religiosity in tri-faith terms. That propaganda served effectively to contrast U.S. democracy against the racial triumphalism of the Nazis. As the Cold War unfolded in the decades that followed, the tri-faith framework would define Americans as both religious and free, over and against the antireligious totalitarianism of the Soviets. By challenging hatreds they understood as religious, the NCCJ and its tri-faith collaborators would manage to incorporate Judaism and Catholicism alongside Protestantism as legitimately American religious identities. In so doing they expanded the dominant image of the (white) American beyond the Protestant to include Catholics and Jews as well.[120]

In the process, the tri-faith emphasis on religious freedom tended to obscure the ongoing American problem with race. The onset of the Great Depression had only reinforced a racialized public sentiment against new immigrants who might compete for already scarce jobs. The southern racial order had become even more firmly entrenched through the reforms of the New Deal, as Roosevelt compromised with the white southern Democrats whose support he needed to pass its major programs.[121] While many Americans looked the other way on the problems of racial discrimination and violence, or even endorsed the existing order as part of a divine plan, they took great pride in religious freedom as an all-American constitutional ideal. For all of these reasons, Jewish leaders across movements and organizational affiliations had identified the growing tide of anti-Semitism in Germany as an assault on religious freedom, even though they knew that the Nazis had defined the "Jewish problem" in essentially racial terms. If Americans saw anti-Semitism not through a racial lens but as a threat to the global freedom of religion, then perhaps they would be more open to some form of assistance to the persecuted Jews.

The tri-faith move toward religious inclusivity thus had the unintended consequence of redrawing and even solidifying American lines of racial difference. By framing its concerns in religious rather than racial terms, defining both anti-Semitism and anti-Catholicism as *religious* hatreds, the tri-faith movement helped to fold those once considered racially distinct from the Anglo-Saxon—the Irish, Italians, Poles, and especially Jews—into a singular category of whiteness. Eliminating that older multiplicity of racial classifications effectively hardened the black-white binary, making it even more difficult for African Americans to escape the burdens of race. This consequence was quite evident to African American observers at the time. In one editorial titled "Tolerant Ostriches," the influential black-owned *Pittsburgh Courier* commented on the NCCJ's "traveling discussion unit comprising a rabbi, and Catholic priest, and a Protestant minister." Despite "the lynching and ruthless exploitation and shameless discrimination against the colored folk," the *Courier* went on to say, "no Negro is a member of this discussion unit." These "nice liberals" may have been tackling the bigotries of religion, but they had nothing to say about "the worst intolerance of all: color prejudice." The *Pittsburgh Courier* had no doubt that the Jews, the Catholics, and the Protestants active in the NCCJ were all racially white. As its editorial image of the ostrich implied, the tri-faith concern for religious freedom had the effect of obscuring the more intractable racial barriers of American life.[122]

The NCCJ's enthusiastic endorsement of a specifically religious toleration and religious freedom placed the emphasis on inclusion for those Americans (Catholics and Jews) whose difference was coming to be defined in overwhelmingly religious rather than racial terms. Both Jews and Catholics had been able to deploy the ideal of religious freedom to claim equal status on the landscape of American religion. In so doing they established themselves not only as fully American but also as racially white. The flip side of all this is that those who were unable to claim that status—African Americans in particular—had very little access to the promise of religious freedom. The tri-faith emphasis on religious brotherhood and religious freedom thus worked to solidify the black-white binary in American life. The final chapter of this book will explore the utility and the limits of religious freedom talk for African Americans, some of whom attempted to use this principle to redefine the terms of their communal identity. Their inability to do so, and the larger society's insistence on defining them solely through the lens of race, helps us see the racial contours and the limits of religious freedom in American history.

CHAPTER FIVE

Defining a People

African Americans and the
Racial Limits of Religious Freedom

In a 1944 essay titled "The Negro Has Always Wanted the Four Freedoms," Wilberforce University president and historian Charles H. Wesley surveyed the long African American struggle for liberation, from the nineteenth-century abolitionist movement all the way through the recent battles against lynching and Jim Crow. President Franklin Delano Roosevelt's statement of the Four Freedoms that Americans would be prepared to defend at war—freedom of speech, freedom of worship, freedom from want, and freedom from fear—offered a timely and patriotic way to frame the African American cause. This model required attention to the topic of religious freedom, and as an ordained minister in the African Methodist Episcopal (AME) Church, Wesley certainly cared about religion. Yet he devoted far less space to this freedom than to the other three, noting simply the restrictions that had been imposed on slave worship, the past "humiliation of the Negro pew," and the ongoing barriers to "Negro . . . membership in a 'white' church." These brief statements offered important insights into the barriers African Americans had faced in their religious lives. But Wesley's historical narrative and the list of seven "wants" that followed made no further mention of the freedom of worship, stressing economic and social issues instead.[1]

As Wesley's essay suggests, religious freedom was a relatively minor theme within a much broader African American struggle for freedom. Black cultural and religious traditions in the United States had been forged in and through an insistently racialized oppression and maintained a comprehensive and deeply embodied vision of freedom that did not generally single out religion as its focus. Before the Civil War most African Americans had faced lifetimes of slavery or the constant threats of (re-)enslavement.

Most were less interested in a specifically religious freedom than they were in securing their freedom from physical bondage. This is not to question the importance of religious practices and religious modes of meaning making in African American life. African Americans had developed distinctive forms of Christianity that stressed the liberatory themes of the Bible, patterning their hopes for emancipation after the Exodus account of the Jews' liberation from slavery in Egypt.[2] However, unlike the American Jews described in chapter 4, they did not typically narrate this story in the language of religious freedom. These cultural patterns remained in place as a new white supremacist racial order took hold after the Civil War. The larger society insistently defined and denigrated African Americans as a racial minority rather than as a religious one. For all these reasons and more, religious freedom did not provide the primary lens through which African Americans articulated their concerns.

Yet as they sought new ways to advance communal interests, some African Americans did invoke this principle as a way to defend themselves and their traditions. Religious freedom talk provided African Americans with one way to assert their full humanity against the dehumanizing civilizational assemblages of the dominant society—and to reassemble the cultural components of that society in the hope that their people could not only survive but also thrive. To demand this freedom was also to claim an interiority of experience, to define oneself as a human subject, one with a soul and a spirit and a concern for the eternal. In his pioneering *Appeal to the Colored Citizens of the World* (1829), for example, the former slave David Walker had attacked the hypocrisies of the "christian Americans" who professed allegiance to liberty while holding "our fathers, our mothers, ourselves, and our children in eternal ignorance and wretchedness." Walker called on all "colored citizens" to resist the "tyrants" who denied slaves even the freedom to read the Bible and assemble for worship, rights that the predominantly Protestant slaveholders otherwise claimed to value. The same slaveholders who "[sent] out missionaries to convert the heathen" and congratulated themselves on their Christian virtue, he wrote, would "*absolutely beat a colored person nearly to death, if they catch him on his knees, supplicating the throne of grace.*"[3] Rejecting a system that classified and dehumanized them in such insistently racial terms, black abolitionists like Walker identified African Americans as a *religious* people with convictions and consciences of their own.

The language of religious freedom remained as a minor theme in the black freedom struggles of the early twentieth century, one means of resistance against a white supremacist racial order. Among those who celebrated this ideal were the leaders of the black Baptist and Methodist churches, who spoke of it as the one freedom that they had managed to secure. By asserting their fidelity to this constitutional principle, black church leaders sought to locate themselves alongside white Protestants, Catholics, and Jews as patriots and civilized moderns, squarely within the American mainstream. Other African American leaders who moved outside the bounds of conventional Christianity, claiming religious identities that the larger society deemed illegitimate, also came to defend their interests in this way. Religious freedom talk helped the new movements they created—including Father Divine's Peace Mission Movement, the Moorish Science Temple, and the Nation of Islam—to renegotiate their social location by rejecting the negatively racialized identity of the Negro and reformulating African American identity in primarily religious or ethno-religious terms.[4] As in the case of American Jews, the members of these movements invoked the freedom of religion not only to defend themselves from persecution but also to redefine the terms of their peoplehood, either replacing race with religion or infusing their blackness with a new spiritual and even cosmic significance.

Black churches and the new ethno-religious movements all participated in an ongoing set of debates over the prospects of African Americans within the United States. Should black people seek equal rights as U.S. citizens, or were such hopes impossibly naive? Rather than demanding inclusion in a white-dominated and racially stratified society, should they instead build their own institutions, their own sense of peoplehood, and perhaps even their own nation? James Cone, the leading black theologian of the later twentieth century and an astute analyst of African American religious life, has described the history of the black freedom struggle as an ongoing argument between two competing impulses. On one side were the integrationists, who grounded their appeals in the classically liberal (and all-American) ideals of freedom and equality. Cone points to Martin Luther King Jr. as the twentieth century's exemplary integrationist, and most of the historically black church leaders shared King's approach. On the other side stood the nationalists, who saw no way to reform white America and contended instead that the best prospects for African Americans lay in building themselves up as a distinct people, either in the United States or elsewhere. Cone's paradigmatic nationalist is Malcolm X, who gained fame as a charismatic minister and powerful orator in the Nation of Islam. These two impulses existed on a continuum, two poles of an ongoing debate, with many black leaders moving back and forth between them.[5]

The varieties of African American religious freedom talk reflected these competing but always overlapping impulses. On one side, integrationists tended to conceive of religious freedom as a right belonging to individuals and religious groups in American life. Father Divine's Peace Mission Movement, which began in the late 1920s and flourished in the Great Depression, shared this approach with the majority of black Protestant leaders. Father Divine rejected both the nationalist paradigm and the racial categorization of the Negro, redefining his followers primarily through the language of religion. Enthusiastically endorsing the principles of the U.S. Constitution, his movement skillfully wielded the principle of religious freedom to gain a measure of religious legitimacy within the framework of U.S. law. In contrast, ethno-religious movements like the Moorish Science Temple and the Nation of Islam argued that black people in America must reclaim their lost identity above all as a *nation*—a distinct people group with its own national heritage—and that each nation rightfully possessed its own religion. In some respects their efforts paralleled those of Native Americans who hoped to restore their sovereignty as tribal nations and of the Jewish nationalists who demanded minority group rights within the nations of eastern Europe. Like them, black nationalists asserted the collective right to define and practice their own religion, not so much as individuals but rather as an entire people.

Constrained by the insistent racializing assemblages of the larger society, none of these movements secured the redefinitions of identity for which they worked. Finding themselves denigrated as dangerous "cults" or political subversives and increasingly trapped in the jaws of the criminal justice system, members of the ethno-religious movements would increasingly emphasize their individual rights to the freedom of religion under the U.S. Constitution. While they continued to define their peoplehood in national and religious terms, the available tools of the U.S. legal regime encouraged them to emphasize the religious side of that equation. But however they defined themselves, the larger society most often denied the legitimacy of their claims and viewed them solely through the lens of race. Media outlets and government authorities overwhelmingly dismissed such movements as fraudulent, inauthentic, and overly political rather than as legitimately religious. Once again, the dominant society posited and policed a religious-political divide in ways that served the interests of a majority that defined itself as white and Christian. For the vast majority of African Americans, religious freedom provided little escape from the confines of a racialized oppression.

African Americans had good reason to be suspicious of religious freedom talk because those who claimed the mantle of whiteness had most often employed it to bolster rather than to challenge the institutionalized hierarchies of race. Before the Civil War, the dominant logics of religious freedom had served to ward off any challenges to the institution of slavery. In the North as well as in the South, many white Protestants sought to silence abolitionist agitation and to avoid denominational conflicts by insisting that the slavery issue must be resolved at the level of the individual conscience. Churches could not impose an antislavery standard, they argued, when practicing Christians disagreed on the implications of biblical teachings for this issue. In the 1840s and 1850s, proslavery leaders more and more directly invoked the freedom of religion to defend an institution they had come to define as part of their religion. They denounced abolitionists as radicals who threatened not only the constitutional rights of private property and state sovereignty but religious freedom as well. "We detest Abolitionism because it trespasses upon our rights of conscience," explained members of a South Carolina citizens' committee as part of their argument for secession. "It does not allow us to judge for ourselves the morality of slaveholding." These proslavery southerners increasingly defended the "sacred right" of slavery as a divinely ordained institution. Alongside the principles of states' rights and property rights, they used religious freedom talk to name the abolitionists of the North as the true oppressors.[6]

After the war, white southerners and the northerners who wanted to re-establish social and economic ties with them would update these ideologies of religious freedom to support the new Jim Crow regimes of racial segregation. The Southern Baptist Convention—by this time the largest denomination in the region—was especially committed to the historically Baptist principles of religious freedom and the separation of church and state. But these ideals were more than a prized denominational legacy. Southern Baptists determinedly maintained their independence from any external authority that might impose its standards upon them, whether it was the specter of "popery," federal government mandates, or the northern "carpetbaggers" who repudiated southern norms. They refused to join the Federal Council of Churches (FCC), for example, arguing that any such federation would violate the free spirit of the Reformation by imposing a single orthodoxy on all its member churches.[7] But their most urgent concerns revolved around the question of race. Confronted with FCC appeals for "racial brotherhood" in the 1920s, Southern Baptists and other white evangelicals retorted that segregation was a "political" question in which the churches had no right to intervene. Christians should stick with strictly "religious" concerns, they insisted, such as saving souls. At the same time, in what Paul Harvey has described as "segregationist folk theology," some white southerners defended segregation as divinely ordained: God had created the races separate and did not intend for them to mix. In all of these ways, religious freedom talk contributed to the racializing assemblages of the segregationist South.[8]

The southern strategy of the Democratic Party in former New York governor Al Smith's run for the presidency in 1928—a campaign I described in chapter 4 as an avenue for liberal tri-faith cooperation—further clarifies the racial politics of religious freedom in this era. Baltimore's *Afro-American* reported that Democratic operatives were distributing publicity materials designed "to convince 'Dixie' that it could 'Trust Al on Any Question.'" The party asked southerners who disliked the candidate's Catholicism to remember the mostly Catholic "Tammany Democrats" who had "resisted the reconstruction measures of the Republican Party," enabled the erection of new barriers to African American voter registration, and generally supported the reimposition of "white government" in the post-Reconstruction South. The *Afro-American* reported that the campaign had referred to Smith as "Woodrow Wilson's friend" and advised "Dixie . . . to recall that Thomas Jefferson, founder of the Democratic Party, believed in religious freedom." The racial politics of these associations were all too clear. Both southern Democrats and readers of the *Afro-American* would have been familiar with Jefferson's legacy as a slaveholder and states' rights advocate and with Wilson's active support for the politics of segregation. In this way the Democrats positioned themselves as allies of both white supremacy and religious freedom. The religious freedom they invoked spoke most directly to the right of a Catholic to run for the presidency. At the same time, Smith's campaign literature built on and reinforced a long pattern of religious freedom talk in defense of the white supremacist racial order. All too often, this ideal supported the racial subordination of African Americans and their erasure from the body politic.[9]

Even when they were not pursuing explicitly segregationist ends, an exclusive emphasis on religious freedom often enabled white Americans to avoid confronting the problem of race. Consider the activities of the Baptist Joint Committee on Public Affairs (BJC), organized in the 1930s to lobby for persecuted Baptists in Romania and other parts of the world. The BJC represented most of the major Baptist denominations but received the bulk of its funding from the Southern Baptists and immediately identified the historic Baptist ideal of religious freedom as its primary sphere of interest. During the Second World War, when the leading black Baptist denominations were finally invited to participate, an African American delegate proposed that the "public affairs" that the BJC addressed should include the issue of racial discrimination. The other delegates approved this proposal "in principle" but quickly closed it off by resolving that "from now on" the committee "should concern itself primarily with the question of making effective the Baptist position on religious liberty in the [postwar] peace settlement." Tackling racial discrimination would have alienated significant portions of the committee's white constituency, especially in the South. Its focus on religious freedom allowed the BJC to maintain its tentative (and always fragile) collaboration between northern and southern white Baptists. In so doing the BJC avoided taking up the concerns most pressing to black Baptist churches, and for that reason those churches rarely bothered to send delegates to its meetings over the course of the next two decades. Again, the celebratory rhetorics of religious freedom helped obscure the problem of racism and often worked to exclude African Americans from the conversation.[10]

Through the 1940s and 1950s, segregationists regularly invoked religious freedom alongside the freedom of choice and the freedom of association to defend racially exclusive schools, neighborhoods, and workplaces.[11] Donald R. Richberg, who had previously served in FDR's New Deal administration, condemned the "civil rights hysteria" and specifically President Truman's proposed Federal Fair Employment Practices Act (1948) as a threat to individual liberties, including the freedom of religion. Richberg argued that by forbidding employers to discriminate on racial grounds, the act would violate religious convictions sincerely held by many Americans. For anyone to freely "exercise . . . his religion, he must be free to restrict his associations with others in accordance with his feelings and his convictions as to what is necessary and desirable," he wrote. Such legislation would force associations that many Americans found "repulsive . . . not because of any narrow prejudice, but because of . . . profound religious convictions." For Richberg the distinctions of "race and color" were in no way arbitrary. Rather, they were divinely ordained, part of the order of the world and the history of mankind. In fact he painted any federal action on racial questions as a limit on individual freedom that veered toward communism. Any attempt to force integration represented "an intolerant violation of individual liberty," destroying the fundamental freedoms that Americans had so recently fought to defend.[12]

Those invested in the U.S. racial order in the North as well as in the South found this logic compelling. When the Wisconsin Council of Churches passed a resolution in 1948 endorsing state action against "prejudice" and "discrimination" in the name of "human rights," an ideal that had gained new prominence that year through the United Nations Declaration on Human Rights, board member F. A. Wirt strenuously objected. Citing Richberg among others, he argued that the current agitations for "human rights" and "civil rights" were essentially communistic, endangering individual liberties including the freedom of religion, and that the desired goals should be achieved through "education" rather than "legislation." Such calls for "education" served as a way to sidestep demands for meaningful change without coming out directly in favor of racial discrimination. Indiana congressman Samuel B. Pettengill, another of Wirt's sources, argued that the "crusade against lynching and for civil rights [was] a job for the home, the school and the church, and not for the mailed fist of Big Government in a wild stampede around the barriers and limits of the American Constitution." Yet those who opposed civil rights legislation inevitably spoke out against church- or school-based campaigns that aimed to combat racial segregation, as well as against those emanating from Washington. "With thousands of individuals in Wisconsin opposed to the legislation suggested when one mentions 'civil rights,'" Wirt concluded, "it would seem highly undesirable for the Board of Directors of the Wisconsin Council of Churches to pass resolutions on such controversial subjects." The racial stakes of his argument could not have been more clear.[13]

Although by the late 1930s most U.S. political leaders had condemned the Nazis and their racial ideologies, many voices in the public sphere continued to associate whiteness—or the even more exclusive category of the Anglo-Saxon—with the virtues of freedom, democracy, and civilization. L. L. Gwaltney, editor of the *Alabama Baptist*, argued in 1943 that religious freedom would be essential to an enduring peace after the war. Championing the model set by the United States, Gwaltney titled one section "Anglo-Saxons Lead in Freedom." While he criticized England for "the anachronism of a State Church," he also credited it with the cultural and legal traditions that undergirded American freedoms. "Britain and America, the two great Anglo-Saxon Protestant and democratic nations," he wrote, were now "saving the liberties of the world" in the war against fascism. Gwaltney aimed his polemic against the "huge ecclesiastical system" (Catholicism) that dominated the rest of Europe and, he believed, had inhibited any comparable impulses there. By memorializing Anglo-Saxon Protestants as the pioneers of "civil and religious liberty," his account not only conflated whiteness with American identity but also denied the racial and imperial systems of domination in which both the United Kingdom and the United States were implicated. Here again, religious freedom talk contributed to the racializing assemblages of U.S. empire.[14]

Despite the eventual successes of the civil rights movement, white supremacist articulations of religious freedom would remain very much alive as an impediment to racial integration across the urban and suburban landscapes of the United States. I do not mean to suggest that religious freedom talk has always or necessarily worked in the service of whiteness. Like any other ideal—and like the principle of freedom more generally— religious freedom has been invoked and (re)configured in any number of ways.[15] Nevertheless, the cultural and legal stature of this ideal made it a prominent feature of the racial-religious assemblages that worked more often than not to protect the privileges of whiteness.

ASSERTING MODERNITY: BLACK PROTESTANTS AND THE PROMISE OF FREEDOM

Against the grain of these dominant assemblages, African Americans used religious freedom talk to assert their own rights to equality and self-determination in the United States. Among those who invoked this ideal were the leaders of the independent black churches, generally recognized then and now as the leading institutions of nineteenth- and twentieth-century African American life.[16] While the freedom of religion was never their primary concern, black church leaders invoked this ideal to celebrate the achievements of denominational pioneers who had, they explained, founded free black churches and so secured this freedom for their people against the barriers of racial oppression. Like other racial-religious minorities, they were eager to highlight African American accomplishments and to demonstrate their allegiance to the nation's fundamental ideals. When they experienced new assaults on the integrity and autonomy of their churches, this freedom served as a useful weapon in their defensive arsenal, a way to defend these vital communal institutions against the threats of a hostile world. As black Protestants in a majority white Protestant society, the terms of their marginalization were primarily racial rather than religious. Their claims for religious freedom were less about theology or religious dissent—although these factors certainly played a role—and more about the control of their own institutions and lives.[17] Invoking this ideal worked in tandem with their broader appeals for freedom. It worked also to identify them as civilized moderns, committed to the all-American principles of freedom and democracy, and as moral subjects grounded like other Americans in the values of religion.

The paradigmatic origin story for the black church is that of "Mother Bethel" African Methodist Episcopal Church, founded in 1794 by the former slave Richard Allen, who later became the first bishop of the new AME denomination. By the time of the Civil War, African Methodists were narrating their history through a religious freedom talk that asserted their allegiance to national as well as Christian ideals. The "unchristian conduct" of white Methodists in Philadelphia, said the Reverend John Turner in a wartime sermon, had motivated Allen and the other church founders "to build a house of their own, to worship God under their own vine and fig tree." The moral of the story was clear: "All the religious liberty which the colored people enjoy in this country . . . is attributable to the organization of the A.M.E. Church."[18] As national plans developed for the U.S. centennial celebration in 1876, the denominational paper the *Christian Recorder* made the (ultimately unsuccessful) case for African American participation by proposing a monument in Philadelphia's Fairmont Park "dedicated to religious liberty" and "crowned with a bronze statue of Allen." At a time when the abilities of the "negro race" were so often denigrated, the editorial continued, such a monument would "tell mightily in the interests not only of our Church, but of our whole race." AME leaders had come to see their church's founding as a triumph of religious freedom and to define this freedom as a signal accomplishment for African Americans in the United States. By narrating it as such, they identified themselves as fully committed to the nation's highest ideals, worthy of equal inclusion across the cultural, religious, and political landscapes of the United States.[19]

In many places the language of religious freedom worked to support the formation of new African American churches and to defend existing churches from their detractors. The storied history of Emanuel AME Church in Charleston, South Carolina, began in 1816 when white Methodists insisted on segregating their worship services and burial grounds. Confirming the fears of local white authorities, Emanuel became a nucleus for antislavery activism in the city. After the slave revolt planned by lay leader Denmark Vesey in 1822 was exposed, a white mob burned down the church building. Faced with new legal restrictions on black church activities, the congregation was forced underground. After the Civil War, its leaders fought to regain their property and rebuild. They answered white Methodist allegations that the AME Church was a segregationist organization by lauding their original founders as "the lovers of Christ and of religious liberty." Their church and by extension African Americans themselves were more committed to the ideals of Christianity and the Constitution than the white supremacists arrayed against them were.[20]

Black church leaders presented their achievement of religious freedom as a model for all African Americans, a key dimension of racial advancement. In the fall of 1865 three thousand people gathered in Charleston to watch AME leaders lay the cornerstone for Emanuel's new church building, with Denmark Vesey's son as its chief architect. Capturing the sense of hope that many felt on that occasion, one minister remarked that the "great central . . . idea of self-government and religious liberty has at last been enthroned in the minds of the citizens of Charleston." The church was growing rapidly among the freed people of South Carolina, AME missionary Theophilus Gould Stewart reported several years later, adding, "[We are] conferring religious freedom and responsibilities upon the people who join us." For Stewart the growth of the church was essential to the growth and progress of the race. Its activities, he wrote, were sparking "activity, reformation, revivals and rising manhood."[21]

Here the language of religious freedom also worked in a gendered register, identifying "manhood" and the quest to restore it to black men with the formation of the autonomous but also internally driven and controlled self. This was the ideal liberal subject, whose depictions more often assumed the norms and privileges of the white heterosexual male.[22] The AME Church had achieved and could now confer the freedom of religion, Stewart explained. In so doing, it empowered former slaves to face the future, claiming their rights and fulfilling their responsibilities as free people—or as free and manly men in particular—and as full citizens of the United States. In all these cases, religious freedom talk sought to locate African Americans as authentically Christian, fully American, and thoroughly modern subjects.

As the twentieth century dawned and the legal regimes of segregation in the United States grew ever more impenetrable, black church leaders continued to employ the language of religious freedom to assert the historic achievements of their people and their right to a place in the American mainstream. AME minister H. C. C. Astwood celebrated the memory of Richard Allen with flowery hyperbole typical of the times. Of all the "world's greatest reformers," Astwood said, Allen was "the greatest of them all." His achievements surpassed even those of Martin Luther, who had not faced enslavement and "stood the equal of his fellows"; of Charles Wesley, who had "dissented from a church where he stood foremost among its clergy"; and of the Haitian revolutionary hero Toussaint L'Ouverture, who had "erected the standard of Negro civil government" and so proved the civilizational capabilities (and the true manliness) of the race. While all these heroes merited the honors they had received, Allen towered over them all. "Our religious freedom was beyond the sight of human ken, when Richard Allen struck, with a blow from our limbs, the shackles of religious slavery and made us free indeed," Astwood said. "The world never knew what the Fatherhood of God and the brotherhood of men meant, until Allen, the giant of religious freedom, liberated the sons of Ham, fulfilling the prophecy that 'Ethiopia shall stretch forth her hands to God.'" The fatherhood of God and the brotherhood of man were ideals just coming into vogue at the time Astwood gave this address in 1897; they would increasingly help orient the goodwill and tri-faith movements that I described in chapter 4. Astwood presented Allen and by extension the African American churches as their manliest and indeed their most important pioneers.[23]

African American church leaders well beyond the AME Church similarly celebrated their founders as manly and modern champions of religious freedom. According to the *Washington Bee*, the featured speaker at the fifty-eighth anniversary of Galbraith African Methodist Episcopal Zion Church of Washington, D.C., in 1909—a leading congregation in this rival black Methodist denomination—"made the great men of Zion loom up like spiritual heroes of the stature of Luther, Knox, and Wesley." The African Methodist Episcopal Zion Church had been "brought into existence," he said, "by the sainted Richard Varicks, who was seeking religious liberty and striving to worship God according to the dictates of his own conscience." Other speakers at the anniversary event described an increasingly enforced racial segregation within a number of predominantly white church bodies. Their "colored communicants" should follow Varicks's example, they said, "and come into the great colored Methodist church[es] which welcomed [them] with open arms."[24] The black-owned *Savannah Tribune* similarly praised one Elder Sheafe, who had recently departed from the Seventh-day Adventist Church after experiences of racial discrimination to found the Free Seventh-day Adventists, as a "fearless champion of religious liberty."[25] As long as white churches continued to discriminate on racial grounds, these black church leaders and journalists contended, African Americans could secure the freedom of religion only within their own independent churches and denominations.

Given the historic Baptist commitment to religious freedom, it is not surprising that black Baptists too narrated their congregational histories and commitments through this lens. In sharp contrast to the white Southern Baptists profiled earlier in this chapter, they invoked this freedom against the practice of racial segregation whether in Baptist circles or in the larger society. Meeting in Washington, D.C., in 1914, members of one "council of colored Baptist ministers" protested their recent expulsion from the United Ministers Conference. Their offense had been to join in the newly formed Emergency Baptist Association, which had convened to tackle the problems of racial discrimination and violence. The United Ministers Conference considered that membership a violation of its rules prohibiting ministers from joining "any other Association or Convention." But these African American ministers argued that expelling them on such grounds was "unBaptistic, unprecedented, unchristian, inconsistent, and a violation of the principles of religious liberty for which Baptists have always contended even unto death." The Emergency Baptist Association and its members were in no way a threat to the conference, they explained, but should instead "be commended for the splendid work they are accomplishing and their steady loyalty to the Baptist Church, practices, and principles." In this case, religious freedom talk served as a challenge to the disciplinary practices of a predominantly white Baptist ministerial association.[26]

African Americans sometimes invoked religious freedom to challenge segregationist laws and municipal regulations that infringed on church activities or on their ability to attend the churches of their choice. One new ordinance, enacted by the city of Baltimore in 1911 with the stated purpose of "preserving peace" between the races, made it illegal "for white or colored people to start a new church or mission anywhere in the city without first securing a permit from the Board of Police Commissioners." It specified that all such churches or missions must be limited to either "white or colored people exclusively," thus outlawing racially integrated worship services in newly formed ministries. An editorial in the Baltimore-based *Afro-American* condemned this measure on religious freedom grounds. Under the new law, the editors explained, "it is not lawful for white and colored people, if they so desire, to meet together and worship their common 'Our Father who art in Heaven.'" The ordinance not only was dangerous to upstart churches, they noted, but also potentially criminalized the members of the Roman Catholic and Episcopalian churches, some of which had continued to hold racially integrated masses "as a matter of convenience" despite the segregated standards of the larger society. City authorities could now arrest a Catholic or Episcopal priest who presided over such services, particularly when a new priest was appointed or a new church building erected. Conceding that many churches were racially segregated as a matter of "custom" or preference, the editors asserted that any truly Christian "house of worship" should be on principle "open and free to whoever may come." No sincere "disciple of Jesus Christ" could support this "supreme affront to the supreme law of Christ." The measure violated both the Christian gospel and the basic constitutional principles of freedom.[27]

Beyond the achievements of the black churches, African American leaders defended black aptitudes by pointing to the achievements of a global African diaspora and especially of those African peoples who had demonstrated their commitments to democracy and freedom. The independent republic of Haiti had emerged from its anticolonial and antislavery revolutions in 1804 to become just the second nation in the Americas to gain its independence from European colonial rule. Like the Filipino leaders profiled in chapter 2, Haitians defended their right to independence by asserting their commitment to the principles of modernity, including the freedom of religion. A government circular issued in 1860 urged "Blacks, Men of Color, and Indians in the United States and British North American Provinces" to immigrate to Haiti. It promised new arrivals "a welcome, a home, and a free homestead," as well as "sites for the erection of schools and chapels . . . without regard to [their] religious belief." The circular went on to guarantee "the fullest religious liberty" and specifically that the predominantly Protestant emigrants would "never be called on to support the Roman Catholic Church." Haiti's constitution, modeled after that of the French Republic, had disestablished Catholicism and guaranteed complete religious freedom to all citizens. In the 1860 government circular, religious freedom talk served to reassure nervous black Protestants that Haiti's prevailing Catholicism would pose them no threat—and to identify Haitians in the eyes of a skeptical world as a modern people who were entirely capable of governing themselves.[28]

While they praised Haiti's achievement in gaining its independence, African American Protestants had real reservations about what they viewed as the superstitions of Catholicism and even more so about the African diasporic tradition of vodou that the majority of Haitians practiced. For the AME missionary Mary Ella Mossell, vodou ceremonies were "rites the most abominable and dissipations the most obscene."[29] Mossell prized a measured Protestant piety, one consistent with the politics of respectability that she and most middle-class African Americans at the time saw as the only realistic means of racial uplift. She saw vodou as an embarrassing regression to African "heathenism," discrediting Haiti's achievements and potentially imperiling the larger project of black emancipation. Refusing to accept any denigration of the Haitians' racial capacities, Mossell pointed to a rapidly growing missionary church as evidence of their immense potential. "Tired of the husks upon which they have been fed," she wrote, "they are seeking for greener pastures." The way forward into modernity, for Mossell, lay in Protestantism. Americans needed the gospel "to strengthen and perpetuate our free, liberal and republican institutions," she wrote, while Haitians needed it to "give birth to such institutions" and "break the spell" of "ignorance and superstition."[30] Haitians had managed to secure their independence, and AME leaders along with other African Americans had defended their right to that status even through the previous decade's riots and rebellions against an unstable government. But black Protestants like Mossell were convinced that they needed Protestant Christianity to enable the birth of a truly free republic. Once again, despite their presumed universality, the liberal values of freedom were predicated upon—and indeed helped constitute—civilizational assemblages of race and religion that were stacked against the peoples and traditions of the African diaspora.[31]

For many African Americans, Haiti was a less ambiguous source of racial pride. Its very existence as an independent republic proved that people of color were not racially inferior but possessed the same capacities for self-government, the same longing for freedom, as everyone else. Black Baptist missionary Solomon Porter Hood, a future U.S. minister to Liberia, attributed Haiti's political unrest to the "color question," or in other words to internal racial hierarchies that were the result of its colonial history.[32] The Haitians "stand alone in the Latin republics in their love of a broad-based religious liberty," asserted the *Colored American* in 1899. "Be it said to the glory of the Haitian people that they alone of all the Roman Catholic nations of the earth, not only guarantee perfect liberty of conscience and of worship to all men of whatever faith, but that . . . their Government grants state aid to the educational institutions of other bodies not of their religion. In this they give a unique example to the world."[33] Against the negative images of Haiti that were so widespread in the press, this writer invoked religious freedom to depict Haitians as *more* capable than others, not less, of honoring this cardinal principle of modernity. A decade later, the black-owned *Cleveland Gazette* reported that a traveler to Haiti had found not "barbarous rites" but "full religious liberty" and a people "very tolerant religiously." Both Protestants and Catholics had erected impressive buildings in Port-au-Prince that "would do credit to any city in the world," the traveler said, and the businessmen of Haiti were "fully alive to the commercial possibilities" of the soon-to-be-completed Panama Canal. The message was that the Haitians were a thoroughly modern people whose free and vibrant religion shaped an environment in which free commerce and capitalism could also flourish. The Haitians and by extension other African diasporic peoples did not need the pretended benevolence of imperial or white supremacist rule.[34]

As the United States claimed new colonies around the world—Hawai'i, the Philippines, Puerto Rico, Guam, and later Haiti—African Americans continued to invoke the idea of religious freedom both to celebrate their communal achievements and to assert their racial equality against the civilizational assemblages of an imperial world. Most black leaders supported President McKinley in the Spanish-American War and at least initially in the colonization of the Philippines. They did so partly in reaction against the racial politics of an anti-imperialist movement that impugned "colored races" as permanently inferior, incapable of joining equally in American democracy, and partly out of loyalty to a Republican Party that—however tepid its support for civil rights in recent years—had enabled their emancipation. But this support created a real dilemma because, as we saw in chapter 1, the majority case for imperialism also assumed white racial superiority. Sympathizing with Filipinos as the targets of racial and imperial violence, a growing number of black leaders repudiated U.S. imperialism altogether. Others, however, walked the tightrope of denouncing imperialist racism while supporting the civilizing and Christianizing agendas of U.S. empire. Like Mossell in Haiti, they positioned themselves as uniquely capable of bringing the gifts of freedom to America's new imperial subjects because they did not carry with them the poison of racial prejudice.[35]

Through a long history of involvements in Liberia and its environs, some African Americans had come to see themselves as the guardians of African freedoms, religious and otherwise.[36] In 1935 AME missionaries invoked the principle of religious freedom to challenge British and French colonial policies that limited their evangelical activities in West Africa. Llewellyn Berry, secretary-treasurer of the AME Missionary Department, urged that a bishop travel to Washington to defend Liberia—dominated since its founding by African American settlers—against the growing threat of an imperial annexation. Such lobbying efforts "would be most effective in ensuring that this open door to Christian endeavor in Africa will not be closed to the free operation of Negro Christian denominations," Berry wrote. "Only in Liberia are their hands untied by subtle restrictions. Every effort is exerted to block their orderly progress in other sections of West Africa." Liberia had become mired in debt, and its legitimacy as an independent nation was being challenged on all sides. White Americans and Europeans were using its plight as further proof that Africans were racially incapable of self-government. In this context, black church leaders highlighted their own commitments to Christianity, civilization, and freedom as a way to demonstrate the racial capacities of African diasporic peoples around the world.[37]

Through these representational strategies, African Americans rearticulated the civilizational hierarchies that others used to demean them. By asserting their own allegiance to the "civilized" standards of modernity and freedom and by distancing themselves from a "savage" or "heathen" past, black leaders implicitly accepted the dominant society's assignment of Africa and its people to a lower stage of civilizational development and its claims for Europe as the standard for modernity. At the same time, they extolled the potential of all people of color and identified themselves, black people presumably untainted by the stain of racial prejudice, as the bearers of a truly free Christian civilization. As participants in an imperial world, then, African Americans inevitably engaged in but also reworked the racial-religious assemblages of empire. "It must be the aim of the Church of Allen to enlarge itself so as to embrace the millions of the darker races who now plead admission," wrote AME missionary advocate Elder C. J. Powell in 1903, "and to raise them to their highest honor and use by bringing them in touch with the best types of Christian civilization, as well as into direct contact with the Savior of the world."[38] In their efforts to evangelize and civilize Haiti, Liberia, South Africa, and other parts of Africa and its diaspora, the men and women of the AME Church envisioned themselves as civilizing pioneers, uniquely equipped to bring the intertwined blessings of Christianity, freedom, and civilization to the members of their own race.

Not all African Americans accepted the black church leaders' formulations of religious freedom. Pointing to the racial segregation that characterized the nation's Baptist and Methodist church families, critics rejected the premise that these traditions even under black leadership could bring freedom in any meaningful way. Some turned instead to Catholicism for its proclaimed universality and for a posited refusal of racial distinctions within the church. The only challenge for "the colored Christian" in entering the Catholic Church, one black Catholic asserted in 1906, was the limits it imposed on their "shouting proclivities." In his view it had definite advantages that outweighed such devotional preferences. Given the option of a church that "offers protection to his body," he wrote, African Americans "should be willing to let shouting alone and pray in silence and conform to the rules governing that church." While white Baptists and Methodists refused to associate with the black people in their own church commun- ions, white Catholics treated "colored Catholics . . . as human beings and not as cattle." This was a rosy picture of race relations in the Catholic Church. While its structure and polity had indeed left Catholicism less segregated than its Protestant counterparts, Catholic parishes were hardly havens of racial equality and were becoming more and more segregated in prac- tice. Nevertheless, this black Catholic argued that the ideal universality of Catholicism offered superior resources for racial equality than anything the Protestant churches could provide.[39]

For my purposes, this critic's cynicism about the freedom of religion is more important than his claims for Catholic universality. "What the colored man wants today is not only religious freedom and protection," he con- cluded, "but civil and political freedom and protection."[40] In his view, the achievements of the independent black churches were limited to the sphere of religious expression, and ultimately he judged the cause of racial equal- ity to be more important. The promises of religious freedom that Method- ists and Baptists advanced were quite simply bankrupt, he had concluded, powerless to further the larger cause of African American freedom. He would not be the last to advance such claims.

REDEFINING PEOPLEHOOD: ETHNO-RELIGIOUS MOVEMENTS AND THE PROBLEM OF RACE

African Americans turned away from mainstream Christianity in signifi- cant numbers during the 1920s and 1930s as they sought new models for communal meaning and action and new ways to imagine themselves and their collective identities into the future. Against the backdrop of the dem- ocratic ideals that President Wilson had articulated in the First World War, they found not an expansion of civil rights but a resurgence of white Prot- estant nativism and racial violence. In that context many lost patience with the integrationist solutions for racial inequality that the established black Protestant churches and civic organizations such as the National Associa- tion for the Advancement of Colored People had for so long advanced. In their quest for new solutions, some forged new worlds of artistic expression in what came to be known as the Harlem Renaissance; others embraced the radical politics of the labor movement or the Communist Party; and still others joined one of the many new religious or ethno-religious movements that swept across African American communities in these years.

Particularly in the cities of the North and Midwest, these diverse new movements—including the United Negro Improvement Association, the Moorish Science Temple, the Peace Mission Movement, and the Nation of Islam—offered new ways to envision African American identities beyond the demeaning racial categories to which the dominant society had consigned them. These movements variously redefined the people commonly called "Negroes" as a nation, as a religion, or according to a more complex vision of collective identity that refused to disentangle the categories of race, nation, and religion. Whether or not they understood themselves in primarily religious terms, all of these groups found the all-American principle of religious freedom valuable in their efforts to make themselves intelligible within the cultural landscape of the United States and to defend against the threat of government suppression. The difficulties they faced reveal the racial assemblages that policed the boundaries of religious legitimacy and so set the limits of American religious freedom.

Black Nationalism and the Prospects of Religious Freedom

The cultural value of religious freedom had an impact even within movements that did not primarily identify themselves through the lens of religion. Those inclined to redefine black identity in nationalist terms—to envision themselves as a nation, a minority people within the United States who might one day be restored to an ancestral nation—invoked the principle of religious freedom first of all to advance their collective right to practice the religion they identified as their true national inheritance. But over time, the legal regimes of American religious freedom as well as the pragmatic realities of African American diversity would push these movements to endorse more individualist formations of religious freedom as well.

The largest black nationalist movement of the early twentieth century was the United Negro Improvement Association (UNIA). Founded in the 1910s under the leadership of Jamaican immigrant Marcus Garvey, the UNIA advocated self-improvement and self-reliance and redefined the American "Negro" as part of a pan-African diaspora. Garvey identified his movement with other anticolonial nationalisms, forging ties, for example, with the Irish anticolonial movement in Philadelphia and New York.[41] In other words, he articulated a diasporic nationalism that many African Americans found compelling. Unlike the majority of black church leaders, Garvey advocated the eventual return of African peoples to the African continent. This vision required the elimination of European colonial rule in Africa, which Garvey insisted was to be governed by Africans themselves. During the 1920s the UNIA attempted to help the Liberian government escape what had become an overwhelming burden of debt to the United States and sponsored several groups of emigrants to Liberia. For a variety of reasons this "back to Africa" effort faltered, but the UNIA maintained immense influence within the United States, where it advanced a powerful vision of pan-African identity and pride.[42]

At first glance, the category of religion had little to do with the UNIA's program. Garvey consciously modeled his pan-African nationalism after other diasporic nationalisms—Irish and Jewish in particular—that sought to call a nation-state into being in order to re-envision the future of an oppressed people. As we saw in chapter 4, Zionism defined what it meant to be Jewish in national far more than racial or religious terms. Both Zionists and the UNIA argued that freedom from racial oppression would ultimately require the secure foundation of a racially identified nation-state. "The culmination of all the efforts of the UNIA must end in Negro independent nationalism on the continent of Africa," Garvey asserted in the correspondence school curriculum that he named the School of African Philosophy. "No race is free until it has a strong nation of its own, its own system of government and its own order of society."[43] But the UNIA had even greater barriers to overcome than its Zionist counterpart. In contrast to Palestine, the continent of Africa was vast, and its people had never existed as a single entity outside of the diasporic imagination. Moreover, in Africa the global configurations of race and empire posed far greater barriers to self-rule. As the Communist newspaper the *Daily Worker* put it in 1924, "The Great Powers and the League of Nations can cheerfully give a few thousand Jews a chance to settle in Palestine, but cannot tolerate for one instance the propaganda for Negro independent nationalism in any quarter of Africa . . . especially not in the 'fanatical' form in which alone this movement is founded." The racializing assemblages of empire made it difficult for white Americans to see such aspirations on the part of the "Negro" as anything but delusional.[44]

Yet for the UNIA as for the Zionists, reconfigurations of race and nation also had implications for the category of religion. In fact Garvey consciously articulated a religious vision that corresponded to his nationalist vision. He taught that God had created each people "for a particular purpose" and that in order to fulfill that purpose they must develop their own institutions, their own ideals, and their own nations. Even further, he rejected the idea of a "white God" and argued that, although in reality "God [had] no color," Negroes should "worship Him through the spectacles of Ethiopia."

The UNIA Constitution required each chapter to appoint a chaplain to tend to members' "spiritual concerns." Their meetings followed the general format of a Protestant church service, complete with hymns from the UNIA hymnal and often Bible readings and prayers as well. God had chosen the American Negro to bring about "the redemption of Africa" at last, Garvey taught, and they would restore Africa and Africans to their rightful stature on the world stage. Pointing to these aspects of the movement, one historian has identified Garvey as a pioneering black theologian and the UNIA movement as a kind of "black civil religion."[45]

Much of the religious freedom talk within the UNIA directly supported the movement's nationalist vision. For some UNIA leaders, this freedom signified the collective right of the "Negro Peoples" to define their own religion. Alexander McGuire was a longtime UNIA officer and the founding bishop of the African Orthodox Church, which he envisioned as the unifying church for all African peoples. McGuire explained in 1924 that when the UNIA Constitution named the promotion of "a conscientious spiritual worship among the native tribes of Africa" as a primary object, it meant a "religion . . . [that] we consider conscientious for us as Negroes." McGuire understood the freedom of religion as a right accruing not simply to individuals but also, and more important, to the racial or national collectivity. "Spiritual freedom is the basis of all other freedoms," he said. "And in the exercise of this freedom we claim the right to set forth theology as we understand it." Understood in this way, a fully developed nation required its own religious identity and vision. Religion could not be separated from race and nation.[46]

Rather than operating at the level of the individual conscience, then, religious freedom served to defend the religion that defined a people. At times Garvey articulated much the same vision. According to the curriculum of his School of African Philosophy, the Negro would ideally "have his own Church" and should not "adopt the peculiar articles of faith of the churches of alien races." The Negro "is not a Hebrew, therefore he would not adopt the Hebrew faith," the lesson continued. "He is not by origin a Roman Catholic nor an Anglican, because these faiths or religions were founded by white men with an idea of their own." Since the historical Jesus was not a white man, Christianity as a whole did not belong to the white race. Thus the Negro could "safely . . . adopt articles of faith to link him to the godhead of the Christian faith" as long as they reflected the Negro's racial character and national interests. Understood in this way, the freedom of religion supported the UNIA's vision for a proudly independent African people.[47]

This was not, however, the only variety of religious freedom that the UNIA articulated. Garvey ultimately sought to incorporate all the peoples of the African diaspora, and he insisted quite pragmatically that the movement must be religiously inclusive. The UNIA's "Declaration of the Rights of the Negro Peoples of the World" (1920) called for "the freedom of religious worship" for African diasporic peoples everywhere, and Garvey also applied this principle within the movement. "You may be a Christian; you may be a Mohammedan; that is your religion," he explained at the Sixth International UNIA Convention in 1929. "Some of us are Catholics, some of us are Presbyterians, some of us are Baptists, and we deem it a right to adhere to our particular belief."[48] By legitimating the movement's existing diversity of religious commitments, this statement helped alleviate simmering conflicts over which church best served African American interests and discouraged any effort to impose a single religious orthodoxy on all its members. Ultimately, Garvey's insistence that the movement could have no single "state religion" made it impossible for the African Orthodox Church to become the UNIA's official church.

This more individualist articulation of religious freedom enabled the UNIA to welcome all African Americans into its ranks, whether they were Baptists, Methodists, Catholics, or otherwise. In so doing, it contradicted the communalist vision of one religion for all African peoples. Both versions of religious freedom countered racial stereotypes by positioning its leaders and the "Negro Peoples" they aimed to represent as committed to this all-American ideal, as products of the American experiment and equal participants in the modern world. Thus for the UNIA, religious freedom talk worked simultaneously to shape a collective sense of peoplehood, to navigate the movement's internal diversities, and to identify African Americans with the liberal principles of modernity.

The Moorish Science Temple and the Quest for Religious Legitimacy

For African American movements that defined themselves in explicitly religious terms but moved outside the bounds of Christianity, the promise of religious freedom would prove far more difficult to claim. Among the earliest of these groups was the Moorish Science Temple of America (MST), established in 1926 by a recent arrival in Chicago who soon assumed the name Noble Drew Ali. Building on a wide variety of sources, Drew Ali redefined the people others called Negroes as "Asiatic Moors" whose rightful religion was Islam.[49] Stolen from their homeland in Africa and sold into slavery, the Moors had lost all knowledge of their true history and identity. Like Garvey, Drew Ali articulated a diasporic nationalism that linked his followers to a proud lineage and a history that transcended the United States. Indeed, he named Garvey as a "forerunner . . . divinely prepared [to] teach and warn the nations of the earth to prepare to meet the Prophet," just as John the Baptist had prepared the way for Jesus. Moorish Americans, he said, had to reclaim their true identity and true religion if they were to throw off the shackles of slavery and inequality at last.[50] Drew Ali taught that the Moors, like any other people, should practice the religion of their national inheritance: "Every nation shall and must worship under their own vine and fig tree, and return to their own and be one with their Father God—Allah." This was a collectivist ideology of religious freedom much like McGuire's, identifying Islam rather than the African Orthodox Church as the proper religion for the redefined Moorish nation.[51]

Unlike Garvey, however, Drew Ali did not teach that the Moorish Americans should immigrate to Africa or anywhere else. Indeed, he consistently denounced any "back-to-Africa" schemes as unrealistic for such a large number of people and even against their best interests. Rather, he encouraged his followers to reclaim their true identities as Moorish Americans precisely so they could claim their constitutional rights and freedoms and participate on equal terms in the life of the United States. In so doing they would be following the example of every other proud immigrant nationality in the United States: the Germans, the Irish, the Poles, the Hebrews, and many more. Thus the incorporation papers for the "Moorish Temple of Science" in November 1926 listed the goals of "uplift[ing] fallen humanity and teach[ing] those things necessary to make men and women become better citizens."[52] In an article that may have been contributed by the MST itself, the black-owned *Chicago Defender* praised the movement's "economic program," its impressive growth across fifteen states, and the success of its business enterprises in several cities. Without commenting on its claim to an Islamic identity, the paper stressed the movement's contributions to a distinctly American future. "This organization is playing a useful and definite part in advancing the sacred obligations of American citizenship," the article explained. Indeed, it was "blazing the trail and marking the pathway over which our posterity may travel unhampered and unafraid." The *Defender* reported that the movement's upcoming convention would begin with "an interesting parade," featuring a camel along with "regalia similar to that worn in eastern countries." Economic success and ultimately civic equality would come with the people's recovery of and pride in their true Moorish American identity.[53]

Within the Moorish Science Temple, then, religious freedom talk facilitated a process of communal redefinition away from the negative racial formation of the Negro and toward the new ethno-religious identity of the Moorish American. At the same time, it underlined the movement's commitment to the United States and its constitutional ideals and in so doing sought to locate these new Moorish Americans as fully modern subjects. The *Moorish Guide*, launched in the fall of 1928 with "the Prophet Noble Drew Ali" as its publisher and editor, noted that the guarantee of "religious freedom" under the U.S. Constitution protected the right of the Moors to "believe in, and foster the Moslem religion." This freedom empowered MST members to embrace Islam and so supported a shift in the way they categorized their peoplehood. "It is only from a purely religious standpoint (it seems at this time) that we differ from other Americans," the *Moorish Guide* proclaimed. Moorish Americans were fully American, fully committed to the constitutional ideals of the United States and to the freedom of religion that supported their right to claim their true national religion of Islam.[54]

The parenthetical in the quote above was significant: in fact Moorish Americans asserted their difference in ways they understood to be more than religious. Drew Ali granted each new member a new surname, either Bey or El, to mark their freedom from the false names and identities that had continued to enslave them. All this was profoundly liberating for many of those who joined the movement, as Judith Weisenfeld has shown. One convert named Sister L. Blakey Bey explained that when new members received their Moorish Nationality Cards, some experienced for the first time a sense of "freedom from slavery, freedom from Negro, black, colored, and likewise from the fetters of Christianity."[55] When they identified themselves as Moors and Moslems, the MST faithful did not simply reject the negatively racialized category of the Negro but redefined themselves as an ethno-religious people who could, through that redefinition, enjoy the rights and freedoms of American citizenship on equal terms.

This communal redefinition, however, would never gain traction in the larger society. To the extent that outsiders noticed the Moorish Science Temple at all, they portrayed it as a fraudulent or primitive "cult." The group gained its first sustained media coverage after the tragic shooting death of Claude Greene, the MST's business manager and a well-known figure in Chicago's African American community. Investigators claimed that Greene was among the leaders of "a faction opposing the Prophet" and that Drew

Ali himself had ordered his execution.[56] After questioning more than forty people, the police arrested the prophet and temporarily imprisoned him pending trial. In an unexpected turn of events, Drew Ali died quite suddenly after his release on bail. His death certificate listed the cause of death as tuberculosis, but many of his followers believed that he had died of injuries inflicted by the police. Worse yet, newspapers reported that the prophet had taken several wives, two of them still in their teens. Newspapers jumped on the story of a "love cult" and a "Moorish leader's amours." This initial wave of coverage depicted the movement as a deceptive cult, allegedly created by Drew Ali to defraud his followers and to enable his seduction of young girls. Certainly it was not a legitimate religion.[57]

City authorities defined the Moorish Science Temple as a "fanatical" threat to the city's racial order. The Chicago Police Department escalated the crisis through military-style displays of force, deemed necessary because of the racial attributes that authorities assigned to the "Negro." Hearing of continuing conflicts over the movement's leadership—six different men apparently claimed to be the new leader after Drew Ali's death, ultimately fracturing the movement—officials sent five hundred police officers to quell "what they thought was going to be a riot."[58] In another incident, reports of a kidnaped "cult member" led to a police raid and a shootout that killed one policeman and two Moorish Americans. Authorities viewed the predominantly African American neighborhood of the South Side as a problem, a likely trouble spot requiring regular disciplinary attention. A large-scale police presence thus appeared essential to keeping the peace.[59]

Newspaper accounts dismissed the movement's claims to the status of religion, using a variety of representational strategies to police the boundaries of religious orthodoxy. One article described the MST as "semi-political . . . with racketeering activities directed against the poor and ignorant." Using the historically constructed dichotomy between religion and politics, this piece located the MST in the latter sphere. At the same time, the charge of "racketeering" portrayed the entire movement as a deliberate fraud. The article went on to posit that the MST had marshaled the elements of religion in service of its deceit. Its leaders had assembled "a strange jumble of mysticism, Mohammedanism, Buddhism, and Confucianism, all mixed with a dash of Christianity and a lot of buncombe," the writer claimed, and "outfitted themselves with regalia and pretentious ceremonials for the purpose of impressing their dupes." Such descriptions portrayed any blending of traditions—the sort of creative hybridity that scholars of religion have attributed to all new religious movements—as inconsistent with religious authenticity.[60] Reporters drew on the stereotype of black religiosity as irrational, emotional, and out of control, attributing the violence in Chicago to a "Negro fanatic's plot" and to the "ignorance" of a "Negro cult."[61] This coverage rearticulated familiar civilizational assemblages of race and religion to portray the Moorish Science Temple in racialized terms as a threat to the social order.

African American newspapers were almost as dismissive as their white counterparts. Like most black professionals, African American journalists participated in a middle-class politics of respectability that contended for racial equality by championing middle-class values and virtues in black communities.[62] They tended to see groups like the MST as an embarrassment, tainting their own hard-earned respectability and so inhibiting progress for all black people in America. But rather than attributing its "fanaticism" to the racial failings of the "Negro" as such, they emphasized the familiar trope of the "fanatical Muslim." In language that echoed earlier depictions of the Moros in the Philippines, Baltimore's *Afro-American* claimed that this "cult" had fed its members a false "Mohammedanism, the basis of which is that it is better to die in the cause of the 'prophet' than a natural death." Similarly, the coroner's office investigating the recent deaths in Chicago advised that the state of Illinois should "revoke the license granted the Moorish Science Temple" so that "the imitators of the dress and rites of Mohammedanism" could be required to "return to normalcy." Even as they blamed the violence in Chicago on Islam, which they considered an inherently violent and out-of-bounds religion, these accounts suggested that the MST was not even legitimately Muslim. Thus they doubly rejected the movement's claims to the protected status of religion in the United States.[63]

The earliest Federal Bureau of Investigation report on the Moorish Science Temple, filed in 1931, reflected a lack of accurate information about the group and a complete dismissal of its claims. Investigating the MST chapter in Reading, Pennsylvania, an FBI agent reported that its leader, surnamed Bey, had insisted that he was "not a negro, but a descendant of the Moors." The agent felt the need to comment, however, that Bey had "all of the appearance and characteristics of a full-blooded negro." Because he saw the familiar racial categories of American life as stable and self-evident, the agent viewed the effort to reframe communal identity—whether in national or ethno-religious terms—as evidence of a delusional extremism. Bey was "fanatic on the subject of equality for all races," the agent concluded, "and is attempting to promote and carry on the MST for propaganda purposes." A subsequent report described Bey as "crazy," claiming that locals in Reading considered him "more or less of a joke and no one took him seriously, not even the Negroes." For the time being, while the MST had already appeared on the FBI's radar screen as a potential threat to the racial order, investigators considered the group too small and insignificant to cause serious problems.[64]

The Moorish Science Temple that emerged from the crisis of 1929 invoked the principle of religious freedom to assert its legitimacy as a religion.[65] The booklet *Moorish Literature* (1935) reprinted a number of pieces by Noble Drew Ali and dated its "Authority and Rights of Publishing" to 1928, but it also included two letters clearly written in 1935 and several new articles attributed only to "Prophet Noble Drew Ali Who Has Reincarnated in Another Form." Among these was the "Moorish Leader's Historical Message to America," also published in the *Moorish Guide* for July 1935, which explained that although the MST had first been "incorporated as a civic organization," it had later filed an affidavit changing it "to a religious corporation" because its work was "largely religious." After denouncing the "Christian ministers" who had attacked the movement, the article went on to explain that under the U.S. Constitution, "one of the greatest documents of all time," nobody had the "legal right to oppose citizens, individuals, and organizations . . . for their religious belief."[66]

The message then offered a paean to American religious freedom. Without this freedom, "no search for truth would be possible . . . no discovery of truth would be useful . . . religious progress would be checked," it maintained, "and we would no longer march forward toward the nobler life which the future holds for the races of men." This article strategically deployed the rhetorics of Christian republicanism, exploding the white and Christian boundaries of that tradition to place Moorish Americans clearly within its scope. Here, despite its reputation for militant nationalism, the MST used religious freedom talk as part of an effort to escape the strictures of race and to reclassify those generally called "Negroes" as one of many nationalities or ethno-religious people groups within the United States.[67]

"Father Divine Is God": Domesticating the Peace Mission Movement

Not all of the new religious movements that attracted African American members in the interwar years articulated religious freedom in a primarily nationalist vein. Starting in the late 1920s, Father Divine's Peace Mission Movement rejected the categories of race altogether and advanced a more integrationist model of religious activism. Born George Baker to a working-class black family in Maryland, Father Divine had been profoundly shaped by the New Thought emphasis on the power of mental energies to change one's circumstances in life. As a young man, Baker had visited California in 1909 and apparently had participated, albeit briefly, in the revivals at Azusa Street. His movement therefore linked New Thought themes with the charismatic worship practices of Pentecostalism. After a time of religious seeking, the future Father Divine had moved in 1919 to the predominantly white neighborhood of Sayville in Suffolk County, Long Island, where he gathered about thirty followers, including his wife, Penninah. There he created a small employment agency that helped some of them and many others find work.[68]

Father Divine taught that he was the embodied manifestation of God for the present age and that each person had the ability to access the divine within. He told his followers that race was an illusion, there were no whites or Negroes, and all were equal in the eyes of God. As devotee Priscilla Paul explained to a reporter, "He is the light of the world, and he has come to unify his love in all people. There is no race or creed or sect or nationality or government or color." At their headquarters in Sayville, believers celebrated the presence of the living God with ecstatic worship and lavish, multicourse banquets that by 1931 were attracting busloads of people from across the region. As the woes of the Depression intensified, the bounty of Father Divine's table became a symbol of divine power, a very real attraction to those who suffered the daily realities of poverty and hunger. Father Divine also drew a number of wealthy white followers, most of whom found him through New Thought channels and were drawn to the idealism of his message and to his charismatic presence. At banquets and worship services, Divine had light- and dark-skinned followers seated in an alternating pattern in order to emphasize the erasure of racial distinctions within the movement.[69]

Religious freedom would become important to the Peace Mission Movement as a crucial means of defense against the legal challenges and harassments it faced. Neighbors in Sayville were increasingly disturbed by the large numbers of visitors to the house and by the noise of their activities, particularly when worship continued late into the night. The intensity of their opposition and the seriousness with which local officials took their charges reflected a white community's intertwined fears of racial pollution and religious heterodoxy. Police repeatedly raided the property and issued charges of disorderly conduct. After an undercover investigation failed to find evidence of illegal activities, Father Divine himself was arrested in May

1931 on charges of public nuisance. African Americans even outside the movement viewed all of this as racially motivated harassment. Editorials in black newspapers explained that most whites could not believe that a black man could spend money so freely unless he had some illegal source of funds and that they resented the success of a "Negro" who not only had attracted an interracial group of followers but also had the nerve to claim that he was God.[70] The prominent Harlem lawyer and former assistant U.S. attorney general James C. Thomas offered to provide Divine with legal services to combat "the un-American and prejudiced treatment accorded you and your followers in deprivation of constitutional rights of property and freedom of religious worship." The Peace Mission Movement thus began to define and defend its interests via the First Amendment. In contrast to the communalist and nationalist visions of the UNIA and the Moorish Science Temple, its religious freedom talk would always be linked to the rights of the individual under the U.S. Constitution.[71]

The dramatic events surrounding Father Divine's trial in the spring and summer of 1932 turned the movement into a national sensation. Thomas managed to convince the judge to move Divine's trial out of Suffolk County on the grounds that any jury there would be hopelessly biased. But the neighboring Nassau County was, in the attorney's words, "a change from the frying pan into the fire."[72] After the jury found Divine guilty, Justice Lewis Smith imposed an unusually harsh sentence of a $500 fine and a year in jail. Reflecting the racial-religious assemblages of the dominant society, Smith explained that Divine had lied about his true identity, was not "an ordained minister" in any recognized church, and represented "a menace to society."[73] But a few days later the media exploded with the news that the judge had died unexpectedly of a heart attack and that Divine's followers were attributing his death to the "supernatural powers" of their "God." "Harlem All Agog!" one headline read. Father Divine himself implied that the heart attack had been a regretful but necessary consequence of the judge's actions.[74] When a Superior Court judge subsequently released him from jail pending appeal, the celebrations multiplied. In "a monster hallelujah meeting," seven thousand worshippers greeted Divine with the movement's iconic refrain—"It is wonderful!"—and testified to the miraculous healings he had performed. Observers marveled that although collection plates were never passed at his services, resources were always plentiful. New branches of the movement soon appeared across the East Coast, most notably in New Jersey, and within two years there would be missions as far away as Colorado and California.[75]

Around this time Divine's followers began to link the freedom of religion to his miraculous powers. At a rally in Philadelphia, devotees explained to reporters that Divine had been tried and convicted "for his uncompromising stand for unrestricted worship of God by all races" and had demonstrated his power by walking free ten days later "with a court injunction restraining any and all from interference with his religious worship." Here Father Divine appeared as the champion of religious freedom, victorious over the court that had recently convicted him. For true believers, his successful deployment of religious freedom against the odds of a simultaneously racial and religious discrimination served as one more proof of his divinity. In this instance at least, they described him as a divine guardian of American freedoms against the oppressive hierarchies of a racialized state.[76]

The larger society did not accept this interpretation, however, and the movement continued to contend with competing visions of religious freedom. A series of legal battles in New Jersey pitted this freedom against charges of noise pollution and public nuisance. As on Long Island, these charges could not be separated from the co-constituted hierarchies of race and religion. During a series of services at Brighton Theater in East Orange, white residents complained to the city council about the "shrieking and moaning of the communicants." Some "more candid" residents openly objected to the movement's interracial character and voiced suspicions of sexual improprieties between Father Divine and the "white 'Angels'" among his assistants. The city responded with "a large detachment of policemen and firemen," purportedly sent "to prevent race trouble," who enforced orders for the meeting to adjourn promptly at ten o'clock in keeping with "the city's anti-noise ordinance."[77] Similar complaints emerged in Newark, where a judge for the state's Third Precinct likewise ordered Father Divine to end all worship services by ten o'clock. "The Constitution guarantees religious liberty," the judge commented, "but that doesn't mean that you are allowed to annoy other people. If you want to have wailing and gnashing of teeth, you ought to take a walk out in the desert."[78]

For this judge, the freedom of religion clearly did not protect activities that appeared unorthodox, transgressing the restrained style of the white Protestant churches that set the model of religious legitimacy in America. In a recent book aptly titled *Religion Out Loud*, Isaac Weiner has shown that minority religious expressions, simply because they stand out from a community's expected norms, have been defined and disciplined as "noise" far more than the familiar sounds of mainstream religious practices—church bells, hymn singing, and in some contexts outdoor devotions such as pilgrimages and fiestas—even when their decibel levels are not discernibly different.[79] Faced with a controversial new religious movement, public officials in New Jersey denied that the First Amendment posed any impediment to restrictions on noise that they construed as a public nuisance. That judgment cannot be separated from the controversially heterodox and mixed-race character of the movement.

The legal difficulties of the Peace Mission Movement multiplied over the course of the next year. In August 1932, the East Orange City Council "unearthed a state statute which declares that anyone who leads his followers to believe he is a deity is guilty of a misdemeanor" and sent a police squadron to shut down its services.[80] When the movement's local leaders refused to comply, five of them were imprisoned for "helping Father Divine to pretend he is Jesus Christ."[81] Another controversy developed in Newark, where an abandoned husband filed charges against Divine for "breaking up his home." His wife had followed Divine's teaching against sexual intimacy even within marriage and finally moved with their daughter into the local "kingdom" headquarters. Bishop John Selkridge, who had emerged as Divine's chief lieutenant in Newark, appeared in court to contest the charges. He failed to persuade the judge, who issued a warrant for Divine's arrest and had Selkridge arrested on charges of conspiracy. The judge explained that the principle of religious freedom did not protect any behavior that posed a threat to public morality. "I will not meddle with any religion," he explained, "but when an individual is trying to break up homes in this section I am interested." No matter how its leaders articulated their claims to religious freedom, this unorthodox and predominantly black movement was subject to regular harassment by local authorities.[82]

Yet in the long run Father Divine and his followers emerged victorious. When Bishop Selkridge and four others were imprisoned once again, this time on charges of disorderly conduct, their attorney argued that "the court had no right to interfere with the manner in which either prayer or singing was conducted within the church."[83] They filed a lawsuit contending that they were breaking no law and that Newark's ban on Peace Mission Movement services had "deprived [them] of their constitutional rights" to "enjoy religious liberty." After some deliberation, the Chancery Court issued a restraining order against the city, preventing officials from interfering with services in the temple.[84] A superior court later reversed the sentence against Selkridge, ruling that while "the right to freedom of religious worship did not include the right to commit public nuisance," there was insufficient evidence to convict him in this case. When the judge who had originally sentenced Selkridge was himself arrested on disorderly conduct charges, Father Divine's followers celebrated another divine retribution.[85] Once Divine's own appeal in the Sayville case wound its way through the courts in New York, his conviction too was finally reversed. After the Superior Court judge had heard all the arguments in the case, he "agreed with [Divine's] lawyer that freedom of religious expression was guaranteed to all under the American Constitution" and ordered the trial court to refund all the fines that Divine and his followers had paid.[86]

Despite its unorthodoxies and its challenge to the segregated order of American life, the Peace Mission Movement would gradually gain a degree of legitimacy as a religion in the eyes of the larger society. That acceptance came with a great deal of ambivalence. One committee of prominent white citizens, appointed to investigate Father Divine's activities in New Jersey, produced what they intended to be a balanced report. In condescending and racially coded language, the committee noted the "excessively emotional" and gullible nature of Father Divine's followers. While insisting that they were "not concerned with the religious belief of the members," they criticized Father Divine for presenting himself as God and for destroying his adherents' "belief and faith in medical science." Proper religion, as construed by that category's liberal gatekeepers, was not to be confused with science. Religious leaders were expected to maintain a clear distinction between prayers for healing on one hand, which were to be kept safely in the realm of the spiritual, and the practice of medicine on the other, in which actual healing took place. Proper religion had spiritual but not material efficacy, in other words, and Father Divine's movement had clearly transgressed these bounds.[87]

At the same time, the committee concluded that the Peace Mission Movement had some positive effects, such as encouraging "collective charitable action" and "respect for spiritual aspects of life." One of its members, who ultimately refused to sign the final report because he found it too negative, told reporters that "Father Divine's religious teachings" had improved the lives of many people. Stereotypical views of African American racial capacities ultimately supported the committee's acceptance of the movement as religious. The report commented that many Negroes were attracted to such movements out of an "instinctive search for God and assurance of a life hereafter" and the "desire to escape from the realities of life and impoverished conditions." Negroes were "naturally an emotional people, simple in their beliefs," and "easily influenced by those who offer either economic or social security," it concluded. This committee found it entirely comprehensible that such a people would accept the sort of "deluded" and "emotional" religion that Father Divine offered. They had more trouble accounting for his white followers, some of them possessing "evident respectability and refinement." Ultimately the report depicted these believers as anomalies who were most likely mentally unbalanced. Their stereotypical depictions of black religion allowed the committee to grant the Peace Mission Movement a sort of conditional religious legitimacy. In short, they considered it a simple and emotional religion, ultimately harmless and well suited to the poor situation and limited capacities that they attributed to the Negro.[88]

The perception that Father Divine taught a peaceful and primarily "spiritual" message facilitated the gradual acceptance of his movement. News reports often depicted the movement in this way despite Divine's programs for economic advancement and his active involvement in campaigns against poverty and racism. Divine actually worked with the Communist Party for a time, finding affinities with its emphasis on peace and social equality. In 1934 and 1935, thousands of his followers joined Communist marches in New York City, carrying banners that read "Father Divine Is God!" Party leaders tentatively welcomed these marchers as "fellow workers," hoped they would join the proletarian revolution, and dismissed their religious claims as a temporary delusion.[89] Other observers, however, hoped the influence could flow in the other direction. One *New York Times* headline proclaimed, "Red Rally Dimmed by Harlem Fervor: Negroes' Camp Meeting Spirit Eclipses Radicals' Turnout in Anti-war March." Mocking the Communists for protesting "against virtually everything but communism," this writer presented black religious emotionalism as just the thing to tame them. Here the Peace Mission Movement appeared as a useful if simplistic salve for Communist radicalism. Intellectual elites would keep their distance. But if Divine's "religious fervor" could drown out the Communists, then his movement merited a degree of recognition in religious terms. At least some white liberals had come to see it as a legitimate religion, one that avoided political radicalism and—in contrast to groups like the UNIA or the Moorish Science Temple—instilled a spiritual message of peace and love.[90]

Father Divine's work for economic and racial justice remained controversial. In the midst of the New Deal era, Divine convened a three-day summit in Harlem that drew six thousand people, including representatives from a variety of pacifist, civil rights, and left-wing organizations. Under his leadership they produced a "Righteous Government Platform" that outlined a detailed program for full employment and an end to racial inequality. This platform never received significant attention beyond those who had framed it. According to historian Robert Weisbrot, its most important consequence lay in Divine's own growing involvement in the effort to pass antilynching legislation. But the racially integrated Peace Mission Movement was a red rag to hardline segregationists, and antilynching advocates in Congress generally considered Divine's involvement a political liability rather than a benefit. "Imagine a people in America seriously believing that the son of a slave is God!" commented a Louisiana senator as he made his case against one antilynching measure. For this senator, Divine illustrated the ignorance of the Negro race and the dangers of a "political equality" that would inevitably lead to "social equality" as well. In the racial-religious assemblages of white supremacy, the Peace Mission Movement hardly merited protection under the First Amendment. Rather, it demonstrated the permanence of Negro inferiority and the need to remain vigilant in defense of the southern racial order.[91]

Nevertheless, the Peace Mission Movement increasingly succeeded in invoking the principle of religious freedom against bureaucratic harassments and even violent assaults. Two separate controversies in the spring of 1935, one in New York and one in Colorado, illustrate this point. When officials in Manhattan charged Divine and his lieutenant Faithful Mary with child endangerment and operating a boardinghouse without a license, they were acquitted largely on religious freedom grounds.[92] Soon thereafter in Ivywild, Colorado, more than a hundred white residents protested against a new Peace Mission in their neighborhood as "an invasion of Negroes." Gathering outside as a worship service began, protesters threw stones through the mission's windows and set fire to cans of gasoline outside the building. After a county commissioner denounced the violence and advised the local sheriff "that the Constitution guaranteed the right to worship without molestation," the sheriff forced the crowd to disperse and escorted the mixed-race worshippers to their vehicles. Despite many more threats over the next several years, local authorities continued to protect the mission. Divine ultimately convinced the Colorado governor that his movement merited constitutional protection, and the Ivywild mission remained open without serious difficulties.[93]

Over time, the Peace Mission Movement responded to its legal difficulties by taming its radical edges and conforming more and more closely to the dominant society's norms for religion. In this respect it was similar to some of the Native American movements profiled in chapter 3. As with the Native American Church and the Indian Shakers of the Pacific Northwest, legal incorporation was a key part of this process. Weisbrot writes that incorporation "afforded the Peace Mission legal status on par with other churches, providing at least a partial antidote to the tendency of trial judges to treat the Peace Mission as a barely legitimate 'racket.'"[94] Once it enjoyed the legal status of a church, the movement's religious legitimacy could less easily be dismissed. Also like the Indian Shakers, the process of legal incorporation encouraged the movement to codify a new structure of church trustees and ministers, facilitating institutional continuity but reducing the prospects for new charismatic leadership.

By the 1950s, Father Divine would join tri-faith religious leaders in denouncing communism as a threat to the American values of freedom, democracy, and religion. The "Crusader's Creed," recited by members in this period, identified America as "the Birthplace of the Kingdom of God on Earth" and endorsed the U.S. Constitution "with its Bill of Rights and Amendments" as "Divinely Inspired . . . instruments of the synonymous teachings of Democracy, Brotherhood, Americanism, Christianity, and True Judaism." Blending the Bill of Rights with President Roosevelt's Four Freedoms, the creed went on to assert belief in "the Freedom of Religious Worship, the Freedom of Expression, the Freedom to assemble peacefully, the Freedom from want and the Freedom from fear." These statements were by no means apolitical. But they presented a deeply patriotic and profoundly individualistic vision that was distinguishable from the period's prevailing tri-faith conventions only through its confessional claim that "Father Divine . . . is our Father-Mother-God."[95] Religious freedom talk had enabled the Peace Mission Movement to claim the status of religion in America, one that the racializing assemblages of the larger society made perpetually unstable. Securing that status meant withdrawing from the movement's early radicalism, retreating from involvement in arenas that the larger society designated political, and so conforming to dominant conventions for what counted as authentically religious.

The Nation of Islam and the Racial-Religious Assemblages of a Nation at War

As the Second World War broke out in Europe and Asia and across the Atlantic and Pacific worlds, the ethno-religious movements most active in African American communities faced a rising level of federal suspicion and surveillance. At the end of the 1930s the United States was finding it less and less possible to remain uninvolved in this developing global crisis. Federal authorities feared the threats of German and Japanese infiltration and of more diffuse forms of influence and propaganda that might reshape homegrown disloyalties toward traitorous ends. The civilizational assemblages of U.S. empire turned all this into a recipe for new levels of government harassment against racialized minorities as well as immigrants. For African Americans— especially those involved in heterodox ethno-religious movements that had located themselves outside the bounds of Christianity, such as the Moorish Science Temple and the newer Nation of Islam—religious freedom would provide a limited and always problematic avenue for self-defense. The Nation of Islam shifted in these years from a communalist-nationalist ideology of religious freedom, which it never entirely abandoned, toward a more pragmatic emphasis on the rights of conscience and the movement's legitimacy as a religion under the U.S. Constitution. Yet the larger society would continue to categorize this movement as dangerously political, not authentically religious, thus exposing the racial-religious assemblages that bounded religious freedom in American life.

The Nation of Islam (NOI), founded in Detroit in the early 1930s, joined other black nationalist and ethno-religious movements by redefining the terms of African American peoplehood along the co-constituted lines of race, nation, and religion. Wallace D. Fard had reportedly served as a grand sheik in Chicago's Moorish Science Temple before he moved to the Motor City, where he began to call the "so-called Negroes of America" back to their rightful identity within what he initially named the Lost-Found Nation of Islam. Fard encountered various difficulties, including repeated police harassment, and after several years he simply disappeared. His committed disciple Elijah Muhammad proved to be a gifted and charismatic new leader for the reconstituted NOI. As interpreted and disseminated by Muhammad, Fard's distinctive theology celebrated Black people as the original humans, a divine race once known as the tribe of Shabazz. (My capitalization of "Black" and "White" here follows the NOI's conventions.) The White race had originated as a kind of science experiment gone awry and had multiplied to subjugate Black people for a period of four hundred years. Now that time was finally coming to an end, and Allah had incarnated himself in the person of Fard to restore Black people to their knowledge of themselves and their true racial religion of Islam. In contrast to the Moorish Science Temple, the NOI embraced the racial identity of Blackness. While both movements taught that Islam was the religion that would restore African Americans to their rightful inheritance, the NOI adopted a far more militant tone against Christianity as the "religion of the devil," part of the conspiracy to keep Black people convinced of their own inferiority and so to perpetuate their enslavement.[96]

As with the Moorish Science Temple, an early scandal enabled outsiders to discredit the religious legitimacy of the Nation of Islam. Once again, the racial-religious assemblages of U.S. empire shaped the representational patterns that discredited the movement. Robert Harris, a forty-four-year-old man loosely affiliated with the NOI in Detroit, had reportedly claimed the title "King of the Order of Islam" on the basis of his own prophetic revelation. In November 1932, Harris stabbed a man in what newspapers immediately dubbed a "pagan ceremonial killing," allegedly conducted on a "sacrificial altar." Sensational headlines depicted this "King of Islam" as a violent fanatic driven by the superstitions and passions that reporters associated with his race. The first of these accounts called Harris's "mystic cult . . . as strange and barbarous as the voodoo of the West Indies." Even though the events in Detroit had no connection whatsoever to the much-maligned tradition of vodou, itself forged in the interstices of French, Spanish, and U.S. empires, the headlines that followed translated the comparison as if it provided factual information about the NOI. Some claimed without any clear evidence that a further "Negro Voodoo Murder Plot" had been uncovered in Detroit. When detectives raided NOI headquarters, seizing "records and ritual books" and arresting several people, news reports dubbed the group a "Voodoo-Moslem cult." Ominous accounts of "cult members" being exhorted to "kill devils" framed the news of a protest held by the NOI to protest these arrests.[97]

Desperate to distance his movement from such negative associations and to claim the culturally and legally protected status of religion, Fard wrote to several newspapers in December 1932 explaining that Harris did "not belong to the said Nation of Islam," which along with "two-thirds of the inhabitance [sic] on the planet" practiced the ancient "religion of Mohammed." It was "a perfect insult to any Moslem," he said, "to be called a voodoo or cult of some organization." Fard was quite willing to let the racialized stereotypes of "voodoo" stand, as long as he could uncouple them from Islam. But his attempt to present Islam as a venerable, respectable, and beneficent religion faced an uphill battle against an overwhelming tide of derogatory media representations.[98]

From the beginning, government authorities and the mainstream press categorized the Nation of Islam not as a legitimate religion but a dangerous "cult" and a threat to the racial order. Reporters and public officials reinforced each other's analyses in a sort of self-perpetuating feedback loop. In April 1934 the city learned that the NOI was operating a school called the University of Islam in Detroit. A police raid resulted in the arrest of nineteen "leaders and instructors," who were then charged with "contributing to the delinquency of minors by withdrawing them from the public schools and by subversive teachings." The NOI protested these arrests with a demonstration at police headquarters. Violence erupted when the police attempted to disperse the crowd, injuring eleven demonstrators and five policemen. Newspaper reports linked this "riot" to a "Moslem . . . cult" opposed to "white civilization" and indicated that it had required "fifty policemen swinging their nightsticks to disperse the rioters." The racial-religious qualities that authorities attributed to the NOI had predisposed the police to view this event as a riot. In a clear distortion of the movement's history, reporters identified the University of Islam as a "revival" of the same "cult" that had perpetrated a "human sacrifice" two years earlier.[99] Lacking the racial status of whiteness, the religious status of Christianity, and the financial resources to mount a legal defense, the NOI of the 1930s had little chance of gaining official approval for a school. City authorities simply did not accept its claims to the status of religion. Nor did they take the University of Islam seriously enough to recognize it as a legitimate educational venture.[100]

As the Great Depression gave way to the Second World War, the U.S. government increasingly viewed any heterodox movements—particularly those associated with racial-religious minorities—as a potential threat to national security. Well before the war the FBI had opened files on both the Moorish Science Temple and the Nation of Islam. Even before the bombing of Pearl Harbor propelled the United States into the war, agents had begun to suspect that Japanese agents had infiltrated these movements. One investigation charged that the Jackson, Mississippi, branch of the MST was teaching "that the Japanese are fighting a war of liberation for the Asiatic race, of which race Negroes are members," and that in the event of a Japanese invasion "the Negro (Moorish) members in good standing" would "be treated as brothers."[101] A summary report characterized the MST as "a fast moving colored movement which is now very dangerous" and claimed without any clear evidence that it had "originally [been] started by a Japanese."[102] The FBI leveled similar charges against the Nation of Islam. When agents raided the NOI temple in Chicago and arrested seventy people, regional FBI director Albert Johnson informed the press that although no definite connections had yet been found, "there was a possibility that the groups secured their seditious ideas from a Major Satakata Takahishi, who was imprisoned several years ago for attempting to incite colored Americans against their government."[103] The FBI no longer categorized these movements simply as fraudulent and fanatical cults that threatened the domestic racial order but as an even more ominous danger to the nation's security in a time of war.

These FBI suspicions had their basis in the statements of racial solidarity with the Japanese that emanated from both the MST and the NOI. But these sentiments rested more on these movements' broader analyses of the global systems of race and empire than on any particular Japanese influence or infiltration. Although Elijah Muhammad may well have had some communication with Takahishi, the FBI failed to find concrete evidence that such contact had occurred or of any other Japanese infiltration into either group. Rather, the MST and the NOI were building on long-standing currents of internationalism in African American culture and on the shared conviction—articulated by black leaders as different as Marcus Garvey and W. E. B. Du Bois—that people of color shared a common destiny in a racialized imperial world.[104] The MST had long taught that the people commonly called "Negroes" were in reality Asiatic Moors, giving Moorish Americans a sense of kinship with Asia. In the NOI, meanwhile, Elijah Muhammad identified the African American freedom struggle with the anticolonial struggles of the "darker races" in Asia and Africa and viewed Japan as a part of that struggle. The NOI had positioned itself directly against the white supremacist racial order of the United States, and its members concluded that a Japanese victory would improve the fortunes of the "darker people" everywhere. To the extent that the existing order of the United States was founded on white supremacy, the FBI was quite right to see these Black Muslims as subversives who threatened that order.[105]

The FBI failed to show that the members of either movement were guilty of sedition or any "subversive activities" that might be subject to prosecution. Thus, most of the charges actually filed against them involved draft registration and military service. FBI agents received frequent reports that both the MST and the NOI were instructing their members not to register for the draft, as mandated by the Selective Training and Service Act of 1940. In fact, the two groups were quite different in this respect. Most Moorish Americans did register and many served in the war; others came to the conclusion that they could not fight against fellow Asiatics or for a nation that had not yet recognized their citizenship on equal terms. One investigation in Kansas City, Kansas, found that local MST members had "failed to register for the Selective Service, claiming since they were religious Asiatics they had no interest in a European conflict." Fifteen men were arrested and charged with that offense, but they were the exception within the MST.[106] Far more NOI members actually did object to military service. Many of them refused to register altogether, and many were imprisoned for that reason. While the sedition charges filed against NOI leaders in Chicago were quickly dismissed, thirty-six of the men picked up in that raid, including Elijah Muhammad, were convicted of draft evasion and spent three to five years in prison.[107]

In this situation, both the MST and the NOI began to invoke the principle of religious freedom as a pragmatic way to avoid military service. The legal status of the conscientious objector had been secured on religious freedom grounds, in large part by Quakers and Mennonites who had argued against compulsory military service as a violation of their religious convictions. Moorish Americans and Black Muslims echoed these claims. One MST member in Cleveland, Ohio, registered as a conscientious objector on the basis of his faith in "the divine creed of Islam" as taught by Prophet Noble Drew Ali.[108] Another in Richmond, Virginia, informed an FBI agent that he had filed for conscientious objector status because "the Koran teaches that Moslems shall not kill anything."[109] Members of the NOI often refused to register entirely and justified that refusal on the grounds of religion. Two Black Muslims in Washington, D.C., reportedly "declared that the laws of their faith forbade them to carry arms for the United States." One explained, "I follow the teaching of Allah brought to me through Allah's Apostle, [Elijah] Mohammed Rassoull, and when any law interferes with the teaching of Allah I will follow Allah's teaching."[110] These Moorish Americans and Black Muslims followed models set by other conscientious objectors who had similarly refused military service on the basis of their allegiance to a higher authority.

The contrast between the MST and the NOI on the question of draft registration reflected their differing views about the utility of U.S. citizenship. The former maintained loyalty to the United States and sought equality under its laws precisely on the basis of participants' rediscovered peoplehood as Moorish Americans. In a message to President Roosevelt, MST leaders explained that the United States had always recognized potential citizens by "the land of their fathers, 'by their nation and religion.'" The racial term "Negro," a product of slavery rather than a national identity, had made them ineligible for that recognition. As Moorish Americans they would be able to participate as loyal U.S. citizens in all the "affairs of the people."[111] One MST member in Grand Rapids, Michigan, explained to the FBI "that he [was] now a Moorish American similar to the German Americans and the Irish Americans only that his people are the Moors."[112] Moorish Americans thus saw this reclaimed national or ethno-religious identity as the foundation for a new equality of citizenship within the United States.

In contrast, most Black Muslims rejected the legitimacy of the U.S. government entirely and appealed to a higher authority in its place. At his trial for draft evasion in November 1942, Elijah Muhammad reportedly "told the court he was a 'citizen of the Universe,' and as such was not required to submit to United States laws." The "nation of Islam" was "opposed to armed aggression," he said, and "Allah . . . had issued no declaration of war."[113] NOI members refused to register for the draft because they owed their allegiance to Allah and the Nation of Islam. They rejected the authority of the United States because they viewed it as a white supremacist power, allied with whiteness and Christianity against Islam and the "darker races" of the world. "Mr. Rassoull [Muhammad] has told us that we should be on the side of our nation Islam, which is composed of the dark peoples of the earth," testified Joseph Nipper in Washington, D.C. "I am opposed to fighting in this war on the side of the United States since this is a war between Christianity and Islam. Christianity is on the side of the white people and Islam is on that of the Asiatics, and I don't wish to fight against the Moslems." Nipper's testimony illustrates how the NOI reversed dominant ideologies of race, nation, and religion. Rejecting Christianity as the religion of the white oppressor, he sided with an Islam that belonged to the "black, brown, red, and yellow peoples." Because he viewed the United States as a white Christian nation whose enemies included the Asian superpower of Japan, he could not in good conscience fight on its behalf.[114]

Yet these NOI members had little choice but to work within the legal framework of the United States. As they battled the charges of draft evasion, they defined their movement more and more in the language of religion— and defended it via the constitutional principle of religious freedom. At his hearing in Washington, one Elijah X denounced the label "religious 'cult'" and insisted instead "on the unadorned term 'religion.'"[115] Such assertions supported the claim to conscientious objector status more effectively in court than the NOI's challenge to U.S. sovereignty or its Black nationalist assertions ever could. As time went on, Black Muslims in prison also used the language of religious freedom to protest prison rules that infringed on their understanding of Islamic practice. Malcolm X, who would become the NOI's most famous minister, first joined the movement while in prison for a series of minor criminal offenses. Soon after his conversion he led a group of his fellow prisoners in a protest against prison food and mandatory typhoid inoculations. By framing their cause in the language of religious freedom, he defined their identity and practice as *religious*—a defensive strategy and a claim to legitimacy that even then had a chance of succeeding. In the shifting legal environment of the 1960s, courts would begin to grant Muslim prisoners the right to food that fulfilled their dietary requirements on First

Amendment grounds. But prison officials in 1950 refused to accommodate such requests and, in hopes of silencing these prisoners, transferred Malcolm X to a different facility.[116]

Dominant formations of race and religion in the mid-twentieth century had made it virtually impossible for either the MST or the NOI to gain religious legitimacy in the eyes of the law or the larger society. Federal agents and media reports had continually described these movements in derisive terms that denied their claims to the protected status of religion in the United States. During the war, for example, a summary report to J. Edgar Hoover on the MST concluded that this "Negro cult" showed "strong traces of Japanese influence" and had "influenced its members to refuse to comply with the provisions of the Selective Service Act because of their 'Mohammedan Religion.'" The scare quotes around this term reflected the FBI's utter dismissal of the movement's self-definition as such.[117] Even more telling is an FBI report from 1955 on the Nation of Islam, which the agency misnamed the "Muslim Cult of Islam" (MCI). The summary portion of the report began, "The MCI is a fanatic Negro organization purporting to be motivated by the religious principles of Islam, but actually dedicated to the propagation of hatred against the white race. The services conducted throughout the temples are bereft of any semblance to religious exercises."[118] The Nation of Islam would become even more controversial at the height of the Black Power movement in the 1960s, when Malcolm X rose to national prominence and media coverage branded the movement as a black supremacist "hate group," refusing yet again to recognize it as a real religion.[119]

Through the first half of the twentieth century, the agents of the U.S. government and the larger white society denied religious legitimacy to most predominantly black ethno-religious movements by classifying them instead as fraudulent cults and politically motivated hate groups. Recent scholarship has fundamentally challenged such dismissals. Every religious commitment has political implications of one kind or another, and the divide between religion and politics has always been a definitional ideal rather than a clear distinction on the ground. These implications have simply been less noticeable and less controversial when they support the status quo. As the story of the Nation of Islam reveals, American religious freedom has been limited not only by religious barriers—although a racially inflected anti-Muslim bias clearly played a role—but also by deeply racialized assumptions about what does and does not count as religion in the first place.[120]

The Power of Race and the Irrelevance of
Religious Freedom

For African Americans, this chapter has argued, religious freedom was at best a limited and ambivalent ideal. In the case of the Peace Mission Movement and for some black church leaders, this principle could provide a way to defend against racialized forms of harassment. But as we have seen throughout this book, successful religious freedom claims required a certain degree of conformity to the dominant society's model for acceptable or proper religion. Father Divine and his followers were initially anathematized as a cult not only because of their theological unorthodoxies but also because they challenged the lines of racial segregation that were so fundamental to American society at the time. In the midst of the Great Depression, when American elites increasingly felt threatened by labor movements, communism, and other forms of political radicalism, the Peace Mission Movement managed to gain a degree of acceptance and to win legal battles on First Amendment grounds. It did so, I have suggested, because authorities came to see this movement as mostly apolitical, a spiritual salve for the strains and stresses of African American life. Despite his long-term involvement in campaigns for racial and economic justice, Father Divine was able to frame the identity of his movement in terms that the larger society recognized as religious and so managed to win limited acceptance as a quaint and misguided but relatively harmless religious leader in African American life.

The situation was very different for the Moorish Science Temple and the Nation of Islam, which attempted to escape the negative racial formation of the Negro by redefining African American communal identities as simultaneously national and religious. Religious freedom for them was above all a collective right that protected—or at least ought to protect—a redefined vision of peoplehood that they defined partly in the language of religion. For some, particularly in the NOI, the new ethno-religious identity was fundamentally incompatible with citizenship in what they identified as the White Christian nation of the United States. They shared this dilemma with Filipinos and Native Americans, those other racialized subjects of U.S. empire described in chapters 2 and 3 of this book. In all three cases, alternative claims to nationhood and sovereignty grounded communalist articulations of religious freedom that drew on U.S. cultural ideals even as they rejected the racial and imperial assemblages—and sometimes even the political sovereignty—of the United States. Conquered by the U.S. military or policed by local, state, and federal authorities, all three of these peoples found that they had no alternative but to work within the legal and constitutional systems of the United States. In the process, their articulations of religious freedom changed subtly in an individualist direction and, ultimately, altered the shape of the traditions that they aimed to protect.

Precisely because the larger society discriminated against African Americans in such insistently racial terms, African American invocations of religious freedom could provide no more than a limited relief. Those located within the traditional black churches appealed to this ideal to celebrate their founders as pioneers who had expanded its racial contours, to confront the racial exclusions of the white churches, and to challenge the segregationist laws that in one way or another limited their own church activities. Much like the Catholic and Jewish immigrants of the time, they stressed their allegiance to religious freedom as an attempted point of entry into equal citizenship in the United States. As I argued in chapters 1 and 4 of this book, religious freedom talk helped Catholics and Jews to gain general recognition as fully American subjects and, in the process, to act as agents of U.S. empire. For Jews especially, an emphasis on this principle further helped establish the terms of their peoplehood as primarily religious, rather than racial, and thus supported their movement into the racial status of whiteness in American life. In contrast, African Americans were trapped at the bottom of a black-white racial binary that this expansion of whiteness seemed only to solidify. Even when African Americans stressed their religious values and commitments and even when they denied that existing racial categories fairly described them at all, the larger society continued to define and denigrate them almost entirely in racial terms. For them, in short, religious freedom talk simply did not have the power to transcend the racialized terms of their oppression.

Conclusion

Race, Empire, and the Multiplicities of Religious Freedom

"The Supreme Court holds that freedom of religion under the Constitution takes precedence over the rights of private property," commented African American columnist Ralph Matthews on the court's recent decision in *Marsh v. Alabama* (1946). "Just as the Japanese and the Hebrews have been able to tie their religion into every phase of their social, national, and economic life, we could do the same thing and use it as a weapon to abolish segregation and discrimination on the basis of this decision." The Supreme Court had applied the First Amendment to forbid a company-owned town in Alabama from banning proselytizing activities on its streets, in this case (as in so many others) by a Jehovah's Witness. Tongue firmly in cheek, Matthews proposed that the case opened up a new strategy for the fight against racial discrimination. As an admitted skeptic—he commented, for example, that "it makes precious little difference whether anybody gets to heaven or not, if it operates on the pattern conceived by most Christians in America"—he saw no harm in editing "the hand-me-down rituals and dogmas" of the churches to suit contemporary needs. "Every organized colored religious body," he suggested, could simply add to its creed an affirmation of faith in something like "THE UNIVERSAL BROTHERHOOD OF MAN, REGARDLESS OF RACE, CREED, OR COLOR, THE IRREPRESSIBLE DIGNITY OF THE HUMAN SPIRIT AND THE IRREPEALABLE LAW THAT ALL MEN, UNDER GOD, ARE CREATED EQUAL." They could then file lawsuits claiming "that the very existence of jim-crow laws compel us to defile our souls and prevent us from worshipping God in our own way." In this way, Matthews proposed, the newly expanded scope of religious freedom could provide an airtight case against racial segregation as well.[1]

Although it is not well remembered today, *Marsh v. Alabama* was part of a series of cases in the 1940s that ushered in a new era of religious freedom jurisprudence. Its distinguishing feature was the fact that a private company, the Gulf Shipbuilding Corporation, owned and operated the town. Justice Hugo Black's majority opinion cited several recent precedents, most notably *Cantwell v. Connecticut* (1940), to show that the court had already applied the free exercise and free speech clauses to prevent state and local government authorities from significantly restricting religious activities. In more general terms, the equal protection clause of the Fourteenth Amendment— which was passed during Reconstruction but had been far more narrowly interpreted—was now being incorporated to require the states and not just the federal government to honor the individual rights guaranteed in the Constitution. The specific issue in *Marsh* was whether or not these rights could be protected on private property; the court ruled that because the public spaces of the town functioned like those in any other, it had to follow the same constitutional standard. As Sarah Barringer Gordon has argued, this was a new constitutional landscape that encouraged Americans from all walks of life, far more than they ever had before, to challenge whatever they saw as restrictions on their religious practices in the courts. Along with the dramatic cultural changes that followed the Second World War, this constitutional transformation marks the opening of a new era of religious freedom talk and the end of this book.[2]

Matthews provides a helpful way to conclude this book not just because his analysis highlighted the new constitutional landscape of the 1940s but also, and more important, because he managed to weave together several of my central themes. First, his proposed creedal amendments drew directly on the tri-faith discourse of racial and religious brotherhood that I described in chapter 4. The mass movement for civil rights that took shape in the next decade would sound many of the same notes; Martin Luther King Jr.'s powerful speeches prominently stressed the integrationist ideals of racial equality, inclusion, and justice for all. In this sense, the tri-faith agenda helped lay the groundwork for the successes of the civil rights movement.[3]

As far as I know, however, no African American churches or civil rights organizations picked up on Matthews's proposal to define the black freedom struggle in the language of religious freedom. The mainstream civil rights movement took advantage of the Supreme Court's new emphasis on equal protection under the U.S. Constitution, but it did not adopt religious freedom either as a public rallying cry or as a legal principle to be deployed in the courts. No doubt one of the reasons for this absence is that few church leaders would have countenanced changes to their statements of faith simply for legal advantage, as Matthews had so wryly suggested. In addition, as

I argued in chapter 5, African Americans were relatively uninterested in the freedom of religion because the terms of their peoplehood and the discrimination against them had been shaped so insistently as a matter of race—and because the dominant strains of American religious freedom talk, as we have seen, functioned to bolster racial discrimination and the civilizational hierarchies that sustained it. This was the case not only in African American history but also among missionaries and government agents on Native American reservations, as chapter 3 described, and in the politics of U.S. imperial conquest and governance in the Philippines, as we saw in chapters 1 and 2. In all these cases, white American Christians used religious freedom talk as a way to mark their own superiority and the civilizational inadequacies of those they governed.

Religious freedom has emerged in this book as an eminently malleable discourse, a shared cultural value that has been defined and deployed in a wide variety of ways. Matthews's proposal for African Americans to fight segregation on the grounds of religious freedom was not taken seriously, and he does not seem to have imagined that it would be. Nonetheless, he reminds us that the targets of racial and imperial oppression also rearticulated this principle in their own defense. While religious freedom remained a minor theme in their cultural vocabularies, African American church leaders regularly deployed it to celebrate the founding of their churches and sometimes to fight for their very survival as independent institutions. The predominantly black ethno-religious movements of the Great Migration period had also used it as part of their effort to claim the status of religion and redefine the terms of their identities in American life.

Native Americans too had been quick to define their indigenous ceremonial traditions and the new prophetic movements that swept through Indian country in the late nineteenth and early twentieth centuries as *religion*—and to insist, against the settler-colonial discourses that denigrated these traditions as savage, that they, like other religions, must be protected as such. Likewise, although the people of the Philippines had not previously framed their protests against Spanish rule in the language of religious freedom, they began to invoke this ideal as soon as they faced the prospect of American imperial rule. Recognizing the cultural significance of this principle to the Americans, Filipinos claimed their own right to political sovereignty and their own identity as modern subjects by framing a constitution that enshrined religious freedom and, far more ambivalently, the separation of church and state as political ideals for their nascent Republic of the Philippines.

Like most Americans who have commented on the freedom of religion, Matthews did not mention (and probably did not see) its frequent intersections either with the discursive apparatus of U.S. empire or with the diverse modes of resistance to that empire. Subaltern claims to political sovereignty and nationhood coincided—for African Americans, Native Americans, Filipinos, and Moros alike—with assertions of distinctive communal or national religious traditions and the right to shape the contours of those traditions without interference from the United States. On the other hand, when forced to concede U.S. sovereignty and perhaps even finding themselves confined to prisons, on reservations, or within other institutions of racial-imperial control, the members of all these groups had little alternative but to articulate their appeals under the laws of the United States. In this case, the constitutional principle of religious freedom at least offered them a way to defend, often at an individual level, the distinctive practices and identities that gave them meaning and hope for a better world to come.

When Matthews proposed that African Americans follow the model set by the "Japanese and the Hebrews" by similarly tying "their religion into every phase of their social, national, and economic life," he hinted at the connection this book has found between religious freedom talk and the contours of peoplehood in U.S. history. Because religious freedom held so much weight as a basic national value and a marker of the modern subject, Americans of all descriptions were motivated to defend their practices and traditions in its terms. When they did so, religion often became a more significant component of their communal identities and their ways of representing themselves to the world. American Jews, as I argued in chapter 4, successfully deployed the ideal of religious freedom to transform the larger society's understanding of who they were as a people. Race, nation, and religion have never been entirely separate categories of identity—indeed, the task of separating them can be seen as a part of modernity's ideological project—and being Jewish had long been construed in simultaneously racial, national, and religious terms. When they defended their interests in the language of religious freedom, American Jews publicly highlighted the religious dimensions of that identity. In the process, I have argued, they worked subtly against the idea that Jews were a distinct race and so facilitated their gradual incorporation into the racial status of whiteness in American life.

The same outcome did not always follow for others. Although unrecognized by Matthews, and although they adopted nationalist platforms rather than the more integrationist religion of "universal brotherhood" that he proposed, the Moorish Science Temple and the Nation of Islam had done precisely what he suggested when they insisted on the inseparability of race, nation, and religion in their identities as Moorish Americans and Black Muslims. In so doing, they hoped to escape or transcend the constraints and denigrations of a negatively racialized identity in the United States, reassembling the terms of their peoplehood to emphasize instead the dimension of religion and to give a positive valence to nation and race. Their failure to gain recognition and legitimacy in such terms from the larger society, which rejected their claims to the status of religion by denigrating their movements as overly "political" and refused to see their members as anything other than "Negroes," reflects the staying power of the black-white racial binary in American life.

The situation was different again for Native Americans, whose conquest and subordination had been confirmed and reinforced by white settler depictions of Indians as an essentially "tribal" and therefore primitive people. Tribal peoples were seen as premodern at least in part because they did not culturally differentiate between the categories of race, nation, and religion. U.S. governing officials criticized them for that reason, insisting that they must separate religious from political authority within their tribal governments and even eliminate their tribal identities altogether before they could be recognized as civilized and modern people. As I argued in chapter 3, the language of religious freedom on Native American reservations often worked to reinforce such separations by creating new distinctions that would divide the religious from those aspects of life newly designated as secular. Native Americans managed to maintain their sense of distinctiveness as peoples—a goal that their appeals to religious freedom sometimes also helped them achieve. For that very reason, the larger society continued to denigrate them as a tribal people not yet equipped to govern themselves. In their case, articulations of religious freedom that were only marginally successful by any measure had the unintended consequence of reinforcing the demeaning white settler category of the tribal.

The word "secularism" can be defined as a system or an ideology that separates out something called "religion" from other dimensions of life. Religious freedom talk is an important component or tool of secularism in this sense because, as we have seen throughout this book, it tends to highlight the religious and so distinguish it from other presumably nonreligious aspects of identity and tradition. (The more familiar way of seeing religious freedom as a basic constitutional principle of the modern secular state is linked to this broader process; as such, this freedom distinguishes the religious from the secular or the political in the life of the nation.) As

Talal Asad has most influentially argued, secularism has historically served as part of the racial and civilizational assemblages of empire because it enabled those peoples targeted for imperial conquest to be labeled as premodern, in need of an imperial hand to instruct them in its purportedly universal principles. At the same time, it served to consign (and so restrict) subaltern lifeways and modes of governance to the realm of the religious, forcing their separation from the spheres of political and imperial authority in the modern world.[4] This book has documented the role of religious freedom as a mechanism in such imperial processes both on Indian reservations and in the southern Philippines, where Muslim Moros used religious freedom talk in an effort to defend an expansive view of traditional authority—but ultimately had to accept the redefinition of their sultans and *datus* as purely religious figures, their ruling authority appropriated by the new imperial power.

In recent years, some scholars have argued that the rising U.S. foreign policy emphasis on global religious freedom has actually exacerbated the tensions that it purports to solve. This emphasis, they contend, has a tendency to reduce complex and multidimensional conflicts to the single question of religion and encourages even those most caught up in a conflict to view their differences in primarily religious terms. In the process, other sources of tension and violence—most of all the geopolitical inequities produced by a long colonial history and by contemporary neoliberal and neo-imperial coercions—are obscured. As in some of the cases described in this book, this neo-imperial discourse of religious freedom can justify U.S. military interventions, purportedly to solve conflicts that American policy makers have interpreted as products of an unyielding (fanatical and pre- or antimodern) religious hate. In more general terms, this discourse presents the United States—which offers itself as a secular and neutral arbiter, dedicated to freedom—as the solution to conflicts that it has misdiagnosed as religious.[5]

At one level, this book has provided a longer history of these contemporary discourses, mapping earlier implications of religious freedom with the exercise of U.S. imperial power. At the same time, I have attempted to paint a broader and more complex picture of the cultural work performed by religious freedom talk in early twentieth-century America and its colonial possessions. Just as the proponents and administrators of empire made powerful use of this ideal, so too did the racialized minorities of an imperial world who rearticulated it as a resource for their own resistance. Their assertions of religious freedom had ambivalent consequences, to be sure.

If they were to have any hope of success, they required the reconfiguration of indigenous and minority traditions to fit a Christian and often specifically Protestant model for what the dominant society considered religion (or proper or legitimate or acceptable religion) to be. Religious freedom talk provided a valuable way for some marginalized minorities to defend their own traditions and perhaps even to maintain their own identities under imperial rule. Yet as they did so, the traditions they so designated and defended were often subtly transformed. Minorities who were relatively well positioned on the racial-religious landscape, as in the case of American Catholics and Jews, could leverage the freedom of religion to establish their credentials as patriotic Americans and agents of empire, perhaps even to relocate themselves on that racial-religious landscape. Others, trapped by the racial assemblages of empire, found their subaltern status little affected by the effort.

Despite the deconstructive frequencies in which so much of this book is written, I do not see the ideal of religious freedom as inherently imperial or tied to the racial hierarchies of modernity. I have emphasized these less savory aspects of its history because they have been far less noticed or observed—a silence that has enabled the celebratory accounts that in turn facilitate the uses and abuses of U.S. imperial power. Ultimately no discourse is singular in meaning or limited in the kinds of cultural work it can perform, and no ideal can be contained by its history or the apparent logic of its significations. The principle of religious freedom seems necessarily to define the practices and traditions it defends as religious, placing them in opposition to that which is not so designated. To define religion is to limit religion, to set its boundaries and hence to delineate its other. But the potential shape of such definitions and oppositions are infinite in their possibilities. Whatever the streams of its dominant configurations and however powerful they might be, this ideal (like any other) has the potential to overflow their limits and to carve out new channels that have yet to be imagined.

Notes

ABBREVIATIONS

CCF	Bureau of Indian Affairs, Record Group 75, Central Classified Files, 1907–1939, National Archives and Records Administration, Washington, D.C.
FBI MST Files	Federal Bureau of Investigation, Moorish Science Temple of America Files, Department of Justice, Washington, D.C., http://vault.fbi.gov/Moorish%20Science%20Temple%20of%20America
Kohler Papers	Max James Kohler Papers, P-7, American Jewish Historical Society, New York, N.Y.
MST Collection	Moorish Science Temple Collection, MG 435, Schomburg Center for Research in Black Culture, New York Public Library, New York, N.Y.
Philipson Papers	David Philipson Papers, MS 35, American Jewish Archives, Cincinnati, Ohio
Richards Papers	Bernard G. Richards Papers, P-868, American Jewish Historical Society, New York, N.Y.

INTRODUCTION

1. Said, *Culture and Imperialism*, 282–336; Go, *Patterns of Empire*, 26–27.

2. Weheliye, *Habeas Viscus*, 4. The concept of assemblage originates in the collaborations of Gilles Deleuze and Felix Guattari, especially in their book *Thousand Plateaus*. See also Puar, *Terrorist Assemblages*.

3. The literature on the history of race and modernity is immense. Among the best recent works are Garrigus and Morris, *Assumed Identities*; Seth, *Europe's Indians Producing Racial Difference*; Smedley, *Race in North America*; Allen and Perry, *Invention of the White Race*; and Wolfe, *Traces of History*.

4. Said, *Culture and Imperialism*, 9. My definitions in this paragraph build also on Burbank and Cooper, *Empires in World History*, 8; Byrd, *Transit of Empire*, xix–xxvi; Go, *Patterns of Empire*, 7; and A. Goldstein, *Formations of United States Colonialism*, 7–21.

5. Patterson, *Freedom in the Making of Western Culture*.

6. Among others on these themes, see Mehta, *Liberalism and Empire*; Holt, *Problem of Freedom*; and Muthu, *Empire and Modern Political Thought*.

7. Cavanaugh, *Myth of Religious Violence*, chapter 3. On the early modern history of the category of religion, see Harrison, *"Religion" and the Religions in the English Enlightenment*; W. Smith, *Meaning and End of Religion*; J. Smith, *Relating Religion*; and Nongbri, *Before Religion*.

8. Chidester, *Savage Systems*; Chidester, *Empire of Religion*. On the imperial implications of the category of religion and the global politics of its translation, see also R. King, *Orientalism and Religion*; Fitzgerald, *Ideology of Religious Studies*; Masuzawa, *Invention of World Religions*; Mandair, *Religion and the Specter of the West*; Wenger, *We Have a Religion*; and Josephson, *The Invention of Religion in Japan*.

9. Locke's involvements in empire were intimate and extensive. After his work with the Carolina colony he served as secretary and treasurer to the English Council for Trade and Foreign Plantations (1673–74) and secretary to the English Board of Trade (1696–1700). He also became a shareholder in the Royal African Company when it was chartered in 1672. See Armitage, *The Ideological Origins of the British Empire*, 166; and Arneil, *John Locke and America*, chapters 3–5.

10. Locke, "The Fundamental Constitutions of Carolina," articles 95, 97, and 100; Underwood, *Constitution of South Carolina*, 4–5.

11. Locke, *Letter Concerning Toleration Humbly Submitted*.

12. Quoted in Armitage, *Foundations of Modern International Thought*, 109–10; Seed, *Ceremonies of Possession*; Banner, *How the Indians Lost Their Land*.

13. Locke, "Fundamental Constitutions of Carolina," article 104, emphasis added.

14. Irons, *Origins of Proslavery Christianity*, 23–30; Goetz, *Baptism of Early Virginia*, 86–111.

15. Irons, *Origins of Proslavery Christianity*, 31–54; Goetz, *Baptism of Early Virginia*, 138–67.

16. Goetz, *Baptism of Early Virginia*.

17. Goldschmidt and McAlister, *Race, Nation, and Religion in the Americas*.

18. Mehta, *Liberalism and Empire*; Pitts, *Turn to Empire*; Lowe, *Intimacies of Four Continents*. As Lowe puts it, the material and intellectual economics of liberalism supported "freedoms for 'man' in modern Europe and North America, while relegating others to geographical and temporal spaces that [were] constituted as backward, uncivilized, and unfree" (3).

19. See Sehat, *Myth of American Religious Freedom*, 13–69; Beneke and Grenda, *First Prejudice*.

20. On the racial and imperial politics of religious freedom in nineteenth-century America see Jordan, *Church, State, and Race*.

21. Notable exceptions include Fessenden, *Culture and Redemption*; Jordan, *Church, State, and Race*; Weiner, *Religion Out Loud*; F. Curtis, *Production of American Religious Freedom*; and Su, *Exporting Freedom*.

Recent examples include Kidd, *God of Liberty*; Sehat, *Myth of American Religious Freedom*; Gunn and Witte, *No Establishment of Religion*; Meyerson, *Endowed by Our Creator*; and Green, *Inventing a Christian America*.

Legal scholars have focused their attention on First Amendment jurisprudence since the 1940s, when the Supreme Court applied the Fourteenth Amendment to expand the scope of its authority in this arena. See Greenawalt, *Religion and the Constitution*; Gordon, *Spirit of the Law*; Koppelman, *Defending American Religious Neutrality*; and S. Smith, *Rise and Decline of American Religious Freedom*.

22. The term "ethno-religious" comes from S. Johnson, "Rise of Black Ethnics."

23. Mahmood and Danchin, "Politics of Religious Freedom"; Hurd, *Beyond Religious Freedom*; Mahmood, *Religious Difference in a Secular Age*; Sullivan et al., *Politics of Religious Freedom*.

CHAPTER ONE

1. The United States formally honored its promise to recognize Cuba's independence after the war but exerted indirect control over its affairs for the next half century. On this history and the politics of naming the war, see Pérez, *War of 1898*.

2. "Spain Must Give Up: Island of Luzon the Least We Will Take," *Los Angeles Times*, August 24, 1898, 2.

3. On the U.S. colonization of the Philippines, see Wexler, *Tender Violence*; Kramer, *Blood of Government*; Go, *American Empire and the Politics of Meaning*; Brody, *Visualizing American Empire*; McMahon, *Dead Stars*; and Beredo, *Import of the Archive*. But even those who have attended to themes of religion—as in Harris, *God's Arbiters*; McCullough, *The Cross of War*; and Walther, *Sacred Interests*—have not highlighted the theme of religious freedom. The exceptions are in the fields of foreign policy and political science: Preston, *Sword of the Spirit*; and Su, *Exporting Freedom*.

4. "Waged for Humanity," *Washington Post*, May 9, 1898, 10.

5. Stanwood, "Catholics, Protestants, and the Clash of Civilizations."

6. The Whig Party, dominated by northern Protestants, had opposed the annexation of Texas, the war with Mexico, and the ensuing conquest of California and New Mexico because all of these new territories added to the political power of the slaveholding South. Many feared, as well, that the United States could not successfully absorb so many non-white and non-Protestant subjects without corrupting its democracy. See Howe, *What Hath God Wrought*, 701–8, 762–70; and Pinheiro, *Missionaries of Republicanism*.

7. Murray, *Decline of Popery and Its Causes*, 29–30.

8. Schaff, "Development of Religious Freedom," 351, 361; Schaff, *Church and State in the United States*, 9–14.

9. Preston, *Sword of the Spirit*; Fessenden, *Culture and Redemption*; Modern, *Secularism in Antebellum America*.

10. Goldschmidt and McAlister, *Race, Nation, and Religion in the Americas*.

11. Strong, *Our Country*; Berge, "Voices for Imperialism"; Luker, *Social Gospel in Black and White*, 268–75.

12. Van Dyke, *Cross of War*, 1, 6; "Spain and Her People," *Trenton Evening Times*, April 9, 1898, 2; Greer, Mignolo, and Quilligan, *Rereading the Black Legend*; Sánchez, *Comparative Colonialism*.

13. Van Dyke, *Cross of War*, 1, 6.

14. "Waged for Humanity," *Washington Post*, May 9, 1898.

15. "The Outcome of the War," *New York Times*, May 16, 1898, 10.

16. Ibid.

17. Cited in McCartney, *Power and Progress*, 109–10.

18. Blanco, *Frontier Constitutions*.

19. White, *Our New Possessions*, 49, 58.

20. Quoted in Eardley, *Christianity in Turkey*, 22.

21. "The Carolines," *Outlook*, September 17, 1898, 161.

22. "Editorial Notes," *New York Observer and Chronicle*, August 18, 1898, 209.

23. "Current History Notes," *Congregationalist*, May 19, 1898, 726; "The Religious Consequences of the War," ibid., June 2, 1898, 799.

24. "The Church and Expansion: Attitude of the Religious Press of the Country on the Philippine Question," *Washington Post*, September 5, 1898, 6.

25. J. King, *Facing the Twentieth Century*, 1, 3, 583, 588.

26. "Episcopal Council Opens," *New York Times*, October 6, 1898, 6.

27. "Dr. Abbott on America's Destiny," ibid., May 30, 1898, 10.

28. Van Dyke, *American Birthright*, 6; Cullinane, *Liberty and American Anti-imperialism*, 57.

29. Anti-imperialist League, *Moral and Religious Aspects of the So-Called Imperial Policy*, 6.

30. Leonard Bacon, "A Grave Danger in the Philippines," *Congregationalist*, January 26, 1899, 120.

31. Anti-imperialist League, *Moral and Religious Aspects of the So-Called Imperial Policy*, 3.

32. "Bryan Attacks Expansion," *New York Times*, January 8, 1899, 4.

33. Love, *Race over Empire*.

34. "Opposition to Expansion," *New York Times*, January 7, 1899, 4.

35. Kipling, "The White Man's Burden." On the U.S. debates over and deployments of Kipling's poem, see Murphy, *Shadowing the White Man's Burden*; and Brantlinger, *Taming Cannibals*, 203–23.

36. Washington Gladden, "The Nation's Opportunity," *Independent*, January 12, 1899, 103; on the Spanish-American War as a social gospel crusade, see Wetzel, "American Crusade," 119–68.

37. Gladden, "Nation's Opportunity," 103.

38. Sullivan, *Exemplar of Americanism*; for an account of Worcester's performance as secretary of the interior, see Edgerton, *People of the Middle Ground*, 100–178.

39. Worcester, *Philippine Islands and Their People*, 125, 340–42, 472–75.

40. Ibid., 125, 340–44, 472–75.

41. Ibid., 150–59, 170, 473, emphasis in original.

42. "The Transvaal Crisis," *Outlook*, October 7, 1899, 281.

43. Ibid.

44. Ibid., 284; Evans, *Burden of Black Religion*.

45. "Transvaal Crisis," 286–87.

46. Thomas Hughes, "Catholic Spain—Its Politics and Liberalism," *American Catholic Quarterly Review*, July 1897, 493.

47. O'Brien, *Isaac Hecker*.

48. "Editorial Notes," *Catholic World*, August 1898, 715; Charleson Shane, "A Sketch of Catholicity in the Philippines," ibid., August 1898, 695; Henry E. O'Keeffe, "A Word on the Church and the New Possessions," ibid., December 1898, 319.

49. "Methodists Assail Spain," *New York Times*, April 6, 1898, 5.

50. "Article 2—No Title," *Catholic World*, May 1898, 279.

51. John Jerome Rooney, "A Catholic Soldier," *Catholic World*, August 1898, 698–99.

52. "Editorial Notes," *Sacred Heart Review*, October 22, 1898.

53. Bryan J. Clinch, "Imperialism as a Policy for America," *American Catholic Quarterly Review*, January 1899, 150. On Clinch's career as an architect and amateur historian in California, see Avella, *Sacramento and the Catholic Church*, 60–61, 291.

54. "Editorial Notes," *Sacred Heart Review*, December 17, 1898.

55. "Ours Is Not a Protestant Nation," *Sacred Heart Review*, December 31, 1898, 4.

56. Doyle, *Irish Americans*, 287–88.

57. "Editorial Notes," *Sacred Heart Review*, December 17, 1898.

58. "Welcomes American Control," *Chicago Daily Tribune*, October 27, 1898, 2.

59. Rev. A. P. Doyle, "Religious Problem of the Philippines," *Catholic World*, October 1898, 119–24.

60. "Religious News and Views," *New York Times*, August 27, 1898.

61. Bryan J. Clinch, "The Truth about the Church in the Philippines," *Catholic World*, June 1899, 292.

62. "Editorial Notes," *Catholic World*, February 1899, 711.

63. John Ireland, "The Religious Conditions in Our New Island Territory," *Outlook*, August 26, 1899, 933–34.

64. George McDermot, "English Administrators and the Ceded Possessions," *Catholic World*, March 1, 1899, 733.

65. "A Catholic Federation," *New York Times*, November 30, 1900; for a more detailed account of these Catholic complaints, see M'Faul, "Catholics and American Citizenship."

66. I put the word "white" in parentheses here to signal that not all American Catholics would be able to claim the racial status of whiteness.

67. "The Spanish Administration in the Philippines," *Catholic World*, January 1899, 531, 538–41.

68. W. A. Jones, "The Religious Orders in the Philippines," *Catholic World*, February 1899, 579.

69. "Do We Want These Citizens?," *Sacred Heart Review*, November 26, 1898, 427.

70. Philip E. Nylander, "A Cloudy Pearl of the Pacific," *Catholic World*, January 1899, 498.

71. "Spanish Friars' Reports," *New York Times*, March 21, 1899, 3.

72. Ibid.

73. "The Roman Church in Our New Possessions," *New York Times*, September 3, 1898, 5.

74. "Filipinos Have New Creed," *New York Times*, May 6, 1900, 6. On the figure of the bandit and the role of messianic and prophetic religious movements (including the Gabinistas) in the history of the Philippines, see Ileto, "Outlines of a Nonlinear Employment of Philippine History."

75. "Freedom Contra Church," *American Israelite*, August 4, 1898, 4.

76. Cited in Maskell, "'Modern Christianity Is Ancient Judaism.'"

77. "Freedom Contra Church," 4.

78. "Editorial Article 3," *American Israelite*, June 26, 1902, 4.

79. GOG [pseud.], "Used Rose-Colored Glasses," *New York Times*, September 2, 1898.

80. McCartney, *Power and Progress*, 150–53.

81. E. Goldstein, "Editor's Introduction"; Michels, "Is America 'Different'?"

82. "American Expansion," *Jewish Messenger*, October 21, 1898, 4.

83. Paul Kramer argues that Anglo-Saxonism reached its high point at the end of the nineteenth century and went into decline with the practical exigencies of governing the Philippines. My research suggests that the anti-Catholicism accompanying the war with Spain encouraged Anglo-Saxonism and that the tactical cooperation between American Protestants and Catholics in governing the Philippines was one factor in its decline. See Kramer, "Empires, Exceptions, and Anglo-Saxons."

84. Blum, *Reforging the White Republic*.

85. "Sword Must Now Decide," *Washington Post*, May 2, 1898, 9.

86. Jacobson, *Roots Too*.

87. "Allen Names a Test: Opposition to Cheese Not a Lack of Patriotism," *Washington Post*, June 30, 1898, 4.

88. "American Brotherhood," *New York Times*, August 27, 1898, 5. This reference to interreligious "brotherhood" predates by several decades the tri-faith brotherhood movement, as described by Kevin Schultz, that would become a crucial dimension of public discourse in the Second World War. See Schultz, *Tri-faith America*.

89. Robert S. MacArthur, "The Golden Rule versus Racial Prejudice and Religious Intolerance," *American Hebrew*, March 29, 1901, 570; "Brotherhood, with the Golden Rule as Guide," *New York Times*, March 27, 1901, 3.

90. "Terms of the Treaty," *Washington Post*, December 14, 1898, 1.

CHAPTER TWO

1. Gregorio Aglipay "The Independent Catholic Church in the Philippines," *Independent*, October 29, 1903, 2571; for an admiring portrait of Aglipay, see Scott, *Aglipay before Aglipayanism*.

2. Dressler and Mandair, *Secularism and Religion-Making*.

3. Majul, *Political and Constitutional Ideas of the Philippine Revolution*, 9.

4. Filipino visions of modernity must be understood on their own terms, not as an incomplete or somehow inadequate copy of either Spanish or American molds. See Blanco, *Frontier Constitutions*; and Thomas, *Orientalists, Propagandists, and Ilustrados*. For a similar argument in regard to Mexico, see Coronado, *World Not to Come*.

5. Blanco, *Frontier Constitutions*, chapter 4; Majul, *Political and Constitutional Ideas of the Philippine Revolution*, 1–2; Marcelo H. del Pilar, "Monastic Supremacy in the Philippines," 1889, in Agoncillo, *Filipino Nationalism, 1872–1970*, 184–205.

6. Majul, *Political and Constitutional Ideas of the Philippine Revolution*, 4–7; "Extracts from the Correspondence of Rouseville Wildman, Et Al.," Exhibit 82: 86–89 in Taylor, *Philippine Insurrection*, vol. 1.

7. My primary sources for addressing these questions do not represent the voices of all Filipinos but rather the small cadre of elites whose roles in the revolution made them visible in the colonial archive. In 1906 the U.S. colonial official John R. M. Taylor compiled a six-volume set of sources with the goal of documenting, and ultimately discrediting, the recently defeated Filipino revolution. These aims are clear in his introduction. The collection consists of memos, reports, articles, and letters written by

and to Filipino leaders during the prior decade's revolutionary struggle against Spanish and then American rule. These leaders were all male, all Catholic, and mostly ethnic Tagalogs from the island of Luzon. This set of documents offers no access to a multiplicity of other perspectives in this diverse archipelago. But however partial and problematic, these sources provide an important window into the evolving views of Filipino leaders as they fought for the survival of their nascent republic. On the controversy and delayed publication of this set of documents, see Beredo, *Import of the Archive*, 30–41.

8. Emilio Aguinaldo, "Message from the Honorable President of the Republic to Congress," January 23, 1899, Exhibit 410: 21–22, in Taylor, *Philippine Insurrection*, vol. 4.

9. Felipe Buencamino, "Speech to U.S. Congress," August 20, 1899, Exhibit 738: 61–63, in ibid., vol. 5. As an address to Congress, this speech was also published in United States, *Affairs in the Philippine Islands*, 45–52.

10. Apolinario Mabini, "Constitutional Programme of the Philippine Republic," June 5, 1898, Exhibit 18: 12–20, in Taylor, *Philippine Insurrection*, vol. 3.

11. Sixto López, "Memorandum to the U.S. Secretary of State," January 5, 1899, Exhibit 530: 57, in ibid., vol. 4.

12. "Brush Fighting," *Boston Daily Globe*, February 19, 1899, 2.

13. Cited in Parker, *Church and State in the Philippines*, 150.

14. Vicente Lukban, "Proclamation," February 4, 1901, Exhibit 1344: 68–69, in Taylor, *Philippine Insurrection*, vol. 5. For a history of Samar, including the role of Lukban as governor and military commander under the Philippine Republic, see Cruikshank, *Samar*.

15. *"Benevolent Assimilation" in the Philippines*.

16. Asad, *Formations of the Secular*.

17. Majul, *Political and Constitutional Ideas of the Philippine Revolution*, 153–55.

18. Cited in ibid., 157–58.

19. J. Sandico, "Bases of the Committee," September 1898, Exhibit 265: 83–84, in Taylor, *Philippine Insurrection*, vol. 3.

20. Majul, *Muslims in the Philippines*, 76–103.

21. José Roa, "Letter to Emilio Aguinaldo," January 26, 1899, Exhibit 1427: 4–6, in Taylor, *Philippine Insurrection*, vol. 5.

22. Both quotes are in Majul, *Political and Constitutional Ideas of the Philippine Revolution*, 157–58.

23. Majul, *Muslims in the Philippines*; Gowing, *Mandate in Moroland*, chapters 1 and 2.

24. Cited in Majul, *Muslims in the Philippines*, 315.

25. "Letter to the General of Iloilo, January 4, 1899," Exhibit 1211: 12, in Taylor, *Philippine Insurrection*, vol. 5.

26. Mariano Trías, "Circular to Joló and Mindanao," August 10, 1899, Exhibit 1430: 7, in ibid.

27. Majul, *Muslims in the Philippines*, 314–16; Gowing, *Mandate in Moroland*, 33–34.

28. Majul, *Political and Constitutional Ideas of the Philippine Revolution*, 159–60.

29. Apolinario Mabini, "For the Council of Government," December 13, 1898, Exhibit 320, in Taylor, *Philippine Insurrection*, vol. 3.

30. Apolinario Mabini, "Letter to E. Aguinaldo," January 1899, Exhibit 351: 2, in ibid., vol. 4.

31. Salanga, *Aglipay Question*, 2–5; Scott, *Aglipay before Aglipayanism*, 23–25.

32. Salanga, *Aglipay Question*, 5; Scott, *Aglipay before Aglipayanism*, 26–29.

33. Salanga, *Aglipay Question*, 18.

34. Ibid., 6–8.

35. Cited in Scott, *Aglipay before Aglipayanism*, 35.

36. Salanga, *Aglipay Question*, 21–22; Bennett, *Religion and the Rise of Jim Crow*, 190–92.

37. Cited in Scott, *Aglipay before Aglipayanism*, 38–39.

38. Florentino Torres, "Manifesto and Comprehensive Platform of the Creed and Proceedings of the Federal Party," December 23, 1900, Exhibit 1182: 95–97, in Taylor, *Philippine Insurrection*, vol. 5.

39. Lukban, "Proclamation."

40. Trías had also served as secretary of the treasury for the Republic of the Philippines and before his surrender was a lieutenant general for the republic, commanding the department of the south. He would become the first provincial governor of Cavite under U.S. rule. United States, *Fifth Annual Report of the Philippine Commission*, 357.

41. Mariano Trías and Victor Celis, "To My Dear Compatriots," March 1901, Exhibit 1148: 79, in Taylor, *Philippine Insurrection*, vol. 5; Emilio Aguinaldo, "Letter to the Filipino People," April 19, 1901, Exhibit 1017: 36, in ibid.

42. Vicente Rafael names this imperial logic "white love." See Rafael, *White Love and Other Events in Filipino History*.

43. "Peace Is Declared," *Washington Post*, July 4, 1902.

44. Scott, *Aglipay before Aglipayanism*, 39–40; Salanga, *Aglipay Question*, 11.

45. Stuntz, *Philippines and the Far East*, 490.

46. Parker, *Church and State in the Philippines*, 361.

47. Salanga, *Aglipay Question*, 12; Parker, *Church and State in the Philippines*, 366–67.

48. Parker, *Church and State in the Philippines*, 363–81.

49. Salanga, *Aglipay Question*, 24–26.

50. Cited in Whittemore, *Struggle for Freedom*, 121–22.

51. Salanga, *Aglipay Question*, 24.

52. Parker, *Church and State in the Philippines*, 367–68.

53. Laubach, *People of the Philippines*, 142; Parker, *Church and State in the Philippines*, 367–69; Salanga, *Aglipay Question*, 23–24.

54. Parker, *Church and State in the Philippines*, 374–75; United States, *Fifth Annual Report of the Philippine Commission*, 20.

55. "The Catholic Hierarchy," *New York Sun*, April 24, 1903.

56. Ibid., 12.

57. Ambrose Coleman, "The Inside of the Aglipayan Church," *American Catholic Quarterly Review*, April 1905, 368.

58. After reviewing the evidence, however, this report concluded that despite the unruly elements in his movement, Aglipay's own purpose was "to build up a church of his own . . . a purely Filipino church." United States, *Fifth Annual Report of the Philippine Commission*, 19.

59. Ambrose Coleman, "The Inside of the Aglipayan Church," *American Catholic Quarterly Review*, April 1905, 374, 376; Reyes y Florentino, *Religion of the Katipunan*.

60. Cited in Parker, *Church and State in the Philippines*, 417–18.

61. Ibid., 425.

62. Cited in Whittemore, *Struggle for Freedom*, 8–9, 123; for more on Aglipay and de los Reyes's interests in scientific rationality, see Gealogo, "Religion, Science, and Bayan."

63. Brown and Presbyterian Church in the U.S.A., *Report of a Visitation of the Philippine Mission*, 9–10.

64. Brown, *New Era in the Philippines*, 146.

65. Stuntz, *Philippines and the Far East*, 376.

66. Brown, *New Era in the Philippines*, 146.

67. Stuntz, *Philippines and the Far East*, 392, 490, 495; "The Bible in the Philippines," *Outlook*, September 15, 1906, 104. On the Protestant missionaries' views of Aglipay, see Clymer, *Protestant Missionaries in the Philippines*.

68. Gregorio Aglipay, "The Independent Catholic Church in the Philippines," *Independent*, October 29, 1903, 2571–72.

69. Ibid., 2575.

70. Parker, *Church and State in the Philippines*, 451–58; Salanga, *Aglipay Question*, 27–28.

71. Whittemore, *Struggle for Freedom*, 140–51, 168–218; Achútegui and Bernad, *Religious Revolution in the Philippines*, 245–52.

72. The question was whether under Spanish colonial law these properties had belonged to the state or to the church. By compensating the church, the U.S. government legitimated its claims, saving face for the Catholic hierarchy without actually returning the estates to the unpopular religious orders. The U.S. government then resold the estates with the announced goal of aiding the Filipino people, including the tenants who had always farmed them. But the vast majority went to commercial interests in a process that often favored the friends and relatives of colonial administrators, sparking a new controversy in subsequent years. See United States, *Sale of Friar Lands in the Philippines*; and Forbes, Worcester, and Carpenter, *Friar-Land Inquiry*.

73. "Chapelle Is Dead," *Washington Post*, August 10, 1905, 1.

74. Quezon, *Philippine Independence*, 29.

75. "Problem of Religion," *Washington Post*, December 18, 1898, 23; "Governed by a Sultan," ibid., January 8, 1899, 19.

76. Walther, *Sacred Interests*.

77. On "bad religion," see Orsi, "Snakes Alive"; on the imperial politics of religious-secular distinctions, see Stack, Goldenberg, and Fitzgerald, *Religion as a Category*.

78. This promise also reflected the secularizing reforms underway in Spain at the time, where liberal reformers were attempting to reduce the power of the church. Majul, *Muslims in the Philippines*, 103.

79. U.S. Senate, *Report of the Philippine Commission to the President*, 100–105. While the sultan had no authority on Mindanao Island, most of the local chiefs or *datus* of the Sulu Archipelago recognized him as their head, making him the single most important Moro leader at the time.

80. McKinley, "Report of John C. Bates," 27.

81. Salman, *Embarrassment of Slavery*, 54, 60–64; see also Warren, *Sulu Zone*.

82. John Elfreth Watkins, "Philippine Slaves," *Los Angeles Times*, March 5, 1899, B10.

83. "The Sultan of the Sulus," *Washington Post*, August 23, 1899, 6.

84. "America's New Slave Dominion," *St. Louis Post-Dispatch*, October 30, 1899, 3.

85. "Slavery and Polygamy Recognized," *Baltimore Sun*, August 28, 1899, 4.

86. "Severe on the Sultan," *Washington Post*, February 7, 1900, 4.

87. "Treatment of the Sulus," *New York Times*, November 1, 1899, 5. The identical interview with Schurman appeared on the same date in multiple newspapers, including the *Baltimore Sun*, the *Los Angeles Times*, the *Detroit Free Press*, and the *New York Tribune*.

88. "Serious Dangers in the Philippines," *Washington Post*, May 20, 1900, 22.

89. Salman, *Embarrassment of Slavery*.

90. On Roberts's life, see Roberts, *Autobiography*; and Madsen, *Defender of the Faith*.

91. Bitton, *Ritualization of Mormon History*, 150–70. A similar controversy flared again four years later when Utah elected Reed Smoot to the U.S. Senate. Smoot was an apostle in the LDS church but had never been a polygamist, and after three years of debate the Senate finally dismissed the case against him—a decision that symbolized the Mormons' gradual movement into the American mainstream. See Flake, *Politics of American Religious Identity*.

92. Melusina Fay Peirce, "The Only Cure for Mormon Polygamy," *New York Times*, November 26, 1899, 23; U.S. House of Representatives, *Constitutional Amendment to Prohibit Polygamy*. On nineteenth-century comparisons between Mormons and Muslims, see Perciaccante, "Mormon-Muslim Comparison"; Fluhman, *Peculiar People*; and Peterson, "Mormons and Muslims."

93. Reeve, *Religion of a Different Color*.

94. S. S. Laws, "Religious Liberty," *Washington Post*, January 8, 1900, 10.

95. U.S. House of Representatives, "Case of Brigham H. Roberts," 10.

96. "Problem of Religion," *Washington Post*, December 18, 1898, 23. The *Post* later chided Democratic papers for their "show of righteous indignation" against the administration for making payments under the Bates Treaty to a "harem-keeper," arguing that it would be "impossible" to "convert the Mohammedan polygamists to monogamous Christianity" and noting that not so long ago, "among Caucasian Americans in one of our Territories that is now a State," the U.S. president had appointed a polygamist (Brigham Young) as governor of Utah. "In making a treaty with the Sultan of Sulu we do not indorse polygamy," the editors opined, "any more than we have indorsed the heathenish, idolatrous, and barbarous beliefs and rites of Indian tribes in our own country in the numerous treaties we have made with them." "Our Harem-Keeper," *Washington Post*, November 2, 1899, 6.

97. Anna Northend Benjamin, "Our Mohammedan Wards in Sulu," *Outlook*, November 18, 1899, 675; on Benjamin's career, see Keenan, *Encyclopedia of the Spanish-American and Philippine-American Wars*, 39.

98. J. N. Taylor, "Sultan of Sulu," *Boston Daily Globe*, March 14, 1900, 1.

99. Ibid., 4.

100. "Tour of the Philippines," *New York Times*, July 3, 1899, 3.

101. "Approved by Schurman," *Baltimore Sun*, November 1, 1899, 9.

102. McKinley, "Report of John C. Bates," 31.

103. Ibid., 66.

104. Ibid., 26, 58.

105. Ibid., 109–10.

106. "Sulu Slaves to Be Gradually Emancipated," *San Francisco Chronicle*, October 27, 1899, 2.

107. Gowing, *Mandate in Moroland*, 122n28.

108. William McKinley, "President's Policy in the Philippines," *New York Times*, September 18, 1900, 5.

109. Cited in Gowing, *Mandate in Moroland*, 48.

110. "Schurmann [*sic*] on Islands," *Los Angeles Times*, August 3, 1902, 2.

111. Quoted in Walther, *Sacred Interests*, 180.

112. Barrows, *Bureau of Non-Christian Tribes for the Philippine Islands*, 3.

113. Walther, *Sacred Interests*, 184–85. In fact many reformers in Indian affairs would similarly advocate an end to reservations, contending that Native Americans would be better served if they were forced to adapt immediately to the advancing tides of white "civilization." Barrows was no doubt familiar with this debate, but he considered it even more true in the case of the "Mohammedan" Moros.

114. Brent emphasized missions to the non-Christian tribes in part because he refused to send Episcopal missionaries to evangelize the Filipino Catholics. His resulting reputation as an even-handed and fair-minded cleric strengthened his positive relationships with colonial officials. See ibid., 222–24; Clymer, *Protestant Missionaries in the Philippines*, 51–54, 160–69; and Jones, *Christian Missions in the American Empire*, 89–102.

115. Cited in Walther, *Sacred Interests*, 221, 191.

116. Gowing, *Mandate in Moroland*, 108–18; Walther, *Sacred Interests*, 205–7.

117. Gowing, *Mandate in Moroland*, 72–75; Salman, *Embarrassment of Slavery*, 112–18.

118. Gowing, *Mandate in Moroland*, 118–20.

119. Quoted in ibid., 351.

120. "Appendix D: Memorandum Agreement between the Governor-General of the Philippine Islands and the Sultan of Sulu," in ibid., 352–53.

121. Ibid.

122. Chidester, *Savage Systems*; Chidester, *Empire of Religion*.

123. "The Problems of the Pacific," *Los Angeles Times*, November 18, 1927, A4.

124. "Urges Philippines for Rubber Fields," *New York Times*, June 27, 1926, 23.

125. Cited in Abinales, *Mindanao, Nation, and Region*, 12–13.

126. Abinales, *Mindanao, Nation, and Region*; Graf, Kreuzer, and Werning, *Conflict in Moro Land*.

127. Abinales, "American Colonial State," 89–117.

128. Islam, *Politics of Islamic Identity*.

CHAPTER THREE

1. Pawnee Chiefs to Sells, August 18, 1914, Indian Customs: Pawnee, reel 7, CCF.

2. Hultkrantz, *Religions of the American Indians*, 9; Sando, *Pueblo Indians*, 22–23.

3. On the term "doings," see Fowles, *Archaeology of Doings*.

4. Non-Indian observers often remarked—whether in critical or in admiring tones—on how much individual freedom Native Americans enjoyed. On themes of visionary

experience and prophecy in Native American traditions, see Irwin, *Dream Seekers*; and Irwin, *Coming Down from Above*.

5. Silverman, *Red Brethren*, 39–40; Richter, *Before the Revolution*, 365–66; Soderlund, *Lenape Country*, 196–97.

6. Fisher, *Indian Great Awakening*.

7. McLoughlin, *Cherokees and Missionaries*, 199–238.

8. U.S. Office of Indian Affairs, *Annual Report*, 1873, 227–28.

9. Wenger, *We Have a Religion*, chapter 1.

10. U.S. Office of Indian Affairs, *Annual Report*, 1882, vii.

11. U.S. Office of Indian Affairs, *Annual Report*, 1883, xv; U.S. Office of Indian Affairs, *Sixty-First Annual Report*, 1892, 27–29.

12. Quoted in Wunder, *"Retained by the People,"* 35; see also Wenger, "Indian Dances and the Politics of Religious Freedom," 857–58.

13. The Dawes Act was a tragedy almost everywhere it was implemented. It eventually resulted in the wholesale loss of Indian land, not only by opening up the sale of "surplus" land to non-Indians (a provision that blatantly violated treaty provisions) but also because many impoverished allottees were forced to sell their land to speculators. See Hoxie, *Final Promise*, 70–81; and Nugent, *Into the West*, 98–108, 131–32, 181–94.

14. U.S. Office of Indian Affairs, *Annual Report*, 1885, v–viii.

15. Quoted in Prucha, *The Great Father*, 875; Hoxie, *Final Promise*, 211–38.

16. U.S. Office of Indian Affairs, *Report of the Commissioner of Indian Affairs*, 1906, 119–24.

17. Crane, *Indians of the Enchanted Desert*, 17.

18. C. J. Crandall to H. B. Peairs, April 24, 1924, Records of the Bureau of Indian Affairs, RG 75, Northern Pueblos Agency, General Correspondence File, 1904–1937, file 806.1, National Archives and Records Administration, Washington, D.C.

19. Lindquist, *Red Man in the United States*, v–vi, xv.

20. Mormons were fascinated by the new movement; for a time some of them placed the Ghost Dance within the framework of Mormon revelation and viewed Wovoka as a legitimate prophet, perhaps even the Messiah whose imminent return Joseph Smith had predicted. See Mooney, *Ghost-Dance Religion*, 777–93; and Barney, *Mormons, Indians, and the Ghost Dance Religion of 1890*.

21. Duratschek, *Crusading along Sioux Trails*, 142.

22. Quoted in Coleman, *Voices of Wounded Knee*, 57.

23. Blaine, *Some Things Are Not Forgotten*, 56; Mooney, *Ghost-Dance Religion*, 782–83.

24. Mooney, *Ghost-Dance Religion*, 656, 782–83. As Raymond DeMallie argues in his introduction to Mooney's text (xix–xxi), there is no evidence that the Ghost Dance had warlike connotations among the Sioux, any more than it did among the other Native peoples who practiced it. On the persistence of these representational patterns, see Hale, "Hostiles and Friendlies."

25. Raymond DeMallie, introduction to Mooney, *Ghost-Dance Religion*, xix.

26. Lesser, *Pawnee Ghost Dance Hand Game*.

27. Quoted in Mooney, *Ghost-Dance Religion*, 809.

28. Ruby and Brown, *Dreamer-Prophets of the Columbia Plateau*, 33–39.

29. U.S. Office of Indian Affairs, *Sixty-First Annual Report*, 1892, 499–501; Ruby and Brown, *John Slocum and the Indian Shaker Church*, 109–23.

30. Myron Eells, "The Indians: S'kokomish Agency, W. T.," *American Missionary* 38, no. 5 (May 1884): 152; Eells, *Ten Years of Missionary Work*, 162–65.

31. Eells, *Ten Years of Missionary Work*, 180–83.

32. U.S. Office of Indian Affairs, *Sixty-First Annual Report*, 1892, 495.

33. Wickersham is quoted in Mooney, *Ghost-Dance Religion*, 757–59; U.S. Office of Indian Affairs, *Annual Report*, 1893, 333. Wickersham's motives were hardly unmixed. His more profitable clientele included Tacoma businessmen eager to buy up Indian lands, and the citizenship rights he wished to advance included the sale of Indian lands to speculators. The Shakers nevertheless considered him a valuable ally. See Ruby and Brown, *John Slocum and the Indian Shaker Church*, 112–15.

34. Mooney, *Ghost-Dance Religion*, 750.

35. Wilson to Commissioner of Indian Affairs, January 29, 1917, Indian Customs: Klamath, reel 4, CCF.

36. James Wickersham to James Mooney, June 25, 1893, reprinted in Mooney, *Ghost-Dance Religion*, 759.

37. Ruby and Brown, *John Slocum and the Indian Shaker Church*, 118–21.

38. U.S. Office of Indian Affairs, *Report of the Commissioner of Indian Affairs*, 1901, 386.

39. U.S. Office of Indian Affairs, *Report of the Commissioner of Indian Affairs*, 1904, 356.

40. U.S. Office of Indian Affairs, *Report of the Commissioner of Indian Affairs*, 1906, 381.

41. Ruby and Brown, *John Slocum and the Indian Shaker Church*, 124–25.

42. Ibid., 126–30.

43. See, for example, Mack, *Visionary Women*; Humez, *Mother's First-Born Daughters*; and Brekus, *Strangers and Pilgrims*.

44. Johnson to Commissioner of Indian Affairs, February 6, 1915, Indian Customs: Klamath, reel 4, CCF.

45. Sells to Johnson, March 12, 1915, ibid.

46. Freer to Commissioner of Indian Affairs, October 9, 1915, ibid.

47. Freer to Jackson, Moore, and Jackson, January 2, 1917, ibid.; for a more detailed account of the origins and difficulties of the Klamath Shaker Church, see Ruby and Brown, *John Slocum and the Indian Shaker Church*, 157–71.

48. Moore to Wickersham, January 16, 1917, Indian Customs: Klamath, reel 4, CCF; Anderson to Assistant Secretary of the Interior, February 14, 1917, ibid.

49. Brown, "Affidavit of Charlie Brown, January 24, 1917," ibid.; Brown, "Affidavit of Sargent Brown, January 24, 1917," ibid.

50. Freer to Commissioner of Indian Affairs, February 16, 1917, ibid.

51. Bradley to Anderson, May 2, 1917, ibid.

52. Schaefer and Furst, *People of the Peyote*; Anderson, *Peyote*; Maroukis, *Peyote Road*.

53. Quoted in Hagan, *Quanah Parker*, 57.

54. Less biased research has consistently supported practitioners' claims that peyote is not addictive and, at least as used in their ceremonies, has no harmful or long-term physiological effects. As early as the 1920s, key psychological and pharmacological studies concluded that there was no evidence to support the allegations against peyote

and that there was no scientific basis to suppress its use. These conclusions significantly weakened the BIA's case against the Peyote movement. See Maroukis, *Peyote Road*, 112.

55. Stewart, *Peyote Religion*, 68–127; Maroukis, *Peyote Road*, 14–58.

56. U.S. House of Representatives, *Peyote*, 17–18.

57. Johnson had gained notoriety as a temperance activist in Nebraska during the 1890s when he posed as a brewer in order to uncover and incriminate pro-alcohol businessmen. His predilection for nighttime sleuthing in that effort earned him the nickname "Pussyfoot," which stuck with him for the rest of his career. See McKenzie, *"Pussyfoot" Johnson*; Maroukis, *Peyote Road*, 39–40.

58. U.S. Office of Indian Affairs, *Report of the Commissioner of Indian Affairs*, 1909, 14.

59. Hauke to Sewell, May 6, 1912, Indian Customs: Creek Indians, reel 2, CCF; U.S. Office of Indian Affairs, *Report of the Commissioner of Indian Affairs*, 1916, 62.

60. U.S. House of Representatives, *Peyote*, 1918, 59–114. The letter from Bull Bear is reprinted on pp. 103–6.

61. Ibid, 149–50.

62. Maroukis, *Peyote Road*, 33; Slotkin, *Peyote Religion*, 56.

63. U.S. House of Representatives, *Peyote*, 88–89; Maroukis, *Peyote Road*.

64. Maroukis, *Peyote Road*, 30–39, quotes from Hensley on 37 and 39. Maroukis is drawing on the work of Paul Radin, the well-known ethnologist who did fieldwork among the Winnebagos from 1908 to 1913.

65. U.S. House of Representatives, *Peyote*, 128.

66. Stewart, *Peyote Religion*, 219–26; Moses, *Indian Man*, 179–205.

67. Slotkin, *Peyote Religion*, 58–64, quote on 137n20; Maroukis, *Peyote Road*, 46–58, 183–233.

68. Burke to Ziebach, December 12, 1925, Indian Customs: Fort Hall, reel 4, CCF; Ziebach to Burke, December 17, 1925, ibid.; Burke to Ziebach, December 20, 1925, ibid.

69. Rhodes, "American Tradition," 39; Stewart, *Peyote Religion*, 128–47, 213–38; Sikkink, "From Christian Civilization to Individual Civil Liberties."

70. Edgar McCarthy, "Petition to the Senate Committee of Indian Affairs, October 1921," Indian Customs: Osage, reel 5, CCF.

71. U.S. House of Representatives, *Hearing to Investigate Indian Conditions*, 334; Wood, *Taos Pueblo*, 33–34; Stewart, *Peyote Religion*, 31–38, 202–8.

72. U.S. House of Representatives, *Hearing to Investigate Indian Conditions*, 316.

73. This section of the chapter reworks material from my essay "Indian Dances and the Politics of Religious Freedom."

74. Kracht, "Kiowa Religion in Historical Perspective."

75. Big Tree to Secretary of the Interior, February 15, 1916, Indian Customs: Kiowa, reel 4, CCF.

76. Rhinefort to Red Buffalo, June 23, 1915, ibid.

77. Wolf Tail to Bradley, June 9, 1917, Indian Customs: Blackfeet, reel 1, CCF.

78. Lastman and Cheyenne River Indians to Norbeck, McMaster, and Williamson, February 1927, Indian Customs: Cheyenne River, reel 1, CCF.

79. Pawnee Chiefs to Stanion, February 11, 1915, Indian Customs: Pawnee, reel 7, CCF.

80. Stanion to Commissioner of Indian Affairs, February 18, 1915, ibid.

81. Vecsey, *Traditional Ojibwa Religion*, 174–90.

82. Dickens to Commissioner of Indian Affairs, November 15, 1916, Indian Customs: Red Lake, reel 8, CCF.

83. Ah-see-ne-we-nee and Chippewa Indians to Commissioner of Indian Affairs, August 30, 1916, ibid.

84. Warren and Chippewa Indians to Commissioner of Indian Affairs, January 21, 1917, ibid.

85. Perkins to Commissioner of Indian Affairs, June 28, 1917, ibid.

86. Wakonabo to Burnquist, April 28, 1918, Indian Customs: Leech Lake, reel 5, CCF.

87. Meritt to Perkins, July 23, 1917, Indian Customs: Red Lake, reel 8, CCF.

88. Meritt to McGregor, November 15, 1918, Indian Customs: Cheyenne River, reel 1, CCF.

89. Martin to Commissioner of Indian Affairs, June 24, 1913, Indian Customs: Uintah and Ouray, reel 13, CCF.

90. Stecker to Commissioner of Indian Affairs, June 26, 1914, Indian Customs: Kiowa, reel 4, CCF.

91. Stinchecum to Commissioner of Indian Affairs, August 1, 1915, ibid.

92. Troutman, "Citizenship of Dance."

93. Tidwell to Commissioner of Indian Affairs, August 8, 1918, Indian Customs: Pine Ridge, reel 8, CCF.

94. Indians of Standing Rock Reservation to Commissioner of Indian Affairs, June 7, 1919, Indian Customs: Standing Rock, reel 11, CCF.

95. Meets the Enemy to Sells, December 1920, Indian Customs: Cheyenne River, reel 1, CCF; LeBeau and Cheyenne River Indians to Commissioner of Indian Affairs, June 27, 1921, ibid.

96. Munro to Commissioner of Indian Affairs, 1921, ibid.

97. Kelsey to Commissioner Valentine, July 25, 1912, Indian Customs: Creek Indians, reel 2, CCF.

98. Meritt to McGregor, November 15, 1918, Indian Customs: Cheyenne River, reel 1, CCF.

99. *Lander Eagle*, "Sun Dance Called Off," July 4, 1913, Indian Customs: Shoshone, reel 11, CCF.

100. Ellis, *Dancing People*, 46–54, 115–21.

101. Clyde Ellis has shown how Indian dancing served as a crucial means of cultural resistance and how, in the process, Native people actively and strategically modified their dances in order to maintain them under suppression. Although Ellis recognizes that the powwow culture he studies "lost" at least part of its "spiritual" dimension, he does not interrogate the process of making distinctions between "religious" and "social" dances in the first place. See ibid.

102. Lassiter, "Southwestern Oklahoma, the Gourd Dance, and 'Charlie Brown'"; Fitzgerald, *Religion and the Secular*; Stack, Goldenberg, and Fitzgerald, *Religion as a Category*.

103. Browning to Burke, August 29, 1925, Indian Customs: Fort Hall, reel 4, CCF.

104. Ziebach to Burke, August 25, 1925, ibid.

105. Browning to Burke, August 29, 1925, ibid.

106. Estep to Commissioner of Indian Affairs, July 3, 1913, ibid.

107. Browning to Burke, August 29, 1925, ibid.

108. Ibid. See Twain, *Following the Equator*. Chapter 21 concludes: "There are many humorous things in the world; among them the white man's notion that he is less savage than the other savages" (126).

109. Wenger, *We Have a Religion*.

110. Ziebach to Burke, August 25, 1925, Indian Dances: Fort Hall, reel 4, CCF.

111. Wenger, *We Have a Religion*; Wenger, "Indian Dances and the Politics of Religious Freedom."

112. U.S. House of Representatives, Committee on Indian Affairs, "Readjustment of Indian Affairs: Hearings on H.R. 7902," 1934, John Collier Papers, reel 30, Sterling Memorial Library, Manuscripts and Archives, Yale University; Deloria, *Indian Reorganization Act*, 127–201.

113. Elaine Goodale Eastman, "Does Uncle Sam Foster Paganism?," *Christian Century*, August 8, 1934, 1016–18.

114. John Collier, "A Reply to Mrs. Eastman," *Christian Century*, August 8, 1934, 1018–20.

115. Collier to Ortiz, July 8, 1935, Indian Customs: Santa Fe, reel 10, CCF.

116. Wenger, "'New Form of Government.'"

CHAPTER FOUR

1. O. Straus, *Religious Liberty in the United States*, 11–12.

2. O. Straus, *Roger Williams*.

3. O. Straus, *Origin of Republican Form of Government*.

4. See, for example, "Jewish Historical Society," *American Hebrew*, December 31, 1897, 277.

5. O. Straus, *Roger Williams*, 241–41.

6. R. Straus, *Religious Liberty and Democracy*, x.

7. On the Jews as a foreign nation in early modern Europe, see Kaplan, *Divided by Faith*, 328–29; on the Reform movement and the category of religion, see Batnitzky, *How Judaism Became a Religion*; on the ambivalent figure of the Jew as a key problematic for European modernity, see Mufti, *Enlightenment in the Colony*.

8. American Jews' appeals to religious freedom were by no means the only factor in their racial redefinition as white. A number of historians have traced the emergence of ethnicity as a new way of defining communal identity that escaped the stigmas of race, thus assisting the movement of various European immigrant groups into the racial status of whiteness. Jewish intellectuals played a crucial role in the development of ethnicity as a concept and very clearly benefited from its capacious potential. See Jacobson, *Whiteness of a Different Color*; Jacobson, *Roots Too*; Greene, *Jewish Origins of Cultural Pluralism*; and Brodkin, *How Jews Became White Folks*.

9. "The City: Sacrifice for Principle," *American Hebrew*, August 17, 1894, 482; W. B. Capps, "In the Land of Religious Liberty," ibid., October 5, 1894, 676.

10. "Religious Liberty a Farce," ibid., August 16, 1895, 354. For more on these battles, see Cohen, *Jews in Christian America*, 72–79, 109–15. Cohen describes the shifting debate among Jews on whether to make strong protests against such laws or to simply accept them as an unfortunate consequence of living in a predominantly Christian

country. Jewish leaders were more likely to take the latter position at times when public anti-Semitism seemed to be on the rise, she finds, because they feared a backlash against any public expression of Jewish dissent.

11. Jones, *Sound the Tocsin of Alarm*, 29, 17, 130. Jones elaborated a similar argument, referencing the events of the Spanish-American War and the U.S. occupation of the Philippines, in *Politics of the Nazarene*.

12. Michels, "Is America 'Different'?," 29–40.

13. "Baron Hirsch's Argentine Colonization," *American Hebrew*, December 11, 1891, 122–24.

14. This editorial from the *New York Herald*, along with many other sympathetic pieces, is cited in "The Oppressor's Rod," *American Hebrew*, October 2, 1891, 201.

15. Gurock, *Orthodox Jews in America*.

16. "The Best Teacher," *American Hebrew*, May 3, 1889, 214.

17. "It Has the True Ring," *Los Angeles Times*, June 10, 1892, 6; "Democratic Doctrine," ibid., June 23, 1892, 6.

18. "Censure for Russia," *Washington Post*, June 1, 1903, 4; "Bishop Potter on Kishineff Outrage," *New York Times*, June 2, 1903, 5; "Philadelphia Protests," *New York Times*, June 4, 1903, 5; "Urges a National Protest to Russia," *New York Times*, June 3, 1903, 7.

19. "Count Cassini Confers with the President," *New York Times*, June 13, 1903, 9; "President Hears the Case of the Jews," ibid., June 16, 1903, 1.

20. "Russia Will Resent the Jewish Petition," ibid., July 4, 1903, 7.

21. "God Hasten the Time," *Afro-American*, December 30, 1911, 4.

22. For a history of the Zionist movement in the United States, see Cohen, *Americanization of Zionism*.

23. Gurock, *Orthodox Jews in America*; Stern, *Genius*; Levitt, "Other Moderns."

24. David Philipson, "Partisanship in Office," November 28, 1909, box 5, folder 4, Philipson Papers.

25. Abram Isaacs, "Is Judaism Necessary Today?," *North American Review*, July 1, 1911, 108; Abram Isaacs, "The Jew's Opportunity in America," ibid., March 1, 1915, 431.

26. "The City: West End Synagogue," *American Hebrew*, February 10, 1899, 522.

27. Ibid.

28. "Zionist Congress," ibid., August 17, 1900, 378.

29. "President Accepts a Flag," *New York Times*, September 28, 1903, 1. As Naomi Cohen has argued, the Zionist movement took on distinctive contours in the American context. Whether they were recent immigrants or not, while American Zionists embraced a symbolic vision of Judaism as a nation, they rejected the most radical forms of Jewish nationalism. And even as they advocated for a national homeland in Palestine for persecuted Jews, they continued to celebrate the principles of U.S. citizenship for American Jews. See Cohen, *Americanization of Zionism*.

30. Wolf to Executive Committee of the Union of American Hebrew Congregations, August 18, 1899, box 16, folder 10, Union for Reform Judaism Records, MS 72, American Jewish Archives, Cincinnati, Ohio; Myer Cohen, "Minutes of a Meeting of the Executive Committee of the Board of Delegates on Civil Rights," box 29, folder 6, Union for Reform Judaism Records.

31. American Jewish Committee, *Jews in the Eastern War Zone*, 9.

32. Kohler, *Jewish Rights at International Congresses*, 55.

33. Bernard G. Richards, "The American Jewish Congress," 1918, pamphlet, box 6, folder 6, Richards Papers.

34. The text of the Balfour Declaration (including preliminary drafts) can be found in Stein, *The Balfour Declaration*, 664; see also Schneer, *Balfour Declaration*.

35. David de Sola Pool, "The British Capture of Jerusalem," *American Hebrew and Jewish Messenger*, December 14, 1917, 177, 196.

36. American Jewish Committee, "Statement on Balfour Declaration," April 28, 1918, box 2, folder 21, Morris D. Waldman Papers, MS 23, American Jewish Archives, Cincinnati, Ohio.

37. "Messages Favoring and Opposing Zionism Sent President Wilson by American Jews," *Jewish Independent*, September 13, 1918, 1.

38. Wolsey to Philipson, September 12, 1918, box 2, folder 4, Philipson Papers.

39. "Messages Favoring and Opposing Zionism."

40. Schulman to Philipson, September 26, 1918, box 2, folder 1, Philipson Papers.

41. David Philipson, "Dear Sir," August 1918, box 1, folder 15, Philipson Papers; Straus to Philipson, September 2, 1918, folder 19, ibid.; Cohen, *Americanization of Zionism*.

42. Henry Berkowitz, "An Appeal to Members of the World's Peace Conference in Behalf of the Full Rights of Jews in Every Land," December 1918, box 1, folder 27, Henry Berkowitz Papers, MSS 25, American Jewish Archives, Cincinnati, Ohio.

43. Landman to Berkowitz, March 5, 1919; Isaac Landman, "The League of Nations and the Jews," *American Hebrew and Jewish Messenger*, May 23, 1919, 741.

44. "League Draft Completed; Monroe Doctrine Left Out," *Boston Daily Globe*, March 28, 1919, 1; Henry Wales, "Seek Church Freedom in League," *Los Angeles Times*, March 20, 1919, 11.

45. Pedersen, *Guardians*.

46. Landman, "League of Nations and the Jews," 740.

47. Brecher, *Reluctant Ally*; Rappaport, *Hands across the Sea*.

48. Preston, *Sword of the Spirit*, 279–80. Preston argues that religious liberty "was a peculiarly American preoccupation" at the peace conference, grounded in U.S. religious and political traditions that "had little resonance elsewhere."

49. Janowsky, *Jews and Minority Rights*, 351–56.

50. Ibid., 351–63.

51. D. Johnson, *Challenge to American Freedoms*; Cottrell, *Roger Nash Baldwin*.

52. Kennedy, *Freedom from Fear*, 14.

53. Evans, "Klan's Fight for Americanism," 36, 54, 57–60; see also Evans, *Public School Problem in America*.

54. On the KKK of the 1920s, see Baker, *Gospel According to the Klan*; and Pegram, *One Hundred Percent American*.

55. Jewish periodicals offered alarming news of these developments; see, for example, "Foreign News," *American Israelite*, January 11, 1923, 1.

56. Cohen, *Jews in Christian America*.

57. David Philipson, "Henry Ford's Campaign of Hatred," *American Israelite*, November 25, 1920, 4. On Ford's anti-Semitism, see Wallace, *American Axis*; and Curcio, *Henry Ford*.

58. Max Kohler, "College Entrance Examination and Civil Rights," *Jewish Advocate*, October 19, 1922, 11.

59. "The Fight in the Open at Last," *American Israelite*, March 19, 1925, 4.

60. Kohler to Zepin, June 21, 1921, box 10, folder 4, Kohler Papers.

61. "Mr. Post on Immigration," *American Israelite*, March 24, 1921, 3.

62. Wolf to Kohler, November 23, 1922, box 10, folder 4, Kohler Papers.

63. Federal Council of the Churches of Christ in America and Cavert, *Churches Allied for Common Tasks*, 143–44, 184–87, 347–48.

64. Federal Council of Churches, *Bulletin, Vol. 5*, 16, 73.

65. Federal Council of Churches, *Bulletin, Vol. 6*, 17.

66. Ariel, *Evangelizing the Chosen People*.

67. Anthony and Herring, "Annual Report to the Members and Advisors of the Committee on Goodwill between Jews and Christians," box 11, folder 15, Kohler Papers.

68. On Wilson's vision of social Christianity, see Burnidge, "Business of Church and State."

69. Brown, *Foreign Missions and the War*, 10.

70. Brown and Presbyterian Church in the U.S.A., *Report of a Visitation of the Philippine Mission*; Brown, *New Era in the Philippines*.

71. David Philipson, "Religious Liberty," 1926, box 5, folder 5, Philipson Papers.

72. Schulman to Philipson, December 11, 1924, box 2, folder 1, ibid.

73. Ibid.

74. "Enemies of Liberty," *Jewish Exponent*, January 18, 1924, 4.

75. "Keynote of Dinner Is Religious Amity," *New York Times*, February 24, 1926, 19. Both of these were standard arguing points for Catholics, too, particularly in the debates over religion in public education, providing a point of connection for Catholics and Jews against the persistent threat of Protestant hegemony in the schools.

76. "Christians and Jews Come Together," *American Israelite*, March 19, 1925, 5.

77. "Aims to Harmonize National Groups," *New York Times*, December 11, 1927, N1.

78. Where Catholics generally demanded control over the religious education of their own children, most Protestants argued for a shared standard of supposedly "non-sectarian" religious instruction for all. On the history of these debates, see Green, *Bible*.

79. "Russia Proclaims Religious Freedom," *New York Times*, April 5, 1917, 13.

80. "Religious Liberty for Russia," *American Israelite*, April 19, 1917, 1.

81. "Dr. Hartman Says Russia's Revolution Is Genuine," *Boston Daily Globe*, September 9, 1923, A1.

82. "Liberty or Communism—Which?" *Washington Post*, April 13, 1923, 6; "Pope Plans Appeal for Curb on Soviet," ibid., April 16, 1923, 1.

83. "17,000 Catholics March," *Baltimore Sun*, October 11, 1915, 2; "Wilson Attacked at Catholic Week," *St. Louis Post-Dispatch*, August 22, 1916, 3; "Catholics Avoid Giving Wilson Mexican Blame," *New York Tribune*, August 23, 1916, 9. See Fallaw, *Religion and State Formation*; and Redinger, *American Catholics*.

84. "Allied with Bolshevism," *Boston Daily Globe*, November 10, 1926, A7; "K. of C. Disavow Aid to Mexican Rebels," *New York Times*, November 6, 1926, 13. See also Vinca, "American Catholic Reaction."

85. See, for example, Inter-American Peace Committee, "Minutes of the Inter-American Peace Committee," July 6, 1916, Mexican Commission Correspondence, box 4,

Moorefield Storey Papers, Library of Congress, Manuscript Division, Washington, D.C.; Inman, *Again the Mexican Question*; and Inman, *Church and State in Mexico*.

86. "Prof. Lord Speaks on Religious Freedom," *Boston Daily Globe*, April 9, 1923, 29.

87. "President Coolidge," *Commonweal*, November 12, 1924, 1–2.

88. "Jews an Asset to America Says Governor Smith," *American Israelite*, September 10, 1925, 6; "Best Wishes from Governor," *New York Times*, September 8, 1926, 11. Any Catholic who wanted to succeed in electoral politics at the state or national level had to demonstrate allegiance to these ideals. Smith, already a prospective Democratic nominee in 1924, had long-standing presidential aspirations and excellent instincts as a politician. For more on his articulations of religious freedom, see F. Curtis, *Production of American Religious Freedom*, 87–112.

89. "Smith Issue Raised at Good-Will Fete," *New York Times*, December 9, 1927, 13.

90. Van Dyke, *In Defense of Religious Liberty*.

91. Stephen S. Wise, "Religious Tolerance and the American Ideal," *Free Synagogue Pulpit* 8, no. 10 (1928): 11, 14–15, box 5, folder 6, Stephen S. Wise Collection, American Jewish Archives, Cincinnati, Ohio.

92. For Williams's take on the role of Catholics in the First World War, see Williams, *American Catholics in the War*. Under his leadership, *Commonweal* became the leading journal of liberally oriented lay Catholic opinion, a stature it still holds today. See Clements, "Michael Williams and the Founding of 'The Commonweal'"; see also Allitt, *Catholic Converts*, 192–94. Despite Allitt's title, Williams was not a convert to Catholicism but had returned to the church after a long drift away from it as a young man.

93. Michael Williams, "Columbus Day, 1928," *Commonweal*, September 19, 1928, 566–67.

94. Nolan, "Men of Good Will."

95. "Religious Liberty Conference Is Set," *Washington Post*, January 25, 1932, 4.

96. "National Conference of Catholics, Jews, and Protestants," *Jewish Exponent*, February 19, 1932, 7.

97. Hayes, "J. Elliot Ross and the National Conference of Christians and Jews," 327–29; Montavon to Burke, January 26, 1932, folder 5, box 19, Records of the United States Conference of Catholic Bishops, Office of the General Secretary, Collection 10, American Catholic History Research Center and Archives, Catholic University of America, Washington, D.C.

98. National Conference of Jews and Christians, "Catholic Leader Commends Conference Methods," *Information Bulletin*, no. 8, May 1931, box 4, folder 2, Patrick Henry Callahan Papers, American Catholic History Research Center and Archives, Catholic University of America, Washington, D.C.

99. "War on Intolerance Planned by Laymen," *Atlanta Constitution*, September 12, 1933, 2.

100. Freedman, *Klezmer America*.

101. Clinchy to Philipson, March 8, 1933, box 1, folder 2, Philipson Papers; "Religious Leaders Ask Social Reform," *New York Times*, March 27, 1933, 10.

102. Dochuk, *From Bible Belt to Sunbelt*; Kruse, *One Nation under God*.

103. "Land of the Free," *Commonweal*, March 22, 1933, 561–63.

104. American Jewish Congress and American Jewish Committee, "Memorandum on Conference on German Situation," box 6, folder 8, Richards Papers. Like the

American Jewish Committee, the CCAR feared that dramatic protests were likely to fuel anti-Semitism in the United States as well as in Europe and that the German Jews would be better served through quieter methods of philanthropy and lobbying behind the scenes. See "Central Conference of American Rabbis Condemns Oppression of Catholics," *American Israelite*, June 29, 1933, 1–2.

105. American Jewish Congress, "For Immediate Release: Outstanding Representatives of Three Faiths Describe Menace of Hitlerism," February 27, 1933, box 5, folder 4, Stephen S. Wise Collection.

106. Cyrus Adler and Alfred Cohen, "Statement by Jewish Committee, B'nai B'rith," *Jewish Advocate*, March 21, 1933, 1.

107. "Unbelievable Prejudice Exists in America Today," *Jewish Advocate*, March 11, 1932, 1; "Vivisecting Religious Prejudices at Washington Conference," *Jewish Exponent*, 4.

108. Joseph Proskauer, "For the Information of Members of the Executive Committee," June 26, 1933, box 11, folder 3, Kohler Papers; Irving Lehman et al., "Copy of Statement by the Joint Council of the American Jewish Committee, the American Jewish Congress and the B'nai B'rith," 1933, ibid.

109. Guido Enderis, "Protestants Balk at Curb by Nazis," *New York Times*, November 20, 1933, 1; "Americans Aided in Reich Protest," ibid., November 21, 1933, 10.

110. Williams to Richards, April 3, 1933, box 1, folder 26, Richards Papers.

111. "Week by Week: Justice for Jews," *Commonweal*, April 5, 1933, 620.

112. Michael Williams, "Nazis Think Democracy Must Yield to Socialism," *Daily Boston Globe*, July 16, 1933, C6. Several newspapers published this series of articles on the Nazis.

113. Michael Williams, "Burning Books—and Bridges," *Daily Boston Globe*, July 9, 1933, C5; "Declares Catholics, Protestants Suffer," ibid., June 26, 1933, 3.

114. American Jewish Congress, *Case of Civilization against Hitlerism*, 20.

115. Proskauer, "For the Information of Members of the Executive Committee."

116. "Ohio Group to Protest on Nazis," *New York Times*, May 20, 1933, 3.

117. David Philipson, "Reactions to the German Jewish Situation," May 29, 1933, box 5, folder 5, Philipson Papers.

118. "Takes Up Cause of German Jews," *Baltimore Sun*, June 6, 1933, 3; "Gov. Ritchie Exalts Religious Freedom," *New York Times*, February 2, 1928, 10.

119. "Against Anti-Jewish Action," *Palestine Post*, June 8, 1933, 2.

120. Schultz, *Tri-faith America*; Wenger, "Freedom to Worship."

121. Kennedy, *Freedom from Fear*, 411–13.

122. "Tolerant Ostriches," *Pittsburgh Courier*, October 28, 1933, 10.

CHAPTER FIVE

1. Wesley, "The Negro Has Always Wanted the Four Freedoms," 91. After a long conflict with the Wilberforce University board of directors, Wesley would be removed from the presidency in 1947. See Gomez-Jefferson, *Sage of Tawawa*, 229–45.

2. Raboteau, *Slave Religion*; Glaude, *Exodus!*

3. Walker, *Walker's Appeal in Four Articles*, 41, emphasis in original. On Walker's life and significance, see Hinks, *To Awaken My Afflicted Brethren*.

4. The term "ethno-religious" is Sylvester Johnson's. Weisenfeld describes them as "religio-racial" movements, emphasizing the various ways in which they employed the categories and practices of religion to redefine their racial identities. See S. Johnson, "Rise of Black Ethnics"; S. Johnson, *African American Religions*; and Weisenfeld, *New World a-Coming*.

5. Weisenfeld, *New World a-Coming*; Cone, *Martin and Malcolm and America*.

6. Furman et al., "To the Citizens of Greenville District" [1861], Correspondence of Rev. Franklin Wilson, MSS 833, box 3, Franklin Wilson Papers, Maryland Historical Society, Baltimore. See also Jordan, *Church, State, and Race*, and Noll, *God and Race in American Politics*.

7. Baptist minister H. M. Lawson, editor of the virulently anti-Catholic *American Sentinel of Religious Liberty*, described the FCC as a "Romanizing" organization aimed at "a union of church and state right here in America." "Is There Not a Cause?," *American Sentinel of Religious Liberty*, June 1920, 6–7. See also Kelsey, *Social Ethics among Southern Baptists*, 23–27, 206–30.

8. Harvey, *Freedom's Coming*, 229–45; Haynes, "Distinction and Dispersal."

9. "Al Smith Is Declared to Be a Friend of the South," *Afro-American*, July 7, 1928, 5.

10. Joint Conference Committee on Public Relations Representing the Northern Baptist Convention and the Southern Baptist Convention, "Records of Meeting," April 27, 1943, box 1, folder 1, Baptist Joint Committee on Public Affairs Minutes, 1938–1979, AR 378, Southern Baptist Historical Library and Archives, Nashville, Tenn.

11. Kruse, *White Flight*.

12. Richberg, *Nor Can Government*; see also Richberg, *My Hero*.

13. Wirt, "To Members, Wisconsin Council of Churches, Re: Human Rights, Property Rights, Civil Rights," December 28, 1948, Wisconsin Council of Churches Records, Wis MSS WB, box 11: Human Rights, Wisconsin Historical Society Archives, Madison.

14. Gwaltney, "Religious Liberty the Only Basis for a Just and Durable Peace" [1943], box 9, folder 9, Rufus Washington Weaver Papers, AR 99, Southern Baptist Historical Library and Archives, Nashville, Tenn.

15. Foner, *Story of American Freedom*.

16. There was never a singular "black church," but black churches—Baptist, Methodist, Holiness, Pentecostal, and more—were key social institutions, gathering places for spiritual sustenance, cultural expression, and leadership development. All of these functions became even more important for black communities in the wake of the Civil War. Anxious to refute the slanders of black immorality and criminality, the African American elite and aspiring classes relied on churches to nurture communal values of education and ethics. On these points, among others, see Higginbotham, *Righteous Discontent*; Harvey, *Redeeming the South*; and Miller, *Elevating the Race*.

17. I am indebted to Judith Weisenfeld for help in clarifying this point.

18. Allen, *Life, Experience, and Gospel Labours*; "A Copy of Rev. John M. Turner's Address," *Christian Recorder*, May 3, 1862, 1.

19. "Why Can't We Do It?," *Christian Recorder*, March 5, 1874. For more on African American historical narrations, see Maffly-Kipp, *Setting Down the Sacred Past*. On the role of the AME Church in this period, see C. Walker, *A Rock in a Weary Land*, and Montgomery, *Under Their Own Vine and Fig Tree*.

20. "Charleston Correspondence," *Christian Recorder*, June 3, 1865. Emanuel would also take a leading role in the civil rights movement of the mid-twentieth century and gained a renewed, tragic fame in 2015 when an avowed white supremacist shot and killed nine church members, including the pastor and state senator Clementa Pinckney. See Sarah Kaplan, "For Charleston's Emanuel AME Church, Shooting Is Another Painful Chapter in Rich History," *Washington Post*, June 18, 2015.

21. Theophilus Gould Stewart, "From Charleston, S.C.," *Christian Recorder*, March 23, 1867; for more on the life and theology of Stewart, see Miller, *Elevating the Race*.

22. On the gendered politics of African American culture in this period, see Carby, *Race Men*; and Mitchell, *Righteous Propagation*.

23. Astwood, "Africa's Redemption or Religious Patriotism," *Christian Recorder*, February 14, 1897.

24. "Fifty-Eighth Anniversary," *Washington Bee*, November 27, 1909, 5.

25. "The Man and His Work," *Savannah Tribune*, May 13, 1916.

26. "Emergency Baptists Treated Unfairly," *Afro-American*, April 11, 1914, 4.

27. "That Wicked Law," *Afro-American*, June 3, 1911, 4.

28. "Emigration to Hayti," *Douglass' Monthly*, May 1861; Maffly-Kipp, "Serpentine Trail," 40. On the Haitian revolution and subsequent Haitian history, see Sheller, *Democracy after Slavery*; Girard, *Slaves Who Defeated Napoleon*; and M. Smith, *Liberty, Fraternity, Exile*.

29. Cited in Maffly-Kipp, "Serpentine Trail," 39. For more on the Mossells and the AME mission in Haiti, see Dandridge, *History of the Women's Missionary Society*.

30. Mary Ella Mossell, "Father Forgive Them; They Know Not What They Do," *Christian Recorder*, May 9, 1878; on the tangled history and legal regulation of vodou, see Ramsey, *Spirits and the Law*.

31. On AME views of Haiti, see Little, *Disciples of Liberty*, 134–44.

32. Ibid., 137–38.

33. "The Round Table," *Colored American*, September 23, 1899, 2.

34. "Hayti Maligned," *Cleveland Gazette*, January 22, 1910, 1.

35. Little, *Disciples of Liberty*, 84–146. For an excellent sampling of African American opinion on imperialism after the Spanish-American War, see Marks, ed., *The Black Press Views American Imperialism, 1898–1900*.

36. Liberia was founded in 1822 as Africa's first republic, part of a controversial effort to resettle freed American slaves on that continent. Although the idea of escaping the racial order of the United States appealed to some African Americans, especially at times of economic distress and when the racial order of the United States seemed to be deteriorating, most black leaders had opposed such schemes as driven less by African American interests and more by whites' desire to rid themselves of a free black population. Among others, see Little, *Disciples of Liberty*, 66–76; Sundiata, *Brothers and Strangers*; Mitchell, *Righteous Propagation*, 17–50; and Clegg, *Price of Liberty*.

37. Berry, "Report of L. L. Berry, Secretary-Treasurer of the Missionary Department of the A.M.E. Church," March 1, 1934, box 1, folder 6, Llewellyn L. Berry Papers, MG 282, Schomburg Center for Research in Black Culture, New York Public Library, New York; on the complex role of African Americans in Liberia during this period, see especially Sundiata, *Brothers and Strangers*.

38. C. J. Powell, "Mission of the A.M.E. Church," *A.M.E. Church Review*, January 1903, 592.

39. "The Catholic Church," *Washington Bee*, May 5, 1906, 4. On racial segregation in American Catholicism, see Bennett, *Religion and the Rise of Jim Crow*; and McGreevy, *Parish Boundaries*. On African Americans in the Catholic Church, see Davis, *History of Black Catholics*; and Mosely and Raboteau, *Uncommon Faithfulness*.

40. "The Catholic Church," 4.

41. S. Johnson, *African American Religions*, 284–85.

42. The dynamics of class and power in Liberia were complex, and the UNIA's efforts faltered both because of the conflicts within Liberian society and because neither indigenous Liberians nor the Liberian elite—most of whom were earlier emigrants from the United States—shared Garvey's pan-African vision. See Sundiata, *Brothers and Strangers*; and Ewing, *Age of Garvey*. On the sexual and gender politics of the UNIA and black nationalism more broadly, see Mitchell, *Righteous Propagation*, 219–37.

43. Garvey and Universal Negro Improvement Association, "School of African Philosophy, Lesson One," 1938, School of African Philosophy Collection, MG 482, Schomburg Center for Research in Black Culture, New York Public Library, New York.

44. Sundiata, *Brothers and Strangers*, 24–27.

45. Burkett, *Garveyism as a Religious Movement*.

46. Quoted in ibid., 98–99, 62–65. For the UNIA Constitution and Statement of Principles, see Hill, Garvey, and Universal Negro Improvement Association, *Marcus Garvey*, 571–80.

47. Garvey and Universal Negro Improvement Association, "School of African Philosophy, Lesson One."

48. Burkett, *Garveyism as a Religious Movement*, Garvey quotes on 46–47.

49. E. Curtis, *Islam in Black America*.

50. *Holy Koran of the Moorish Science Temple* (48:3), FBI MST Files, part 1 of 31, p. 56. Noble Drew Ali compiled portions of his "Holy Koran" from other sources, including several New Thought texts, but wrote the key concluding chapters himself. This text was first published in 1927. See E. Curtis, *Islam in Black America*, 52–62; and Weisenfeld, *New World a-Coming*, 56–67.

51. This quote appears repeatedly in Moorish Science Temple publications, starting with *Holy Koran of the Moorish Science Temple* (48:3), FBI MST Files, part 1 of 31, p. 56.

52. Moorish Temple of Science, "Certificate for Corporation, Cook County, State of Illinois," box 1, folder 3, MST Collection.

53. "Moorish Head Makes Plans for Conclave," *Chicago Defender*, July 21, 1928, A4.

54. "Moorish Science Temple of America," *Moorish Guide*, January 1929, box 1, folder 7, MST Collection. My arguments throughout this section are profoundly influenced by S. Johnson, *African American Religions*, 294–311.

55. Cited in Weisenfeld, *New World a-Coming*, 67–68.

56. "Hold Moorish Temple 'Prophet' in Murder Plot," *Chicago Defender*, March 23, 1929, 1. While the details of Greene's murder are otherwise uncertain, there is clear evidence of a power struggle within the MST in Noble Drew Ali's writings from 1928, which called on all Moors to "amend [their] ways," demanded fiscal accountability, and warned their "Grand Sheiks and Head Officials of All Temples" that the movement had

only "one prophet." See Noble Drew Ali, "Prophet Drew Ali Speaks to the Nations," 1928, box 1, folder 5, MST Collection.

57. "Love Cult Thot [*sic*] Responsible for Slaying," *Afro-American*, March 23, 1929, 2; "Murder Exposes Moorish Leader's Amours," *Pittsburgh Courier*, March 23, 1929, 10.

58. "Murder Exposes Moorish Leader's Love Affairs," *New Journal and Guide*, March 30, 1929, 6.

59. "Seize 60 after South Side Cult Tragedy," *Chicago Daily Tribune*, September 26, 1929, 1.

60. Ibid. On media policing of "religion" through the category of the "cult," see McCloud, *Making the American Religious Fringe*.

61. "'Grand Sheik' Fired the Shot," *Boston Daily Globe*, September 27, 1929; "Three Deaths Laid to Fanatical Plot," *Washington Post*, September 27, 1929.

62. Washburn, *African American Newspaper*; the classic account of the "politics of respectability" is Higginbotham, *Righteous Discontent*.

63. "Police to Silence Mohammedans," *Afro-American*, October 5, 1929, 3. Edward Curtis argues eloquently against framing scholarship on the Moorish Science Temple in terms of its authenticity as a Muslim movement. As he explains, this question not only replicates the terms of the MST's critics but also assumes an essential Islamic core that cannot account for the global and historical diversity of Islam. As he argues, scholars of religion are better served by taking seriously all who identify themselves as Muslim— even if, like the Moorish Science Temple, they lack concrete ties to prior Islamic traditions—because they are participants in an ongoing process of defining the contours of Islam. See E. Curtis, "Debating the Origins of the Moorish Science Temple."

64. Acting Special Agent Rhea Whitley to FBI Director, September 12, 1931, in FBI MST Files, part 1 of 31, pp. 32–37.

65. Several distinct organizations emerged from the crisis, all of which claimed the name Moorish Science Temple. The largest of them maintained the group's Chicago headquarters, with C. Kirkman Bey as its Supreme Grand Advisor and Moderator. Its main competitor was the Brooklyn-based Moorish Science Temple, under the leadership of R. Francis-Bey. These two organizations had a series of legal disputes over the right to use the name. See R. Francis-Bey, "Afro Readers Say: There Is But One God and Mahomet Is His Prophet," *Afro-American*, September 23, 1933; "Col. C. Kirkman-Bey Declared the Only Supreme Grand Advisor and Moderator," *Moorish Guide*, July 12, 1935, box 1, folder 7, MST Collection.

66. Noble Drew Ali and Moorish Science Temple of America, *Moorish Literature* [1935], 13–15, box 1, folder 5, MST Collection; reprinted in "Moorish Leader's Historical Message to America," *Moorish Guide*, July 12, 1935, box 1, folder 7, ibid.

67. Ibid.

68. Watts, *God, Harlem U.S.A.*

69. Weisenfeld, *New World a-Coming*, 96–99, Paul quote on 97; Watts, *God, Harlem U.S.A.*

70. "N.Y. Court Jails 'God' Who Had 'Long Green': Mystery of Father Divine's Money Made Neighbors Sore," *Afro-American*, June 4, 1932, 3; "A 'Colored' Sentence," *New York Amsterdam News*, June 9, 1932, 8.

71. "Offers His Aid to 'Heaven,'" *New York Times*, November 29, 1931, 31; "Thomas Quits Divine Case," *Chicago Defender*, February 11, 1933, 3.

72. "Father Divine's Attorney Will Use Scottsboro Decision to Help Prove Client Was Railroaded," *New Journal and Guide*, November 26, 1932, 1–2.

73. "A 'Colored' Sentence," 8.

74. "Harlem All Agog!," *Pittsburgh Courier*, June 11, 1932, 1.

75. "Divine Hailed Here by 7,000 as He Quits Jail," *New York Amsterdam News*, June 29, 1932, 1–2; "'God' Out of Prison," *New Journal and Guide*, July 2, 1932, 1–2.

76. Sam Reading, "Becton Loses Grip as Father Divine Invades Quaker City," *Philadelphia Tribune*, January 12, 1933, 1–2.

77. "Police, Firemen Close Divine Meeting in N.J.," *Afro-American*, July 30, 1932, 4.

78. "Order God to Stop Services at 10:00 p.m.," ibid., August 20, 1932, 1–2.

79. Weiner, *Religion Out Loud*.

80. "Father Divine Forced Out of N.J. Theatre," *Afro-American*, August 27, 1932, 1.

81. "Divine Crowd Is Jailed in Orange, N.J.," ibid., June 10, 1933, 1.

82. "New Warrant Is Issued for Father Divine," ibid., June 10, 1933, 5; "Gets Warrant for Divine When Wife's Love Chills," *New York Amsterdam News*, June 14, 1933, 1–2.

83. "Newark Man Fights Jail," *New York Amsterdam News*, July 19, 1933, 9.

84. "Father Divine's Flock Seeks Police Injunction in Jersey," ibid., August 9, 1933, 1; "Divine Flock Supported in Jersey Fight," ibid., September 6, 1933, 1.

85. "Father Divine Follower Wins In Court Case," *Philadelphia Tribune*, March 8, 1934, 9; "Arrest of Newark Judge Called Vengeance of Father Divine," *Afro-American*, April 14, 1934, 2.

86. "Divine Followers Win Appeal in Case," *New York Amsterdam News*, March 17, 1934, 2.

87. "'Father' Divine under Scrutiny of Committee," *Philadelphia Tribune*, October 5, 1933, 1; "Are Father Divine's Angels Deluded?," *Afro-American*, December 30, 1933, 12.

88. "Are Father Divine's Angels Deluded?"; Evans, *Burden of Black Religion*.

89. "10,000 'Young' Men in Father Divine Parade," *Philadelphia Tribune*, June 14, 1934, 9; "Divine Leads 4,000 in the Peace Parade," *New York Amsterdam News*, August 11, 1934, 2. For more on this temporary alliance, see Weisbrot, *Father Divine*, 148–52.

90. "Red Rally Dimmed by Harlem Fervor," *New York Times*, August 5, 1934, N3.

91. Weisbrot, *Father Divine*, 152–61, quote on 157.

92. "Divine Is Freed; Ovation by 700 Disrupts Court," *New York Herald Tribune*, April 16, 1935, 3; "Father Divine and 'Faithful Mary' Are Freed Again," *Afro-American*, April 20, 1935, 2.

93. "Father Divine Colorado Cult Is Under Fire," *New York Herald Tribune*, April 7, 1935, 5; Weisbrot, *Father Divine*, 109.

94. Weisbrot, *Father Divine*, 210.

95. Burnham, *God Comes to America*, 95–96.

96. S. Johnson, *African American Religions*, 320–22; E. Curtis, *Islam in Black America*.

97. "Ritual Knife Plunges, Cult's Victim Expires on Sacrificial Altar," *Toronto Globe*, November 21, 1932, 1–2; "Negro Voodoo Murder Plot Aimed at Jurist," *Los Angeles Times*, November 22, 1932, 1; "Cult Sacrifice-Murder Stirs Country as Police Reveal Fantastic Story of Detroit Tragedy," *New Journal and Guide*, December 3, 1932, 1–2.

98. Wallace D. Fard, "No Connection between Islam and Robert Harris," *Afro-American*, December 31, 1932, 6.

99. "Detroit Cult Members and Police in Battle," *Atlanta Daily World*, April 19, 1934, 1.

100. Left unmentioned in the coverage of the University of Islam was the ongoing public debate over Catholic parochial schools, similarly attacked as subversive and anti-American. But the Catholic Church was obviously much larger and better established than the Nation of Islam, and its legitimacy as a religion was never seriously questioned. For the most part the Catholic Church had successfully invoked the freedom of religion to defend its control over parochial schools. The Nation of Islam was not granted that luxury. On the history of the "School Question," see especially Green, *Bible*; and McGreevy, *Catholicism and American Freedom*.

101. FBI Report No. 100–793 on Moorish Science Temple, Jackson, Mississippi, May 26, 1942, in FBI MST Files, part 1 of 31, p. 64.

102. Confidential Report to the War Department, August 6, 1942, in FBI MST Files, part 2 of 31, pp. 92–94.

103. "Sedition and Draft the Charges Jail 'Moslems,'" *New Journal and Guide*, September 26, 1942, 1–2.

104. On African American internationalism, see Gallicchio, *African American Encounter with Japan and China*; Slate, *Colored Cosmopolitanism*; and Lubin, *Geographies of Liberation*.

105. S. Johnson, *African American Religions*.

106. J. Edgar Hoover to Special Agent in Charge, Kansas City, November 6, 1942, in FBI MST Files, part 2 of 31, p. 103. See also Weisenfeld, *New World a-Coming*.

107. "Cultists 'Guilty,' 32 Given Jail Sentences," *Chicago Defender*, October 10, 1942, 1; "The Muslim Cult of Islam," June 1955, in Federal Bureau of Investigation, Nation of Islam Files, U.S. Department of Justice, Washington, D.C., https://vault.fbi.gov/Nation%20of%20Islam/Nation%20of%20Islam, part 1 of 3, pp. 46–48.

108. Cleveland, Ohio File No. 100–9538, in FBI MST Files, part 11 of 31, pp. 60, 63.

109. Richmond, Virginia File No. 100–5698, in FBI MST Files, part 10 of 31, p. 19.

110. "Members of D.C. Moslem Sect Charged with Draft Violation," *Washington Post*, April 2, 1942, 10; "Moslem Says He 'Registered' with Islam," *Washington Post*, August 2, 1942, 8.

111. Transcript of Message Sent to President Roosevelt, FBI MST Files, part 12 of 31, pp. 32–24.

112. Grand Rapids File No. 100–4460, July 20, 1943, in ibid., p. 59.

113. "Moslem, Tried as Draft Evader, Says Allah Didn't Declare War," *Washington Post*, November 25, 1942, 22.

114. "Members of D.C. Moslem Sect Charged with Draft Violation," 10.

115. "Moslem Says He 'Registered' with Islam," 8.

116. Turner, *Islam in the African-American Experience*, 197, 182–88; Gordon, *Spirit of the Law*.

117. Report on Moorish Science Temple of America, February 26, 1943, in FBI MST Files, part 5 of 31, p. 48.

118. "The Muslim Cult of Islam," June 1955, in Federal Bureau of Investigation, Nation of Islam Files, U.S. Department of Justice, Washington, D.C., https://vault.fbi.gov/Nation%20of%20Islam/Nation%20of%20Islam, part 1 of 3, p. 8.

119. Turner, *Islam in the African-American Experience*, 148, 163, 151.

120. Ibid., 168, 170; S. Johnson, "Religion Proper and Proper Religion"; on the racialization of Islam, see S. Johnson, *African American Religions, 1500–2000.*

CONCLUSION

1. Matthews, "Behind the Scenes," *Afro-American*, January 19, 1946, 24.
2. Gordon, *Spirit of the Law.*
3. Schultz, *Tri-faith America.*
4. Asad, *Genealogies of Religion.*
5. Hurd, *Beyond Religious Freedom*; Cavanaugh, *Myth of Religious Violence.* Mahmood, *Religious Difference in a Secular Age*, offers a compatible analysis of the workings of secularism in the Islamic world.

Bibliography

ARCHIVAL COLLECTIONS

Baltimore, Maryland
    Maryland Historical Society
        Franklin Wilson Papers, MSS 833
Cincinnati, Ohio
    American Jewish Archives
        Henry Berkowitz Papers, MSS 25
        David Philipson Papers, MS 35
        Union for Reform Judaism Records, MS 72
        Morris D. Waldman Papers, MS 23
        Stephen S. Wise Collection, MS 49
Denver, Colorado
    National Archives and Records Administration
        Records of the Bureau of Indian Affairs, RG 75, Northern Pueblos Agency
Madison, Wisconsin
    Wisconsin Historical Society Archives
        Wisconsin Council of Churches Records, Wis MSS WB
Nashville, Tennessee
    Southern Baptist Historical Library and Archives
        Baptist Joint Committee on Public Affairs Minutes, 1938–1979, AR 378
        Rufus Washington Weaver Papers, AR 99
New Haven, Connecticut
    Yale University, Sterling Memorial Library, Manuscripts and Archives
        John Collier Papers, Part II, Series III, Commissioner's Subject File: Pueblo
            Indians Microfilm edition, Reel 30
New York, New York
    American Jewish Historical Society
        Max James Kohler Papers, P-7
        Bernard G. Richards Papers, P-868
    Schomburg Center for Research in Black Culture, New York Public Library
        Llewellyn L. Berry Papers, MG 282
        Moorish Science Temple Collection, MG 435
        School of African Philosophy Collection, MG 482
Washington, D.C.
    Catholic University of America, American Catholic History Research Center and
        Archives

Patrick Henry Callahan Papers
Records of the United States Conference of Catholic Bishops, Office of the
    General Secretary, Collection 10
Library of Congress, Manuscript Division
    Moorefield Storey Papers
National Archives and Records Administration
    Central Classified Files, 1907–1939, Bureau of Indian Affairs, Record Group
        75 Microfilm edition, project editor Robert Lester, Bethesda, Md.: University
        Publications of America, 1995
U.S. Department of Justice
    Federal Bureau of Investigation, Moorish Science Temple of America Files. http://
        vault.fbi.gov/Moorish%20Science%20Temple%20of%20America.
    Federal Bureau of Investigation, Nation of Islam Files. https://vault.fbi.gov/
        Nation%20of%20Islam/Nation%20of%20Islam.

PUBLISHED PRIMARY SOURCES

Allen, Richard. *The Life, Experience, and Gospel Labours of the Rt. Rev. Richard Allen.*
    Chapel Hill: University of North Carolina Press, 2000. Electronic ed.
American Jewish Committee. *The Jews in the Eastern War Zone.* New York: American
    Jewish Committee, 1916.
American Jewish Congress. *The Case of Civilization against Hitlerism, Presented under
    the Auspices of the American Jewish Congress at Madison Square Garden, New York,
    March 7, 1934; the Pleaders, Bainbridge Colby, Bernard S. Deutsch, Arthur R. Brown
    [and Others].* New York: R. O. Ballou, 1934.
Anti-imperialist League. *The Moral and Religious Aspects of the So-Called Imperial
    Policy.* Washington, D.C.: Anti-Imperialist League, 1899.
Barrows, David Prescott. *The Bureau of Non-Christian Tribes for the Philippine Islands.*
    Manila, 1901.
"Benevolent Assimilation" in the Philippines. From the *Independent.* N.p., 1899. Pamphlet
    in the collections of Sterling Memorial Library, Yale University.
Brown, Arthur Judson. *Foreign Missions and the War: Address . . . at the General
    Assembly in Columbus, Ohio, May 23, 1918.* New York: Board of Foreign Missions of
    the Presbyterian Church in the U.S.A., 1918.
————. *The New Era in the Philippines.* New York: F. H. Revell, 1903.
Brown, Arthur Judson, and Presbyterian Church in the U.S.A. *Report of a Visitation of the
    Philippine Mission: Of the Board of Foreign Missions of the Presbyterian Church in the
    United States of America.* New York: The Board, 1902.
Crane, Leo. *Indians of the Enchanted Desert.* Boston: Little, Brown, 1925.
Duratschek, Mary Claudia. *Crusading along Sioux Trails: A History of the Catholic Indian
    Missions of South Dakota.* Yankton, S.D.: Benedictine Convent of the Sacred Heart, 1947.
Eardley, Culling, ed. *Christianity in Turkey: Correspondence of the Governments of
    Christendom, Relating to Executions in Turkey for Apostacy from Islamism.* London:
    Partridge, Oakey and Co., 1855.

Eells, Rev. Myron. *Ten Years of Missionary Work among the Indians at Skokomish, Washington Territory, 1874–1884*. Boston: Congregational Sunday-School and Publishing Society, 1888.

Evans, Hiram Wesley. "The Klan's Fight for Americanism." *North American Review* 223, no. 830 (March 1, 1926): 33–63.

———. *The Public School Problem in America: Outlining Fully the Policies and the Program of the Knights of Ku Klux Klan toward the Public School System*. K.K.K., 1924.

Federal Council of Churches. *Federal Council Bulletin, Vol. 5*. New York: Religious Publicity Service of the Federal Council of the Churches of Christ in America, 1922.

———. *Federal Council Bulletin, Vol. 6*. New York: Religious Publicity Service of the Federal Council of the Churches of Christ in America, 1923.

Federal Council of the Churches of Christ in America, and Samuel McCrea Cavert. *The Churches Allied for Common Tasks: Report of the Third Quadrennium of the Federal Council of the Churches of Christ in America, 1916–1920*. New York: Federal Council of the Churches of Christ in America, 1921.

Forbes, W. Cameron, Dean C. Worcester, and Frank W. Carpenter, eds. *The Friar-Land Inquiry, Philippine Government: Reports*. Manila: Bureau of Printing, 1910.

Hill, Robert A., Marcus Garvey, and Universal Negro Improvement Association, eds. *The Marcus Garvey and Universal Negro Improvement Association Papers*. Vol. 2. Berkeley: University of California Press, 1983.

Inman, Samuel Guy. *Again the Mexican Question*. N.p., 1927.

———. *Church and State in Mexico*. [Chicago], 1928.

Janowsky, Oscar Isaiah. *The Jews and Minority Rights (1898–1919)*. Studies in History, Economics and Public Law 384. New York: Columbia University Press, 1933.

Jones, Orville Davis. *Politics of the Nazarene, or, What Jesus Said to Do*. Edina, Mo.: Press of Appeal to Reason, 1901.

———. *Sound the Tocsin of Alarm*. 2nd ed. The Economic Library, vol. 3, no. 2. Indianapolis: Vincent Bros., 1892.

King, James Marcus. *Facing the Twentieth Century: Our Country, Its Power and Peril*. New York: American Union League Society, 1899.

Kipling, Rudyard. "The White Man's Burden." *McClure's Magazine* 12, no. 4 (February 1899): 290–91.

Kohler, Max J. *Jewish Rights at International Congresses*. Philadelphia: Jewish Publication Society of America, 1917.

Laubach, Frank Charles. *The People of the Philippines, Their Religious Progress and Preparation for Spiritual Leadership in the Far East*. New York: George H. Doran Company, 1925.

Lindquist, Gustavus Elmer Emanuel. *The Red Man in the United States*. New York: George H. Doran Company, 1923.

Locke, John. "The Fundamental Constitutions of Carolina," March 1, 1669. The Avalon Project: Documents in Law, History and Diplomacy. Lillian Goldman Law Library, Yale Law School, http://avalon.law.yale.edu/17th_century/nc05.asp.

———. *A Letter Concerning Toleration Humbly Submitted, Etc.* London: Printed for Awnsham Churchill, 1689.

McKenzie, F. A. *"Pussyfoot" Johnson: Crusader—Reformer—A Man among Men*. New York: Fleming H. Revell Company, 1920.

McKinley, William. "Report of John C. Bates on Agreement with Sultan of Sulu." S. Doc. No. 136, 56th Cong., 1st sess., February 1, 1900.

Mead, Edwin D. *The Two Englands and Their Lessons for America*. Boston: Reprinted from the Editor's Table of the New England Magazine, 1899.

M'Faul, James A. "Catholics and American Citizenship." *North American Review* 171, no. 526 (1900): 320–32.

Mooney, James. *The Ghost-Dance Religion and the Sioux Outbreak of 1890*. Lincoln: University of Nebraska Press, 1991.

Murray, Nicholas. *Decline of Popery and Its Causes: An Address Delivered in the Broadway Tabernacle, on Wednesday Evening, January 15, 1851*. New York: Harper and Brothers, 1851.

Quezon, Manuel Luis. *Philippine Independence: Speech in the House of Representatives, March 2, 1911*. Washington, D.C.: Government Printing Office, 1911.

Reyes y Florentino, Isabelo de los. *Religion of the Katipunan: Which Is the Religion of the Ancient Filipinos, Now Being Revived by the Association of the "Sons of the Country" ("Katipunan"), the Agitator of Philippine Revolution*. 1901. Manila: National Historical Institute, 2009.

Richberg, Donald R. *My Hero: The Indiscreet Memoirs of an Eventful but Unheroic Life*. New York: Putnam, 1954.

———. *Nor Can Government: Analysis and Criticism of S. 984—"A Bill to Prohibit Discrimination in Employment Because of Race, Religion, Color, National Origin, or Ancestry."* American Affairs Pamphlets. New York: National Industrial Conference Board, 1948.

Roberts, B. H. *The Autobiography of B. H. Roberts*. Salt Lake City: Signature Books, 1990.

Schaff, Philip. *Church and State in the United States, or the American Idea of Religious Liberty and Its Practical Effects*. New York: G. P. Putnam's Sons, 1888.

———. "The Development of Religious Freedom." *North American Review* 138, no. 329 (April 1, 1884): 349–61.

Straus, Oscar S. *The Origin of Republican Form of Government in the United States of America*. New York: Putnam, 1885.

———. *Religious Liberty in the United States*. New York: P. Cowen, 1896.

———. *Roger Williams: The Pioneer of Religious Liberty*. New York: Century, 1894.

Straus, Roger Williams. *Religious Liberty and Democracy*. Chicago: Willett, Clark and Company, 1939.

Strong, Josiah. *Our Country: Its Possible Future and Its Present Crisis*. New York: Baker and Taylor for the American Home Missionary Society, 1885.

Stuntz, Homer C. *The Philippines and the Far East*. Cincinnati, N.Y.: Jennings and Pye; Eaton and Mains, 1904.

Taylor, John R. M., ed. *The Philippine Insurrection against the United States: A Compilation of Documents with Notes and Introduction*. 6 vols. Washington, D.C.: Bureau of Insular Affairs, War Department, 1906. Microfilm ed.

Twain, Mark. *Following the Equator: A Journey Around the World*. 1897. National Geographic Adventure Classics. Washington, D.C.: National Geographic Society, 2005.

United States. *Affairs in the Philippine Islands*. S. Doc. No. 66, 56th Cong., 1st Sess. N.p.: G. Turner, 1900.

———. *Fifth Annual Report of the Philippine Commission*. Washington, D.C.: Government Printing Office, 1905.

———. *Sale of Friar Lands in the Philippines: Hearings before the United States House Committee on Insular Affairs, Sixty-First Congress, Second Session, on June 7, 1910*. Washington, D.C.: Government Printing Office, 1910.

United States, and William McKinley. *Lands Held for Ecclesiastical or Religious Uses in the Philippine Islands, Etc.: Message from the President of the United States*. S. Doc. No. 190, 56th Cong., 2nd Sess. Washington, D.C.: Government Printing Office, 1901.

U.S. House of Representatives. "Case of Brigham H. Roberts, of Utah." 56th Cong., 1st Sess., January 20, 1900.

———. *Constitutional Amendment to Prohibit Polygamy or Polygamous Cohabitation in the United States and All Territory Subject to Its Jurisdiction*. H.J. Res. 45, 56th Cong., 1st Sess., December 5, 1899.

———. *Hearing to Investigate Indian Conditions in the United States*. Washington, D.C.: Government Printing Office, 1944.

———. *Peyote: Hearings before a Subcommittee of the Committee on Indian Affairs on H.R. 2614*. Washington, D.C.: Government Printing Office, 1918.

U.S. Office of Indian Affairs. *Annual Report of the Commissioner of Indian Affairs, for the Year 1873*. Washington, D.C.: Government Printing Office, 1873.

———. *Annual Report of the Commissioner of Indian Affairs to the Secretary of the Interior for the Year 1882*. Washington, D.C.: Government Printing Office, 1882.

———. *Annual Report of the Commissioner of Indian Affairs to the Secretary of the Interior for the Year 1883*. Washington, D.C.: Government Printing Office, 1883.

———. *Annual Report of the Commissioner of Indian Affairs, for the Year 1885*. Washington, D.C.: Government Printing Office, 1885.

———. *Sixty-First Annual Report of the Commissioner of Indian Affairs to the Secretary of the Interior*. Washington, D.C.: Government Printing Office, 1892.

———. *Annual Report of the Commissioner of Indian Affairs, 1893*. Washington, D.C.: Government Printing Office, 1893.

———. *Report of the Commissioner of Indian Affairs*. Washington, D.C.: Government Printing Office, 1901.

———. *Report of the Commissioner of Indian Affairs*. Washington, D.C.: Government Printing Office, 1904.

———. *Report of the Commissioner of Indian Affairs*. Washington, D.C.: Government Printing Office, 1906.

———. *Report of the Commissioner of Indian Affairs*. Washington, D.C.: Government Printing Office, 1909.

———. *Report of the Commissioner of Indian Affairs*. Washington, D.C.: Government Printing Office, 1911.

———. *Report of the Commissioner of Indian Affairs*. Washington, D.C.: Government Printing Office, 1916.

U.S. Senate. *Report of the Philippine Commission to the President*. Washington, D.C.: Government Printing Office, 1900.

Van Dyke, Henry. *The American Birthright and the Philippine Pottage: A Sermon Preached on Thanksgiving Day, 1898*. New York: Charles Scribner's Sons, 1898.

———. *The Cross of War*. New York, 1898.

———. *In Defense of Religious Liberty*. New York: Democratic National Committee, 1928.

Walker, David. *Walker's Appeal in Four Articles Together with a Preamble to the Coloured Citizens of the World, but in Particular, and Very Expressly, to Those of the United States of America*. 3rd and last ed. Boston: Rev. and published by D. Walker, 1830.

Wesley, Charles H. "The Negro Has Always Wanted the Four Freedoms." In *What the Negro Wants*, edited by Rayford Whittingham Logan, 90–112. Chapel Hill: University of North Carolina Press, 1944.

White, Trumbull. *Our New Possessions: Four Books in One: A Graphic Account, Descriptive and Historical, of the Tropic Islands of the Sea Which Have Fallen under Our Sway, Their Cities, Peoples and Commerce, Natural Resources and the Opportunities They Offer to Americans. Book I. The Philippine Islands. Book II. Puerto Rico. Book III. Cuba. Book IV. The Hawaiian Islands. Special Chapters on Tropical Cultivation, Sugar, Coffee, Etc., the Ladrones, the Carolines, and Other Island Groups of the Pacific, and Their Commercial Relations*. Chicago: International Pub. Co., 1898.

Williams, Michael. *American Catholics in the War: National Catholic War Council, 1917–1921*. New York: Macmillan, 1921.

Worcester, Dean C. *The Philippine Islands and Their People: A Record of Personal Observation and Experience, with a Short Summary of the More Important Facts in the History of the Archipelago*. New York: Macmillan, 1898.

NEWSPAPERS AND PERIODICALS

Afro-American (Baltimore, Md., 1893–1988)

A.M.E. Church Review (Nashville, Tenn.)

American Catholic Quarterly Review (Philadelphia, 1876–1924)

American Hebrew (New York, 1879–1902)

American Hebrew and Jewish Messenger (New York, 1903–22)

American Israelite (Cincinnati, 1874–2000)

American Missionary (New York, 1846–1934)

American Sentinel of Religious Liberty (Washington, D.C.)

Atlanta Constitution

Atlanta Daily World (1932–2003)

Baltimore Sun

Boston Daily Globe

Catholic World (New York)

Chicago Daily Tribune

Chicago Defender (1921–67)

Christian Century (Chicago)

Christian Recorder (Philadelphia)

Cleveland Gazette

Colored American (New York)

Commonweal (New York)

Congregationalist (Boston)

Douglass' Monthly (Rochester, N.Y.)

Independent (New York, 1848–1924)

Jewish Advocate (Boston, 1909–90)

Jewish Exponent (Philadelphia, 1887–1990)

Jewish Independent (Cincinnati, 1906–64)

Jewish Messenger (New York)

Los Angeles Times

New Journal and Guide (Norfolk, Va.,
    1916–2003)
New York Amsterdam News (1922–38)
New York Herald Tribune (1926–62)
New York Observer and Chronicle
    (1833–1912)
New York Sun
New York Times
New York Tribune (1911–22)
North American Review
Outlook (1893–1924)

Palestine Post (Jerusalem)
Philadelphia Tribune (1912–2001)
Pittsburgh Courier
Sacred Heart Review (Boston)
San Francisco Chronicle
Savannah Tribune
St. Louis Post-Dispatch (1879–1922)
Toronto Globe
Trenton Evening Times
Washington Bee
Washington Post

SECONDARY SOURCES

Abinales, Patricio. "An American Colonial State: Authority and Structure in Southern
    Mindanao." In *Vestiges of War: The Philippine-American War and the Aftermath of an
    Imperial Dream, 1899–1999,* edited by Angel Velasco Shaw and Luis Francia, 89–117.
    New York: New York University Press, 2002.
———. *Mindanao, Nation, and Region: The Joys of Dislocation.* Manila: Published and
    exclusively distributed by Anvil, 2008.
Achútegui, Pedro S. de, and Miguel Anselmo Bernad. *Religious Revolution in the
    Philippines: Life and Church of Gregorio Aglipay.* Vol. 2. Manila: Ateneo de Manila, 1960.
Agoncillo, Teodoro A., ed. *Filipino Nationalism, 1872–1970.* Quezon City: R. P. Garcia,
    1974.
Allen, Theodore W., and Jeffrey B. Perry. *The Invention of the White Race, Volume 1:
    Racial Oppression and Social Control.* New York: Verso, 2012.
Allitt, Patrick. *Catholic Converts: British and American Intellectuals Turn to Rome.*
    Ithaca: Cornell University Press, 1997.
Anderson, Edward F. *Peyote: The Divine Cactus.* 2nd ed. Tucson: University of Arizona
    Press, 1996.
Ariel, Yaakov S. *Evangelizing the Chosen People: Missions to the Jews in America,
    1880–2000.* Chapel Hill: University of North Carolina Press, 2000.
Armitage, David. *Foundations of Modern International Thought.* New York: Cambridge
    University Press, 2013.
———. *The Ideological Origins of the British Empire.* Ideas in Context 59. New York:
    Cambridge University Press, 2000.
Arneil, Barbara. *John Locke and America: The Defence of English Colonialism.* Oxford:
    Clarendon Press, 1996.
Asad, Talal. *Formations of the Secular: Christianity, Islam, Modernity.* Stanford: Stanford
    University Press, 2003.
———. *Genealogies of Religion: Discipline and Reasons of Power in Christianity and
    Islam.* Baltimore: Johns Hopkins University Press, 1993.
Avella, Steven M. *Sacramento and the Catholic Church: Shaping a Capital City.* Reno:
    University of Nevada Press, 2008.

Baker, Kelly. *Gospel According to the Klan: The KKK's Appeal to Protestant America, 1915–1930*. Lawrence: University Press of Kansas, 2011.

Banner, Stuart. *How the Indians Lost Their Land*. Cambridge, Mass.: Belknap Press, 2007.

Barney, Garold D. *Mormons, Indians, and the Ghost Dance Religion of 1890*. Lanham, Md.: University Press of America, 1986.

Batnitzky, Leora Faye. *How Judaism Became a Religion: An Introduction to Modern Jewish Thought*. Princeton: Princeton University Press, 2011.

Beneke, Chris, and Christopher S. Grenda, eds. *The First Prejudice: Religious Tolerance and Intolerance in Early America*. Philadelphia: University of Pennsylvania Press, 2011.

Bennett, James B. *Religion and the Rise of Jim Crow in New Orleans*. Princeton: Princeton University Press, 2005.

Beredo, Cheryl. *Import of the Archive: U.S. Colonial Rule of the Philippines and the Making of American Archival History*. Series on Archives, Archivists and Society, Number 5. Sacramento: Litwin Books, 2013.

Berge, William H. "Voices for Imperialism: Josiah Strong and the Protestant Clergy." *Border States: Journal of the Kentucky-Tennessee American Studies Association* 1 (1973). Online edition. http://spider.georgetowncollege.edu/htallant/border/bs1/berge.htm.

Bitton, Davis. *The Ritualization of Mormon History, and Other Essays*. Urbana: University of Illinois Press, 1994.

Blaine, Martha Royce. *Some Things Are Not Forgotten: A Pawnee Family Remembers*. Lincoln: University of Nebraska Press, 1997.

Blanco, John D. *Frontier Constitutions: Christianity and Colonial Empire in the Nineteenth-Century Philippines*. Berkeley: University of California Press, 2009.

Blum, Edward J. *Reforging the White Republic: Race, Religion, and American Nationalism, 1865–1898*. Conflicting Worlds. Baton Rouge: Louisiana State University Press, 2005.

Brantlinger, Patrick. *Taming Cannibals*. Ithaca: Cornell University Press, 2011.

Brecher, Frank W. *Reluctant Ally: United States Foreign Policy toward the Jews from Wilson to Roosevelt*. New York: Greenwood Press, 1991.

Brekus, Catherine A. *Strangers and Pilgrims: Female Preaching in America, 1740–1845*. Chapel Hill: University of North Carolina Press, 1998.

Brodkin, Karen. *How Jews Became White Folks and What That Says about Race in America*. New Brunswick, N.J.: Rutgers University Press, 1998.

Brody, David. *Visualizing American Empire: Orientalism and Imperialism in the Philippines*. Chicago: University of Chicago Press, 2010.

Burbank, Jane, and Frederick Cooper. *Empires in World History: Power and the Politics of Difference*. Princeton: Princeton University Press, 2011.

Burkett, Randall K. *Garveyism as a Religious Movement: The Institutionalization of a Black Civil Religion*. Metuchen, N.J.: Scarecrow Press, 1978.

Burnham, Kenneth E. *God Comes to America: Father Divine and the Peace Mission Movement*. Boston: Lambeth Press, 1979.

Burnidge, Cara L. "The Business of Church and State: Social Christianity in Woodrow Wilson's White House." *Church History: Studies in Christianity and Culture* 82, no. 3 (2013): 659–66. doi:10.1017/S0009640713000681.

Byrd, Jodi A. *The Transit of Empire: Indigenous Critiques of Colonialism*. First Peoples: New Directions Indigenous. Minneapolis: University of Minnesota Press, 2011.

Carby, Hazel V. *Race Men*. Cambridge, Mass.: Harvard University Press, 1998.

Cavanaugh, William T. *The Myth of Religious Violence: Secular Ideology and the Roots of Modern Conflict*. New York: Oxford University Press, 2009.

Chidester, David. *Empire of Religion: Imperialism and Comparative Religion*. Chicago: University of Chicago Press, 2014.

———. *Savage Systems: Colonialism and Comparative Religion in Southern Africa*. Charlottesville: University Press of Virginia, 1996.

Clegg, Claude Andrew. *The Price of Liberty: African Americans and the Making of Liberia*. Chapel Hill: University of North Carolina Press, 2004.

Clements, Robert B. "Michael Williams and the Founding of 'The Commonweal.'" In *Modern American Catholicism, 1900–1965: Selected Historical Essays*, edited by Edward R. Kantowicz, 286–321. New York: Garland, 1988.

Clymer, Kenton J. *Protestant Missionaries in the Philippines, 1898–1916: An Inquiry into the American Colonial Mentality*. Urbana: University of Illinois Press, 1986.

Cohen, Naomi Wiener. *The Americanization of Zionism, 1897–1948*. Brandeis Series in American Jewish History, Culture, and Life. Hanover, N.H.: Brandeis University Press/University Press of New England, 2003.

———. *Jews in Christian America: The Pursuit of Religious Equality*. Studies in Jewish History. New York: Oxford University Press, 1992.

Coleman, William S. E. *Voices of Wounded Knee*. Lincoln: University of Nebraska Press, 2000.

Cone, James H. *Martin and Malcolm and America: A Dream or a Nightmare?* 20th anniversary ed. Maryknoll, N.Y.: Orbis Books, 2012.

Coronado, Raúl. *A World Not to Come: A History of Latino Writing and Print Culture*. Cambridge, Mass.: Harvard University Press, 2013.

Cottrell, Robert C. *Roger Nash Baldwin and the American Civil Liberties Union*. New York: Columbia University Press, 2000.

Cruikshank, Bruce. *Samar, 1768–1898*. Historical Conservation Society 41. Manila: Historical Conservation Society; exclusive distributor, Casalinda Bookshop, 1985.

Cullinane, Michael Patrick. *Liberty and American Anti-imperialism, 1898–1909*. New York: Palgrave Macmillan, 2012.

Curcio, Vincent. *Henry Ford*. Lives and Legacies Series. New York: Oxford University Press, 2013.

Curtis, Edward E. "Debating the Origins of the Moorish Science Temple: Toward a New Cultural History." In *The New Black Gods: Arthur Huff Fauset and the Study of African American Religions*, edited by Edward E. Curtis and Danielle Brune Sigler, 70–90. Religion in North America. Bloomington: Indiana University Press, 2009.

———. *Islam in Black America: Identity, Liberation, and Difference in African-American Islamic Thought*. Albany: State University of New York Press, 2002.

Curtis, Finbarr. *The Production of American Religious Freedom*. New York: New York University Press, 2016.

Dandridge, Octavia W. *A History of the Women's Missionary Society of the African Methodist Episcopal Church, 1874–1987*. Women's Missionary Society, 1987.

Davis, Cyprian. *The History of Black Catholics in the United States.* New York: Crossroad, 2016.

Deleuze, Gilles, and Félix Guattari. *A Thousand Plateaus: Capitalism and Schizophrenia.* Minneapolis: University of Minnesota Press, 1987.

Deloria, Vine. *The Indian Reorganization Act: Congresses and Bills.* Norman: University of Oklahoma Press, 2002.

Dochuk, Darren. *From Bible Belt to Sunbelt: Plain-Folk Religion, Grassroots Politics, and the Rise of Evangelical Conservatism.* New York: W. W. Norton, 2012.

Doyle, David Noel. *Irish Americans: Native Rights and National Empires; The Structure, Divisions, and Attitudes of the Catholic Minority in the Decade of Expansion, 1890–1901.* The Irish-Americans. New York: Arno Press, 1976.

Dressler, Markus, and Arvind-pal Singh Mandair, eds. *Secularism and Religion-Making.* Reflection and Theory in the Study of Religion Series. New York: Oxford University Press, 2011.

Edgerton, Ronald King. *People of the Middle Ground: A Century of Conflict and Accommodation in Central Mindanao, 1880s–1980s.* Mindanao Studies Series. Quezon City: Ateneo de Manila University Press, 2008.

Ellis, Clyde. *A Dancing People: Powwow Culture on the Southern Plains.* Lawrence: University Press of Kansas, 2003.

Evans, Curtis J. *The Burden of Black Religion.* New York: Oxford University Press, 2008.

Ewing, Adam. *The Age of Garvey: How a Jamaican Activist Created a Mass Movement and Changed Global Black Politics.* Princeton: Princeton University Press, 2014.

Fallaw, Ben. *Religion and State Formation in Postrevolutionary Mexico.* Durham, N.C.: Duke University Press, 2012.

Fessenden, Tracy. *Culture and Redemption: Religion, the Secular, and American Literature.* Princeton: Princeton University Press, 2007.

Fisher, Linford D. *The Indian Great Awakening: Religion and the Shaping of Native Cultures in Early America.* New York: Oxford University Press, 2012.

Fitzgerald, Timothy. *The Ideology of Religious Studies.* New York: Oxford University Press, 2000.

———, ed. *Religion and the Secular: Historical and Colonial Formations.* Oakville, Conn.: Equinox, 2007.

Flake, Kathleen. *The Politics of American Religious Identity: The Seating of Senator Reed Smoot, Mormon Apostle.* Chapel Hill: University of North Carolina Press, 2004.

Fluhman, J. Spencer. *A Peculiar People: Anti-Mormonism and the Making of Religion in Nineteenth-Century America.* Chapel Hill: University of North Carolina Press, 2012.

Foner, Eric. *The Story of American Freedom.* New York: W. W. Norton, 1998.

Fowles, Severin M. *An Archaeology of Doings: Secularism and the Study of Pueblo Religion.* Santa Fe, N.M.: School for Advanced Research Press, 2013.

Freedman, Jonathan. *Klezmer America: Jewishness, Ethnicity, Modernity.* New York: Columbia University Press, 2008.

Gallicchio, Marc S. *The African American Encounter with Japan and China: Black Internationalism in Asia, 1895–1945.* Chapel Hill: University of North Carolina Press, 2000.

Garrigus, John D., and Christopher Morris, eds. *Assumed Identities: The Meanings of Race in the Atlantic World*. College Station: Texas A&M University Press, 2010.

Gealogo, Francis A. "Religion, Science, and Bayan in the Iglesia Filipina Independiente." In *From Wilderness to Nation: Interrogating Bayan*, edited by Damon L. Woods, 108–21. Diliman, Quezon City: University of the Philippines Press, 2011.

Girard, Philippe R. *The Slaves Who Defeated Napoleon: Toussaint Louverture and the Haitian War of Independence, 1801–1804*. Atlantic Crossings. Tuscaloosa: University of Alabama Press, 2011.

Glaude, Eddie S. *Exodus! Religion, Race, and Nation in Early Nineteenth-Century Black America*. Chicago: University of Chicago Press, 2000.

Go, Julian. *American Empire and the Politics of Meaning: Elite Political Cultures in the Philippines and Puerto Rico during U.S. Colonialism*. Politics, History, and Culture. Durham, N.C.: Duke University Press, 2008.

———. *Patterns of Empire: The British and American Empires, 1688 to the Present*. New York: Cambridge University Press, 2011.

Goetz, Rebecca Anne. *The Baptism of Early Virginia: How Christianity Created Race*. Baltimore, Md.: Johns Hopkins University Press, 2012.

Goldschmidt, Henry, and Elizabeth A. McAlister, eds. *Race, Nation, and Religion in the Americas*. New York: Oxford University Press, 2004.

Goldstein, Alyosha, ed. *Formations of United States Colonialism*. Durham, N.C.: Duke University Press, 2014.

Goldstein, Eric L. "Editor's Introduction." *American Jewish History: An American Jewish History Society Quarterly Publication* 96, no. 3 (September 2010): v–lx.

Gomez-Jefferson, Annetta Louise. *The Sage of Tawawa: Reverdy Cassius Ransom, 1861–1959*. Kent, Ohio: Kent State University Press, 2002.

Gordon, Sarah Barringer. *The Spirit of the Law: Religious Voices and the Constitution in Modern America*. Cambridge, Mass.: Belknap Press of Harvard University Press, 2010.

Gowing, Peter G. *Mandate in Moroland: The American Government of Muslim Filipinos, 1899–1920*. Diliman, Quezon City: Philippine Center for Advanced Studies, University of the Philippines System, 1977.

Graf, Arndt, Peter Kreuzer, and Rainer Werning, eds. *Conflict in Moro Land: Prospects for Peace?* Academic Imprint Series / Penerbit USM. Pulau Pinang: Penerbit Universiti Sains Malaysia, 2009.

Green, Steven K. *The Bible, the School, and the Constitution: The Clash That Shaped Modern Church-State Doctrine*. New York: Oxford University Press, 2012.

———. *Inventing a Christian America: The Myth of the Religious Founding*. New York: Oxford University Press, 2015.

Greenawalt, Kent. *Religion and the Constitution*. Princeton: Princeton University Press, 2006.

Greene, Daniel. *The Jewish Origins of Cultural Pluralism: The Menorah Association and American Diversity*. Bloomington: Indiana University Press, 2011.

Greer, Margaret Rich, Walter Mignolo, and Maureen Quilligan, eds. *Rereading the Black Legend: The Discourses of Religious and Racial Difference in the Renaissance Empires*. Chicago: University of Chicago Press, 2007.

Gunn, T. Jeremy, and John Witte, eds. *No Establishment of Religion: America's Original Contribution to Religious Liberty*. New York: Oxford University Press, 2012.

Gurock, Jeffrey S. *Orthodox Jews in America*. The Modern Jewish Experience. Bloomington: Indiana University Press, 2009.

Hagan, William Thomas. *Quanah Parker, Comanche Chief*. The Oklahoma Western Biographies 6. Norman: University of Oklahoma Press, 1993.

Hale, Tiffany. "Hostiles and Friendlies: Memory, U.S. Institutions, and the 1890 Ghost Dance." Ph.D. diss., Yale University, forthcoming.

Harris, Susan. *God's Arbiters: Americans and the Philippines, 1898–1902*. New York: Oxford University Press, 2011.

Harrison, Peter. *"Religion" and the Religions in the English Enlightenment*. New York: Cambridge University Press, 1990.

Harvey, Paul. *Freedom's Coming: Religious Culture and the Shaping of the South from the Civil War through the Civil Rights Era*. Chapel Hill: University of North Carolina Press, 2005.

————. *Redeeming the South: Religious Cultures and Racial Identities among Southern Baptists, 1865–1925*. Chapel Hill: University of North Carolina Press, 1997.

Hayes, Patrick J. "J. Elliot Ross and the National Conference of Christians and Jews: A Catholic Contribution to Tolerance in America." *Journal of Ecumenical Studies* 37, no. 3–4 (September 2000): 321–32.

Haynes, Stephen R. "Distinction and Dispersal: Folk Theology and the Maintenance of White Supremacy." *Journal of Southern Religion* 17 (2015). http://jsreligion.org/issues/vol17/haynes.html.

Higginbotham, Evelyn Brooks. *Righteous Discontent: The Women's Movement in the Black Baptist Church, 1880–1920*. Cambridge, Mass.: Harvard University Press, 1993.

Hinks, Peter P. *To Awaken My Afflicted Brethren: David Walker and the Problem of Antebellum Slave Resistance*. University Park: Pennsylvania State University Press, 1997.

Holt, Thomas C. *The Problem of Freedom: Race, Labor, and Politics in Jamaica and Britain, 1832–1938*. Johns Hopkins Studies in Atlantic History and Culture. Baltimore: Johns Hopkins University Press, 1992.

Howe, Daniel Walker. *What Hath God Wrought: The Transformation of America, 1815–1848*. Oxford History of the United States. New York: Oxford University Press, 2007.

Hoxie, Frederick E. *A Final Promise: The Campaign to Assimilate the Indians, 1880–1920*. New York: Cambridge University Press, 1989.

Hultkrantz, Åke. *The Religions of the American Indians*. Berkeley: University of California Press, 1979.

Humez, Jean McMahon. *Mother's First-Born Daughters: Early Shaker Writings on Women and Religion*. Bloomington: Indiana University Press, 1993.

Hurd, Elizabeth Shakman. *Beyond Religious Freedom: The New Global Politics of Religion*. Princeton: Princeton University Press, 2015.

Ileto, Reynaldo C. "Outlines of a Nonlinear Employment of Philippine History." In *The Politics of Culture in the Shadow of Capital*, edited by Lisa Lowe and David Lloyd, 98–126. Durham, N.C.: Duke University Press, 1997.

Irons, Charles F. *The Origins of Proslavery Christianity: White and Black Evangelicals in Colonial and Antebellum Virginia*. Chapel Hill: University of North Carolina Press, 2008.

Irwin, Lee. *Coming Down from Above: Prophecy, Resistance, and Renewal in Native American Religions*. The Civilization of the American Indian Series 258. Norman: University of Oklahoma Press, 2008.

———. *The Dream Seekers: Native American Visionary Traditions of the Great Plains*. Norman: University of Oklahoma Press, 1994.

Islam, Syed Serajul. *The Politics of Islamic Identity in Southeast Asia*. Singapore: Thomson, 2005.

Jacobson, Matthew Frye. *Roots Too: White Ethnic Revival in Post–Civil Rights America*. Cambridge, Mass.: Harvard University Press, 2006.

———. *Whiteness of a Different Color: European Immigrants and the Alchemy of Race*. Cambridge, Mass.: Harvard University Press, 1998.

Johnson, Donald. *The Challenge to American Freedoms: World War I and the Rise of the American Civil Liberties Union*. Lexington: For the Mississippi Valley Historical Association, University of Kentucky Press, 1963.

Johnson, Sylvester A. *African American Religions, 1500–2000: Colonialism, Democracy, and Freedom*. New York: Cambridge University Press, 2015.

———. "Religion Proper and Proper Religion." In *The New Black Gods: Arthur Huff Fauset and the Study of African American Religions*, edited by Edward E. Curtis and Danielle Brune Sigler, 145–70. Bloomington: Indiana University Press, 2009.

———. "The Rise of Black Ethnics: The Ethnic Turn in African American Religions, 1916–1945." *Religion and American Culture* 20, no. 2 (Summer 2010): 125–63.

Jones, Arun W. *Christian Missions in the American Empire: Episcopalians in Northern Luzon, the Philippines, 1902–1946*. New York: P. Lang, 2003.

Jordan, Ryan P. *Church, State, and Race: The Discourse of American Religious Liberty, 1750–1900*. Lanham, Md.: University Press of America, 2012.

Josephson, Jason Ananda. *The Invention of Religion in Japan*. Chicago: University of Chicago Press, 2012.

Kaplan, Benjamin J. *Divided by Faith: Religious Conflict and the Practice of Toleration in Early Modern Europe*. Cambridge, Mass.: Belknap Press of Harvard University Press, 2007.

Keenan, Jerry. *Encyclopedia of the Spanish-American and Philippine-American Wars*. Santa Barbara, Calif.: ABC-CLIO, 2001.

Kelsey, George D. *Social Ethics among Southern Baptists*. Metuchen, N.J.: Scarecrow Press, 1973.

Kennedy, David M. *Freedom from Fear: The American People in Depression and War, 1929–1945*. New York: Oxford University Press, 1999.

Kidd, Thomas S. *God of Liberty: A Religious History of the American Revolution*. New York: Basic Books, 2010.

King, Richard. *Orientalism and Religion: Postcolonial Theory, India and "The Mystic East."* New York: Routledge, 1999.

Koppelman, Andrew. *Defending American Religious Neutrality*. Cambridge, Mass.: Harvard University Press, 2013.

Kracht, Benjamin R. "Kiowa Religion in Historical Perspective." In *Native American Spirituality: A Critical Reader*, edited by Lee Irwin, 236–55. Lincoln: University of Nebraska Press, 2000.

Kramer, Paul A. *The Blood of Government: Race, Empire, the United States, and the Philippines*. Chapel Hill: University of North Carolina Press, 2006.

———. "Empires, Exceptions, and Anglo-Saxons." In *The American Colonial State in the Philippines: Global Perspectives*, edited by Anne L. Foster and Julian Go, 43–91. American Encounters/Global Interactions. Durham, N.C.: Duke University Press, 2003.

Kruse, Kevin Michael. *One Nation under God: How Corporate America Invented Christian America*. New York: Basic Books, 2015.

———. *White Flight: Atlanta and the Making of Modern Conservatism*. Politics and Society in Twentieth-Century America. Princeton: Princeton University Press, 2005.

Lassiter, Luke. "Southwestern Oklahoma, the Gourd Dance, and 'Charlie Brown.'" In *Contemporary Native American Cultural Issues*, edited by Duane Champagne, 145–66. Walnut Creek, Calif.: AltaMira Press, 1999.

Lesser, Alexander. *The Pawnee Ghost Dance Hand Game*. New York: Columbia University Press, 1933.

Levitt, Laura. "Other Moderns, Other Jews: Revisiting Jewish Secularism in America." In *Secularisms*, edited by Janet R. Jakobsen and Ann Pellegrini, 107–38. Durham, N.C.: Duke University Press, 2008.

Little, Lawrence S. *Disciples of Liberty: The African Methodist Episcopal Church in the Age of Imperialism, 1884–1916*. Knoxville: University of Tennessee Press, 2000.

Love, Eric Tyrone Lowery. *Race over Empire: Racism and U.S. Imperialism, 1865–1900*. Chapel Hill: University of North Carolina Press, 2004.

Lowe, Lisa. *The Intimacies of Four Continents*. Durham, N.C.: Duke University Press, 2015.

Lubin, Alex. *Geographies of Liberation: The Making of an Afro-Arab Political Imaginary*. John Hope Franklin Series in African American History and Culture. Chapel Hill: University of North Carolina Press, 2014.

Luker, Ralph. *The Social Gospel in Black and White: American Racial Reform, 1885–1912*. Chapel Hill: University of North Carolina Press, 1991.

Mack, Phyllis. *Visionary Women: Ecstatic Prophecy in Seventeenth-Century England*. Berkeley: University of California Press, 1992.

Madsen, Truman G. *Defender of the Faith: The B. H. Roberts Story*. Salt Lake City: Bookcraft, 1980.

Maffly-Kipp, Laurie F. "The Serpentine Trail: Haitian Missions and the Construction of African-American Religious Identity." In *The Foreign Missionary Enterprise at Home: Explorations in North American Cultural History*, edited by Daniel H. Bays and Grant Wacker, 29–43. Tuscaloosa: University of Alabama Press, 2003.

———. *Setting Down the Sacred Past: African-American Race Histories*. Cambridge, Mass.: Belknap Press of Harvard University Press, 2010.

Mahmood, Saba. *Religious Difference in a Secular Age: A Minority Report*. Princeton: Princeton University Press, 2015.

Mahmood, Saba, and Peter G. Danchin. "Politics of Religious Freedom: Contested Genealogies." *South Atlantic Quarterly* 113, no. 1 (December 21, 2014): 1–8. doi:10.1215/00382876-2390401.

Majul, Cesar Adib. *Muslims in the Philippines*. 2nd ed. Quezon City: Published for the Asian Center by the University of the Philippines Press, 1973.

———. *The Political and Constitutional Ideas of the Philippine Revolution*. Quezon City: University of the Philippines Press, 1996.

Mandair, Arvind-Pal S. *Religion and the Specter of the West: Sikhism, India, Postcoloniality, and the Politics of Translation*. New York: Columbia University Press, 2009.

Marks, George P., ed. *The Black Press Views American Imperialism, 1898–1900*. New York: Arno Press, 1971.

Maroukis, Thomas. *The Peyote Road: Religious Freedom and the Native American Church*. Norman: University of Oklahoma Press, 2010.

Maskell, Caleb. "'Modern Christianity Is Ancient Judaism': Rabbi Gustav Gottheil and the Jewish-American Religious Future." *Religion and American Culture* 23, no. 2 (Summer 2013): 139–84.

Masuzawa, Tomoko. *The Invention of World Religions: Or, How European Universalism Was Preserved in the Language of Pluralism*. Chicago: University of Chicago Press, 2005.

McCartney, Paul T. *Power and Progress: American National Identity, the War of 1898, and the Rise of American Imperialism*. Baton Rouge: Louisiana State University Press, 2006.

McCloud, Sean. *Making the American Religious Fringe: Exotics, Subversives, and Journalists, 1955–1993*. Chapel Hill: University of North Carolina Press, 2004.

McCullough, Matthew. *The Cross of War: Christian Nationalism and U.S. Expansion in the Spanish-American War*. Madison: University of Wisconsin Press, 2014.

McLoughlin, William Gerald. *Cherokees and Missionaries, 1789–1839*. Norman: University of Oklahoma Press, 1984.

McGreevy, John T. *Catholicism and American Freedom: A History*. New York: W. W. Norton, 2003.

———. *Parish Boundaries: The Catholic Encounter with Race in the Twentieth-Century Urban North*. Chicago: University of Chicago Press, 1996.

McMahon, Jennifer M. *Dead Stars: American and Philippine Literary Perspectives on the American Colonization of the Philippines*. Diliman, Quezon City: University of the Philippines Press, 2011.

Mehta, Uday Singh. *Liberalism and Empire: A Study in Nineteenth-Century British Liberal Thought*. Chicago: University of Chicago Press, 1999.

Meyerson, Michael. *Endowed by Our Creator: The Birth of Religious Freedom in America*. New Haven, Conn.: Yale University Press, 2012.

Michels, Tony. "Is America 'Different'? A Critique of American Jewish Exceptionalism." *American Jewish History: An American Jewish History Society Quarterly Publication* 96, no. 3 (September 2010): 201.

Miller, Albert George. *Elevating the Race: Theophilus G. Steward, Black Theology, and the Making of an African American Civil Society, 1865–1924*. Knoxville: University of Tennessee Press, 2003.

Mitchell, Michele. *Righteous Propagation: African Americans and the Politics of Racial Destiny after Reconstruction*. Chapel Hill: University of North Carolina Press, 2004.

Modern, John Lardas. *Secularism in Antebellum America: With Reference to Ghosts, Protestant Subcultures, Machines, and Their Metaphors; Featuring Discussions of*

Mass Media, Moby-Dick, Spirituality, Phrenology, Anthropology, Sing Sing State Penitentiary, and Sex with the New Motive Power. Religion and Postmodernism. Chicago: University of Chicago Press, 2011.

Montgomery, William E. *Under Their Own Vine and Fig Tree: The African-American Church in the South, 1865–1900.* Baton Rouge: Louisiana State University Press, 1993.

Mosely, LaReine-Marie, and Albert J. Raboteau. *Uncommon Faithfulness: The Black Catholic Experience.* Edited by M. Shawn Copeland. Maryknoll, N.Y.: Orbis Books, 2009.

Moses, L. G. *The Indian Man: A Biography of James Mooney.* Lincoln: University of Nebraska Press, 2002.

Mufti, Aamir. *Enlightenment in the Colony: The Jewish Question and the Crisis of Postcolonial Culture.* Princeton: Princeton University Press, 2007.

Murphy, Gretchen. *Shadowing the White Man's Burden: U.S. Imperialism and the Problem of the Color Line.* New York: New York University Press, 2010.

Muthu, Sankar, ed. *Empire and Modern Political Thought.* New York: Cambridge University Press, 2012.

Nolan, Lucinda A. "Men of Good Will: The Religious Education Association, J. Elliot Ross, and the National Conference of Jews and Christians." *Religious Education* 104, no. 5 (2009): 509–26.

Noll, Mark. *God and Race in American Politics.* Princeton: Princeton University Press, 2008.

Nongbri, Brent. *Before Religion: A History of a Modern Concept.* New Haven, Conn.: Yale University Press, 2013.

Nugent, Walter T. K. *Into the West: The Story of Its People.* New York: Knopf, 1999.

O'Brien, David J. *Isaac Hecker: An American Catholic.* New York: Paulist Press, 1992.

Orsi, Robert A. "Snakes Alive: Resituating the Moral in the Study of Religion." In *In Face of the Facts: Moral Inquiry in American Scholarship,* edited by Richard Wightman Fox and Robert B. Westbrook, 201–26. Washington, D.C.: Woodrow Wilson Press and Press Syndicate of the University of Cambridge, 1998.

Parker, Donald Dean. *Church and State in the Philippines, 1896–1906.* Manila: University of the Philippines, 1938.

Patterson, Orlando. *Freedom in the Making of Western Culture.* Freedom 1. New York: Basic Books, 1991.

Pedersen, Susan. *The Guardians: The League of Nations and the Crisis of Empire.* New York: Oxford University Press, 2015.

Pegram, Thomas R. *One Hundred Percent American: The Decline of the Ku Klux Klan in the 1920s.* Chicago: Ivan R. Dee, 2011.

Perciaccante, Marianne. "The Mormon-Muslim Comparison." *Muslim World* 82, no. 3–4 (July 1992): 296–314.

Pérez, Louis A. *The War of 1898: The United States and Cuba in History and Historiography.* Chapel Hill: University of North Carolina Press, 1998.

Peterson, Daniel C. "Mormons and Muslims." In *The Oxford Handbook of Mormonism,* edited by Philip L. Barlow and Terryl L. Givens. New York: Oxford University Press, 2015. Online edition. doi:10.1093/oxfordhb/9780199778362.013.44.

Pinheiro, John C. *Missionaries of Republicanism: A Religious History of the Mexican-American War.* Religion in America. New York: Oxford University Press, 2014.

Pitts, Jennifer. *A Turn to Empire: The Rise of Imperial Liberalism in Britain and France.* Princeton: Princeton University Press, 2005.

Preston, Andrew. *Sword of the Spirit, Shield of Faith: Religion in American War and Diplomacy.* New York: Knopf, 2012.

Prucha, Francis Paul. *The Great Father: The United States Government and the American Indians.* Lincoln: University of Nebraska Press, 1984.

Puar, Jasbir K. *Terrorist Assemblages: Homonationalism in Queer Times.* Next Wave. Durham, N.C.: Duke University Press, 2007.

Raboteau, Albert J. *Slave Religion: The "Invisible Institution" in the Antebellum South.* New York: Oxford University Press, 1978.

Rafael, Vicente L. *White Love and Other Events in Filipino History.* Durham, N.C.: Duke University Press, 2000.

Ramsey, Kate. *The Spirits and the Law: Vodou and Power in Haiti.* Chicago: University of Chicago Press, 2011.

Rappaport, Joseph. *Hands across the Sea: Jewish Immigrants and World War I.* Lanham, Md.: Hamilton Books, 2005.

Redinger, Matthew. *American Catholics and the Mexican Revolution, 1924–1936.* Notre Dame, Ind.: University of Note Dame Press, 2005.

Reeve, W. Paul. *Religion of a Different Color: Race and the Mormon Struggle for Whiteness.* New York: Oxford University Press, 2015.

Rhodes, John. "An American Tradition: The Religious Persecution of Native Americans." *Montana Law Review* 52 (1991): 13–72.

Richter, Daniel K. *Before the Revolution: America's Ancient Pasts.* Cambridge, Mass.: Belknap Press of Harvard University Press, 2011.

Ruby, Robert H., and John Arthur Brown. *Dreamer-Prophets of the Columbia Plateau: Smohalla and Skolaskin.* Norman: University of Oklahoma Press, 1989.

———. *John Slocum and the Indian Shaker Church.* Norman: University of Oklahoma Press, 1996.

Said, Edward W. *Culture and Imperialism.* New York: Knopf, distributed by Random House, 1993.

Salanga, Alfrredo Navarro. *The Aglipay Question: Literary and Historical Studies on the Life and Times of Gregorio Aglipay.* A CRISIS Book. Quezon City: Communication Research Institute for Social and Ideological Studies, 1982.

Salman, Michael. *The Embarrassment of Slavery: Controversies over Bondage and Nationalism in the American Colonial Philippines.* Berkeley: University of California Press, 2001.

Sánchez, Joseph P. *Comparative Colonialism, the Spanish Black Legend and Spain's Legacy in the United States: Perspectives on American Latino Heritage and Our National Story.* Albuquerque: National Park Service, Spanish Colonial Research Center, 2013.

Sando, Joe S. *The Pueblo Indians.* San Francisco: Indian Historian Press, 1976.

Schaefer, Stacy B., and Peter T. Furst, eds. *People of the Peyote: Huichol Indian History, Religion, and Survival.* Albuquerque: University of New Mexico, 1996.

Schneer, Jonathan. *The Balfour Declaration: The Origins of the Arab-Israeli Conflict.* New York: Bloomsbury, 2010.

Schultz, Kevin Michael. *Tri-faith America: How Catholics and Jews Held Postwar America to Its Protestant Promise.* New York: Oxford University Press, 2011.

Scott, William Henry. *Aglipay before Aglipayanism.* Quezon City, Philippines: Aglipayan Resource Center, National Priest Organization, Iglesia Filipina Independiente, 1987.

Seed, Patricia. *Ceremonies of Possession in Europe's Conquest of the New World, 1492–1640.* New York: Cambridge University Press, 1995.

Sehat, David. *The Myth of American Religious Freedom.* New York: Oxford University Press, 2011.

Seth, Vanita. *Europe's Indians Producing Racial Difference, 1500–1900.* Durham, N.C.: Duke University Press, 2010.

Sheller, Mimi. *Democracy after Slavery: Black Publics and Peasant Radicalism in Haiti and Jamaica.* Gainesville: University Press of Florida, 2000.

Sikkink, David. "From Christian Civilization to Individual Civil Liberties: Framing Religion in the Legal Field, 1880–1949." In *The Secular Revolution: Power, Interests, and Conflict in the Secularization of American Public Life*, edited by Christian Smith, 310–54. Berkeley: University of California Press, 2003.

Silverman, David J. *Red Brethren: The Brothertown and Stockbridge Indians and the Problem of Race in Early America.* Ithaca: Cornell University Press, 2010.

Slate, Nico. *Colored Cosmopolitanism: The Shared Struggle for Freedom in the United States and India.* Cambridge, Mass.: Harvard University Press, 2012.

Slotkin, James Sydney. *The Peyote Religion: A Study in Indian-White Relations.* Glencoe, Ill.: Free Press, 1956.

Smedley, Audrey. *Race in North America: Origin and Evolution of a Worldview.* 4th ed. Boulder, Colo.: Westview Press, 2011.

Smith, Jonathan Z. *Relating Religion: Essays in the Study of Religion.* Chicago: University of Chicago Press, 2004.

Smith, Matthew J. *Liberty, Fraternity, Exile: Haiti and Jamaica after Emancipation.* Chapel Hill: University of North Carolina Press, 2014.

Smith, Steven D. *The Rise and Decline of American Religious Freedom.* Cambridge, Mass.: Harvard University Press, 2014.

Smith, Wilfred Cantwell. *The Meaning and End of Religion: A New Approach to the Religious Traditions of Mankind.* Minneapolis: Fortress Press, 1991.

Soderlund, Jean R. *Lenape Country: Delaware Valley Society before William Penn.* Early American Studies. Philadelphia: University of Pennsylvania Press, 2015.

Stack, Trevor, Naomi R. Goldenberg, and Timothy Fitzgerald, eds. *Religion as a Category of Governance and Sovereignty.* Boston: Brill Academic Publishing, 2015.

Stanwood, Owen. "Catholics, Protestants, and the Clash of Civilizations in Early America." In *The First Prejudice: Religious Tolerance and Intolerance in Early America*, edited by Chris Beneke and Christopher S. Grenda, 218–40. Philadelphia: University of Pennsylvania Press, 2011.

Stein, Leonard. *The Balfour Declaration.* New York: Simon and Schuster, 1961.

Stern, Eliyahu. *The Genius: Elijah of Vilna and the Making of Modern Judaism.* New Haven, Conn.: Yale University Press, 2013.

Stewart, Omer Call. *Peyote Religion: A History.* Norman: University of Oklahoma Press, 1987.

Su, Anna. *Exporting Freedom: Religious Liberty and American Power*. Cambridge, Mass.: Harvard University Press, 2016.

Sullivan, Rodney J. *Exemplar of Americanism: The Philippine Career of Dean C. Worcester*. Michigan Papers on South and Southeast Asia 36. Ann Arbor, Mich.: Center for South and Southeast Asian Studies, University of Michigan, 1991.

Sullivan, Winnifred Fallers, Elizabeth Shakman Hurd, Saba Mahmood, and Peter G. Danchin, eds. *Politics of Religious Freedom*. Chicago: University Of Chicago Press, 2015.

Sundiata, I. K. *Brothers and Strangers: Black Zionism, Black Slavery, 1914–1940*. Durham, N.C.: Duke University Press, 2003.

Thomas, Megan Christine. *Orientalists, Propagandists, and Ilustrados: Filipino Scholarship and the End of Spanish Colonialism*. Minneapolis: University of Minnesota Press, 2012.

Troutman, John. "The Citizenship of Dance: Politics of Music among the Lakota, 1900–1924." In *Beyond Red Power: American Indian Politics and Activism since 1900*, edited by Daniel M. Cobb and Loretta Fowler, 91–103. Santa Fe: School for Advanced Research, 2007.

Turner, Richard Brent. *Islam in the African-American Experience*. Bloomington: Indiana University Press, 1997.

Underwood, James L. *The Constitution of South Carolina*. Vol. 3, *Church and State, Morality and Free Expression*. Columbia: University of South Carolina Press, 1986.

Vecsey, Christopher. *Traditional Ojibwa Religion and Its Historical Changes*. Philadelphia: American Philosophical Society, 1983.

Vinca, Robert H. "The American Catholic Reaction to the Persecution of the Church in Mexico, 1926–1936." In *Modern American Catholicism, 1900–1965: Selected Historical Essays*, edited by Edward R. Kantowicz, 286–321. The Heritage of American Catholicism. New York: Garland, 1988.

Walker, Clarence E. *A Rock in a Weary Land: The A.M.E. Church during the Civil War and Reconstruction*. Baton Rouge: Louisiana State University Press, 1982.

Wallace, Max. *The American Axis: Henry Ford, Charles Lindbergh, and the Rise of the Third Reich*. New York: St. Martin's Press, 2003.

Walther, Karine V. *Sacred Interests: The United States and the Islamic World, 1821–1921*. Chapel Hill: University of North Carolina Press, 2015.

Warren, James Francis. *The Sulu Zone, 1768–1898: The Dynamics of External Trade, Slavery, and Ethnicity in the Transformation of a Southeast Asian Maritime State*. Quezon City: New Day Publishers, 1985.

Washburn, Patrick Scott. *The African American Newspaper: Voice of Freedom*. Visions of the American Press. Evanston, Ill.: Northwestern University Press, 2006.

Watts, Jill. *God, Harlem U.S.A.: The Father Divine Story*. Berkeley: University of California Press, 1992.

Weheliye, Alexander G. *Habeas Viscus: Racializing Assemblages, Biopolitics, and Black Feminist Theories of the Human*. Durham, N.C.: Duke University Press, 2014.

Weiner, Isaac. *Religion Out Loud: Religious Sound, Public Space, and American Pluralism*. North American Religions. New York: New York University Press, 2014.

Weisbrot, Robert. *Father Divine and the Struggle for Racial Equality*. Blacks in the New World. Urbana: University of Illinois Press, 1983.

Weisenfeld, Judith. *New World a-Coming: Black Religion and Racial Identity during the Great Migration*. New York: New York University Press, 2017.

Wenger, Tisa. "Freedom to Worship." In *The Four Freedoms: FDR's Legacy of Liberty for the United States and the World*, edited by Jeffrey Engel, 73–110. New York: Oxford University Press, 2015.

———. "Indian Dances and the Politics of Religious Freedom, 1870–1930." *Journal of the American Academy of Religion* 79, no. 4 (December 2011): 850–78. doi:10.1093/jaarel/lfr061.

———. "'A New Form of Government': Religious-Secular Distinctions in Pueblo Indian History." In *Religion as a Category of Governance and Sovereignty*, edited by Trevor Stack, Naomi R. Goldenberg, and Timothy Fitzgerald, 68–89. Boston: Brill, 2015.

———. *We Have a Religion: The 1920s Pueblo Indian Dance Controversy and American Religious Freedom*. Chapel Hill: Published in association with the William P. Clements Center for Southwest Studies, Southern Methodist University, by the University of North Carolina Press, 2009.

Wetzel, Benjamin James. "American Crusade: Lyman Abbott and the Christian Nation at War, 1861–1918." Ph.D. diss., University of Notre Dame, 2016.

Wexler, Laura. *Tender Violence: Domestic Visions in an Age of U.S. Imperialism*. Cultural Studies of the United States. Chapel Hill: University of North Carolina Press, 2000.

Whittemore, Lewis Bliss. *Struggle for Freedom: History of the Philippine Independent Church*. Greenwich, Conn.: Seabury Press, 1961.

Wolfe, Patrick. *Traces of History: Elementary Structures of Race*. Brooklyn: Verso, 2016.

Wood, Nancy C. *Taos Pueblo*. New York: Knopf, 1989.

Wunder, John R. *"Retained by the People": A History of American Indians and the Bill of Rights*. Bicentennial Essays on the Bill of Rights. New York: Oxford University Press, 1994.

Index

Abolitionists, 85–86, 188–89, 192

Adler, Cyrus, 171, 182

African Americans: religious freedom invoked by, 13, 188–91, 196–205, 211, 214, 215–18, 221–22, 227–31, 233–35; and black church tradition, 33, 168, 188–90, 196–205, 231; racial stereotypes of, 33, 174–75, 212–14, 216, 219–20, 224–25; and Catholicism, 39, 179, 204–5; and U.S. empire, 39, 203–4, 236; and tri-faith movement, 168, 174–75, 186–87, 222, 234; and integrationism, 190–91, 196–205, 214–15, 231; and black nationalism, 190–91, 206–11, 214, 223, 230–31, 236–37; and ethno-religious movements, 191–92, 205–31, 236–37; and global African diaspora, 201–4, 226; and Islam, 209–14, 222–29; government harassment/ surveillance of, 212–14, 215–18, 222–29. *See also* Racial binary; Racial segregation; Racial violence; Slavery

African Methodist Episcopal Church (AME), 39, 197–99, 201–202, 203–5

African Methodist Episcopal Zion Church, 199

African Orthodox Church, 208, 209, 210

Aglipay, Gregorio, 54–55, 65–68, 71–80. *See also* Philippine Independent Church

Agoncillo, Felipe, 59–60

Aguinaldo, Emilio, 56–57, 58–59, 63–64, 65–66, 69–70, 81, 90

Allen, Richard, 197, 198–99

American Jewish Committee, 157–58, 159, 161, 166, 181–82, 184

American Jewish Congress, 158–59, 161, 181–82, 183

Anglo-Saxons: identified with Protestantism and Americanism, 16–17, 20–21, 26, 33, 195–96; and whiteness, 20, 39, 49, 50, 85, 107, 187; and U.S.-British alliance, 22, 33, 195–96; and gender, 22–23, 26; and U.S. empire, 26, 29, 61, 85; critiques of, 37–39, 49–53. *See also* Whiteness

Anti-Catholicism, 18–23, 25–26, 34–35, 42, 52, 144, 175–77, 187, 246n83, 262n7

Anticolonialism, 14, 136, 201, 206–7, 226

Anti-imperialism: in Spanish-American War, 15, 27–29; racism of, 28–29; Catholics and, 34–35, 37–39, 43–44; and U.S. rule in Philippines, 37–39, 44, 82, 85, 203; African Americans and, 39, 203

Anti-Semitism, 13, 17, 47–49, 52, 144–57, 160, 164–69, 170–71, 178, 179–80, 181–87, 256–57n10, 260–61n104

Arapaho Indians, 111, 112, 123, 132, 134

Balfour Declaration, 158–59

Bannock Indians, 125–26, 132, 135–37

Baptists, 10, 26, 52, 129, 143, 167, 173; African American, 190, 194, 200, 202, 204–205, 209; white Southern, 151, 192–96

Barbarians: Spanish Catholics seen as, 16, 22–23, 61; Filipinos seen as, 17, 30, 37, 43–44, 48; Muslim Moros seen as, 55, 85, 86–87, 94–95; Native Americans seen as, 105, 114, 115–16, 119, 128, 134; Nazis seen as, 185. *See also* Heathens; Primitives; Savages

Barrows, David Prescott, 94–95

Bates, John C. (U.S. general), 65, 83–84, 91–93, 97

Bates Treaty, 65, 83–87, 89, 91–93, 95–97, 250n96

American, 190–91, 206–10, 214, 216, 223, 227–28, 236–37, 264n42

Nation of Islam, 13, 190–91, 206, 222–31, 236–37

Native American Church, 125–28, 138–41, 221

Native Americans, 7, 8–9, 11, 12, 20, 30, 35, 36, 70, 87, 93–95, 101–42, 221–22, 235, 237–38

Navajo Indians, 127, 140

Nazis, 144, 145–46, 179–80, 181–86

New Deal, 127, 139, 179–81, 186, 194, 220

New England, 10, 87, 174

Nozaleda, Bernardino (archbishop of Manila), 60, 66, 68, 71, 73

Ojibwe Indians, 129–31

Orientalism, 88–89

"Orientals," depictions of, 39, 43, 76, 85–86

Orthodox Judaism, 154, 180

Osage Indians, 123, 126

Ottoman Empire, 146, 158, 162

Outlook magazine, 32–34

Palestine, 146, 153, 154, 155–56, 157, 158–61, 207. *See also* Zionists/Zionism

Parker, Quanah, 122, 124

Paulists, 35, 75, 177. See also *Catholic World*

Pawnee Indians, 101, 112, 129

Peace Mission Movement, 190–91, 214–22, 230

Peyote / Peyote religion, 108, 109, 121–28, 138–41, 253n54, 254n57

Philippine-American War, 33, 56–57, 59–70, 93

Philippine Commission, 31, 41, 74, 85, 90, 93, 96

Philippine Constitution (1898), 59–60, 62–66, 69, 82, 235

Philippine Independent Church, 54, 71–81

Philippine Islands: as a Spanish colony, 15, 23–24; American debates over colonizing, 23–34, 37–39; "pagan tribes" in, 31–32, 43; American Catholics in U.S. governance of, 39–41; independence from United States, 99–100

Philippine Republic (1898–1901), 54, 56–57, 58–67, 103. *See also* Aguinaldo, Emilio

Philipson, David, 160, 166, 169–70, 184–85

Pius XI (pope), 180

Political distinctions. *See* Religious-political distinctions

Polygamy: in Philippines, 84–86, 88–89, 92, 250n96; in United States, 84, 86–88, 89, 118

Powell, John Wesley, 111–12

Presbyterians, 21, 50, 78, 114–15, 169, 176, 209

Price, Hiram (commissioner of Indian Affairs), 105–6

Primitives, 5, 9–10; Moros seen as, 43, 56; Native Americans seen as, 105, 134, 137–38, 139, 141, 237. *See also* Barbarians; Heathens; Savages

Protestants/Protestantism: and Protestant Reformation, 18, 19–20, 77, 192; in Philippines, 55–56, 60, 62–63, 68, 74, 77–79; and Mormons, 86–89; and Native American traditions, 108, 120, 121, 127, 128, 139; and American Jews, 165–66, 168–72; and brotherhood/goodwill movement, 49–53, 150, 164, 166, 168–72; and tri-faith movement, 144, 172–87. *See also* African Methodist Episcopal Church; Baptists, Church of England; Congregationalists; Episcopalians; Methodists / Methodist Episcopal Church; Missionaries, Protestant; Presbyterians

—African American: critiques of slaveholders' Christianity, 189; assertions of modernity and racial equality, 190, 196–205

—asserted as: foundation for religious freedom, 2, 6, 16–17, 19–20, 25; optimal religion for modernity, 6, 23, 24; American religious norm, 10, 11, 18, 20–21, 31, 36, 49, 68, 120, 145, 217, 239; imperial civilizing tool, 11–12, 24–26, 29–31, 33, 56; basis of American democracy, 19, 20, 16, 19, 27

—and Catholics/Catholicism: in conflict with, 5–6, 16–17, 18–20, 35–36, 81, 173–74; criticized by, 37–38, 40–44; cooperation with, 174–87

—linked to: American secular, 11–12, 20, 26, 33, 42, 68; whiteness, 20–21, 28–29, 33,

164–65, 195–96; gendered male, 22–23, 34, 198; slavery and segregation, 192–93

Pueblo Indians, 108, 127, 137, 140

Puerto Rico, 15, 27, 39, 42, 45, 53, 81, 203

Puritans, 33, 87, 143, 174

Quezon, Manuel, 81–82

Race, 1–3, 13–14, 20, 236–39; Jews and, 2, 13, 20, 47–50, 142, 144–47, 149–50, 153, 156–57, 160–63, 164–172, 178, 182, 185–87, 207, 236; Catholics and, 2, 17, 20–23, 25–26, 37–39, 42–45, 49–53, 55, 75–76, 164–65, 172–73, 178–79, 185–87, 193, 204–5; white Protestants and, 2–3, 11–12, 20–23, 25–29, 49–53, 164–65, 168–73, 178, 185–87, 192–96; historical invention of, 3–5, 7–9; African Americans and, 13, 33, 50, 186–87, 190, 191, 192–94, 197–204, 207–8, 211–18, 221–26, 228–31, 233, 234–35; in debates over war and empire, 17–18, 22–23, 26, 28–34, 39, 42–44, 45–46, 48–53, 61, 67; in Philippines, 23–24, 30, 31–33, 55–56, 63–65, 75–76; in representing Moros, 32, 55–56, 58, 64–65, 82–89, 93–95, 213; in representing Native Americans, 108, 115–16, 123, 126, 141–42

Racial binary, 50, 185–87, 231, 237

Racial segregation, 29, 50–51, 68, 107, 192–201, 204–5, 219, 220–21, 230, 233–35

Racial violence, 107, 149, 152, 168, 187, 188, 195, 221

Reform Judaism, 144–45, 146, 148, 150–51, 153–55, 157, 160–61, 166–67, 169–70, 182, 184–85

Religion: delineated by religious freedom, 2–3, 10, 11–14, 98, 104, 222, 236–37; emergence of category, 5–9; Christianity as the model for, 6–7, 104, 110–11, 113–32, 138, 142, 145, 239; co-constituted with race and nation, 8–9, 17–18, 20, 25–28, 48–50, 94, 108, 115–16, 118–19, 142, 165, 185–87, 191, 206–12, 217, 223, 227–29; Islam as, 32, 82–83, 85–86, 90–92, 97, 100, 190–91, 206, 209–14, 223–24, 229; racial stereotypes of, 33, 191, 201–2, 211–13, 219–21, 224–25;

229; hierarchies of, 45–46, 55–56, 58, 118–21, 141–42, 162, 165, 202, 222–30; Native American traditions as, 101–2, 104–5, 109, 111, 113–42, 235; Judaism as, 144–47, 150–51, 153–60, 163, 164, 167, 168–73, 178–87. *See also* Religious freedom; Religious-political distinctions; Religious-secular distinctions

Religious Crimes Code (1883), 105

Religious freedom: as defining national ideal, 1, 10–13, 16–20, 23, 25–27, 59, 147, 164, 185–87; Catholic articulations of, 2, 17, 34, 37–45, 49–53, 74–76, 80–81, 164, 172–79, 183–87, 193; whiteness and, 2, 20, 28, 48–53, 192–196; Catholicism seen as a threat to, 3, 10, 16, 18–28, 46, 71–74, 76–79; Protestants and, 6, 11, 16, 28, 40–41, 60, 77–78; in the British Empire, 6–10, 24, 26–27, 83, 158; slavery and, 7–9, 83–86, 89, 97–98, 188–89, 192; Jews and, 10, 11, 13, 17–18, 46–53, 142, 143–187, 189, 231, 236, 239; as individual right, 10, 18–20, 30–32, 55, 59, 69–70, 80, 91–92, 163, 170, 191, 192, 194–95, 206, 208–9, 214, 216–22; secularism and, 11–12, 20, 23, 25–26, 34, 68, 90–100; African American articulations of, 13, 186–87, 188–91, 196–205, 206, 208–11, 214, 215–19, 221–22, 227–31, 233–37; capitalism and, 30, 70, 96, 148, 154, 203; sovereignty and, 58–61, 69–70, 90–93, 97–98, 102–4; Catholic reservations about, 61–62, 65–67, 68; Mormons and, 86–88; Native Americans and, 102–5, 109–132, 133, 136, 137–42; as collective right, 163, 191, 206, 208–10, 230, 236–37

—in Philippines: Moros and, 12, 32, 55–56, 63–65, 82, 85–86, 88–92, 95–100l Filipinos and, 54–55, 57–67, 69–70, 71–80, 81–82, 99–100

—in U.S. Empire: and resistance, 11, 12, 55, 58–61, 76–79, 91, 99–100, 102–4, 109–31, 183, 189–91, 236, 238–39; as governing mechanism, 12, 70, 85–86, 90–92, 95–98; as U.S. diplomatic/imperial priority, 16,

tyrannical and anti-freedom, 17–19, 21–25, 27, 30, 31, 35, 46–47, 61, 146; aftermath of rule in Philippines, 29, 37–45, 54–55, 58–68, 71–74, 77–79; Moros in relation to, 32, 63–64, 83–85, 90, 92; ambivalently portrayed by American Catholics, 34–37, 40, 42–44, 178; Filipino views of, 56–58, 62. *See also* Religious orders, Spanish Catholic; Spanish-Cuban-Filipino-American War

Spanish-Cuban-Filipino-American War, 1, 12, 15–16, 18, 21–23, 25, 34, 49, 61, 68; as basis for U.S. sectional reconciliation, 50–53; from Filipino perspectives, 56–57; African American views of, 203. *See also* Treaty of Paris

Straus, Oscar, 143–46, 160

Strong, Josiah, 20–21

Sulu, sultan of, 65, 83, 88–89, 90–93, 96–98, 99, 249n79

Supreme Court: of United States, 11, 87, 118, 166, 233–34, 242n21; of Philippines, 74, 79–80; of Montana, 126

Taft, William Howard, 72, 73, 74

Thompson, Mary, 113, 117

Tillman, John, 123–24

Toleration, religious: in the British colonies, 6–7, 20; in Philippines, 57, 59; and goodwill/tri-faith movements, 175–77

Treaties: with Moros, 65, 83–87, 89, 90–97; with Native American nations, 105, 126, 250n96. *See also* Treaty of Paris; Treaty of Versailles

Treaty of Paris (1898), 53, 56; terms debated in United States, 15, 25, 28; aftermath of, 29, 48, 79, 81, 82

Treaty of Versailles (1919), 143; and Minorities Treaties, 157, 162–63, 165

Trías, Mariano, 64–65, 69

Tri-faith movement, 49–53, 143–47, 164, 168–87, 193, 199, 222, 234, 246n88

Tutelary regime, U.S.: in Philippines, 41, 53, 68–69, 71–72; and Native Americans, 101, 103–4, 106, 108, 119, 131, 136

Twain, Mark, 136–37

Umatilla Indians, 105

Unitarians, 27, 80, 170

United Negro Improvement Association, 206–9, 216, 220, 264n42. *See also* Garvey, Marcus

U.S. Constitution: and imperialism, 28, 38, 69, 85, 236; Catholic appeals to, 38, 41–42, 166; and religious pluralism, 51; in Philippines, 69, 74, 76–77; and polygamy, 86–88; and slavery, 92, 192; and Native Americans, 106, 115, 116, 118, 123, 126, 128, 137, 138, 140–41; and American Jews, 147, 157, 177, 186; and African Americans, 190–91, 198, 210–11, 214, 216–19, 221–22, 223, 228, 231, 234; and racial segregation, 195, 201. *See also* First Amendment

U.S. House Committee on Indian Affairs, 122, 123, 124, 127

Vodou, 201–2, 224

Wardship, U.S., of Native Americans, 105–7, 114, 118

Whiteness: and U.S. imperialism, 2, 17–18, 23; linked to Christianity, 9; incorporation of Jews into, 12–13, 17–18; 48–53; incorporation of Catholics into, 17–18, 36, 39, 49–53; limited to Anglo-Saxon Protestants, 20, 23

Wickersham, James, 114–15, 253n33

Williams, Michael, 176, 183–84

Wilson, Woodrow, 159–60, 162, 164, 169, 193, 205

Winnebago Indians. *See* Ho-Chunk Indians

Wise, Stephen S., 155, 159, 176, 182

Wolf, Simon, 156–57, 167

Wood, Leonard, 42, 96–97

Worcester, Dean, 30–32, 41, 42–43, 90

World War I: and Native Americans, 132–33; and American Jews, 143, 146, 147, 157–63; and American Protestants, 169; and African Americans, 205

World War II, 2, 195, 234; and the tri-faith movement, 49, 179, 186, 246n88; and

Philippines, 100; and American Jews, 146, 179; and African Americans, 194, 222, 225–28. *See also* Roosevelt, Franklin Delano

Wounded Knee, 109–12, 128. *See also* Ghost Dance

Wovoka (Pauite prophet), 109–10, 252n20

Yakama Indians, 117–18, 120

Ziebach, C. H., 125–26, 135, 137–38
Zionism, 145, 146–47, 153–63, 181, 207, 257n29